A Treatise
on the Family

GARY S. BECKER

A Treatise on the Family

ENLARGED EDITION

Harvard University Press
Cambridge, Massachusetts
London, England

First Harvard University Press paperback edition, 1993

Library of Congress Cataloging-in-Publication Data

Becker, Gary Stanley, 1930–
    A treatise on the family / Gary S. Becker. — Enl. ed.
        p.   cm.
    Includes bibliographical references (p.
    Includes index.
    ISBN 0-674-90698-5 (acid-free paper) (cloth)
    ISBN 0-674-90699-3 (paper)
    1. Family—Economic aspects.   I. Title.
HQ518.B35   1991   90-4975
306.85—dc20   CIP

To Guity

for support and confidence
when progress was slow

Contents

Contents

Preface to the Enlarged Edition

In this book I develop an economic or rational choice approach to the family. The title does not refer to economic aspects of the family, however, because most noneconomists and many economists would interpret the qualifier "economic" to indicate that the discussion is confined to the material aspects of family life, to incomes and spending patterns. My intent is more ambitious: to analyze marriage, births, divorce, division of labor in households, prestige, and other nonmaterial behavior with the tools and framework developed for material behavior. That is to say, this book contains an economic approach to the family, not in the sense of an emphasis on the material aspects of family life, but in the sense of a choice-theoretic framework for analyzing many aspects of family life.

The rational choice approach has been refined during the past two hundred years. It now assumes that individuals maximize their utility from basic preferences that do not change rapidly over time, and that the behavior of different individuals is coordinated by explicit and implicit markets. I argued in an earlier publication that the economic approach is not restricted to material goods and wants or to markets with monetary transactions, and *conceptually* does not distinguish between major and minor decisions or between "emotional" and other decisions.

This volume uses the assumptions of maximizing behavior, stable preferences, and equilibrium in implicit or explicit markets to provide a systematic analysis of the family. I build on my research during the past two decades to analyze the allocation of time to children and to market work, marriage and divorce in polygynous as well as monogamous societies, altruism in addition to selfishness in families, intergenerational mobility, and many other aspects of the family. Although not all are considered, the systematic, unified treatment of the important aspects perhaps justifies the old-fashioned title "treatise."

My book is not written for a lay audience, but much of the material should be understandable to noneconomists familiar with basic economic principles. Chapters 5, 10, and 11, including the supplement to Chapter 11, are the least technical, and appreciable portions of other chapters should also be accessible to persons having only a limited acquaintance with economic analysis. I hope they will not be put off by the terminology and techniques, for their participation is required to achieve a full development and evaluation of the rational choice approach to the family. I say this because many economists are hostile to this application of the approach, whereas increasing numbers of sociologists, anthropologists, lawyers, biologists, psychologists, and historians are using a rational choice approach or related methods to analyze the family. My "treatise" is intended for an interdisciplinary audience—for skeptics as well as for advocates.

I have immensely enjoyed writing this book because of the importance of the subject matter and the intellectual challenges provided by many aspects of family organization and behavior. I would be less than truthful if I did not express my belief that substantial progress has been made in meeting and resolving these challenges. At the same time, I am aware of and disturbed by serious omissions and incomplete analyses; I delayed publication of the earlier edition several times to fill in gaps and improve certain of the discussions. I finally decided to delay no longer and to publish the book because others, noneconomists as well as economists, can better carry on these efforts to understand the major institution throughout history in essentially all human societies.

The remarkable changes in family behavior and structure during the past several decades in countries throughout the world contributed greatly to the attention paid to the first edition of the *Treatise,* despite its technical nature. The book was widely reviewed by economists, sociologists, demographers, and also by a few biologists and psychologists, and has been translated into several languages. Since I have continued to work on the family, I was happy to agree to a proposal by the publisher that I prepare an enlarged edition.

Acknowledgments

I incurred numerous debts in the preparation of this book. Let me begin by thanking colleagues and students at the University of Chicago for creating the stimulating atmosphere I have experienced here. Economics is taken seriously at Chicago, and ideas are considered and analyzed in a frank and searching manner without intellectual inertia or excessive respect for authority or for boundaries between disciplines. I have especially benefited from the following students who wrote dissertations on the family, or relevant to the family, during their participation in our Workshop on Applications of Economics: James Adams, Wallace Blackhurst, Michael Brien, Dennis De Tray, Alan Freiden, Miguel Gomez, Daniel Gros, Amyra Grossbard, Nadeem Haque, Boyan Jovanovic, Michael Keeley, Lawrence Kenny, Ayal Kimhi, Edy Kogut, Sui Fai Leung, Daniel Levy, Luis Locay, Thomas MaCurdy, Indra Makhija, Gabriel Martinez, Haim Ofek, Elizabeth Peters, Seth Sanders, James Smith, Jeffrey Smith, Robert Tamura, Nigel Tomes, Grace Tsiang, Jenny Bourne Wahl, Walter Wessels, Louis Wilde, Richard Wong, and Martin Zelder.

I have prepared a new Introduction for this enlarged edition, and I am including slightly modified versions of four articles published subsequent to the 1981 edition. One article was written jointly with Robert J. Barro, another with Kevin M. Murphy, and a third with Nigel Tomes.

I am indebted to Robert Michael, Richard Posner, Sherwin Rosen, T. W. Schultz, and George Stigler for helpful and detailed suggestions on all the chapters. Valuable comments also came from Stuart Altmann, Michael Aronson, Edward Banfield, Reuven Brenner, Arthur Diamond, Ted Frech, David Friedman, Milton Friedman, Victor Fuchs, David Galenson, Matthew Goldberg, Arthur Goldberger, Zvi Griliches, Reuben Gronau, Amyra Grossbard, Sanford Grossman, James Heckman, David Hirshleifer, Jack Hirshleifer, Arcadius Kahan, Lawrence Kenny, Elisabeth Landes, Richard Layard, H. Gregg

Lewis, Robert Lucas, Jacob Mincer, John Muellbauer, Kevin M. Murphy, Sam Peltzman, Edward Prescott, Sam Preston, Margaret Reid, Paul Romer, Nasser Saidi, José Scheinkman, James Smith, Stephen Stigler, Larry Summers, Robert Tamura, Nigel Tomes, Yoram Weiss, Robert Willis, Edward Wilson, and Kenneth Wolpin. Vivian Wheeler provided excellent editorial assistance in both editions, and Dan Greenway skillfully drew virtually all of the figures. Michael Aronson was again a most cooperative and encouraging editor.

My research on the family has been generously supported by the University of Chicago's Center for the Study of Economy and the State, the Lilly Foundation, the National Institute of Child Health and Human Development (Grant #SSP 1 R37 HD22054), the National Science Foundation (Grants #SES-8012187 and #SES-8520258), the Lynde and Harry Bradley Foundation, and the Sloan Foundation, both of which also aided our Workshops on the Family. The National Bureau of Economic Research, especially the Center for Economic Analysis of Human Behavior and Social Institutions, over a period of years provided funding, encouragement, and freedom to pursue my research in any direction that seemed promising. The views expressed here are my own and not necessarily those of the granting agencies.

Finally, let me express my deep appreciation to: Gale Mosteller, who worked on the first edition, for conscientious, thorough, and remarkably outstanding research assistance; Michael Gibbs, for valuable research aid on the supplements; David Meltzer, for truly excellent work in preparing the index and bibliography and generally in helping with the enlarged edition; Myrna Hieke, for extraordinary typing and other secretarial assistance through many not-so-legible drafts and under trying circumstances during both editions; and my wife, Guity Nashat, for numerous discussions—especially about the family in Islamic societies—as well as for the reasons given in the dedication.

Relation of the Directors to the Work and Publications
of the National Bureau of Economic Research

1. The object of the National Bureau of Economic Research is to ascertain and to present to the public important economic facts and their interpretation in a scientific and impartial manner. The Board of Directors is charged with the responsibility of ensuring that the work of the National Bureau is carried on in strict conformity with this object.

2. The President of the National Bureau shall submit to the Board of Directors, or to its Executive Committee, for their formal adoption all specific proposals for research to be instituted.

3. No research report shall be published by the National Bureau until the President has sent each member of the Board a notice that a manuscript is recommended for publication and that in the President's opinion it is suitable for publication in accordance with the principles of the National Bureau. Such notification will include an abstract or summary of the manuscript's content and a response form for use by those Directors who desire a copy of the manuscript for review. Each manuscript shall contain a summary drawing attention to the nature and treatment of the problem studied, the character of the data and their utilization in the report, and the main conclusions reached.

4. For each manuscript so submitted, a special committee of the Directors (including Directors Emeriti) shall be appointed by majority agreement of the President and Vice Presidents (or by the Executive Committee in case of inability to decide on the part of the President and Vice Presidents), consisting of three Directors selected as nearly as may be one from each general division of the Board. The names of the special manuscript committee shall be stated to each Director when notice of the proposed publication is submitted to him. It shall be the duty of each member of the special manuscript committee to read the manuscript. If each member of the manuscript committee signifies his approval within thirty days of the transmittal of the manuscript, the report may be published. If at the end of that period any member of the manuscript committee withholds his approval, the President shall then notify each member of the Board, requesting approval or disapproval of publication, and thirty days additional shall be granted for this purpose. The manuscript shall then not be published unless at least a majority of the entire Board who shall have voted on the proposal within the time fixed for the receipt of votes shall have approved.

5. No manuscript may be published, though approved by each member of the special manuscript committee, until forty-five days have elapsed from the transmittal of the report in manuscript form. The interval is allowed for the receipt of any memorandum of dissent or reservation, together with a brief statement of his reasons, that any member may wish to express; and such memorandum of dissent or reservation shall be published with the manuscript if he so desires. Publication does not, however, imply that each member of the Board has read the manuscript, or that either members of the Board in general or the special committee have passed on its validity in every detail.

6. Publications of the National Bureau issued for informational purposes concerning the work of the Bureau and its staff, or issued to inform the public of activities of Bureau staff, and volumes issued as a result of various conferences involving the National Bureau shall contain a specific disclaimer noting that such publication has not passed through the normal review procedures required in this resolution. The Executive Committee of the Board is charged with review of all such publications from time to time to ensure that they do not take on the character of formal research reports of the National Bureau, requiring formal Board approval.

7. Unless otherwise determined by the Board or exempted by the terms of paragraph 6, a copy of this resolution shall be printed in each National Bureau publication.

(Resolution adopted October 25, 1926, as revised through September 30, 1974)

A Treatise
on the Family

Introduction

The family in the Western world has been radically altered—some claim almost destroyed—by events of the last three decades. The rapid growth in divorce rates has greatly increased the number of households headed by women and the number of children growing up in households with only one parent. The large increase in labor force participation of married women, including mothers with young children, has reduced the contact between children and their mothers and contributed to the conflict between the sexes in employment as well as in marriage. The rapid decline in birth rates has reduced family size and helped cause the increased rates of divorce and labor force participation of married women. Conversely, expanded divorce and labor force participation have reduced the desire to have large families. Conflict between the generations has become more open, and today's parents are less confident than those of earlier years that they can guide the behavior of their children.

A few statistical highlights provide a quantitative perspective on the magnitude of these changes. Less than 15 percent of the women in the United States who married for the first time in the early 1950s have divorced, whereas about 60 percent of all first marriages of the early 1980s are likely to end in divorce (Preston, 1975; Martin and Bumpass, 1989). The average household size apparently was remarkably stable in England and Wales for three centuries prior to the end of the nineteenth century, whereas it has declined by one-third since then (Laslett, 1972, table 4.4). Spurred by the increased divorce rate and the greater longevity of women, female-headed households increased between 1950 and 1987 from 15 to 31 percent of all households in the

United States (U.S. Bureau of the Census, 1977b, p. 41; 1989, p. 46). The labor force participation rate of married women below age 75 in Sweden went from 39 to 70 percent between 1960 and 1984 (Sweden National Central Bureau of Statistics, 1980, 1986), and even the participation rate of married women with children under age six increased rapidly in the United States from 12 percent in 1950 to 57 percent in 1988 (U.S. Bureau of the Census, 1977b, p. 392; 1989, p. 386). Finally, the reproduction rate in the United States was below replacement in 1989 because the birth rate had declined by more than 40 percent since 1958 (U.S. Bureau of the Census, 1989), and in Japan the birth rate declined by more than 50 percent from 1950 to 1987 (Japan Bureau of Statistics, 1989, p. 53).

Precisely because of these dramatic changes, the family is receiving more attention from laypeople and scholars than ever before. Discussions of its decline and its future course are common fare in newspapers and magazines of the 1990s. At the other extreme, demographers and historians have published painstaking and fascinating accounts of family composition and behavior in villages hundreds of years ago (Henry, 1965; Laslett, 1972; Le Roy Ladurie, 1978). Anthropologists (Goody et al., 1976), biologists (Trivers, 1974; Wilson, 1975), and psychologists (Keniston et al., 1977) also have expanded their interest in the family.

Aside from the Malthusian theory of population change, economists hardly noticed the family prior to the 1950s, when they began to recognize spouses, children, and other family members. Jacob Mincer (1962; also see Long, 1958) argued persuasively that the labor force participation of married women is determined not only by their earnings potential, but also by the earnings of their husbands, the number of children they have, and other family characteristics. A modern economic analysis of fertility began to replace the Malthusian analysis, and the demand for children has been shown to depend on family income, the value of parents' time (especially that of mothers), the "quality" of children, and other family variables (Becker, 1960, 1965; Easterlin, 1968). Studies of investment in human capital treated private expenditures on education as parental investments in the productivity of children (Schultz, 1963; Becker, 1964).

My *Treatise on the Family* builds on these and other studies to present an economic approach to the family. Although I utilize my earlier work, much of the analysis is original. Chapter 2 analyzes the division of household labor between men and women and between intrinsically identical persons; Chapter 3 relates the incidence of polygyny to the demand for children, differences among men, and several other variables; Chapter 9 analyzes mating and the quantity of offspring in nonhuman species; and Chapter 11 considers the role of nuclear and extended families and kin in traditional, modern, and contemporary societies.

I had worked out in previous publications (some with collaborators) the basic analysis in the other chapters, then rewrote the discussions for inclusion in this volume. Considered for the first time are the effects of polygamy, inflexible marital "prices," and differences in preferences on the optimal sorting of mates (Chapter 4); the interaction between quantity and quality of children and its effect on changes in fertility over time and on differences in fertility between groups at a moment in time (Chapter 5); the effect on fertility of the number of siblings and other aspects of family background (Chapter 6); the comparison between altruism and envy in the family and selfishness in the marketplace (Chapter 8); and the stigma attached to divorce (Chapter 10).

Although the main emphasis of the book is on analytical development, most chapters also contain empirical evidence: statistical data for recent periods; historical studies of particular villages, cities, and countries; information on Islamic, African, and Oriental societies; and anthropologic ethnographies of primitive societies. The evidence is covered much less systematically than the theory, but its breadth accurately conveys my intention to present a comprehensive analysis that is applicable, at least in part, to families in the past as well as the present, in primitive as well as modern societies, and in Eastern as well as Western cultures.

This Introduction relates the four new supplements included in this expanded edition to the discussion in the earlier chapters, replies to several criticisms, and comments on a few general issues concerning families.

The model developed in Chapter 2 shows that even if a husband and wife are intrinsically identical, they gain from a division of labor between market and household activities, with one of them specializing more in market activities and the other specializing more in household activities. The gain comes from increasing returns to investments in sector-specific human capital that raise productivity mainly in either the market or the nonmarket sectors. Therefore, even small differences between men and women—presumably related at least partially to the advantages of women in the birth and rearing of children—would cause a division of labor by gender, with wives more specialized to household activities and husbands more specialized to other work. The degree of specialization in a marriage would be less extreme if one of the sectors, perhaps housework, were considered more boring and less worthwhile, or if divorce were common.

Chapter 2 evidently conveyed the impression to many (see for example Boserup, 1987) that I rely only on biological differences—that women are intrinsically more productive at child bearing and rearing than men—to explain this division of labor between household and other activities. That is certainly not my intent, for of course I recognize that working women have suffered from discrimination. Although I do believe that biological differences are very important in explaining why women traditionally have done most of the child rearing, the main lesson from my analysis of an efficient division of labor is not that biology or discrimination causes the traditional division of activities between men and women.

Rather, as emphasized in my 1985 article, "Human Capital, Effort, and the Sexual Division of Labor," included as a supplement to Chapter 2, the message is that even small amounts of market discrimination against women or small biological differences between men and women can cause huge differences in the activities of husbands and wives. Therefore, large market discrimination or strong biological differences are not required to understand why the gender gap in earnings traditionally has been enormous. A sizable gap is expected when women have specialized in household activities, have invested little in market human capital, and have allocated most of their energy to the household.

The supplement also argues that an efficient division of labor is perfectly consistent with exploitation of women by husbands and parents—a "patrimony" system—that reduces their well-being and their command of their lives. Indeed, the gain to men from exploitation tends to increase when the allocation of resources, including the division of labor between men and women, becomes more efficient and raises output of goods and services. Boserup is one of the many writers on exploitation of women who fails to appreciate that exploitation is largely a separate issue from efficiency in the division of labor by gender.

Through their decisions, environments, and genetic constitutions, families transmit culture, abilities, education, earnings, and assets from older to younger generations. Chapter 7, based on Becker and Tomes (1979), models the transmission of endowments and assets from parents to children to analyze the determinants of inequality and intergenerational mobility. But the model has serious limitations, especially its assumption that parents can leave debt as well as wealth to children, and its merging of human and nonhuman capital into a homogeneous asset.

My article with Tomes on the rise and fall of families—published in 1986 but written for a conference in 1984—makes the more realistic assumption that parents cannot leave debt. It also distinguishes human capital from assets by assuming that rates of return on assets are fixed by the asset market, whereas rates of return on investments in the human capital of children depend positively on their endowment of "abilities" and decline (eventually) as more is invested in them.

These assumptions lead to a richer and more relevant set of implications than the analysis in Chapter 7, and I have added the 1986 article as a supplement to Chapter 7. It is also more consistent with the analysis in Chapter 6, which distinguishes human capital from assets, and assumes that rates of return on investments in human capital decline as more is invested in a person.

Arthur Goldberger (1985) claims that the analysis in Chapter 7 adds little to older models of inequality and intergenerational mobility that do not assume utility maximization and rational choices. In the "Rise and Fall" article that is now a supplement to Chapter 7, I show that maximization and other assumptions of the model have many implications not found in these other models. Elsewhere I reply systematically to a restatement of his criticisms (see Goldberger, 1989, and Becker, 1989).

The analysis in Chapter 8 and the supplement to Chapter 7 assume that parents are altruistic: their utility is raised when their children are better off. Altruistic parents are willing to contribute to the cost of investing in their children's human capital, but their contribution is limited by the recognition that greater spending on children means less spending on themselves. Therefore, even altruistic parents may underinvest in children in the sense that the equilibrium marginal rate of return on the children's human capital exceeds the rate on assets owned by parents.

When parents have underinvested, both children and parents would be made better off if the children could borrow from them to finance the wealth-maximizing investment in human capital and then repay the debt when they are adults and their parents are elderly. Poorer families would gain the most from such an arrangement because they are more likely than richer families to underinvest in children.

"The Family and the State," by Kevin M. Murphy and myself, reprinted as a supplement to Chapter 11, analyzes various consequences of parents' inability to bind children to repay loans. Besides too little investment in children, these include insufficient saving for old age in poorer families, and an unusual (some might say bizarre) aspect of the old and difficult question of "optimal" population. Obviously, unborn children cannot commit to compensating parents to induce them to have additional children (see Parfit, 1984, for a philosophical discussion of the weight that should be given to the interests of unborn children). Therefore, parents may not have additional children, even when both parents and the children could be made better off if they did.

Note that such an improvement in the welfare of both parents and additional children is possible only in the (poorer) families that do not leave bequests. Families with bequests do not want compensation from any children, including additional children, inasmuch as they could instead leave smaller bequests if they wanted to.

This supplement to Chapter 11 also suggests that the extensive government involvement in families found everywhere—through subsidies to schooling, social security programs, child allowances, laws regulating marriage and divorce, and many other mechanisms—often helps overcome the difficulties of making binding commitments between parents and children. For example, combining subsidies to education with social security payments may both raise investments in children to more efficient levels and also compensate older persons for the taxes they pay to finance these investments.

The supplements to Chapters 7 and 11 consider the consequences of parental altruism in an overlapping generations framework. "A Reformulation of the Economic Theory of Fertility" (with Robert J. Barro), included as a supplement to Chapter 5, incorporates the demand for children into this framework, where parents choose the number of children along with bequests and investments per child. The approach links fertility in different generations of a single dynastic family (and in different cohorts of an open economy) to the cost of children, incomes, interest rates, the degree of altruism, and other variables.

One implication of this dynamic analysis of fertility over time is that improvements in health knowledge which reduce child mortality must lower birth rates in the very long run (if interest rates do not rise). But births fall by more eventually than they do initially, and may even rise for a while.

If the long-term rate of growth over time in per capita consumption is held constant, fertility responds positively to changes in long-term interest rates. By contrast, the causation is reversed in so-called biological models of interest-rate determination (Samuelson, 1958), where interest rates are related to fertility and other variables that determine the rate of population growth. Although our model appears to be the first that relates fertility to interest rates, this connection has been recognized in fiction. The narrator in *The Forsyte Saga* says:

A student of statistics must have noticed that the birth rate had varied in accordance with the rate of interest for your money. Grandfather 'Superior Dosset' Forsyte in the early nineteenth century had been getting ten per cent. for his, hence ten children. Those ten, leaving out the four who had not married, and Juley, whose husband Septimus Small had, of course, died almost at once, had averaged from four to five per cent. for theirs, and produced accordingly. (Galsworthy, 1949, p. 365)[1]

In our analysis the degree of altruism per child determines the discount rate on the consumption of children and other future generations. With diminishing marginal utility from children, the altruism per child declines as the number of children increases. Then an increase in fertility raises the discount rate on the future, which discourages future consumption. Therefore, a rise in long-term interest rates may not increase the rate of growth in long-term per capita consumption because a higher discount rate offsets the effect of higher interest rates.

---

1. Galsworthy goes on to a further economic analysis: "There were other reasons, too, for this mild reproduction. A distrust of their earning power, natural where a sufficiency is guaranteed, together with the knowledge that their fathers did not die, kept them cautious. If one had children and not much income, the standard of taste and comfort must of necessity go down; what was enough for two was not enough for four, and so on—it would be better to wait and see what Father did. Besides, it was nice to be able to take holidays unhampered. Sooner in fact than own children, they preferred to concentrate on the ownership of themselves, conforming to the growing tendency—*fin de siècle,* as it was called" (p. 366).

The analysis in Chapters 5 to 7, including the supplement to Chapter 5, relies on an interaction between the number of children and the quality per child, where quality is measured by various proxies for the well-being of children. An early paper (Becker and Lewis, 1973; also see Willis, 1973) shows that quantity and quality of children interact partly because they enter multiplicatively in the budget set of parents through total expenditures on children. This interaction means that quantity and quality of children are closely related decisions of parents, even when they are not closely related in parental utility functions.

The link relation between these variables may also result from the way they enter parental utility functions. Since the degree of altruism per child, and hence the weight attached to the future, decreases when the number of children increases, the effect of fertility on the rates of discount of the future is an additional source of interaction between quantity and quality.

Many sociologists and demographers as well as economists now incorporate an interaction between quantity and quality of children into their analysis of fertility (see for example the discussion in Blake, 1981, who earlier [1968] criticized the economic analysis of fertility). Still, some remain skeptical about the analysis of child quality, complaining, among other things, that I base the demand for quality mainly on biological considerations.[2] Yet I explicitly reject biological arguments as inadequate (see for example the early part of Chapter 5 and the concluding remarks in Chapter 9).

Economists almost never discuss why consumers like bananas or other goods, but it is not hard to understand why parents are altruistic toward children. Barro and Becker (1989) show that altruistic parents

---

2. Brian Arthur, in his 1982 review of the *Treatise,* expressed great skepticism about the value of an analysis based on child quality. Apropos of an analysis that relates child quality to parents' expenditures on each child, Arthur asked, "How can expenditures have a price?" (p. 396). Expenditures per child, when used as a proxy for child quality, do have a *shadow* price, which is positively related to the number of children and which enters the first-order condition for utility maximization by parents in the same way other prices do. Arthur claimed too that I rely on a biological foundation for my emphasis on child quality.

I have avoided spending much time in this Introduction on replies to reviews of the first edition. But I explicitly mention Arthur's review because some demographers (such as McNicholl, 1988) believe that it is damaging to the *Treatise.* A lengthy comment on Arthur's critique, which I prepared several years ago, is available on request and shows that the review was full of misconceptions about the analysis in the *Treatise.*

tend both to have larger families and to spend more on each child than selfish parents with equal resources. Their discussion answers the question raised in Chapter 8 regarding whether altruistic parents have more children as well as spend more on each one. If children "inherit" culturally or biologically a tendency to be like their parents, families with greater altruism would become relatively more numerous over time. Such a selection mechanism operating over thousands of years would have made altruism toward children common in modern times.

Yet many economists dispute that altruism is important in families, even though these same economists often deny themselves in order to accumulate gifts and bequests for their children. Moreover, parental love, especially mother love, has been recognized since biblical times. For example, in 1580 the great French essayist Michel de Montaigne stated, "If there is any true law of nature, . . . after the care that all beasts have for their own preservation, and to avoid what does them harm, the affection which the parent feels for its progeny holds the second place" (1958, p. 138).

Even though altruism is important in most families, some parents do abuse their children, and some others want power or financial help from children. But surely interactions between family members are distinguished from those between unrelated persons primarily by the love and caring within the family.

And altruism changes enormously the nature of interactions among people. Chapter 8, based on the analysis in Becker (1974b), shows that a small redistribution of income between a parent and child does not change either's consumption or utility if the parent is altruistic and makes gifts to the child. Barro (1974) also derives such a "neutrality" result in the context of considering the effects on consumption and savings of public debt, social security, and other government transfers between generations. His analysis is one of the most important and controversial in public finance during the past two decades.

These neutrality results use the effect of altruism on the budget constraint only (see Figure 8.1). Altruism also affects incentives and strategy. One important example is the Rotten Kid Theorem, which shows that if several conditions are met, altruistic parents and their children maximize the same utility function, even if children are selfish. The main assumptions are: all goods can be bought and sold (leisure is an example of a good that cannot); there is a single time period; parents provide gifts to children; and parents choose after children do in a two-stage "game."

Several remarks in Chapter 8 suggest unwarranted generalizations of this theorem beyond the assumptions just stated (see especially the discussion of shirking, reading in bed, and manners). But the theorem may not hold when some goods cannot be bought, or when consumption extends over more than one period (see the supplement to Chapter 11; Bruce and Waldman, 1986; Lindbeck and Weibull, 1988; and especially Bergstrom, 1989).

The most unsatisfactory aspect of my discussion, however, is not incorrect applications of the Rotten Kid Theorem—however lamentable they may be—but the failure to combine the discussions of "merit goods" and altruism. By "merit goods" I mean particular traits or behavior of children that parents care about: whether they are lazy, study hard at school, visit often, drink excessively, marry well, or are mean to siblings.

When altruistic parents also want merit goods for children, parents and children do not interact only because children can raise or lower both their own and parental utilities, the effect considered by the Rotten Kid Theorem; in addition, decreased consumption of merit goods by children may lower the degree of altruism toward children, which in turn directly reduces gifts to children. For example, a child who studies little in college may get less from parents because his failure to study angers them. A rational child takes account of parental response to how hard he studies (or how hard they believe he studies).

To analyze this interaction without postulating direct bargaining between parents and children or that parents can commit to gifts in advance, assume that children choose first their merit goods, parents then choose gifts and their own consumption, and, finally, children choose their other goods; the Rotten Kid Theorem assumes a similar sequence. Let a child have the utility function $U = U(x_1, x_2)$ and parents have $V = V(x_3, x_2, U)$, where x_2 is the children's good that is a merit good to parents. Children choose x_1 and x_2, and parents cannot directly affect these choices, but they can indirectly do so by the gifts (g) they give. In a perfect foresight equilibrium, children maximize U subject to their resources that equal $I_c + g$, where I_c is their income. Parents maximize with respect to x_3 and g, subject to their income, I_p, and given the choice of x_2 by children. The first-order conditions for parents are

$$\frac{\partial V}{\partial x_3} = V_3 = \lambda_p p_3 \tag{I.1}$$

and
$$\lambda_p = V_u \frac{dU}{dg} = V_u \lambda_c = \frac{V_u U_1}{p_1}, \tag{I.2}$$

where λ_p and λ_c are the marginal utilities of income to the parents and child, respectively, and p_3 is the price of x_3. The first two terms of Eq. (I.2) starting from the left-hand side constitute the first-order condition for g. The third term from the left recognizes that dU/dg equals the marginal utility of income to the child, and the last term comes from the fact that $\lambda_c = U_1/p_1$ is a first-order condition for the child.

A child realizes that a change in x_2 may affect giving, because x_2 also enters the parents' utility function. The child's first-order condition for x_2 is

$$U_2 = \lambda_c \left[p_2 - \frac{dg}{dx_2} \right] = \lambda_c \Pi_2. \qquad (I.3)$$

The term dg/dx_2 indicates that an increase in the merit good x_2 may change giving. If x_2 and parental altruism are "complements"—for example, if $V_{u2} > 0$ and $V_{32} = 0$—greater x_2 raises giving by making parents more altruistic.

If g increases when x_2 does (if $dg/dx_2 > 0$), the net or shadow price of x_2 is below its market price ($\Pi_2 < p_2$). A lower price tends to increase the demand for x_2 by the child, which makes his parents happier. As with the Rotten Kid Theorem, the *automatic* responses of parents to the x_2 chosen by children—no bargaining, commitment, or threats are allowed—induce children to move in a direction desired by parents. In this case the mechanism is not altruism alone, but the effect of merit goods on the degree of altruism.

Automatic responses of parents induce children to raise x_2, but its level is generally below what parents would choose if they directly controlled the child's behavior. In other words, the first-order conditions above for the child and parents are not equivalent to the first-order conditions for parents when they maximize utility and control x_1, x_3, and x_2, and total income. To illustrate, if U only weakly affects V, and if x_1 and x_2 enter U in fixed proportions, then a child consumes x_1 and x_2 in these proportions when he chooses, but he would get little x_1 relative to x_2 when parents choose.

In an excellent analysis, Bergstrom (1989) demonstrates that children, in fact, choose the same outcomes as parents if there is "transferable" utility, but transferability implies strong restrictions on utility functions. They choose the same outcomes in other cases as well, but no one has yet given a general representation of all cases where Rotten Kid Theorems apply. The interaction of merit goods with parental altruism, however, induces children to increase their consumption of these goods in the *direction* desired by parents, even if children do not behave exactly as parents wish.

Another important aspect of the relation between merit goods and altruism is that merit goods sometimes help offset adverse effects of altruism on children's incentives. Consider the prodigal son example discussed by Bruce and Waldman (1986), Becker and Murphy (1988a), Lindbeck and Weibull (1988), and Bergstrom (1989). Without precommitment by parents, a child with altruistic parents may consume much of his wealth quickly and work very little, because he can count on their altruism to help him out when his income is low. But if parents are less altruistic when children are wasteful or lazy, even a prodigal son may work hard and be frugal to get larger gifts and bequests. In essence, the child's behavior is disciplined by the negative effect of prodigality on his parents' altruism toward him.

This analysis implies that wealthy parents may have more leverage over the behavior of children than poorer parents, in that wealthy parents leave bequests (see my comments in Chapter 8). A 1776 Virginia act abolishing entails on estates relied on this leverage, for it stated that an entail "does injury to the morals of youth by rendering them independent of and disobedient to their parents" (Herning, 1809–1823; I owe this reference to Milton Friedman). Since parents usually like visits from children, a reasonable explanation of why the elderly rich are apparently more frequently visited than are the elderly poor (see the evidence in Bernheim et al., 1986) is that parental control over bequests induces children to please wealthy parents. A similar argument explains why divorced fathers often fall behind in child-support payments, for their altruism declines over time as contact with children is reduced. (Weiss and Willis, 1989, give a different explanation.)

The effect of children's behavior on altruism helps explain why altruistic parents may not compensate less successful children with larger bequests. (Menchik, 1980, among others, presents evidence on the equality of bequests to children.) Bequests to less successful children would be reduced if parents suspect that these children are lazy or wasteful.

Merit goods are not needed to control a prodigal son's behavior if parents' gifts are precommitted and are not contingent on his earnings or wealth. But precommitment has its problems too; parents lose the flexibility to react to exogenous events that affect the child. For example, with fully precommitted gifts, parents cannot help children who have serious accidents or develop debilitating diseases. Merit goods can be more effective than commitment precisely because they do distinguish exogenous events from choices by children. For this reason children with known physical or mental handicaps are likely to receive larger bequests and gifts than their siblings, although I am unaware of any evidence on transfers to children with handicaps.

The relation between merit goods and altruism can introduce strategic elements into children's behavior, for children may be able to increase gifts and bequests from parents partly at the expense of gifts to siblings—a "beggar-thy-sibling" policy. The result may be collusion by children, or excessive production of merit goods as children compete for parents' favors.

The marriage market induces a relation between the altruisms in different nuclear families, because parents-in-law and other relatives may contribute to the joint consumption of their children and grandchildren. And a surprisingly large fraction of all families are related in a few generations through marriage of relatives (see Bernheim and Bagwell, 1988). However, the degree of interaction among the altruisms in different families may be severely limited by incentives to free-ride on gifts from others. For example, a father may fear that if he gives more to his daughter, his in-laws will give less to their son (see my comments in Chapter 8, and the extended discussion in Nerlove et al., 1987).

A redistribution of a fixed total income from children to parents does not change the consumption or utility of either, even when (1) merit goods are important, (2) the Rotten Kid Theorem breaks down, (3) the altruisms of relatives interact, and (4) children behave strategically. A proof of this proposition simply notes that parents could have achieved this redistribution, if they wanted to, by giving children less. Since parents choose not to give less, they must prefer the initial utility position to all others that are feasible after the redistribution of income.

Chapters 3 and 4 analyze the competition for marriage partners among men and women of different incomes, abilities, education, ages, family backgrounds, and other attributes. They examine the characteristics of men and women in polygynous marriages when these are permitted, and assess who gets the more attractive partners. The analysis does not assume that husbands and wives necessarily share equally in the rewards from marriage, and considers how competitive forces determine the distribution of marital output between spouses.

Some authors have claimed that I overemphasize competition in marriage markets, while neglecting "power" and bargaining in marriages (see for example McElroy and Horney, 1981, and Boserup, 1987).[3] Yet I do consider bargaining over whether to divorce; whether divorce laws that require mutual consent have different effects from laws that permit unilateral divorce, sometimes only by husbands (see Chapter 10); the relation between unequal power of husbands and wives and the division of labor by gender (especially see the supplement to Chapter 2); and other examples of bargaining and power in marriage.

What I emphasize is that bargaining within marriages takes place in the shadow of competition in marriage markets, even when laws and customs favor husbands. For example, if only men can divorce—as under traditional Islamic law—before marriage a bride and her family will require the groom and his family to agree to an appropriate settlement in the event she is divorced; otherwise, she will look elsewhere for a husband. Islamic countries do have marriage contracts that stipulate in detail the settlements paid to divorced wives. Since divorce was common in the late Roman republic, fathers seldom endowed their daughters with generous dowries. For "a high probability of divorce was also a considerable disincentive to granting a huge dowry to a husband who might be entitled to keep part of it if the marriage dissolved" (Saller, forthcoming). When divorce is not possible, or when both spouses must agree to a divorce—as was the case in most of the United States prior to 1970—women who fear abuse by their husbands delay marriage until they are more confident about the love and character of their husbands.

Competition in marriage markets can fully offset even highly unequal power of husbands and wives if marriages have binding contracts that provide for resource allocation under all future contingencies. Competition is less effective when marriage contracts are not legally binding, or when they can allow for only a fraction of the many contingencies

---

3. Despite my assumption that competition in marriage markets determines the division of marital outputs between husbands and wives, Boserup claims that "Becker assumes a harmony of interest between the marriage partners and an equal distribution of consumption and leisure between them" (1987, p. 826). But in this book I explicitly deny such an assumption: "Available information on the amounts spent on husband's and wife's clothing or on their leisure time could be related to sex ratios, wage rates, education levels, and other determinants of the division of marital output" (p. 42 of the first edition; p. 84 of this edition).

that arise during a marriage. How can a contract protect a wife against mental or physical abuse that leaves no mark and takes place in private?

My conclusion in Chapter 10 that divorce rates would not be raised by a change to unilateral divorce laws from mutual consent assumes that married persons do not know less about their spouses' gains than about their own gains from a divorce. Peters (1986) shows that such a change to unilateral divorce laws would raise divorce rates if individuals did know more about their own gains. A little empirical work in that chapter and Peters' much more detailed empirical study failed to find any appreciable effect on divorce rates, but several subsequent studies found that the change to unilateral divorce increased these rates (see especially Weiss and Willis, 1989, and Zelder, 1989). But even in these studies the change in laws explains only a small part of the large increase in divorce after 1970, when states began to introduce unilateral divorce laws. Therefore, the conclusion in Chapter 10 that the rise in divorce rates is due mainly to changed economic and social conditions remains valid whether or not one accepts the results of these studies.

Chapter 11 is an early contribution to the so-called new institutionalism—without ever using that language. In this approach, institutions are assumed to evolve in the direction dictated by rational individual responses to changed conditions. The chapter argues that families are much less closely knit and perform far fewer functions in the twentieth century than in earlier centuries primarily because market and government mechanisms have evolved to train and educate young people, and to protect against the hazards of old age, illness, premature death, prolonged unemployment, and other economic disasters. These new institutions have reduced the value of relying on families for these purposes. According to the argument, families changed at the most rapid pace ever during the past few decades primarily because earnings and employment opportunities of women improved greatly, and the welfare state grew rapidly.

Apropos of my emphasis on the welfare state, I have been criticized for claiming that welfare payments to unmarried mothers in the United States discouraged marriage and encouraged fertility among poorer women. Critics say that the growth in numbers of welfare recipients and in birth rates to unmarried women during the 1970s and 1980s cannot be a result of the welfare system because welfare payments per family declined a little in real terms over this period. They also point out (see Vining, 1983) that state differences in the generosity of welfare payments are not closely related to differences across states in birth rates to unmarried mothers.

However, my analysis of marriage markets implies that the incentive to remain single depends on income while single *relative* to income expected if married.[4] Real wage rates of young male high school dropouts and the lowest quartile of graduates dropped by more than 25 percent over the past 15 years (see Juhn et al., 1989), and these young men may have become less attractive marriage partners for other reasons as well (see Wilson, 1987). Therefore, welfare may well have contributed to the propensity of poor women to remain single and become mothers even though real welfare payments per family fell (see also Bernstam and Swan, 1986).

Chapter 9 claims that the optimizing techniques used in studying human families are useful in understanding family patterns in other species as well, even though human behavior is determined by cultural as well as biological factors, and learning and other aspects of behavior are very different in the biological world. This chapter analyzes mating systems in nonhuman species and the trade-off between the quantity and quality of offspring—called K-strategies and r-strategies in the biological literature.

The same kind of optimizing model can shed light on other issues treated in the biological literature. For example, in an influential article Hamilton (1964) argues that altruism in nonhuman species is greater toward close than toward more distant relations because a larger fraction of genes are shared with close relations. Nonetheless, the four grandparents or eight great-grandparents fully share all the genes with grandchildren or great-grandchildren, just as the two parents fully share genes with their children. If the grandparents cooperate totally in spending time and other resources on grandchildren, *jointly* they have a stronger incentive to help their grandchildren than each parent *alone* has to help a child. It would seem that the kin selection model has to be modified to consider the likelihood of cooperation.

Of course, the degree of free-riding tends to rise with the number of relations who must cooperate. But one cannot simply assume away cooperation among parents and other relations, as the usual kin selec-

---

4. I state that "the expansion of welfare, *along with the general decline in the gain from marriage,* explains the sizable growth in the ratio of illegitimate to legitimate birth rates" (italics added; p. 357, this edition).

tion model does; the propensity to cooperate may be a trait with good survival value.

This book does not discuss all aspects of families—even many volumes would be insufficient for that. Rather, it tries to show that an analysis based on rational behavior provides a powerful framework for gaining insights into family organization and structure under different laws, circumstances, and cultures. Some scholars accept the premise that behavior in modern secular societies tends to be rational, but question whether family decisions in underdeveloped and religious countries are also rational. I cannot prove that rationality is found in most places, but let us consider a few examples of religious, poor, or ancient societies.

"Irish family patterns" is a term in the social science literature that connotes men and women who marry late, and married women who remain at home to take care of many small children because their religion forbids birth control. Yet these so-called Irish patterns no longer apply to Ireland! Men and women in the Republic of Ireland marry much younger than they once did; still, fertility has declined sharply. Couples make extensive use of condoms and other birth control methods, despite the Catholic Church's continued opposition to contraceptives (see the analysis in Kennedy, 1988).

Ireland remains a highly religious country, and the Irish constitution even guarantees married women the right to remain at home to care for their families. However, rational family responses to powerful economic and social changes have outweighed church teachings and the constitution. The growing importance to the economy of well-trained workers has persuaded parents to substitute fewer, better-educated children for the traditional large families. Higher earnings and greater employment opportunities for married women have raised their labor force participation, reduced fertility, and encouraged marital breakups. Indeed, Irish families are behaving very much like other families in the Western world. Many devout parents agonize, but end up disregarding church doctrine on contraception and increasingly on divorce and abandonment of spouses as well.

Bukina Faso (formerly Upper Volta) in Africa is one of the poorest countries in the world, where farming methods and life-styles have hardly been touched by modernization. Yet Singh's (1988) intensive study of a sample of farms shows rational marital and fertility responses to their primitive conditions. Men with "large" farms—these are still less than 10 hectares—take several wives (Bukina Faso is polygynous) because women do most of the farm work, as well as produce children who contribute to farm output. Children are especially useful in caring for livestock, and Singh shows that the number of children is greater when there are more livestock.

Roman private law had detailed rules about family relations and inheritance, which could be overridden by marriage contracts (called dotal pacts) and wills. These pacts and women's right to divorce during the late republic and imperial periods often gave wealthy married women considerable power, even when their husbands nominally held most of the authority. The right to raise or lower bequests to children through a will provided wealthy parents a leverage over their children that poorer parents lacked. The poor had to rely on the generosity of children and public pressure on those children for old-age support (see the interesting discussion of Roman families in Saller, forthcoming).

A pleasant, largely unexpected by-product of the analysis in this book is my realization that family decisions crucially impinge on many other issues. Let me illustrate this with brief discussions of economic growth and income inequality.

The implication of Malthus' model of economic growth, that people marry earlier and have more children when their incomes are greater, was decisively contradicted by the experiences of Western and many other countries during the past 150 years. Neoclassical economics reacted by ignoring the family, and usually assumed that fertility and other determinants of population growth did not depend on economic variables.

But Malthus' mistakes in modeling family responses do not mean that marriages and births are independent of the economy. By combining our reformulation of fertility—the supplement to Chapter 5—with the neoclassical growth model, Robert Barro and I (1989) show that a higher rate of technological progress in a closed economy lowers fertility and the rate of population growth, unless more rapid progress sufficiently raises interest rates. We also show that the neoclassical conclusion about tax incidence, that in the long run a tax on capital is fully shifted to other factors, no longer holds when fertility is endogenous. Such a tax is only partially shifted when fertility is positively related to per capita income, and it is shifted by more than 100 percent when fertility and income are negatively related.

Malthus was correct in believing that total expenditures on children rise as parents' incomes increase. But he went astray in assuming that expenditures go up principally because families have more children; they usually have fewer children when their incomes increase. Expenditures on children grow in expanding economies mainly because children's education and other human capital increase. Becker et al. (1990) combine the Barro-Becker reformulation of fertility with a growth model that highlights the effects of human capital on growth in per capita incomes. Greatly amplifying the discussion in Chapter 6, we show that substitution between the quantity and quality of children helps explain why fertility usually falls sharply and human capital increases when a country "takes off" toward growth. We also demonstrate that the Malthusian model may apply when economic changes in poor countries are not large.

That family behavior is an important determinant of inequality is evident from the effect of the growth in female-headed households since the late 1960s on the fraction of families in the United States below the poverty line. These households became more important as divorce rates surged and the fraction of children born to unmarried mothers skyrocketed. Fuchs (1983) and Levy (1987) give valuable discussions of the relation between family structure and inequality.

The analysis in this book is helpful in understanding the degree of inequality among families. Inequality clearly depends on the relation between fertility and family income; on the extent of underinvestment by poorer families in their children's human capital; on the degree of assortative mating by education, family background, and other characteristics; on divorce rates and the amount of child support to divorced women; and on any inequity in the distribution of bequests among children. Inequality also depends on government efforts to redistribute income through subsidies to education, social security programs, and other techniques, although the net effect on inequality of these programs depends crucially on how families respond. For example, a welfare program may widen rather than narrow inequality if women on welfare raise their fertility and reduce their time and effort spent on each child.

This enlarged edition of *A Treatise on the Family* is an effort to demonstrate further that the rational choice interpretation of family behavior has much to offer not only to economists, but also to researchers in the many other disciplines that study the family. The family merits the great attention it receives from both scholars and laypersons, for despite major changes over time and enormous variations across social and economic environments, it remains the most influential of all institutions.

CHAPTER 1

Single-Person Households

The traditional theory of consumer and household behavior developed by economists ignores cooperation and conflict among members, in essence assuming that each household has only one member. This theory focuses on the effects of changes in money income and money prices on the allocation of income among market goods. The theory of single-person households has been greatly expanded during the past twenty years, from a rather limited analysis to a powerful tool with many applications. The new analysis includes allocation of time as well as of money income and introduces household production of skills, health, self-esteem, and various other "commodities."

This short chapter outlines the traditional theory and its recent enlargement as a preparation for the discussion of families in the rest of the book. There is now a sizable amount of relevant literature; interested readers are referred to Michael and Becker (1973) for a more elaborate discussion.

Traditional Theory

In the simplest version of traditional theory, a single person spends his (or her) given income to maximize his utility function U of goods and services (for simplicity, called "goods") purchased in the marketplace. That is, he maximizes the function

$$U = U(x_1, \ldots, x_n), \tag{1.1}$$

subject to the budget constraint $\Sigma p_i x_i = I$, where p_i is the price of the ith good x_i, and I is his money income. The well-known equilibrium condition is that the marginal utility MU of each good is proportional to its price:

$$\frac{\partial U}{\partial x_i} = MU_i = \lambda p_i, \qquad i = 1, \ldots, n, \tag{1.2}$$

where λ is the marginal utility of income.

The main implication of these equilibrium conditions is that the quantity demanded of any good is negatively related to its price: the "law of negatively sloped demand curves." This law has been extremely important in practical applications and is one of the most significant and universal laws in the social sciences, even though it results more from limited resources than from utility maximization (Becker, 1962).

A rise in income increases the demand for most goods because the additional income must be spent, where "spent" includes adding to cash balances and other assets. The equality between total expenditures and income implies that

$$\sum s_i \eta_i = 1, \tag{1.3}$$

where $\eta_i = [(dx_i)/(dI)] \cdot (I/x_i)$ is the income elasticity of demand for the ith good, and s_i is the fraction of income spent on that good. The average income elasticity equals unity, so that "luxuries" ($\eta_i > 1$) must be balanced by "necessities" ($\eta_i < 1$).

A more complicated and more realistic version of the theory recognizes that each person allocates time as well as money income to different activities, receives income from time spent working in the marketplace, and receives utility from time spent eating, sleeping, watching television, gardening, and participating in many other activities. The utility function, Eq. (1.1), then is extended to

$$U = U(x_1, \ldots, x_n, t_{h_1}, \ldots, t_{h_r}), \tag{1.4}$$

where t_{h_j} is the time spent at the jth activity. A time-budget constraint joins the money-income constraint:

$$\sum_{j=1}^{r} t_{h_j} + t_w = t, \tag{1.5}$$

where t is the total time available during some period, such as 24 hours a day or 168 hours a week, and t_w is the time spent working for pay.[1]

One important implication of this extension is that money income is no longer "given" but is determined by the allocation of time, inasmuch as earnings are determined by the time allocated to work. Therefore, the goods and time-budget constraints are not independent and can be combined into one overall constraint:

$$\sum p_i x_i = I = wt_w + v = w(t - \sum t_{h_j}) + v, \tag{1.6}$$

or

$$\sum p_i x_i + w \sum t_{h_j} = wt + v = S, \tag{1.7}$$

where w is the earnings per hour of work, v is property income, and S is "full" or potential income (or the money income when all time is allocated to the market sector). The terms on the left show that full income is spent in part directly on market goods and in part indirectly on the time used to produce utility rather than earnings.[2]

The equilibrium conditions from maximizing the utility function (Eq. 1.4) subject to the full-income constraint, Eq. (1.7), include

$$MU_{t_{h_k}}/MU_{t_{h_j}} = 1, \quad \text{and} \quad MU_{t_{h_j}}/MU_{x_i} = w/p_i. \tag{1.8}$$

The marginal utility from all uses of time are equal in equilibrium because they have the same price (w), and the marginal rate of substitution between time and each good equals the "real" wage rate, where the price deflator is the price of that good.[3]

The main implications of these equilibrium conditions are generalizations of the negatively sloped demand curves derived with the simpler model. A compensated rise in the price of any good—a rise

---

1. For simplicity I have assumed that working time does not enter the utility function.

2. After division by w, Eq. (1.7) becomes

$$\sum \left(\frac{p_i}{w}\right) x_i + \sum t_j = t + \frac{v}{w} = \frac{S}{w}.$$

The terms on the right now give the total time available plus the value of property income in time units, and the terms on the left show that time is spent in part directly on producing utility and in part indirectly on buying goods, where p_i/w is the time spent on a unit of the ith good.

3. In Becker (1965) the cost of time is allowed to differ among uses because of "productive consumption."

offset by a sufficient rise in property income to keep real income constant—reduces the demand for that good and increases the demand for "most" other goods. It also reduces the time spent at work and increases the time spent at most nonmarket (or household) activities, because a rise in the price of a good reduces the real wage rate in units of that good. Similarly, a compensated rise in the wage rate increases working time and demand for goods and reduces the time allocated to most household activities. For example, a compensated rise in the wage rate reduces the time spent on child care, standing in queues, or shopping, and thereby increases the demand for nursery schools, inventory of goods in the household, and consumer durables that require less maintenance. Finally, a growth in full income without any change in the wage rate reduces working time and increases the demand for most goods and household time (for more details see Becker, 1965).

If all time were spent in the household sector, the value of time would not be measured by the wage rate but by a shadow price equal to the marginal product of time in the household sector. The equilibrium condition in the second equation of (1.8) would be replaced by

$$MU_{t_{h_j}}/MU_{x_i} = \mu/p_i, \tag{1.8'}$$

where μ, the shadow price of time, equals the marginal rate of substitution between goods and time after conversion into monetary units. An increase in property income increases the consumption of goods and thereby raises the marginal product and shadow price of household time. If time is spent working in the marketplace, the wage rate has to equal the shadow price of household time:

$$\mu = w, \qquad t_w > 0; \tag{1.9}$$

otherwise, the marginal value of working time would be less than the marginal value of household time.

Household Production Functions

I have been assuming that time and goods directly provide utility, yet a more intuitive and useful assumption is that time and goods are inputs into the production of "commodities," which directly provide utility. These commodities cannot be purchased in the marketplace but are produced as well as consumed by households using market purchases, own time, and various environmental inputs. These commodities include children, prestige and esteem, health, altruism, envy, and pleasures of the senses,[4] and are much smaller in number than the goods consumed.

The utility function can be rewritten as

$$U = U(Z_1, \ldots, Z_m), \tag{1.10}$$

where $Z_1, \ldots, Z_m$ are the various commodities consumed. Each is self-produced according to

$$Z_i = f_i(x_i, t_{h_i}; E_i), \quad i = 1, \ldots, m, \tag{1.11}$$

where x_i and t_{h_i} represent the possibly many goods and types of time used to produce the ith commodity, and E_i represents household ability, human capital, social and physical climate, and other environmental variables. Commodities do not have market prices because they are not purchased, but they do have shadow prices equal to the cost of production:

$$\pi_i = p_i \frac{x_i}{Z_i} + w \frac{t_{h_i}}{Z_i}, \tag{1.12}$$

where π_i is the average cost of the goods and time spent on each unit of Z_i. The full-income constraint given by Eq. (1.7) can be simply expressed using these shadow commodity prices as

$$\sum p_i x_i + w \sum t_{h_i} \equiv \sum_{i=1}^{m} \pi_i Z_i = S. \tag{1.13}$$

If the utility function of commodities is maximized subject to this full-income constraint, one set of equilibrium conditions equates the ratio of the marginal utilities of different commodities to the ratio of their shadow prices:[5]

$$\frac{\partial U/\partial Z_i}{\partial U/\partial Z_k} = \frac{MU_i}{MU_k} = \frac{\pi_i}{\pi_k}, \quad \text{for all } i \text{ and } k. \tag{1.14}$$

---

4. Bentham (1963, chap. 5) lists about 15 fundamental sources of "pleasure and pain."

5. The relevant shadow prices are determined by marginal, not average, costs of production. However, if all production functions are homogeneous of the first degree, and if each unit of a good or of time is used to produce only one commodity (no joint production), then marginal and average costs are equal and the average prices in Eq. (1.12) would be appropriate. Joint production is considered in Grossman (1971) and in Pollak and Wachter (1975).

An increase in the relative price of Z_k reduces the demand for Z_k and for the goods and time used to produce it.

The distinction between the commodities consumed and the goods and services purchased is not only plausible, but also of considerable value in interpreting behavior. The general utility function given by Eq. (1.4) does not provide insight into special substitution or complementarity relations between different goods and time. We cannot even rule out a compensated increase in the wage rate that would *increase* the time spent at most household activities. The household production approach, on the other hand, implies a special relation between goods and time used to produce the same commodity. Fish and meat are inputs into the production of health and taste; or parental time and nursery schools are substitutes in the production of children.

Put more technically, the utility function given by Eq. (1.10) is separable in the goods and time used to produce the same commodity:

$$\frac{\partial U/\partial x_i}{\partial U/\partial t_{h_i}} \equiv \frac{(\partial U/\partial Z_i) \cdot (\partial Z_i/\partial x_i)}{(\partial U/\partial Z_i) \cdot (\partial Z_i/\partial t_{h_i})} = \frac{\partial Z_i/\partial x_i}{\partial Z_i/\partial t_{h_i}} = MP_{x_i}/MP_{t_{h_i}}$$

$$= \phi(x_i, t_{h_i}), \qquad i = 1, \ldots, m. \tag{1.15}$$

This separability property implies, for example, that an increase in the wage rate necessarily decreases the ratio of time to goods spent on each commodity, and that it tends also to decrease the output of time-intensive commodities relative to goods-intensive commodities.

Investment in Human Capital

The utility function, Eq. (1.10), must be generalized to distinguish consumption at different ages because people are not indifferent between earlier and later consumption. Therefore, assume that

$$U = U(Z_{11}, \ldots, Z_{1n}, \ldots, Z_{m1}, \ldots, Z_{mn}), \tag{1.16}$$

where Z_{ij} is the consumption of the ith commodity at the jth age; n, the length of remaining life, is taken as given but can be treated endogenously (Grossman, 1972). The subsequent presentation is simplified without any significant loss in generality by combining all commodities at a given age into a single aggregate commodity. The utility function can then be written as

$$U = U(Z_1, \ldots, Z_n), \tag{1.16'}$$

where Z_j is the aggregate consumption at age j.

Wage rates change with age because of the accumulation of human capital that results from decisions about the time and other resources to spend on investments. The stock of human capital evolves according to the relation

$$H_j = H_{j-1}(1 - \delta) + Q_{j-1}, \tag{1.17}$$

where H_j is the stock at age j, δ is the given depreciation rate, and Q_{j-1}, the gross investment at age $j - 1$, is produced according to

$$Q_{j-1} = Q(x_{q_{j-1}}, t_{q_{j-1}}; H_{j-1}), \tag{1.18}$$

where x_q and t_q are the goods and time spent on investment. Wage rates in competitive labor markets are determined by

$$w_j = a_j H_j, \tag{1.19}$$

where a_j is the earnings per hour of a unit of human capital at age j.

The total time available at any age can be allocated to the household, market, or investment sector:

$$t_{h_j} + t_{w_j} + t_{q_j} = t, \qquad j = 1, \ldots, n. \tag{1.20}$$

In perfect capital markets the present value of expenditures on goods would equal the present value of earnings and other income:

$$\sum_{j=1}^{n} \frac{p_j x_j + p_{q_j} x_{q_j}}{(1 + r)^j} = \sum_{j=1}^{n} \frac{w_j t_{w_j}}{(1 + r)^j} + A, \tag{1.21}$$

where r is the interest rate and A is the value at time 0 of nonhuman assets. By substituting the time constraints into the goods constraint, we can derive the equation for "full" wealth, W:

$$\sum_{j=1}^{n} \frac{\pi_j Z_j + \pi_{q_j} Q_j}{(1 + r)^j} = \sum_{j=1}^{n} \frac{p_j x_j + p_{q_j} x_{q_j} + w_j(t_{h_j} + t_{q_j})}{(1 + r)^j}$$

$$= \sum \frac{w_j t}{(1 + r)^j} + A = W. \tag{1.22}$$

The utility function in Eq. (1.16′) is maximized subject to this full-wealth constraint, the various commodity and investment production functions, and the evolution of human capital and wage rates. The optimal investment at any age is determined by marginal investment costs and marginal returns, according to the following equation (see Mathematical Appendix, note A):

$$MC_{q_j} = R_j = \sum_{k=j+1}^{n} \frac{\{[\pi_k(\partial Z_k)/(\partial H_k)] + a_k t_{w_k}\}(\partial H_k)/(\partial Q_j)}{(1 + r)^{k-j}}. \quad (1.23)$$

The far left-hand side gives the marginal cost of investment at age j, and R_j equals the discounted value to age j of subsequent market and household returns.

Equation (1.23) implies that investments tend to decline with age because fewer years remain at older ages to receive the annual returns; moreover, investment costs tend to be lower at younger ages because the foregone value of time spent investing is cheaper then. The optimal stock of human capital would rise at a diminishing rate, reach a peak, then decline toward the end of life as depreciation exceeds gross investment. If life went on forever, the capital stock would rise to a peak during the "investment period" and be maintained at that level indefinitely.

If human capital directly raised the output of commodities only by augmenting the effective amount of household time,

$$t_h' = t_h \, \psi(H), \quad \text{and} \quad \frac{\partial Z}{\partial H} = \frac{\partial Z}{\partial t_h'} \, t_h \psi', \quad (1.24)$$

where $d\psi/dH = \psi' > 0$. Investment returns can then be written simply (see Mathematical Appendix, note B) as:

$$R_j = \sum_{k=j+1}^{n} \frac{w_k \left(\frac{\psi'}{\psi} t_{h_k} + \tilde{w}_k t_{w_k}\right)}{(1 + r)^{k-j}} \frac{\partial H_k}{\partial Q_j}, \quad (1.25)$$

where $\tilde{w}_k = (d \log w_k)/dH_k$.

Returns would depend on the allocation of time between the market and household sectors only if human capital affects the productivity of household and market time differently (if $\psi'/\psi \neq \tilde{w}$). As Eq. (1.25) implies, the incentive to invest in capital that mainly raises household productivity is greater when more time is spent in the household sector, and the incentive to invest in capital that mainly raises market productivity is greater when more time is spent at work. Some investments, such as on-the-job training, mainly raise the productivity of market time; others, such as classes in child care, cooking, or art history, mainly raise the productivity of household time. The time spent at a work or consumption activity is a measure of the scale of the activity, or of the intensity of use of capital, and affects the rate of return on investments in capital specialized to that activity.

Returns are independent of the allocation of time between the market and household sectors not only when wage rates and the effective amount of household time are raised by the same percent, but also when wage rates are not raised at all if the effective amount of goods is raised as much as that of time. If

$$x' = x \, y(H), \quad \text{and} \quad \frac{y'}{y} = \frac{\psi'}{\psi} = s(H), \tag{1.26}$$

where $dy/dH = y' > 0$, then

$$Z[x_k y(H_k), t_{h_k}\psi(H_k)] = y(H_k)^g Z(x_k, t_{h_k}\ell), \tag{1.27}$$

where $\ell = \psi(H_k)/y(H_k)$ is independent of H_k, and Z is assumed to be homogeneous of the gth degree in x' and t'_h. Hence (see Mathematical Appendix, note C):

$$R_j = \sum_{k=j+1}^{n} \frac{\pi_k \dfrac{\partial Z_k}{\partial H_k}}{(1 + r)^{k-j}} = \sum_{k=j+1}^{n} \frac{g \, s(H_k)\pi_k Z_k}{(1 + r)^{k-j}}. \tag{1.28}$$

Returns do depend on the value of commodity output, but not in any other way on the allocation of time between the market and household sectors.

Mathematical Appendix

A. If the Lagrangean expression

$$L = U - \lambda \left[\sum \frac{p_j x_j + w_j t_{h_j} + p_{q_j} x_{q_j} + w_j t_{q_j} - w_j t}{(1 + r)^j} \right] - A$$

is maximized with respect to the x_j, x_{q_j}, t_{h_j}, and t_{q_j}, and if H_j has a negligible effect on the output of Q_j, the equilibrium conditions for x_{q_j} where $j = 1, \ldots, n$, are

$$\sum_{k=j+1}^{n} \frac{\partial U}{\partial Z_k} \frac{\partial Z_k}{\partial H_k} \frac{\partial H_k}{\partial Q_j} \frac{\partial Q_j}{\partial x_{q_j}} + \lambda \sum_{k=j+1}^{n} \frac{a_k t_{w_k}(\partial H_k/\partial Q_j)(\partial Q_j/\partial x_{q_j})}{(1 + r)^k} = \lambda \frac{p_{q_j}}{(1 + r)^j}.$$

Since utility maximization also implies

$$\frac{\partial U}{\partial Z_k} = \lambda \frac{\pi_k}{(1 + r)^k} \quad \text{and} \quad MC_{q_j} = p_{q_j} \Big/ \frac{\partial Q_j}{\partial x_{q_j}},$$

the first condition can be written as

$$\sum_{k=j+1}^{n} \left(\frac{[\pi_k(\partial Z_k/\partial H_k)] + a_k t_{w_k}}{(1 + r)^{k-j}} \right) \frac{\partial H_k}{\partial Q_j} = MC_{q_j}.$$

B. Since

$$\frac{\partial Z_k}{\partial t_{h_k}} = \frac{\partial Z_k}{\partial t'_{h_k}} \psi,$$

and equilibrium requires (if $t_{w_k} > 0$) that

$$w_k = \mu_k \equiv \frac{\partial Z_k}{\partial t_{h_k}} \frac{p_k}{(\partial Z_k/\partial x_k)} = \frac{\partial Z_k}{\partial t_{h_k}} \pi_k,$$

then

$$\pi_k \frac{\partial Z_k}{\partial H_k} = \pi_k \frac{\partial Z_k}{\partial t'_{h_k}} t_{h_k} \psi' = t_{h_k} w_k \frac{\psi'}{\psi}.$$

Hence

$$\pi_k \frac{\partial Z_k}{\partial H_k} + a_k t_{w_k} = w_k \left(\frac{\psi'}{\psi} t_{h_k} + \frac{a_k}{w_k} t_{w_k} \right).$$

C.

$$\frac{\partial Z_k}{\partial H_k} = \frac{\partial Z_k}{\partial x'_k} x_k y' + \frac{\partial Z_k}{\partial t'_{h_k}} t_{h_k} \psi'$$

$$= \frac{\partial Z_k}{\partial x'_k} (x_k y) \frac{y'}{y} + \frac{\partial Z_k}{\partial t'_{h_k}} (t_{h_k} \psi) \frac{\psi'}{\psi}$$

$$= s(H_k) \left(\frac{\partial Z_k}{\partial x'_k} x'_k + \frac{\partial Z_k}{\partial t'_{h_k}} t'_{h_k} \right)$$

$$= s(H_k) g Z_k$$

if Z is homogeneous of degree g in x' and t'_h.

CHAPTER 2

Division of Labor in Households and Families

This chapter begins my analysis of the purposes and effects of families by considering the division of labor within households and families. The most pervasive division is between married women, who traditionally have devoted most of their time to childbearing and other domestic activities, and married men, who have hunted, soldiered, farmed, and engaged in other "market" activities. The various divisions of labor among family members are determined partly by biological differences and partly by different experiences and different investments in human capital. Specialization in the allocation of time and in the accumulation of human capital would be extensive in an efficient family even if all members were biologically identical; indeed, this chapter argues that biological differences probably have *weakened* the degree of specialization.

Since married women have been specialized to childbearing and other domestic activities, they have demanded long-term "contracts" from their husbands to protect them against abandonment and other adversities. Virtually all societies have developed long-term protection for married women; one can even say that "marriage" is defined by a long-term commitment between a man and a woman. These commitments are briefly considered in this chapter.

Shirking of duties, pilfering, and cheating is made easier by the extensive specialization and division of labor within families. Such conflict between the interests of members can be reduced by monitoring behavior, including invasions of the "privacy" of members, by expulsion from the family and other punishments, and by altruism. These and other methods are briefly discussed in this chapter and more completely in Chapters 8 and 11.

Specialization in Households

We shall consider the optimal investment in two types of human capital, H^1 and H^2. Each person maximizes utility by choosing the optimal path of H^1 and H^2 and the optimal allocation of time at all ages between the market and household sectors. If a person lives forever, does not age, and faces a stationary environment, our previous discussion indicates that H^1 and H^2 would be accumulated during an initial investment period, after which the equilibrium stock of H^1 and H^2 would be maintained indefinitely.

If consumption were stationary after the investment period, a single-person household would use a fixed amount of time to maintain its capital stocks and would allocate its remaining time between the market and household sectors to maximize consumption. If H^1 only raises market wage rates and H^2 only raises the effective amount of household time, aggregate consumption Z during each year would be given by

$$Z = Z(x, t'_h) = Z\left[\frac{a\hat{H}^1 t_w}{p_x}, t_h \psi(\hat{H}^2)\right], \tag{2.1}$$

where $\hat{H}^1$ and $\hat{H}^2$ are the optimal capital stocks, $a\hat{H}^1$ is the wage rate, $t_h \psi(\hat{H}^2)$ is the effective amount of household time, and p_x is the price of market goods. The allocation of time is constrained by

$$t_w + t_h = t', \tag{2.2}$$

where t_w and t_h are the hours allocated to the market and household sectors respectively, and t' is the total time available each year after allowance for the time spent maintaining capital. The allocation of time would be optimal if the marginal product of working time equaled the marginal product of household time:

$$\frac{\partial Z}{\partial t_w} \equiv \frac{\partial Z}{\partial x} \frac{a\hat{H}^1}{p_x} = \frac{\partial Z}{\partial t_h} \equiv \frac{\partial Z}{\partial t_h'} \psi(\hat{H}^2). \qquad (2.3)$$

Optimal decisions for those in a multiperson household must take into account the skills of the different household members and conflicts in their incentives. The theory of comparative advantage implies that the resources of members of a household (or of any other organization) should be allocated to various activities according to their comparative or relative efficiencies. A major assumption of the present section is that at the beginning everyone is identical; differences in efficiency are not determined by biological or other intrinsic differences. Variations in skill result from different experiences and other investments in human capital. Even with this extreme assumption, efficient multiperson households will be shown to have a pronounced division of labor among members in the allocation of time and in the accumulation of specialized capital.

I also assume that members do not have to be supervised because they willingly allocate their time and other resources to maximize the commodity output of their household. Since all persons are intrinsically identical, each member would receive an equal share of household output (if the market for members is competitive). Consequently, each member gains from a costless increase in household output. This provides only a weak justification, however, for the assumption that members do not have to be supervised; some may gain individually from shirking their duties and other malfeasance even though household output is reduced.

Since all persons are assumed to be intrinsically identical, they supply basically the same kind of time to the household and market sectors. Therefore, the *effective* time of different members would be perfect substitutes even if they accumulate different amounts of household capital (H^2). Similarly, the goods supplied by different members would be perfect substitutes even if they accumulate different amounts of market capital (H^1). Consequently, with no costs of supervision and no fixed costs of allocating time between different sectors, the output of a multiperson household would depend only on the aggregate inputs of goods and effective time. If the optimal accumulation of capital during the investment period were $\hat{H}_i^1$ and $\hat{H}_i^2$ for the ith member, the stationary output after the investment period of a household of n members would be

$$Z = Z\left(\sum_{i=1}^{n} x_i, \sum_{i=1}^{n} t'_{h_i}\right) = Z\left(\sum_{i=1}^{n} \frac{a\hat{H}_i^1 t_{w_i}}{p_x}, \sum_{i=1}^{n} \psi(\hat{H}_i^2)\, t_{h_i}\right). \qquad (2.4)$$

Clearly, if each member accumulated the same capital, Z would depend on the aggregate hours supplied to each sector, Σt_{w_i} and Σt_{h_i} respectively, and not on the distribution of hours between members. However, Z would depend on the distribution of hours if the capital of members differed, because then the household (or market) time of some members would be more productive than that of other members.

Output would be maximized only if marginal products in the household sector equaled marginal products in the market sector for members supplying time to both sectors. That is, only if

$$\frac{\partial Z}{\partial t_{w_j}} = \frac{\partial Z}{\partial x_j}\frac{a\hat{H}_j^1}{p_x} = \frac{\partial Z}{\partial t_{h_j}} = \frac{\partial Z}{\partial t'_{h_j}}\,\psi(\hat{H}_j^2) \quad \text{when } t_{w_j},\, t_{h_j} > 0. \qquad (2.5)$$

Marginal products in the household sector must exceed those in the market sector for members supplying all their time to the household, and conversely for members supplying all their time to the market.

The comparative advantage of a member can be defined by the relation between the ratio of his marginal products in the market and household sectors and the ratios of other members. Since a, p_x, $\partial Z/\partial x_j$, and $\partial Z/\partial t'_{h_j}$ are the same for all members, comparative advantage depends only on $\psi(H^2)$ and H^1. For example, i has a comparative advantage in the market sector relative to j if, and only if,

$$\frac{(\partial Z)/(\partial t_{w_i})}{(\partial Z)/(\partial t_{w_j})} = \frac{\hat{H}_i^1}{\hat{H}_j^1} > \frac{(\partial Z)/(\partial t_{h_i})}{(\partial Z)/(\partial t_{h_j})} = \frac{\psi(\hat{H}_i^2)}{\psi(\hat{H}_j^2)}. \qquad (2.6)$$

We can immediately prove the following theorem:

Theorem 2.1 If all members of an efficient household have different comparative advantages, no more than one member would allocate time to both the market and household sectors. Everyone with a greater comparative advantage in the market than this member's would specialize completely in the market, and everyone with a greater comparative advantage in the household would specialize completely there.

Since a member allocating time to both the market and household sectors must have equal marginal products, all members with a greater comparative advantage in the market sector would have a greater marginal product there than in the household, and conversely for all members with a greater comparative advantage in the household. Consequently, the former would specialize completely in the market and the latter in the household, which proves this theorem.

Since the returns from investing in specialized capital depend on the hours spent in the sector utilizing that capital (see Chapter 1), members specializing entirely in the market sector have strong incentives to invest in market capital (H^1) and no incentive to invest in household capital (H^2). Similarly, members specializing in the household sector have strong incentives to invest in H^2 and no incentive to invest in H^1. Therefore, the sharp division of labor in the allocation of time indicated by Theorem 2.1 implies an equally sharp division in the allocation of investments. This implication can be stated as a theorem:

Theorem 2.2 If all members of a household have different comparative advantages, no more than one member would invest in both market and household capital. Members specializing in the market sector would invest only in market capital, and members specializing in the household sector would invest only in household capital.

This theorem illustrates Adam Smith's often cited but misunderstood and seldom used theorem that the division of labor is limited by the extent of the market. The extent of the market for human capital that raises productivity at particular activities is measured by the time spent at these activities. Theorem 2.2 can be read to state that the division of labor in the accumulation of specialized capital is greater when differences in the allocation of time are greater, or when differences in the extent of the market are greater.

Theorems 2.1 and 2.2 assume that all comparative advantages are different, but could several members have the same comparative advantage and invest in both market and household capital and allocate time to both sectors? The answer, which can be stated as follows, is clearly no.

Theorem 2.3 At most one member of an efficient household would invest in both market and household capital and would allocate time to both sectors.

A simple and instructive proof assumes the contrary—that, say, two members allocate time to both sectors and have the same investments and comparative advantages. If they spent $\hat{t}_w$ hours in the market sector (say $\hat{t}_w < t'/2$), output would not be changed if one of them spent $2\hat{t}_w$ hours in the market and the other specialized completely in the household. However, every member could be made better off if the member now specializing in the household did not invest in market capital and increased his investment in household capital. They would also be better off if the member now supplying $2\hat{t}_w$ hours to the market increased his investment in market capital and reduced his investment in household capital. Consequently, we have contradicted the assumption that two members allocate time to both sectors and invest in both kinds of capital, and the theorem is proved.

None of these theorems on the division of labor and investment make any assumption about returns to scale in commodity production functions or the sorting of persons into different households. If returns to scale are constant or increasing, and if inefficient households cannot survive, specialization would be even more extreme, as shown by the next theorem:

Theorem 2.4 If commodity production functions have constant or increasing returns to scale, *all* members of efficient households would specialize completely in the market or household sectors and would invest only in market or household capital.

To prove this, assume that one member of an n-person household spends time in both sectors (less in the market sector) and that he invests in both market and household capital. If two n-person households form a single $2n$-person household, one member alone can supply the total time to the market that was supplied by him and by a member of the other household. If they continue to make the same investments, constant or increasing returns to scale in the commodity production function imply that the output of the combined household will be no smaller than the sum of the outputs of the smaller households. The combined household can do even better, however; one member can eliminate his investment in market capital, and the other can invest more in market capital and less in household capital since he spends more time in the market. Hence, a small household will be less efficient than larger households if some members do not completely specialize.

These theorems are readily generalized to many commodities in the household sector if commodities are produced independently of one another (no joint production) with their own specialized capital.

Theorem 2.5   All but possibly one member of households with more members than independent commodities would completely specialize their investments and time to the market or to a particular commodity. Moreover, with constant or increasing returns to scale, *all* members of efficient households must be completely specialized.

This theorem is readily proved following the reasoning used for Theorems 2.1 to 2.4 and implies that an increase in the number of independently produced commodities raises the size of efficient households because greater specialization becomes more profitable.

I have assumed that each type of human capital raises efficiency at only a single activity, but we do not need to hold to this limitation. For example, Theorems 2.1 to 2.4 would hold if H^1 and H^2 raise efficiency in both the market and the household sectors, as long as H^1 is more market-intensive in the sense that a dollar spent on H^1 raises wage rates more and household efficiency less than a dollar spent on H^2. A household would not be efficient if two members supplied time to both sectors and invested in both H^1 and H^2, for one of the members could supply all of their combined time to the market, and the other could specialize entirely in the household and eliminate any investment in H^1. Theorem 2.3 can be extended in the same way.

Returns on investments in types of human capital that raise either wage rates or effective goods by the same percent as effective household time would be independent of the allocation of time between the market and household sectors (see Chapter 1). All members of an efficient household might invest in these types regardless of their investment in more specialized types or of their allocation of time.

The analysis developed here is relevant not only to households, but also to countries and to the explanation of comparative advantage in international trade. Modern trade theory explains the gain from trade by international differences in endowments of labor, human and physical capital, and natural resources. I would argue, however, that differences in endowments are often only a proximate explanation of the gains from trade; the fundamental source of much of the gain is, as with households, the advantage of specialized investment and the division of labor.

Even intrinsically identical countries could increase the rate of return on their investments by specializing in particular types of human and physical capital and products that utilize such capital intensively. These products would be traded for products that are intensive in the capital specialized in by other countries. The proximate explanation of the gain from trade is differences in endowments of different kinds of capital, or the comparative advantage of traditional theory. However, the ultimate explanation is the gain from specialization.

Although the importance of intrinsic differences cannot be denied, the gain from international specialization in capital resolves some of the paradoxes besetting the traditional approach. An example of these paradoxes is that countries with apparently similar intrinsic endowments, such as Great Britain and Germany, tend to trade more with each other than do countries with apparently different intrinsic endowments, such as India and Japan;[1] another example is that trade does not decrease in the long run when factor endowments are supposed to become more similar.

The Sexual Division of Labor in Families

Although the sharp sexual division of labor in all societies between the market and household sectors is partly due to the gains from specialized investments, it is also partly due to intrinsic differences between the sexes. A man completes his biological contribution to the production of children when his sperm fertilizes a woman's egg, after which she controls the reproductive process: she biologically houses and feeds the fetus, delivers the baby, and often feeds the infant with her own milk. Sexual reproduction along these lines is all but universal among vertebrates: not only mammals, but also fish, reptiles, birds, and amphibians reproduce sexually (Ghiselin, 1974, chaps. 3 and 4; Wilson, 1975, p. 315).

Women not only have a heavy biological commitment to the production and feeding of children, but they also are biologically committed to the care of children in other, more subtle ways.[2] Moreover, women have been willing to spend much time and energy caring for their children because they want their heavy biological investment in produc-

---

1. I owe this enigma to lectures by Jacob Viner at Princeton University many years ago. Kleiman and Kop (1978, pp. 11-13, 22-23) find that trade is greater between countries with more similar incomes (see also Linder, 1961).

2. A discussion of some different ways is presented in Rossi (1977).

tion to be worthwhile. In addition, a mother can more readily feed and watch her older children while she produces additional children than while she engages in most other activities. This complementarity between bearing and rearing children has been important because, until the last century, practically all women spent most of their prime adult lives with children. Indeed, as recently as 1880 in the United States they averaged 5.4 births (see U.S. Bureau of the Census, 1975c, p. 53, 1910 census). Men have been less biologically committed to the care of children, and have spent their time and energy on food, clothing, protection, and other market activities.

From biological differences emerges the not-very-startling conclusion that the sex of household members is an important distinguishing characteristic in the production and care of children, and perhaps also in other household commodities and in the market sector. Analytically, these differences can be distinguished by the assumption that an hour of household or market time of women is not a perfect substitute for an hour of the time of men when they make the same investments in human capital. These differences between men and women illuminate several aspects of the composition of households and the division of labor within households that are not explained solely by the advantages of specialized investments in human capital.

If women have a comparative advantage over men in the household sector when they make the same investments in human capital, an efficient household with both sexes would allocate the time of women mainly to the household sector and the time of men mainly to the market sector. Indeed, either men or women would be completely specialized to one of these sectors if the time of men and women were perfect substitutes at a rate different from unity.[3] Households with only

---

3. For example, a household with one man and one woman would maximize

$$Z(x,t_h') = Z\left(\frac{wt_w^m}{p} + \frac{\alpha w t_w^f}{p}, \, t_h^m + \beta t_h^f\right),$$

where by Eq. (2.2) $t_w + t_h = t'$, and where $\beta > \alpha$ because women are assumed to have a comparative advantage in the household. If the man allocates time to both sectors,

$$\frac{\partial Z}{\partial x}\frac{w}{p} = \frac{\partial Z}{\partial t_h'}.$$

Then the woman would allocate all her time to the household because her marginal product would be greater there than in the market:

$$\alpha\frac{\partial Z}{\partial x}\frac{w}{p} < \beta\frac{\partial Z}{\partial t_h'}.$$

men or only women are less efficient because they are unable to profit from the sexual difference in comparative advantage.

Consequently, biological differences in comparative advantage between the sexes explain not only why households typically have both sexes, but also why women have usually spent their time bearing and rearing children and engaging in other household activities, whereas men have spent their time in market activities. This sexual division of labor has been found in virtually all human societies, and in most other biological species that fertilize eggs within the body of the female (Barash, 1977, pp. 188–201).

The analysis of specialized investments given earlier implies that women invest mainly in human capital that raises household efficiency, especially in bearing and rearing children, because women spend most of their time at these activities. Similarly, men invest mainly in capital that raises market efficiency, because they spend most of their working time in the market. Such sexual differences in specialized investments reinforce any biologically induced sexual division of labor between the market and household sectors and greatly increase the difficulty of disentangling biological from environmental causes of the pervasive division of labor between men and women.

Since the biological natures of men and women differ, the assumption that the time of men and women are perfect substitutes even at a rate different from unity is not realistic. Indeed, their times are complements in sexual enjoyment, the production of children, and possibly other commodities produced by the household. Complementarity implies that households with men and women are more efficient than households with only one sex, but because both sexes are required to produce certain commodities complementarity reduces the sexual division of labor in the allocation of time and investments.

Introducing complementarity alters the notion of comparative advantage. Women can be said to have a comparative advantage in the household sector when there are complementarities between men and women if the ratio of the marginal product in the household to the wage rate in the market is higher for women than for men when both supply the same amount of time to the household and when both invest in the same human capital. A woman with such a comparative advantage supplies more time to the household and less to the market than a man, and these time allocations are more different when the time of the two members is less complementary and more substitutable. Since specialized investments depend on the allocation of time, the investments of men and women more strongly reinforce their biological differences when differences in comparative advantage are larger and complementarities weaker.

Apparently, differences in comparative advantage and in investments have been more important than complementarities because women traditionally have allocated much more time to the household than men have. Yet complementarities cannot be unimportant, especially in modern times; women are becoming less specialized in household activities, and men are spending more time at household activities.

Since investment differences reinforce biological differences, biological comparative advantage cannot be readily disentangled from specialized investments. There is an additional reason for the difficulty of separating the two. Since specialized investments begin while boys and girls are very young (rates of return to human capital investments are higher at younger ages; see Chapter 1), they are made prior to full knowledge of the biological orientation of children, which is often not revealed until the teens and even later. If only a small fraction of girls are biologically oriented to market rather than household activities, and if only a small fraction of boys are biologically oriented to household activities, then in the face of no initial information to the contrary, the optimal strategy would be to invest mainly household capital in *all* girls and mainly market capital in *all* boys until any deviation from this norm is established.

In this manner investments in children with "normal" orientations reinforce their biology, and they become specialized to the usual sexual division of labor. Investments in "deviant" children, on the other hand, conflict with their biology, and the net outcome for them is not certain. For some, their biology might dominate and they would seek a deviant division of labor, with men in the household and women in the market.[4] For others, however, their investments would dominate, and they would become oriented, less strongly than normal persons, to the conventional sexual division of labor. Presumably the discrepancy between investments and biology is a source of conflict and even agony for the biologically deviant.

---

4. I say "seek" rather than "engage in" a deviant division of labor because each deviant should be matched with another deviant, yet normal persons can be matched more easily because they are more common. Consequently, a larger fraction of deviants either remain single, marry and then divorce, or remain in unsuccessful marriages (see also the discussion of homosexual marriages in Chapter 10). Let me emphasize that "deviance" is used only in a statistical, not in a pejorative, sense.

Note that in this analysis parents and society are not irrational, nor do they willingly discriminate against deviants. Rather, they respond rationally and without discrimination in the face of imperfect information about the biological constitutions of children and the much greater incidence of normal constitutions. Deviant investments would presumably be more common if deviant biology were more common—or if it were revealed at younger ages.

Specialized investments and time allocation together with biological differences in comparative advantage imply that married men specialize in the market sector and married women in the household sector. Therefore the market wage rates of married men will exceed those of married women, partly because women spend more time in the household and invest more in household human capital. Table 2.1 shows that average hourly earnings in the United States have been 60 percent higher for married men than for married women, and married men have spent considerably more time at work and less time at child care and in other domestic activities.

Since single persons anticipate marriage and the sexual division of labor of married persons, single working men are likely to be more specialized toward the market sector than single working women. However, single persons cannot as readily take advantage of the sexual division of labor because they do not have mates. Table 2.1 indicates that

TABLE 2.1   Earnings and hours and weeks worked in the marketplace in the United States, by sex and marital status.

	Male	Female
Average hourly earnings in 1970		
Single (never married)	3.53	3.07
Married (spouse present)	4.79	2.98
Average hours worked per week in 1977[a]		
Single (never married)	35.6	32.5
Married (spouse present)	43.5	34.2
Average weeks worked in 1977[b]		
Single (never married)	27.2	24.2
Married (spouse present)	41.0	22.5

SOURCES: The figures on hourly earnings are from Polachek (1978, p. 119). Hours worked come from the U.S. Bureau of Labor Statistics (1978, table A-35). Weeks worked are calculated from the U.S. Bureau of Labor Statistics (1979, tables A-6 and A-9) and from additional data supplied by the bureau.

[a] Nonagricultural working population only.
[b] Includes population outside the labor force.

wage rates and hours per week and weeks worked in the marketplace are greater for single men than single women, although the differences are much smaller than between married men and women because single men tend to work fewer hours and earn less per hour than married men, while single women tend to work and earn more than married women.

Wage rates are lower for women at least partly because they invest less than men in market human capital, while the productivity of household time is presumably greater for women partly because they invest more than men in household capital. The time of women is worth less than the time of men at younger and older ages, but is worth more during the peak child-rearing years when women are very busy and productive. Since women are more likely to enter the labor force when their household time is worth less, a false inference is drawn from their lower earnings in the labor force about the time value of all women compared to all men.

Figure 2.1 illustrates this point with typical age–wage-rate profiles for men and women and an age–household-productivity profile for women when they spend all their time in the household. Women would be in the labor force prior to age t_1 and after age t_2, because during these periods their wage rates exceed their household marginal productivities. During these ages women supply sufficient hours to the market sector to equate their household marginal product and their wage rate. Clearly, in this illustration women in the labor market have a lower

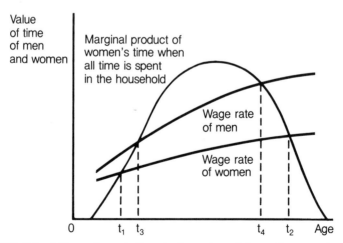

FIGURE 2.1 Life-cycle variations in the value of time of men and women.

value of time than men. However, women are not in the labor force between ages t_1 and t_2 because their time is worth more at home; moreover, between t_3 ($>t_1$) and t_4 ($<t_2$) their home time is worth more than the market time of men. In this illustration the *average* value of time over the lifetime may not be lower for women than for men, even though women's time is less valuable whenever they work in the marketplace.

Chapter 3 shows that women have less incentive to invest in human capital than men do when the number of children is the main result of marriage, and that the incentives of men and women are more equal when the "quality" of children is important. Women do receive considerably less schooling than men in poor countries that emphasize numbers, and about equal schooling in rich countries that emphasize quality (see Table 3.1). Therefore, in poor countries the average value of the time of women tends to be lower than that of men; in rich countries the value of the time of women is more equal to that of men. Explanations of behavior in rich countries that assume a much lower value of time for women may be misled by the much lower market earnings of women.[5]

Specialization of tasks, such as the division of labor between men and women, implies a dependence on others for certain tasks. Women have traditionally relied on men for provision of food, shelter, and protection, and men have traditionally relied on women for the bearing and rearing of children and the maintenance of the home. Consequently, both men and women have been made better off by a "marriage," the term for a written, oral, or customary long-term contract between a man and a woman to produce children, food, and other commodities in a common household.[6]

The nature of the division of labor between married men and women has meant that men have been more able than women to enter into marriages with several mates, simultaneously via polygyny or sequentially

---

5. See, for example, Azzi and Ehrenberg's discussion (1975) of participation in religious activities.

6. "Any marriage contract preserved in the Geniza shows that the first and foremost obligation of the husband was to provide his wife with food and clothing and to maintain her in general" (Goitein, 1978, pp. 118–119). However, in parts of Africa and Asia that did not use the plow, farming was often women's work along with child care and other domestic activities (see Boserup, 1970, chap. 1, and Goody, 1976, chap. 4). Moslems and Jews have had written contracts, whereas Chinese, Japanese, and Christians usually relied on oral and customary agreements.

through divorce or abandonment (see Chapters 3 and 10). Consequently, marriage law and contracts have mainly protected domestically specialized women against divorce, abandonment, and other unfair treatment—as when Moslem law stipulates that all the wives of a polygynous male must be treated equally and that the bride price is forfeited in whole or in part when a wife is divorced without cause (Goode, 1963, pp. 155 ff.), or when Jewish marriage contracts stipulate the amounts paid to wives in the event they are divorced or widowed,[7] or when Anglo-Saxon law provides alimony and child support to divorced women with children.

The biological differences between men and women in the production and care of children, and the specialized investments in market and household skills that reinforce the biological differences, explain why the institution of marriage has been important in all societies. The dominance of marriage as a form of household organization and the close ties between marriage and child rearing are shown in Table 2.2. Row (8) shows, for example, that married couples headed 71 percent of the households in sixteenth-century England and 94 percent in colonial America, and in 1970 headed 69 percent in the United States and 85 percent in rural India. Row (7) shows that 72 percent of the households in sixteenth-century England, 87 percent in colonial America, 46 percent in the United States, and 84 percent in rural India had children. Many of the households without children either planned to have them or raised children who left to form separate households; for example, from columns (3) and (4) we see that 83 percent of the households in the United States headed by males in their prime years have children compared to 46 percent of all households.

Practically all married couples have and rear their own children instead of hiring persons in separate households to rear them (as proposed long ago by Plato and practiced today in some kibbutzim) or

---

7. "The principal function of the Ketuba [the Jewish marriage contract that originated thousands of years ago] is therefore to serve as a document that safeguards the position of the woman after she has entered the marital state," and "following . . . the prohibition of divorcing and dismissal of a woman against her will, the practical importance of the Ketuba declined . . . and there was no longer any major significance to its monetary safeguards" (Davidovitch, 1968, pp. 112, 109). Many marriage contracts for Jews living in the Arab world between the tenth and fifteenth centuries have been found (Goitein, 1978, appendix). Invariably, the husband or his heirs had to return the wife's dowry and provide an additional payment if he terminated the marriage through divorce or death (ibid., pp. 95–142).

adopting children produced by others.[8] Of course, most societies forbid the purchase and sale of children, but it is easy to forbid what would be uncommon. One could postulate a "taste for own children," which is no less (and no more) profound than postulating a taste for good food or for any other commodity entering utility functions. Fortunately, the demand for *own* children, the distinguishing characteristic of families, need not be postulated but can be derived.

Women producing children can use their own milk as food and can more readily take care of young children while pregnant than while working in the marketplace.[9] Moreover, most women have been reluctant to commit so much time, effort, emotion, and risk to producing children without considerable control over rearing. Presumably the genetic similarity between parents and children further increases the demand for own children.

Own children are preferred also because of the value of information about children when investing in them. Information is more readily available about the intrinsic characteristics of own than adopted children, because parents and own children have half their genes in common and the health and some other characteristics of own children at birth and during infancy are directly observed. (See the discussion of a baby market in Chapter 5.) This may also explain why orphaned children of siblings and other close relatives are more frequently adopted than are orphaned children of strangers (Goody, 1976), and even why adopted children are less valued as marriage partners.

Since each woman is biologically limited to a relatively small number of own children,[10] and since the incidence of polygyny is limited by the

---

8. Of course, many upper-class families have reared their children with the help of nurses and tutors, and some have sent their infants to the homes of wet nurses: "the infants of the landed, upper bourgeois and professional classes [in England] in the sixteenth and seventeenth centuries [were] sent out to hired wet-nurses for the first twelve to eighteen months" (Stone, 1977, p. 107).

Goody (1976, chap. 6) discusses adoption in different societies. The Chinese, especially those on Taiwan, have had the unusual practice of adopting young girls as future brides for their own sons (on Taiwan, see also Wolf, 1968, pp. 100–101).

9. Labor force participation by mothers may also reduce the health of their children; see Popkin and Solon (1976) for evidence from a poor country and Edwards and Grossman (1978) for evidence from the United States.

10. A typical woman marrying at age twenty can produce no more than ten children, whereas by contrast a female oyster lays millions of eggs. Women who are unable to produce children usually either have been divorced, have become part of a polygynous household, or have adopted the children of others (Goody, 1976, pp. 81, 91–92).

TABLE 2.2 Number of members per household in various countries at different times. (NA = data not available.)

	Florence (Tuscany), 1427	England, 1599	England, 100 communities, 1574–1821	Colonial America, 1689	Japan, 1713	Serbia, 1733–1734	France, 1778	Mormons, U.S., 1860	Thailand, 1970	Syria, 1970	U.S., 1970, households headed by males ages 35–44 years	U.S., 1970, all households except group quarters	India, 1970–1971	Taiwan, 1975
(1) Average household size	3.92	4.75	4.75	5.85	4.97	5.46	5.04	5.54	5.82	5.91	4.58	3.11	6.64	5.27
(2) Standard deviation of household size	2.42	3.35	2.56	2.88	2.49	2.92	2.55	3.15	2.81	3.00	1.94	1.82	3.61	2.11
(3) Coefficient of variation	0.62	0.71	0.54	0.49	0.50	0.54	0.51	0.57	0.48	0.51	0.42	0.58	0.54	0.40
(4) Skewness A (see below)	0.14	0.43	0.33	0.14	0	0.33	0.14	0.14	0.03	0.15	0.20	0.20	0.25	0.20
(5) Skewness B (see below)	0.94	1.44	0.99	0.99	0.83	1.14	0.97	1.16	0.88	0.67	0.88	1.07	1.20	0.79
(6) Percentage of persons in the average household who are head, spouse of head, or children	NA	72.2	76.9	86.2	72.2	62.6	80.3	70.0[a]	NA	NA	94.1	89.4	69.0	NA
(7) Percentage of households with children[b]	NA	71.8	74.6	87.0	81.9	76.5	77.3	85.1	NA	NA	83.4	46.4	84.4	NA

(8) Percentage of households headed by a married couple	NA	85.3	69.0	91.7	NA	NA	86.7	71.0	82.2	64.0	93.9	70.4	71.0	58.3
(9) Percentage of single-member households	3.1	2.7	17.5	5.0	5.7	3.2	4.0	0	3.1	7.1	4.0	5.6	9.1	20.5
(10) Percentage of households with more than nine members	6.0[c]	16.0	0.5	1.5	11.8	8.2	8.7	5.0	8.2	5.0	9.1	5.0	5.0	NA

SOURCES: Computer tape created by the U.S. Bureau of the Census, 1970 Census of Population, 1/1000 Public Use Sample—15% County Group Sample; private communications from Indra Makhija and Wallace Blackhurst; United Nations (1974, table 24); Taiwan Directorate-General of Budget, Accounting and Statistics (1976, table 18); Laslett (1972, tables 1.7, 1.8, 1.10, 1.13); and Klapisch (1972).

Skewness A = [(90th pct − 50th pct) − (50th pct − 10th pct)]/(90th pct − 10th pct), where pct = percentile.

Skewness B = $\left(\dfrac{\Sigma[(X_i - \bar{X})/\sigma]^3}{N}\right)^{1/3}$, where $\bar{X}$ = mean, σ = standard deviation, N = number of cases.

[a] Children under eighteen years old.
[b] For U.S., children are family members under eighteen years of age related to family head (regardless of marital status); for India, children are fourteen years old and under; for other cultures, all unmarried offspring in the household are children, but servants are not children.
[c] Percentage of households with more than eight members.

sex ratio and other considerations (see Chapter 3), a nuclear family containing parents and their own children usually is small. For example, Table 2.2 shows that even the polygynous Mormons averaged less than six persons to a household.

Shirking, Household Size, and the Division of Labor

I have assumed that a household assigns its members to investments and activities that maximize the household's output of commodities without regard to incentives. Yet shirking, cheating, pilfering, and other malfeasance of members may not be readily detected, for the division of labor due to biological and investment specialization implies that a household's output is produced by members performing separate tasks.

Malfeasance within a family is not simply a theoretical possibility but one that has been recognized for thousands of years, starting with the biblical recommendation to trust wives: "The heart of her husband trusts in her, and he will have no lack of gain" (Proverbs 31:11). Jewish marriage contracts sometimes expressly stipulated that the bride should be trusted: her "complete and absolute trustworthiness," or "she is trustworthy in her statements concerning everything" (from two contracts written in the Middle Ages). Her trustworthiness was sometimes in doubt, partly because of the division of labor and her divided loyalties: "Because of the strong attachment of the wife to her paternal family she could be suspect of pilfering from her husband's house," or "Since [her] earnings were mostly derived from needlework, spinning, or weaving, or from serving as a sales woman to other women, it was difficult for her husband to know her actual takes, and suspicion might rear its ugly head." Of course, grooms frequently were not trusted either: for example, one marriage contract stipulated, "His father stands security for him" (Goitein, 1978, pp. 143–145).

Female adultery is a serious offense in traditional societies, mainly because men are reluctant to rear children fathered by others. These societies have tried to control the incidence of adultery by limiting the opportunities of their women, as when Moslem women are secluded or are forced to cover their faces and their arms and legs in the presence of men, or when married Jewish women must cut their hair and wear wigs.

The ideal Chinese household contains parents, unmarried children, and the families of married sons, yet shirking and lack of trust make such households far from serene:

> This ideal is occasionally achieved by the wealthy, but among the poor, *two married brothers rarely maintain a joint household after the death of their father.* The wife of one is too sure that the wife of the other feeds her children more when it is her turn to cook, or that she shirks her share of the housework. While the brothers' mother is still living and active, she can control or at least mediate disputes in the kitchen, but the loser of any dispute is sure to whisper to her husband about the favoritism his parents are showing to the other brother's children (Wolf, 1968, p. 28; italics added).

and

> She refuses to accept, however, that a man [her brother-in-law] who must obtain custom from city businessmen must dress better than a farmer [her husband]; . . . to [her], it is a simple case of one half of the family working very hard and the other half [her brother-in-law's] living better, sweating less (ibid., pp. 142–143).

Malfeasance in families in different societies has been punished by fines,[11] divorce, religious oaths (Goitein, 1978), or in various other ways, including disgrace for adultery (see Hawthorne, 1864). Moreover, because parents and siblings in some societies have been responsible for the actions of kin who marry into other households, they have had an incentive to limit the malfeasance of family members. In addition, a senior and successful person has sometimes been appointed head of a household or extended family and asked to adjudicate disputes and otherwise determine and punish the malfeasance of members.

Shirking, pilfering, or other malfeasance would be suspected if someone were frequently intoxicated, spent more than his legal income, had secret rendezvous, or engaged in other suspicious behavior. Malfeasance could sometimes be detected, therefore, by invading the privacy of members to gather evidence on the fidelity of their behavior to the interests of the household (see the more extensive discussion in Chapter 11). This suggests that specialization and the division of labor could actually reduce the privacy of members, in that their behavior would then be scrutinized more carefully for malfeasance.

---

11. Jewish marriage contracts of the Middle Ages in the Arab world often provided that a groom breaching his contract would be fined specified amounts (Goitein, 1978, p. 144).

If greater specialization did reduce the net privacy of members in view of this relation between specialization and malfeasance, and if the marginal utility of privacy were positive (privacy as a good is discussed in Posner, 1979), the increased output from greater specialization would be weighed against the reduction in privacy, and the optimal degree of specialization and privacy determined. The growth of separate households for single persons, especially elderly widows, in the United States, illustrates this trade-off. Over the past thirty years widowed parents have become less valuable as baby-sitters, cooks, and the like in their children's households because fertility has declined sharply and nursery schools and child-care centers have become more common. Moreover, social security payments have reduced transfers to elderly parents from their children. As a result of these developments, the gain from living with children has been reduced and the trade-off between privacy and specialization in this case has shifted toward privacy (see Michael et al., 1980).

The effect on malfeasance and privacy of the greater specialization of larger households constitutes a diseconomy of household scale.[12] If this effect were important, households would be considerably smaller than suggested by our analysis of specialized investments and division of labor. And in virtually all societies the average household has indeed been quite small. For the communities shown in Table 2.2, which span the fifteenth to the twentieth centuries in Western and Eastern Europe, Asia, and the United States, the average household comprised less than seven members; only in rural India did it comprise more than six.[13] Moreover, row (6) shows that the nuclear family—the head, his wives, and their own children—usually contributed more than 70 percent of the members.

---

12. Many years ago Wesley Mitchell blamed the small and allegedly inefficient size of modern households on the demand for privacy: "We have jealously insisted upon maintaining the privacy of family life; . . . most of us still prefer a large measure of privacy, even though we pay in poor cooking," and "If housekeeping were organized like business, these efficient managers [of their households] would rapidly extend the scope of their authority, and presently be directing the work of many others" (1937, pp. 5, 6, 10).

13. The average household in some Serbian towns of the nineteenth century had more than nine members (Halpern, 1972), and the average zadruga (extended household) in sixteenth-century Serbia may have had more than ten members (Hammel, 1972, p. 362). The *effective* size of households is perhaps understated by the data in Table 2.2, because siblings and other relatives frequently live near one another and cooperate in the production of defense, celebrations, and other commodities.

Household size can be placed in perspective by a comparison with the size of business establishments. The data in Table 2.3 indicate that more than half the establishments in retailing, minerals, farming, and law have fewer than four paid employees, and more than one-third in retailing and about two-thirds in farming have no paid employees. The average establishment in retailing, farming, and law is smaller than the average household in rural India, colonial America, and Mormon Utah.

Yet the data also indicate that large establishments are much more prevalent than large households. Almost 50 percent of the establishments in manufacturing and 29 percent in wholesaling have more than nine paid employees, whereas only 16 percent of the households in rural India and less than 1 percent in the United States have more than nine members. The coefficient of variation in household size ranges

---

TABLE 2.3   Number of paid employees per establishment in different sectors of the United States. (NA = data not available; * = fewer than five employees.)

	Manufactures, 1972	Retail services, 1967	Wholesale services, 1967	Mineral industries, 1972	Law firms, 1972	Agriculture, 1969 (seasonal workers)
(1) Average establishment size	57.7	5.4	11.3	23.6	1.9	1.9
(2) Standard deviation of establishment size	254.5	17.8	27.7	88.5	6.9	6.9
(3) Coefficient of variation	4.4	3.3	2.5	3.8	3.7	3.7
(4) Skewness A (see below)	0.9	1.0	0.8	1.0	0.5	1.0
(5) Skewness B (see below)	2.5	2.2	2.7	2.5	2.6	2.1
(6) Percentage of establishments with no paid employees ("family firms")	NA	36.5	4.1	NA	48.3	64.7
(7) Percentage of establishments with fewer than four paid employees	35.9*	68.9	42.5	51.3*	85.8	90.6*
(8) Percentage of establishments with more than nine paid employees	49.2	12.7	28.6	35.0	3.2	4.4

SOURCE: U.S. Bureau of the Census, 1971a and b; 1973a; 1975a; 1976a and b.

Skewness A = [(90th pct − 50th pct) − (50th pct − 10th pct)]/(90th pct − 10th pct), where pct = percentile.

Skewness B = $\left(\dfrac{\Sigma[(X_i - \bar{X})/\sigma]^3}{N}\right)^{1/3}$ where $\bar{X}$ = mean, σ = standard deviation, N = number of cases.

A Treatise on the Family

between 0.40 and 0.65 for 13 of the communities in Table 2.2, and between 0.50 and 0.59 for eight communities.[14] By contrast, the coefficient of variation in establishment size exceeds 2.4 for all the sectors in Table 2.3 and is at least 3.7 for four sectors. The distribution of firms is also much more skewed to the right than the distribution of households, as is evident from row (5) of Tables 2.2 and 2.3.

The distributions plotted in Figures 2.2 and 2.3 clearly reveal that large establishments are much more common than large households. The distribution of households usually rises to a peak and then declines slowly. The distribution of establishments peaks immediately, then declines very slowly in a long tail.

Presumably establishments have more incentive to expand to take advantage of the gains from increased specialization because they are more capital intensive than households: the ratio of nonhuman capital

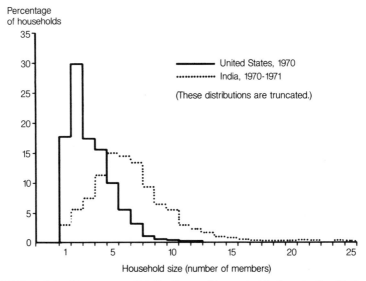

FIGURE 2.2   Frequency distributions of household sizes in the United States, 1970, and in India, 1970–1971.

SOURCES: See Table 2.2.

---

14. Whereas the range of average household size is from 3.1 to 6.6, or 113 percent, the range of the coefficient of variation is 75 percent. The relative inequality in household size is stable across highly diverse communities, probably even more stable than the inequality in income!

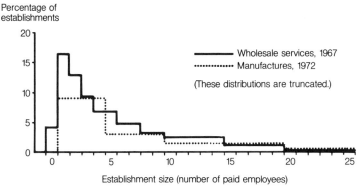

FIGURE 2.3   Frequency distributions of establishment sizes in wholesale services, 1967, and manufactures, 1972.

SOURCES: See Table 2.3.

to labor in firms is about eight times the ratio in households (Michael, 1966).[15] In addition, the diseconomies of scale that result from a loss in privacy may be less important in the marketplace than in the home.[16] Owners and other residual-income recipients of firms profit from limiting the malfeasance of employees and consumers; household members may be less inclined to engage in malfeasance, however, since altruism is more common in families than in firms (see Chapter 8). Indeed, the many firms with only a few paid employees are probably run by families that rely on altruism to organize production efficiently.

---

15. The capital-labor ratio is also much greater in farming than in households (based on U.S. Department of Agriculture, 1976, 1979), although the average farm has less than two paid seasonal employees.

16. In Mitchell's words, "Reluctantly we have let the factory whistle, the timetable, the office hours impose their rigid routine upon our money-making days; but our homes we have tried to guard from intrusion by the world of machinery and business" (1937, pp. 5–6).

Human Capital, Effort, and the Sexual Division of Labor

The labor force participation of married women in Western countries has increased enormously during the last 35 years. Initially the increase was concentrated among older women, but eventually it spread to younger women with small children. Although this supplement is not primarily concerned with the causes of the increase, it will be useful first to sketch an "economic" explanation that can be tested against the evidence in studies of the growth of labor force participation, such as Smith and Ward (1985) and O'Neill (1985).

The major cause of the increased participation of married women

This supplement originally appeared in the *Journal of Labor Economics* 3 (1985): S33–S58. Reprinted here, in slightly amended form, by permission.

during the twentieth century appears to be their increased earning power as Western economies developed, including the rapid expansion of the service sector. The growth in the earning power of married women raised the forgone value of their time spent at child care and other household activities, which in turn reduced the demand for children and encouraged a substitution away from parental, especially mothers', time. Both of these changes raised the labor force participation of married women.

The gain from marriage is reduced, and hence the attractiveness of divorce is raised, by higher earnings and labor force participation of married women, because the sexual division of labor within households becomes less advantageous. Consequently, this interpretation also implies a large growth in divorce rates over time. The decline in the gain from marriage is reflected also in the greater number of "consensual unions" (unmarried couples living together), the substantial increase in families headed by women, and even to some extent in the higher ratio of illegitimate birth rates to legitimate rates during recent decades.

Labor force participation rates, fertility, and divorce rates of women interact in various other ways. For example, fertility is reduced when divorce becomes more likely, because child care is more difficult after a marriage dissolves. There is evidence that couples who anticipate relatively high probabilities of divorce do have fewer children (see Becker et al., 1977). The labor force participation of women is also affected when divorce rates increase, not only because divorced women participate more fully, but also because married women participate more as protection against the financial adversity of a possible divorce.

One difficulty with this explanation is that economic progress and the growth in earning power of women did not accelerate in developed countries after 1950, yet both divorce rates and labor force participation rates of married women have risen far more rapidly since that time. I tentatively suggest that threshold effects of increased female earning power on labor force participation rates, fertility, and divorce rates are responsible for much of the acceleration. As the earning power of women continued to grow, fertility continued to fall until the time spent in child care was reduced enough so that married women could anticipate spending appreciable time in the labor force prior to the birth of their first child and subsequent to the birth of their last child. Women then had much greater incentive to invest in market-oriented human capital, which accelerated the increase in their earning power, participation, and divorce rates, and accelerated the reduction in fertility.

The modest increase in the hourly earnings of women relative to men during the last 35 years in the United States and many other Western countries (but not all; see Gregory et al., 1985; Gustafsson and Jacobsson, 1985) has been an embarrassment to the human capital interpretation of sexual earnings differentials, since this interpretation seems to imply that increased participation of married women would induce increased investment in earnings-raising market human capital. Instead, the increased participation may have temporarily reduced the earnings of women because increased supply generally lowers price, the average labor force experience of working women would be initially reduced, and observed earnings are temporarily reduced by increased on-the-job investments (see O'Neill, 1985; Smith and Ward, 1985).

Nevertheless, the evidence suggests, although it does not demonstrate, that the earnings of men and women would not be equal even if their participation were equal. Some have inferred substantial discrimination in the marketplace against women, perhaps supported by the evidence for Great Britain in Zabalza and Tzannatos (1985). These authors argue that responsibility for child care, food preparation, and other household activities also prevents the earnings of women from rising more rapidly.

Child care and other housework chores are tiring and limit access to jobs requiring travel or odd hours. These effects of housework are captured by a model of the allocation of energy among different activities developed in this supplement. If child care and other housework demand relatively large quantities of "energy" compared to leisure and other nonmarket uses of time by men, women with responsibility for housework would have less energy available for the market than men. This would reduce the hourly earnings of married women, affect their jobs and occupations, and even lower their investment in market human capital when they worked the same number of market hours as married men. Consequently, the housework responsibilities of married women may be the source of much of the difference in earnings and in job segregation between men and women.

In the next section I set out a model of the optimal division of labor among intrinsically identical household members who invest in different kinds of activity-specific human capital. Increasing returns from investments in specific human capital encourage a division of labor that reinforces differences in market and household productivity of men and women due to other forces, including any discrimination against women. I then model an individual's optimal allocation of energy among different activities. Many implications are derived, including a measure of the value of time in different activities, the forces encouraging the production of energy, and especially a very simple equation for the optimal supply of energy per hour of each activity. Following this, I apply the analysis of specialized investment and of the allocation and production of energy to earnings and occupational differentials between married men and women. I show that married women with responsibility for child care and other housework earn less than men, choose "segregated" jobs and occupations, and invest less in market human capital even when married men and women work the same number of market hours.

Human Capital and the Division of Labor

The human capital approach has recognized from the beginning that the incentive to invest in human capital specific to a particular activity is positively related to the time spent at that activity (see Becker, 1964, pp. 51–52, 100–102). This recognition was early used to explain empirically why married women have earned significantly less than married men, because women have participated in the labor force much less than married men (see Oaxaca, 1973; Mincer and Polachek, 1974).

It was not recognized immediately, however, that investments in specialized human capital produce increasing returns and thereby provide a strong incentive for a division of labor even among basically identical persons. This is taken into account in Chapter 2 of this book, where economies of scale from investments in activity-specific human capital are shown to encourage identical members of a household to specialize in different types of investments and to allocate their time differently. I also suggest there that the advantages of specialized investments provide more insight into comparative advantage in international trade than does the conventional emphasis on differences in factor supplies. These increasing returns to scale and advantages of specialization are illustrated in this section with a simple model heavily influenced by discussions with and examples in Rosen (1982) and Gros (1983).

Assume that a person's earnings in each of m market activities are proportional to his time spent at the activity and to his stock of human capital specific to the activity:

$$I_i = b_i t_{w_i} h_i, \qquad i = 1, \ldots, m, \tag{2S.1}$$

where h_i is capital completely specific to activity i. To simplify further, assume that h_i is produced only with investment time (t_{h_i}):

$$h_i = a_i t_{h_i}, \qquad i = 1, \ldots, m. \tag{2S.2}$$

If the total time spent at all work and investment activities is fixed, then

$$\sum_{i=1}^{m} (t_{w_i} + t_{h_i}) = \sum t_i = T, \tag{2S.3}$$

where $t_i = t_{w_i} + t_{h_i}$. By summing over earnings in all activities, and substituting from (2S.2),

$$I = \sum I_i = \sum c_i t_{w_i} t_{h_i}, \tag{2S.4}$$

where $c_i = a_i b_i$.

Since earnings in each activity are determined by the product of work and investment time, total earnings are maximized when these times are equal:

$$I = \frac{1}{4} \sum c_i t_i^2, \tag{2S.5}$$

when $t_{h_i} = t_{w_i}$. The increasing returns from the total time allocated to an activity (t_i) arise from the independence between the cost of accumulating human capital and the amount of time spent using the capital. These increasing returns imply that earnings are maximized when all time is spent on just one activity:

$$I^* = \frac{c_k}{4} T^2, \tag{2S.6}$$

where $c_k \geq c_i$, all i. Examples of complete specialization in human capital specific to a single "activity" include doctors, dentists, carpenters, economists, and so on.

The same formulation is applicable to time allocated among consumption activities produced under constant returns to scale, where the effective time input is proportional to both consumption-specific human capital and consumption time, as in

$$Z_i = b_i t_{z_i} h_i. \tag{2S.7}$$

If $h_i = a_i t_{h_i}$, then

$$Z_i = c_i t_{z_i} t_{h_i}, \tag{2S.8}$$

and the output of each commodity is maximized by equating the time spent on production and investment:

$$Z_i^* = \frac{c_i t_i^2}{4}, \tag{2S.9}$$

where $t_i = t_{z_i} + t_{h_i}$.

If the utility function is a simple Leontief function of these commodities,

$$U = \min (Z_1, \ldots, Z_m), \tag{2S.10}$$

and if $c_i = c$ for all i, utility would be maximized by allocating equal time to each commodity:

$$U^a = Z_i^* = \frac{cT^2}{4m^2}. \tag{2S.11}$$

This indirect utility function depends positively on the total time available and negatively on the number of commodities produced and consumed in fixed proportion.

The link between production and consumption would be severed if other persons also produced these commodities. To eliminate any *intrinsic* comparative advantage, I assume that all persons are basically identical. Even though all commodity production functions have constant returns to scale in effective time, there is still a gain from trade because each person can concentrate his investment and production on a smaller number of commodities and trade for the others. By reducing the number of commodities produced, an individual can take advantage of the increasing returns to the *total* time spent on a commodity (see Eq. 2S.9). For example, if two persons each produce half the commodities and trade their excess production unit for unit, the output of each commodity equals

$$Z_i^1 = \frac{cT^2}{4(m/2)^2}, \qquad i = 1, \ldots, \frac{m}{2}$$

$$Z_j^2 = \frac{cT^2}{4(m/2)^2}, \qquad j = \frac{m}{2} + 1, \ldots, m. \tag{2S.12}$$

Since they trade half the production, the indirect utility function of each person becomes

$$U^t = \frac{1}{2} \frac{cT^2}{4(m/2)^2} > \frac{cT^2}{4m^2} = U^a. \qquad (2S.13)$$

Increasing returns from investments in specialized human capital are the source of the gains from increasing the "extent of the market." Trade permits a division of labor in investments that effectively widens the market and thereby raises the welfare even of basically identical traders. The gain from specialization and trade in this example is simply proportional to the number of traders; each of p traders, $p \leq m$, would specialize in m/p commodities and produce

$$Z_j^k = \frac{c}{4} \frac{T^2}{m^2} p^2, \qquad j \in \frac{m}{p}, \qquad k = 1, \ldots, p \leq m. \qquad (2S.14)$$

If $(p - 1)/p$th of the output were traded unit for unit, the level of utility would be proportional to the number of traders:

$$U^t = \frac{1}{p} Z_j^k = \frac{c}{4} \frac{T^2}{m^2} p, \qquad p \leq m. \qquad (2S.15)$$

The effect of specialization and trade on welfare is shown in Figure 2S.1 (suggested by John Muellbauer). A person without access to trade has a convex opportunity boundary between Z_1 and Z_2 because of increasing returns from specific investments; his utility is maximized at the point of tangency with an indifference curve (U^0). A market with many basically identical persons has better opportunities and can obtain by specialization and trade any point on the straight line joining the intercepts, Z_1^s and Z_2^s. If b persons specialize completely in Z_1 and $n - b$ specialize in Z_2, trading provides each person with $(b/n)Z_1^s$ units of Z_1 and $(1 - b/n)Z_2^s$ units of Z_2. This opportunity to trade defines a straight-line opportunity boundary between Z_1^s and Z_2^s as b varies from zero to n. The improvement in welfare from trade (U^*/U^0) is determined by the degree of increasing returns or by the convexity of the opportunities for a person without trade.

The analysis is readily generalized to permit substitution among a continuum of commodities. The number of commodities consumed along with the degree of specialization in production by any trader would then also depend on the extent of the market (see the analysis in Gros, 1983). Moreover, goods and services as well as time can be inputs into the production of commodities and human capital. The following proposition survives all reasonable generalizations.

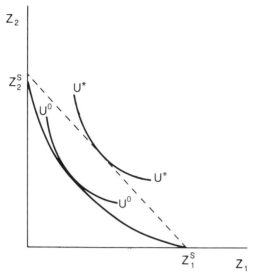

FIGURE 2S.1   The gains from specialization and trade.

PROPOSITION: If n basically identical persons consume in equilibrium $m \ll n$ commodities produced under constant or increasing returns to scale with specific human capital, each person will completely specialize in producing only one commodity and accumulate only the human capital specific to that commodity. The other $m - 1$ commodities will be acquired by trades with other specialized producers. If $n > 1$ is smaller or not much larger than m, or with decreasing returns to scale, specialization may be incomplete, but *some* commodities *must* be produced by only one person.[1]

This analysis is applicable to the division of labor and specialization within households and families because the production of children, many aspects of child care and investments in children, protection against certain risks, altruism, and other "commodities" are more efficiently produced and consumed within households than by trades among households. Most societies in all parts of the world have had a substantial division of labor, especially by age and sex, in the activities of household members. Although the participation of women in agriculture, trade, and other nonhousehold activities varies greatly in dif-

---

1. This proposition essentially combines Theorems 2.2, 2.3, and 2.4 in Chapter 2 of this book.

ferent parts of the world, women are responsible for the lion's share of housework, especially child care and food preparation, in essentially all societies. Moreover, even when they participate in market activities, women tend to engage in different activities than men do (see Boserup, 1970, for evidence from less-developed countries that supports these statements).

The advantages of investments in specific human capital encourage a sharp division of labor among household members but do not in and of themselves say anything about the *sexual* division of labor. In Chapter 2 I suggest that men and women have intrinsically different comparative advantages not only in the production of children, but also in their contribution to child care and possibly to other activities. Such intrinsic differences in productivity determine the direction of the sexual division by tasks and hence sexual differences in the accumulation of specific human capital that reinforce the intrinsic differences.

Some object to the presumption that intrinsic differences in comparative advantage are an important cause of the sexual division of labor, and have argued instead that the sexual division is due primarily to the "exploitation" of women. Yet a sexual division of labor according to intrinsic advantage does not deny exploitation. If men have full power both to determine the division of labor and to take all household output above a "subsistence" amount given to women (a competitive marriage market would divide output more equally), men would impose an efficient division of labor because that would maximize household output and hence their own "take." In particular, they would assign women to child care and other housework *only if* women have a comparative advantage at such activities.[2]

This argument is suggestive but not conclusive, because it assumes that sexual differences in comparative advantage are independent of the exploitation of women. Yet exploited women may have an "advantage" at unpleasant activities only because the monetary value of the disutility tends to be smaller for exploited (and poorer) persons, or because exploited persons are not allowed to participate in activities that undermine their exploitation.[3]

---

2. The advantage to slaveowners of an efficient division of labor probably explains why slaves were sometimes assigned to highly skilled activities (see Finley, 1980).

3. Guity Nashat has pointed out to me, however, that even slaves sometimes had major military responsibilities (see for example Inalcik, 1970, for a discussion of the Janissaries).

No definitive judgment need be made for the analysis in this supplement, because it does not depend on the *source* of the comparative advantage of women at household activities, be it discrimination or other factors. It requires only that investments in specific human capital reinforce the effects of comparative advantage. Indeed, the analysis does not even require that the initial difference in comparative advantage between men and women be large: a small initial difference can be transformed into large observed differences by the reinforcing effects of specialized investments.

This conclusion is highly relevant to empirical decompositions of earnings differentials between men and women. Suppose, for example, that men and women have the same basic productivity, but that discrimination reduces the earnings of women 10 percent below their market productivity. Given the advantage of specialization, such discrimination would induce a sexual division of labor, with most women specialized to the household and most men specialized to the market. As a result, earnings of the average woman would be considerably less than those of the average man, say only 60 percent. A decomposition of the 40 percent differential would show that sexual differences in investments in human capital explain 30 percentage points, or 75 percent, and that only 25 percent remains to be explained by discrimination. Yet in this example the average earnings of men and women would be equal without discrimination, because there would be no sexual division of labor. More generally, discrimination and other causes of sexual differences in basic comparative advantage can be said to explain the *entire* difference in earnings between men and women, even though differences in human capital may appear to explain most of it.

This magnification of small differences in comparative advantage into large differences in earnings distinguishes differences between men and women from those between blacks and whites or other groups. A little market discrimination against blacks would not induce a large reduction in their earnings, because there is no racial division of labor between the market and household sectors. (Even slightly greater market discrimination against black men compared with black women, however, could be magnified into much larger reductions in the earnings of black men than of black women, because black women would be induced to spend more time in the labor force than white women, and black men would spend less time than white men.) Consequently, the empirical decomposition of earnings differences into discrimination and other sources should be interpreted more cautiously for men and women than for other groups because of the division of labor between men and women.

The Allocation of Effort

The huge increase in the labor force participation of married women in developed countries should have encouraged much greater investment by women in market capital, which presumably would raise their earnings relative to men's. Yet sexual differences in earnings are very large (perhaps 40 percent) in the Soviet Union, where women participate almost as much as men (see Ofer and Vinokur, 1981), and they have not declined much in the United States. The persistence of these large differences may be evidence of substantial market discrimination against women (see the evidence for Great Britain in Zabalza and Tzannatos, 1985) or of a countervailing temporary depression in the earnings of women due to the entrance of many women with little market experience (see Mincer, 1983; O'Neill, 1985; Smith and Ward, 1985).

An additional factor is the continuing responsibility of women for housework. For example, married women in the Soviet Union have responsibility for most of the child care and other housework even though they participate in the labor force almost as much as married men, and Ofer and Vinokur (1981) argue that the earnings of married Soviet women are much lower than the earnings of married men in good part because of these responsibilities. O'Neill (1983) has a similar argument regarding the lower earnings and segregated occupations of married women in the United States. Time-budget studies clearly show that women have remained responsible for a large fraction of the child care and other housework even in advanced countries (see for example Gronau, 1976, for Israel; Stafford, 1980, for the United States; and Flood, 1983, for Sweden).

The earnings of women are adversely affected by household responsibilities even when they want to participate in the labor force as many hours as men, because they become tired, must stay home to tend to sick children or other emergencies, and are less able to work odd hours or take jobs requiring much travel. Although many effects of these responsibilities on the earnings and occupations of women have been frequently recognized, apparently the only systematic analysis is in my unpublished paper (Becker, 1977). A model of the allocation of energy (or effort) among various household and market activities is developed there, and many implications are derived, including some relating to differences in earnings and the allocation of time between husbands and wives.

This section further develops that model and shows how the allocation of energy is affected by the energy intensities of different activities, and also how energy allocation interacts with the allocation of time and with investments in market and nonmarket human capital. The incentive to increase one's supply of energy is shown to depend positively on market human capital and other determinants of wage rates.

Firms buy a *package* of time and effort from each employee, with payment tied to the package rather than rendered separately for units of time and effort. Earnings depend on the package according to

$$I = I(t_m, E_m) \qquad (2S.16)$$

with $\partial I/\partial E_m$ and $\partial I/\partial t_m > 0$, and $I(0, t_m) = I(E_m, 0) = 0$, where E_m is effort and t_m is time. By entering E_m explicitly, I am assuming that firms can monitor the effort supplied by each employee, perhaps indirectly (see Mirrlees, 1976; Shavell, 1979). If firms were indifferent to the distribution of hours among identical workers, earnings would be proportional to hours worked for a given effort per hour:

$$I = w(e_m)t_m, \qquad (2S.17)$$

with $\partial w/\partial e_m > 0$ and $w(0) = 0$, where $e_m = E_m/t_m$ is effort per hour. A simple function that incorporates these properties is

$$I = \alpha_m e_m^{\sigma_m} t_m = \alpha_m E_m^{\sigma_m} t_m^{1-\sigma_m} = \alpha_m t_m', \qquad (2S.18)$$

with $t_m' = e_m^{\sigma_m} t_m$ and $\alpha_m = \beta_m h_m$, where h_m is market human capital, and σ_m, the effort intensity of work, is assumed to be constant and measures the elasticity of earnings with respect to effort per hour.

Clearly, an increase in hours would raise earnings when total effort (E_m) is held constant only when $\sigma_m < 1$. However, $\sigma_m < 1$ implies that equal effort (e_m) is used with each hour, because increases in effort per hour then have diminishing effects on earnings. Equation (2S.18) implies that earnings are proportional to an "effective" quantity of time (t_m') that depends on effort per hour as well as number of hours.

Each firm chooses σ_m and α_m to maximize its income—subject to production functions, competition from other firms, the methods used to monitor employees, and the effect of σ_m and α_m on the effort supplied by employees. An analysis of these decisions and of market equilibrium is contained in Becker (1977). Here I only indicate that the trade-off between α_m and σ_m depends on the cost to firms of monitoring effort (perhaps indirectly), and on the effect of these parameters on the effort supplied by employees.

Time and effort not supplied to firms are used in the household (or nonmarket) sector. Each household produces a set of commodities with market goods and services, time, and effort:

$$Z_i = Z_i(x_i, t_i, E_i), \qquad i = 1, \ldots, n. \tag{2S.19}$$

If time and effort in the household sector also combine to produce "effective" time, the production function for Z_i can be written as

$$Z_i = Z_i(x_i, t_i'), \tag{2S.20}$$

with $t_i' = w_i(e_i)t_i = \alpha_i e_i^{\sigma_i} t_i = \alpha_i E_i^{\sigma_i} t_i^{1-\sigma_i}$, with $0 < \sigma_i < 1$ and $\alpha_i = \beta_i h_i$, where h_i is human capital that raises the productivity of time spent on the ith commodity and σ_i is the effort intensity of that commodity. The sum of the time spent on each commodity and the time spent at market activities must equal the total time available:

$$\sum_{i=1}^{n} t_i + t_m = t_h + t_m = t, \tag{2S.21}$$

where t_h is the total time spent in the household sector.

The total energy at the disposal of a person during any period can be altered by the production of energy and by reallocation of energy over the life cycle. I first assume a fixed supply of energy that must be allocated among activities during a single period:

$$\sum_{i=1}^{n} E_i + E_m = E, \tag{2S.22}$$

where E is the fixed available supply. This equation can be written as

$$\sum_{i=1}^{n} e_i t_i + e_m t_m = \bar{e}t = E, \tag{2S.23}$$

where $\bar{e}$ is the energy spent per each of the available hours. Since the decision variables e_j and t_j enter multiplicatively rather than linearly, the allocation of time directly "interacts" with the allocation of energy.

Total expenditures on market goods and services must equal money income:

$$\sum p_i x_i = w_m(e_m) t_m + v = I + v = Y, \qquad (2S.24)$$

where Y is money income and v is income from transfer payments, property, and other sources not directly related to earnings. Money income is affected not only by the time but also by the energy allocated to the market sector. Full income (S) is achieved when all time and energy is spent at work, since earnings are assumed to be independent of the time and energy spent on commodities:

$$w_m(\bar{e})t + v = S. \qquad (2S.25)$$

Full income depends on four parameters: property income (v), the wage rate function (w_m), the available time (t), and the supply of energy per unit of time ($\bar{e}$).

Each household maximizes a utility function of commodities

$$U = U(Z_1, \ldots, Z_n), \qquad (2S.26)$$

subject to the time, effort, and spending constraints in Eqs. (2S.21), (2S.22), and (2S.23) and to the production functions given by Eq. (2S.20). The following first-order conditions are readily derived:

$$\frac{\partial U}{\partial x_i} \equiv U_{xi} = \tau p_{xi}$$

$$\frac{\partial U}{\partial t_i'} w_i \equiv U_{ti} = \mu + \varepsilon e_i$$

$$\tau w_m = \mu + \varepsilon e_m \qquad (2S.27)$$

$$\frac{\partial U}{\partial t_i'} \left[t_i \frac{dw_i}{de_i} \right] \equiv U_{ei} = \varepsilon t_i$$

$$\tau t_m \frac{dw_m}{de_m} = \varepsilon t_m,$$

where τ, μ, and ε are the marginal utilities of income, time, and effort, respectively.

The interpretation of these conditions is straightforward. The second and third indicate that the marginal utility of an additional hour spent at any activity must equal the sum of the opportunity cost of this hour in both time (μ) and effort (εe_i). An additional hour has an effort as well as a time cost because some effort is combined with each hour.

The fourth and fifth conditions simply indicate that the marginal utility of effort per hour must equal the opportunity cost of effort (εt_j).

Each household selects the combination of goods and effective time that minimizes the cost of producing commodities. Effective time can be substituted for goods by reallocating either time or effort from work to commodities. Costs of production are minimized when the marginal rate of substitution between goods and effective time equals the cost of converting either time or effort into market goods.

On substituting the third into the second condition, one obtains

$$U_{t_i} = \tau \left[w_m - \frac{\varepsilon}{\tau}(e_m - e_i) \right] = \tau \hat{w}_i, \qquad (2S.28)$$

where $\hat{w}_i$ is the shadow price or cost of an additional hour at the ith activity. Another expression for the marginal cost of time is obtained by combining the last two conditions, and using the relation between U_{t_i} and U_{t_i}:

$$U_{t_i} = \frac{\tau w'_m w_i}{w'_i} = \frac{\tau w_m(1 - \sigma_m)}{(1 - \sigma_i)} = \tau \hat{w}_i, \qquad (2S.29)$$

where $w'_j = \partial w_j / \partial e_j$.

The marginal cost of time is below the wage rate for all activities with effort intensities less than the effort intensity of work, because the saving in energy from reallocating time away from work is also valued. Equation (2S.28) shows that the marginal cost is the difference between the wage rate and the money value of the saving in (or expenditure on) energy: ε/τ is the value of an additional unit of energy, and $e_m - e_i$ is the saving in (or expenditure on) energy.

Consequently, the marginal cost of time would be least for commodities using the least energy per hour. Moreover, the marginal cost is not the same even for persons with the same wage rate, if the money value of energy and the saving in energy differ. Note also that the cost of time *exceeds* the wage rate for highly effort-intensive activities (the care of young children, for instance).

The second and fourth optimality conditions immediately imply that

$$e_i = \frac{\mu}{\varepsilon} \frac{\sigma_i}{1 - \sigma_i}. \qquad (2S.30)$$

(I am indebted to John Muellbauer for pointing this out.) The optimal amount of energy allocated to an hour of any activity is proportional to the marginal cost of time in terms of energy, and also is positively related to the effort intensity of the activity. The cost of time in terms of energy is a sufficient statistic for other variables, including effort intensities of other activities, investments in human capital, property income, and the allocation of time, because they can affect the energy allocation per hour of any activity only by affecting this statistic.

A remarkably simple relation for the ratio of the optimal allocation of energy to any two activities is immediately derived from (2S.30), or from (2S.29) and the fourth condition in (2S.27):

$$\frac{e_j}{e_i} = \frac{\sigma_j(1 - \sigma_i)}{\sigma_i(1 - \sigma_j)},$$
(2S.31)

for all i, j, including m. The optimal ratio of energy per hour in any two activities depends only on their effort intensities and will be constant as long as these intensities are constant, regardless of changes in other effort intensities, the utility function, the allocation of time, and so on.

The ratio of efforts per hour in Eq. (2S.31) does not depend on utility, the allocation of time, and other variables, because it is a necessary condition to produce efficiently, that is, to be on the production possibility frontier between commodities in the utility function. A change in the effort intensity of an activity might change the absolute amount of energy per hour in all activities, but would not change the ratio between the energies per hour in any two other activities. The simple relations in Eqs. (2S.30) and (2S.31) are of great help in determining the effects of different parameters on the allocation of energy.

A few things can be surmised about the ordering of effort intensities in different activities. Sleep is obviously closely dependent on time but not energy; indeed, sleep is more energy producing than energy using. Listening to the radio, reading a book, and many other leisure activities also depend on the input of time but less closely on energy. By contrast, many jobs and the care of small children use much energy. Available estimates of the value of time in nonmarket activities are usually much below wage rates, one-half or less, which suggests by Eq. (2S.29) that the effort intensity of work greatly exceeds the intensities of many household activities.[4]

---

4. Virtually all estimates of the value of time refer to time spent on transportation. Beesley's estimates for commuting time (1965) rise from about 30 percent of hourly earnings for lower-income persons to 50 percent for higher-income persons; similar results were obtained by Lisco (1967) and McFadden (1974). Becker (1965) estimates the time spent in commuting at about 40 percent of hourly earnings. Gronau (1970) concludes that business time during air

A change in property income, human capital, the allocation of time, or other variables that do not change effort intensities would change the effort per hour in all activities by the same positive or negative proportion, equal to the percentage change in the energy value of time; see Eq. (2S.30). This proportionality, and constant energy ratios in different activities, is a theorem following from utility maximization (and other assumptions of our model) and should not be confused with the assumption of a constant effort per hour in each activity (an assumption made, for example, by Freudenberger and Cummins, 1976).

A decrease in hours worked and an increase in "leisure," induced perhaps by a rise in property income, would save on energy and raise the energy value of time, because work is more effort intensive than leisure.[5] Then the energy spent on each hour of work and other activities would increase by the same proportion, which would raise hourly earnings and the productivity of each hour spent on other activities. Conversely, a compensated increase in market human capital that raised hours worked would reduce the energy value of time, and hence also the energy spent on each hour of work.

The effect of increased market human capital on wage rates, a major determinant of the return to investments in market capital, is positively related to the energy spent on each hour of work. Therefore, the incentive to invest in market capital is greater when the energy per hour as well as number of hours of work is greater,[6] since costs of investing

---

travel is valued at about the hourly earnings of business travelers, while personal air travel time is apparently considered free.

5. By Eq. (2S.23), $e_m t_m + e_h t_h = E$, where $e_h = E_h/t_h$. If $e_h = \gamma e_m$, where $\gamma < 1$ because $\sigma_m > \sigma_h$, then

$$\frac{\partial e_m}{\partial t_m} = \frac{-e_m(1 - \gamma)}{\gamma t + t_m(1 - \gamma)} < 0.$$

6. These variables have opposite effects when hours of work change, if work is more effort intensive than the competing household activities. Since

$$MP = \frac{\partial I}{\partial h_m} = w_m t_m,$$

then

$$\frac{\partial MP}{\partial t_m} = (1 + n_m \sigma_m) w_m, \quad \text{where} \quad n_m = \frac{\partial e_m}{\partial t_m} \frac{t_m}{e_m}.$$

in human capital are only partly dependent on wage rates. The same conclusion applies to investments in capital specific to any other activity.

Earnings in some jobs are highly responsive to changes in the input of energy, whereas earnings in others are more responsive to changes in the amount of time. That is, some have larger effort intensities and others have larger time intensities. Persons devoting much time to effort-intensive household activities like child care would economize on their use of energy by seeking jobs that are not effort intensive, and conversely for persons who devote most of their household time to leisure and other time-intensive activities.

The stock of energy varies enormously from person to person, not only in dimensions such as mental and physical energy,[7] but also in "ambition" and motivation. Although Eq. (2S.30) implies that an increase in the stock of energy, and hence in the energy value of time, increases the energy per hour by the same percentage in all activities, the productivity of working time would increase by a larger percentage if work were more effort intensive than the typical household activity. Then persons with greater stocks of energy would excel at work not only because their wage rates would be above average, but also because the productivity of their working time would be especially high.

If the (full) income effect of greater energy is weak,[8] persons with

---

Given that $0 < \sigma_m < 1$, and that $-1 \leq n_m \leq 1$, then $0 < \partial MP/\partial t_m$ and $(\partial MP/\partial t_m) \gtrless w_m$ as $n_m \gtrless 0$. A change in hours worked always changes the marginal product of human capital in the same direction; but the effect can be substantially attenuated if n_m is quite negative, because work is *much* more effort intensive than the competing household activities. Conversely, the effect is strengthened if n_m is quite positive, because work is less effort intensive than these activities.

7. The inequality in energy is dramatically conveyed in the preface to a biography of Gladstone: "Lord Kilbracken, who was once his principal private secretary, said that if a figure of 100 could represent the energy of an ordinary man, and 200 that of an exceptional man, Gladstone's energy would represent a figure of at least 1,000" (see Magnus, 1954, p. xi). I owe this reference to George Stigler.

8. The sign of the income effect is ambiguous even when leisure is a superior good. The elasticity of working hours with respect to an increase in the stock of energy is

$$\frac{\partial t_m}{\partial E} \frac{E}{t_m} = \eta_{tmE} = R[x\delta_c(\sigma_m - \sigma_h) - \sigma_m(x - v)N_t + x\sigma_h N_x],$$

greater energy also tend to work longer hours at more effort-intensive jobs, because their time is relatively more productive at work than at household activities. Consequently, more energetic persons would both work longer hours and earn more per hour.

Since the elasticity of output with respect to energy per hour is less than unity ($\sigma_m < 1$), a given increase in the stock of energy would raise output by a smaller percentage if hours worked were unchanged. But the induced increase in hours would raise output by more than the increase in the stock of energy. Several experimental studies do find that an increase in the consumption of calories by workers doing physically demanding work, where calories are an important source of "energy," apparently raises their output by a larger percent (see UNFAO, 1962, pp. 14–15, 23–25).

Since a person's health affects his or her energy, ill health reduces hourly earnings (see the evidence in Grossman, 1976) in that a lower energy level reduces the energy spent on each working (and household) hour. Ill health also reduces hours worked, because work is relatively effort intensive; that is, sick time is spent at home rather than at work because rest and similar leisure activities use less energy than work. Therefore, more energetic persons can be said to work longer hours and earn more per hour partly because they are "healthier."

The energy available to a person changes not only because of illness and other exogenous forces, but also because of the expenditure of time, goods, and effort on exercise, sleep, physical checkups, relaxation, proper diet, and other energy-producing activities. At the optimal rate of production, the cost of additional inputs equals the money value of additional energy:

$$w'_m = \beta_m \sigma_m e_m^{\sigma_m - 1} h_m = \frac{\varepsilon}{\tau} = w'_m t_s \frac{de_s}{dE} + p_s \frac{dx_s}{dE} + w_m \frac{(1 - \sigma_m)}{1 - \sigma_s} \frac{dt_s}{dE},$$
(2S.32)

---

where t_h and x are the total time and goods used in the household ($p_x = 1$), N_t and N_x are the *full* income elasticities of t'_h and x respectively, δ_c is the elasticity of substitution between x and t'_h in the utility function, and R is positive. The substitution effect is essentially given by $x\delta_c(\sigma_m - \sigma_h) > 0$ if $\sigma_m > \sigma_h$. The income effect is given by $x\sigma_h N_x - \sigma_m(x - v)N_t \gtreqless 0$. It is greater than zero if $(\sigma_h/\sigma_m) > k_e(N_t/N_x)$, where k_e is the share of earnings in money income. This material is based on notes by H. Gregg Lewis.

where e_s, x_s, and t_s are inputs into the production of energy.[9] The term on the right is the cost of inputs used to produce an additional unit of energy; the money value of an additional unit equals the effect on hourly earnings of an increase in energy per hour—see the last condition in (2S.27).

An increase in the marginal wage rate increases the optimal production of energy because marginal benefits increase relative to marginal costs. An increase in market human capital and a decrease in energy per hour of work (perhaps resulting from an increased number of working hours) both encourage the production of energy by raising benefits relative to cost of production; indeed, costs could decline when energy per hour decreased because the value of time would decrease. Increased production of energy would also improve health, given the positive relation between health and energy.

Many have argued that long hours of work substantially reduce productivity because of "fatigue."[10] This argument is questionable for differences among persons, because more energetic persons work longer. Moreover, even if longer working hours by any given person directly reduce his energy (and productivity) per hour, longer hours also encourage his production of energy and of market human capital. Since more energy and market capital raise the productivity of each working hour, longer hours could even indirectly *raise* productivity per hour.

The incentive to invest in energy varies over the life cycle as the stock of market human capital and other determinants of the value of energy vary. Therefore, hourly earnings rise at younger ages probably partly because of increased production of energy, and conversely for declines in earnings at older ages. The stock of energy at a particular age might also be augmentable by "borrowing" from other ages, perhaps with substantial penalty or interest. In extreme forms, borrowing and repayment of energy produce "overwork" and "burnout."[11]

---

9. I assume here that inputs are devoted exclusively to the production of energy, but the analysis is readily extended to "joint production," where, say, a good diet produces both energy and commodities.

10. In his classic study of the sources of economic growth in the United States, Denison (1962) assumed that each hour of work beyond 43 hours per week reduces productivity by at least 30 percent.

11. Bertrand Russell claimed he worked so hard on *Principia Mathematica* that his "intellect never quite recovered from the strain" (1967, p. 230).

Division of Labor in the Allocation of Effort
between Husbands and Wives

Since more energetic persons have a comparative advantage at effort-intensive activities, efficient marriage markets match more energetic with less energetic persons (that is, negative sorting by energy). A larger fraction of the time of energetic spouses would be allocated to effort-intensive activities like work where they have a comparative advantage, and a larger fraction of the time of sluggish spouses would be allocated to the household activities where they have a comparative advantage.

The evidence is much too scanty to argue that a division of labor by energy level helps explain the division of labor between married men and women. Therefore, I assume that women have responsibility for child care and other housework for reasons unrelated to their energy or to the effort intensity of housework. Nevertheless, differences in effort intensities have important implications for sexual differences in earnings, hours worked, and occupations.

To demonstrate this point, I follow the brief discussion in the previous section suggesting that housework activities like child care are much more effort intensive than leisure-oriented activities and may be more or less effort intensive than market activities. Married women with primary responsibility for child care and other housework allocate less energy to each hour of work than married men who spend equal time in the labor force. A simple proof uses the assumption that housework is more effort intensive than leisure, and the implication of Eq. (2S.31) that the ratio of the energy spent on each hour of any two activities depends only on the effort intensities of these activities.[12]

Since married women earn less per hour than married men when they spend less energy on each hour of work, the household responsibilities of married women reduce their hourly earnings below those of married men even when both participate the same number of hours and have the same market capital. These household responsibilities also induce occupational segregation, because married women seek

---

12. By Eq. (2S.31), $e_c = \gamma_1 e_m$ and $e_l = \gamma_2 e_m$, where $\gamma_1 > \gamma_2$ because $\sigma_c > \sigma_e$, where c refers to housework and l to leisure. Since $e_m t_m + e_c t_c + e_l t_l = E$, then $e_m(t_m + \gamma_1 t_c + \gamma_2 t_l) = E$, and

$$\frac{de_m}{dt_c}\bigg|_{dt_m=0} = \frac{-e_m(\gamma_1 - \gamma_2)}{t_m + \gamma_1 t_c + \gamma_2 t_l} < 0.$$

occupations and jobs that are less effort intensive and otherwise are more compatible with the demands of their home responsibilities. The same argument explains why students who attend class and do homework have lower hourly earnings than persons not in school when both work the same number of hours and appear to have similar characteristics (see the evidence and discussion in Lazear, 1977).

Therefore, the traditional concentration on the labor force participation of women gives a misleading—perhaps a highly misleading—impression of the forces reducing the earnings and segregating the employment of married women. Nor is this all. Married women would invest less in market human capital than married men even when both spend the same amount of time in the labor force. Since the benefit from investment in market human capital is positively related to hourly earnings and hence to the energy spent on each hour of market work, the benefit is greater to married men even when they do not work longer hours than married women.

The lower earnings of married women due both to their lower energy spent on work and their lower investment in market human capital discourage their labor force participation relative to that of their husbands. Of course, their lower participation further discourages their investment in market capital (but see note 6), and could even lower their energy spent on each hour of work if they substitute toward housework that is more effort intensive than their market activities. A full equilibrium could involve complete specialization by wives in housework and other nonmarket activities.

Table 2S.1 (brought to my attention by June O'Neill) shows that even married women employed full-time in the United States work much more at home than do unemployed or part-time employed married men, let alone full-time employed married men. Moreover, married women employed full-time work many fewer hours (about 9 hours per week) in the market than do married men employed full-time, although total hours worked are a little higher for these women. There is considerable other evidence that the occupations and earnings of women are also affected by their demand for part-time employment and flexible hours (see Mincer and Polachek, 1974, table 7; O'Neill, 1983).

This analysis implies that the hourly earnings of single women exceed those of married women even when both work the same number of hours and have the same market capital, because child care and other household responsibilities induce married women to seek more

TABLE 2S.1   Use of time by married women and married men in the United States by hours per week at market work and at home, 1975–1976.

Type of activity	Married women			Married men	
	Employed full time	Employed part time	All[a]	Employed full time	All[b]
Market work	38.6	20.9	16.3	47.9	39.2
At job[c]	35.7	18.9	15.0	44.0	36.0
Travel to and from job	2.9	2.0	1.3	3.9	3.2
Work at home	24.6	33.5	34.9	12.1	12.8
Indoor housework	14.6	21.0	20.8	2.8	3.5
Child care	2.8	3.2	4.9	1.7	1.5
Repairs, outside work, gardening	1.6	1.7	2.2	3.8	3.9
Shopping, services	5.6	7.6	7.0	3.8	3.9
Leisure	21.0	25.5	26.7	23.0	27.1
Total work time	63.2	54.4	51.2	60.0	52.0
Sample size	101	51	220	236	307

SOURCE: Hill (1981), based on data from a national sample of U.S. households collected by the Survey Research Center for the University of Michigan.
[a] Includes married women with no market work.
[b] Includes married men with part-time work and no market work.
[c] Includes lunch and coffee breaks.

convenient and less energy-intensive jobs. The analysis can explain also why marriage appears to raise the health of men substantially and that of women only moderately (Fuchs, 1975). Since married men accumulate more market human capital and work longer hours than single men (Kenny, 1983), married men produce larger stocks of energy than single men, which improves their health. The effect of marriage on the energy of women is more ambiguous: the value of energy to women not working in the market is measured by the value of additional energy in the household, which can be sizable. But the value of energy to working women is measured by its value at work, which has been below the value to men because women have invested less in market human capital and have chosen less energy-intensive work.

The large growth in the labor force participation of married women during the last 35 years has been accompanied by a steep fall in fertility and a sharp rise in divorce rates. The fall in fertility obviously raises the hourly earnings of married women because they have more energy and more flexible time to devote to market work instead of child care. The time spent in housework by married women in the United States apparently did decline significantly after 1965 (Stafford, 1980).

The effect of the growth in divorce on the hourly earnings of women is more problematic. On the one hand, married women invest more in market human capital when they anticipate working because they are likely to become divorced. On the other hand, since divorced women in the United States and other Western countries almost always retain custody of their children, the demands of child care on their energy and attention may exceed those of married women, for they have no husbands with whom to share the housework.[13]

Increasing returns from specialized human capital are a powerful force creating a division of labor in the allocation of time and investments in human capital even among basically identical persons. Increasing returns alone, however, do not imply the traditional sexual division of labor, with women having primary responsibility for many household activities, unless men and women tend to differ in their comparative advantages between household and market activities. Whatever the reason for the traditional division—perhaps discrimination against women or high fertility—household responsibilities lower the earnings and affect the jobs of married women by reducing their time in the labor force and discouraging their investment in market human capital.

This supplement also develops a model of an individual's allocation of energy among different activities. More energy is spent on each hour of more energy-intensive activities, and the ratio of the energy per hour for any two activities depends only on their effort intensities and not at all on the stock of energy, utility function, money income, allocation of time, or human capital. Other implications are derived about the cost of time to different activities, the effect of hours worked on hourly earnings, the effect of earnings on investment in health, and the effect of an increase in the energy spent on each hour of work on the benefits from investment in market human capital.

Since housework is more effort intensive than leisure and other household activities, married women spend less energy on each hour of market work than married men working the same number of hours.

---

13. In the film *Kramer vs. Kramer* the character played by Dustin Hoffman lost his job after he became responsible for the care of his child.

As a result, married women have lower hourly earnings than married men with the same market human capital, and they economize on the energy expended on market work by seeking less-demanding jobs. Moreover, their lower hourly earnings reduce their investment in market capital even when they work the same number of hours as married men.

The responsibility of married women for child care and other housework has major implications for earnings and occupational differences between men and women, even aside from the effect on the labor force participation of married women. I submit that this is an important reason why the earnings of married women typically are considerably below those of married men, and why substantial occupational segregation persists, even in countries like the Soviet Union where labor force participation rates of married men and women are not very different.

The persistence of these responsibilities in all advanced societies may be only a legacy of powerful forces from the past and may disappear or be greatly attenuated in the near future. Not only casual impressions but also evidence from time-budgets indicates that the *relative* contribution of married men to housework in the United States has significantly increased during the last decade (Stafford, 1980; personal communication from Stafford about a 1981 survey). The frequency of partial or complete custody of children in the hands of divorced fathers has also increased. A continuation of these trends would increase the energy and time spent at market activities by women, which in turn would raise their earnings and incentive to invest in market human capital. The result could be a sizable increase in the relative earnings of married women and a sizable decline in their occupational segregation during the remainder of this century.

Even if the process continued until married women no longer had primary responsibility for child care and other housework, married households would still gain considerably from a division of labor in the allocation of time and investments if specialized household and market human capital remained important, or if spouses differed in energy. This division of labor, however, would no longer be linked to sex: husbands would be more specialized to housework and wives to market activities in about half the marriages, and the reverse would occur in the other half.

Such a development would have major consequences for marriage, fertility, divorce, and many other aspects of family life. Yet the effect on the inequality in either individual or family earnings would be more modest: all persons specialized to housework would still earn less than their spouses, and the distribution of family earnings would still be determined by the division of labor between spouses, by the sorting of spouses by education and other characteristics, by divorce rates and the custody of children, and so forth.

A person's sex would then no longer be a valid predictor of earnings and household activities. It is still too early to tell how far Western societies will move in this direction.

CHAPTER 3

Polygamy and Monogamy in Marriage Markets

Chapter 2 showed that over the years most households in Western and Eastern societies have been headed by married men and women who raise their own children. Wives usually have specialized in the care of children and other household activities, while husbands usually have specialized in providing necessities and in other market activities. Marriage includes a contract that has protected specialized women with limited alternatives against abandonment, neglect, and other ill treatment by their husbands.

Although the overwhelming majority of men and women have tended to marry—only about 4.6 percent of the women and 6.3 percent of the men aged 45–54 in the United States in 1975 had never married (U.S. Bureau of the Census, 1975b)—there are many differences in the length and quality of married life. In 1970, for example, 57.9 percent of the women aged 30–34 in this country had married by age twenty, whereas 8.6 percent did not marry before they were thirty (U.S. Bureau of the Census, 1973b and d); about 44 percent of all marriages contracted in the 1970s in the United States will end in divorce

(Preston, 1975); about 15 percent of Mormon men in 1870 were polygynous, and 1 percent had more than three wives (private communication from Wallace Blackhurst); in the United States college-educated men are 15 times as likely to marry college-educated women as are men who never completed high school (calculated from the 1967 Survey of Economic Opportunity, computer tape created by the U.S. Bureau of the Census).

This chapter analyzes the incidence of polygyny (meaning that a man has several wives), polyandry (a woman has several husbands), monogamy, and bachelorhood in efficient "marriage markets" where identical persons have the same marginal product and receive the same income. Of course, unmarried persons do not display their talents in markets[1] the way other sellers do in the stock market or in a Middle Eastern bazaar. But persons in a marriage market often use intermediaries as "brokers," participate in church socials, attend coeducational schools, and take part in other activities designed in part to bring eligible persons together, and advertise their services in many ways. The phrase "marriage market" is used metaphorically and signifies that the mating of human populations is highly systematic and structured.

An efficient marriage market develops "shadow" prices to guide participants to marriages that will maximize their expected well-being. These prices, central to the analysis in this chapter and the subsequent one, are responsible for the more powerful implications found in these chapters than in traditional discussions of marriage. Some other approaches are evaluated in Chapter 4.

The incidence of polygyny has declined substantially over time until no more than 10 percent of the world's population lives today in polygynous societies. The decline has been attributed to the spread of Christianity and the growth of women's rights, but I am skeptical of these explanations. Doctrines encouraging monogamy are attractive only when the demand for polygyny is weak; and this chapter shows that women tend to gain from polygyny. I shall analyze the incidence of polygyny in terms of the relative gains to men and women from polygynous and monogamous marriages. These gains depend on the inequality among men and women in income, education, and other variables affecting their efficiency at household and market production; the marginal contributions of men and women to output; and the

---

1. It is interesting, however, that certain species do use arenas or leks to display their talents and attract mates (see Chapter 9).

ease of substituting between the household inputs supplied by men and women. The decline in the incidence of polygyny is related to changes in these gains rather than to the exogenous spread of religious doctrines or women's rights.

Marriage-Market Equilibrium

Monogamy

To simplify the initial presentation, I assume that all male participants and all female participants in the marriage market are identical. An equilibrium allocation of participants to different mates in an efficient marriage market would provide all men and all women with the same expected utility. If the commodity outputs of households can be combined into a single homogeneous commodity, such as the quantity of children (heterogeneous commodities are considered in Chapter 4), if the output of all marriages is known with certainty (uncertainty is considered in Chapter 10), and if the output is distributed as income to mates, the following accounting identity holds for all marriages:

$$Z_{mf} = Z^m + Z^f, \qquad (3.1)$$

where Z_{mf} is the output of a marriage, and Z^m and Z^f are the incomes of male and female mates.

Participants prefer to marry if, and only if, their utility from marriage exceeds their utility from remaining single. Since utility is monotonically related to the command over household commodities, participants prefer to marry if

$$Z^f > Z_{sf} \quad \text{and} \quad Z^m > Z_{sm}, \qquad (3.2)$$

where Z_{sf} and Z_{sm} are the outputs of single female and male households. These marital decisions are shown graphically in Figure 3.1. The supply curve of the N_f women in the marriage market is infinitely elastic when $Z^f = Z_{sf}$, because at that income they are indifferent between marrying and remaining single; the curve is vertical at $F = N_f$ when $Z^f > Z_{sf}$, and vertical at $F = 0$ when $Z^f < Z_{sf}$. Similarly, the supply curve of the N_m men would be infinitely elastic when $Z^m = Z_{sm}$, vertical at $M = N_m$ when $Z^m > Z_{sm}$, and vertical at $M = 0$ when $Z^m < Z_{sm}$.

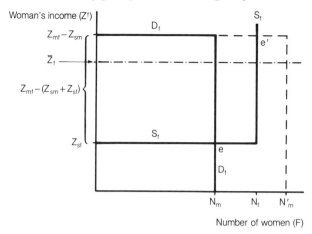

FIGURE 3.1 Equilibrium in a monogamous marriage market relating the income of women to the number of men and women.

If we assume initially that all marriages are monogamous, the supply curve of men to marriage is also a derived demand curve for wives. In effect, each man offers a wife $Z_{mf} - Z_{sm}$ when he is indifferent between being single and being married, and $Z_{mf} - Z^m < Z_{mf} - Z_{sm}$ when he gains from marriage. Therefore, the derived demand curve for wives, also plotted in Figure 3.1, is infinitely elastic when $Z^f = Z_{mf} - Z_{sm}$ and is vertical at $F = N_m$ when Z^f is less than that.

The analysis in Chapter 2 showed that the optimal output of a household requires specialized investments in human capital and specialized allocations of time by different household members. The output of a married household exceeds the sum of the outputs of single male and female households because men and women are biological complements in the production and rearing of children and perhaps of other household commodities, and because rates of return to specialized investments in household and market skills are greater in larger households. The difference between married output and the sum of single outputs is the gain from marriage, and it is measured in Figure 3.1 by the vertical distance between the infinitely elastic sections of the derived demand curve for wives and the supply curve of wives, $Z_{mf} - (Z_{sm} + Z_{sf})$.

Equilibrium in an efficient monogamous marriage market requires that the same number of men and women want to marry, and that participants who remain single have at least as large an income as they

A Treatise on the Family

could receive by marrying. These conditions are satisfied in Figure 3.1 at point e, where N_m men and N_m women want to marry. Since the number of male participants is less than the number of female participants ($N_m < N_f$), all men marry and some women ($N_f - N_m$) remain single. These women are willing to remain single because the income of married women equals the income of single women. Men receive the difference between married output and the single income of women and thereby collect all the "rent" from marriage.

A small increase in the number of eligible men would not change the incomes of men and women but would reduce the number of women remaining single. If the number of men increased sufficiently to exceed the number of women, all women would marry, some men would remain single, the income of men would fall to Z_{sm}, and the income of women would rise to $Z_{mf} - Z_{sm}$, as at point e' in Figure 3.1. Therefore this analysis implies not only that an increase in the ratio of men to women increases the fraction of men and reduces the fraction of women who are single, but also that it redistributes married output away from men and toward women.

Although statistical studies clearly indicate that the fraction of eligible women who are married is positively related to the ratio of the number of eligible men to the number of eligible women,[2] I know only of highly impressionistic evidence on the effect of the sex ratio, or for that matter of any other variable, on the division of output between mates. Little effort has been put into collecting relevant information, because this division has not been considered to be responsive to market forces. Admittedly, data on household consumption cannot readily be separated into those that benefit husbands, wives, or both, but useful empirical relations could be derived. For example, available information on the amounts spent on husband's and wife's clothing or on their leisure time could be related to sex ratios, wage rates, education levels, and other determinants of the division of marital output.[3]

---

2. See the studies of whites in the United States by Freiden (1974), Preston and Richards (1975), and Santos (1975); of blacks in the United States by Reischauer (1971); of Puerto Rico by Nerlove and Schultz (1970); and of Ireland by Walsh (1972). "Eligible" means that a group of women are compared with the men they are most likely to marry; for example, the number of college-educated women are compared with the number of college-educated men, or women aged 20–24 are compared with men aged 25–29.

3. An interesting start has been made by Lazear (1978); see also McElroy and Horney (1981).

Polygamy

Although historically women have only rarely had several husbands (there is clear evidence of polyandry among the Todas of India; see Rivers, 1906) men have been polygynous in early Jewish societies, in Moslem societies, in many parts of ancient Greece, in much of Africa, and in Chinese societies.[4] The analysis given in Figure 3.1 is easily generalized to polygynous or polyandrous marriages. For example, the supply curve of N_f identical women to either monogamous or polygynous marriages is infinitely elastic at their single income until all of them are married, and then it becomes vertical. The derived demand curve for a first wife of N_m identical men is also infinitely elastic at $Z_{mf(1)} - Z_{sm}$ (see Figure 3.2), but does not become vertical when all men have married because they would be willing to take a second wife and offer her

$$Z^f = MP_{f(2)} = Z_{mf(2)} - Z_{mf(1)}$$
$$= Z_{mf(2)} - [MP_{sm} + MP_{f(1)}], \tag{3.3}$$

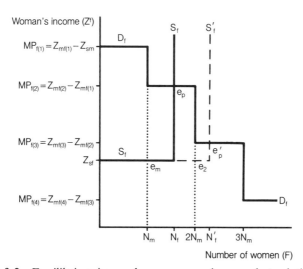

FIGURE 3.2   Equilibrium in a polygynous marriage market relating the income of women to the number of men and women.

---

4. Legally a man in China could not have more than one wife, but often concubines lived in the same household as the wife, bore children, and had various rights (see Goode, 1963, p. 282).

where $MP_{f(2)}$ is the additional output (or marginal product) from a second wife, $Z_{mf(2)}$ is the output of a household with one man and two women, $Z_{mf(1)}$ is the output of a household with one man and one woman, MP_{sm} is the output of a single man, and $MP_{f(1)}$ is the additional output from a first wife. More generally, a man with n wives would be willing to offer an additional wife

$$Z^f = MP_{f(n+1)} = Z_{mf(n+1)} - Z_{mf(n)}$$

$$= Z_{mf(n+1)} - \left[MP_{sm} + \sum_{j=1}^{n} MP_{f(j)} \right]. \qquad (3.4)$$

Even if household output has constant returns with respect to the number of wives and husbands, an increase in the number of wives alone would show diminishing returns because the fixed number of husbands limits the productivity of the wives. For example, the frequency of coition per wife, and thus the number of births per wife, would fall as the number of wives increased; or the husband's time and income spent on each wife and her children would fall as their number increased. Evidence from several polygynous societies indicates that the number of children per wife usually falls a little as the number of wives increases.[5] With diminishing returns from additional wives, the derived demand curve for wives would be a negatively inclined step function, as is D_f in Figure 3.2. Each step has a length equal to N_m, and the nth step has a height equal to the marginal productivity of the nth wife.

Equilibrium in an efficient polygynous marriage market does not require that the same number of men and women want to marry, only that the number of women who want to marry equals the demand for wives. The supply curve of women, S_f, and the derived demand curve for wives, D_f, intersect at point e_p, where all men and women marry and some men have two wives. All men and all women receive the same income, $Z_{mf(1)} - MP_{f(2)}$ and $MP_{f(2)}$ respectively, regardless of whether they are in monogamous or polygynous marriages, since all wives receive the marginal product of the second wife.

Although the number of women exceeds the number of men, the

---

5. Smith and Kunz (1976) review more than ten studies. The negative effect of several wives on the number of children per wife is presumably even stronger than these studies indicate because more "efficient" men, especially wealthier and older men, are more likely to be polygynous. Some evidence indicates that wealthier men tend to have more children per wife than other men with the same number of wives (see Grossbard, 1978).

equilibrium income of women is above their single income (the excess women enter polygynous marriages rather than remain single). If the number of women were to increase from N_f to N'_f (see Figure 3.2), the new equilibrium would be at point e'_p. Some men would take three wives, while the rest would take two wives, and the income of women would be reduced from $MP_{f(2)}$ to $MP_{f(3)}$, which is greater than it would be if no man could have more than two wives (at point e_2).

It is evident that women are better off than they would be if polygyny were forbidden. If the number of women exceeded the number of men and if polygyny were forbidden, the income of women would equal Z_{sf}, considerably less than $MP_{f(2)}$ or even $MP_{f(3)}$. More generally, if all men would have at least $n - 1$ wives and some would have n wives, monogamy would cost each woman the difference between the marginal product of the nth wife and her single income. Monogamy would also reduce the total output of all households by the sum of the differences between the marginal products and the single incomes of multiple wives.

The total income of men, on the other hand, could be increased by enforced monogamy even though total output and the total income of women were decreased. In Figure 3.2 each man receives $Z_{mf(1)} - MP_{f(2)}$ with polygyny (at point e_p), which is smaller than $Z_{mf(1)} - Z_{sf}$, the amount he would receive (at point e_m) if polygyny were forbidden.[6]

The demand for wives has not been the same for all men because they have differed in wealth, occupation, experience, and other relevant ways. In Figure 3.3 the combined demand curve for wives of two types of men, A and the more numerous B, is given by D_f. The marginal product of the second wives of type A is assumed to be above, and that of their third wives below, the marginal product of the first wives of B. The combined demand curve intersects S_f, the supply curve of a group of identical women, at point e_p, where the demand for and supply of wives are equal, and all women receive $MP_{f(1b)}$.

---

6. More generally, if some men were to have n wives with unrestricted polygyny, they would be better off if no man were permitted to have more than $n - 1$ wives (the Koran forbids more than four). However, they might be worse off if they were all restricted to monogamy because the gain from wives $2, 3, \ldots, n - 1$ could dominate the reduced income from the first wife under polygyny. For example, if some men would have three wives, as at point e'_p in Figure 3.2, instead of one wife as at point e_m with compulsory monogamy, all men lose $MP_{f(3)} - Z_{sf}$ from their first wife and gain $MP_{f(2)} - MP_{f(3)}$ from their second wife. If $MP_{f(2)} + Z_{sf} > 2MP_{f(3)}$, men as well as women are better off at e'_p than at e_m.

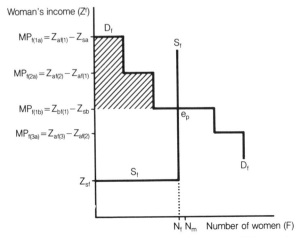

FIGURE 3.3 Equilibrium with polygyny when men differ and women are identical.

All A men take two wives at the same time that some B men remain single. Since the income of each woman equals the marginal product of a first wife to B men, married B men receive their single income and are indifferent between marriage and remaining single. Polygyny can exist when the number of men and women are approximately equal, as in Figure 3.3, because some "inferior" men are induced to remain single by the competition from "superior" men, which permits the "superior" men to become polygynous.

"Superiority" and "inferiority" in this context refer to characteristics that affect the marginal productivity of wives. Grossbard (1976) finds that an increase in several crude measures of wealth, such as the presence of a water standpipe in a household, significantly increases the propensity to be polygynous among men of Maiduguri, Nigeria, even when age, education, tribe, and certain other variables are held constant.[7]

The identical women in Figure 3.3 all receive the same income, $MP_{f(1b)}$, the marginal product of first wives to B men. All A men receive the income $Z_{af(2)} - 2MP_{f(1b)}$, which exceeds their single income by the striped area in the figure. In effect, A men receive a rent because of their superior capacity over other men in marriage. This figure clearly shows that a significant number of men, aboaut 33 percent, can be po-

---

7. For other evidence on the characteristics of polygynous Arabs, Africans, Mormons, Brazilian Indians, and Ugandans, see respectively Goode (1963), Dorjahn (1959), Young (1954), Salzano et al. (1967), and Goldschmidt (1973).

lygynous even when the number of men exceeds the number of women; differences among men in the marginal productivity of wives is a substitute for an excess supply of women.

The same analysis appears to be applicable when women rather than men differ: efficient women would appear to attract several husbands and inefficient women might remain single. Why then has polyandry been rare and polygyny common; more generally, what determines the incidence of monogamy, polygyny, and polyandry in a society? An easy answer is that some laws ban or restrict polygamy. However, laws are more readily passed and enforced when the demand for the affected activity is weak, so this is not a compelling answer. Moreover, polyandry is also rare and polygyny common among nonhuman species (see Chapter 9), which may suggest that more basic considerations than legal restrictions have determined the incidence of polygamy in human societies.

Figures 3.2 and 3.3 show that polygamy would be unimportant unless either men (or women) differed significantly in efficiency, or unless the ratio of eligible men to eligible women differed significantly from unity. These are not, however, the only determinants: the relative marginal contributions of men and women to output, economies or diseconomies of scale in the production of output, and the degree of substitution between men and women are also highly relevant determinants of the incidence of polygamy.

A More General Analysis of Polygamy

To show these effects with a more general analysis,[8] let the output produced by a monogamous marriage of the *i*th man with one of the identical women in the marriage market be given by

$$Z_{m_i 1} = n(\alpha_i)Z[p(\alpha_i)x_m, x_f], \qquad (3.5)$$

where α is an index of male efficiency; x_f represents the total resources of time, energy, and goods of each woman; and $p(\alpha_i) x_m$ represents the total effective resources of the *i*th man; where the function p converts male efficiency into effective amounts of male resources, such as wealth or nonmarket skills, and the function n converts male efficiency into different levels of output from given male and female resources.

---

8. The analysis in this section has been significantly influenced by Chang (1979) and Rosen (1981).

The output of this household, $Z_{m_i 1}$, would be maximized by appropriate allocations of the time and other resources of the ith male and his mate between market and nonmarket activities, and by appropriate specialized investments in human capital (see Chapter 2).

The total output of a polygynous household is assumed to equal the sum of the outputs produced independently with each wife. Independent production is a reasonable assumption when different wives have separate quarters, eat separately, and live largely autonomous existences. The assumption is less reasonable when wives cooperate in food preparation, child care, and the cultivation of land.[9] If all wives are identical and if the outputs with different wives are independently produced, the output of a polygynous family would be maximized by allocating an equal share of the husband's resources to each wife.

If the ith male has w_i wives, the output of his family would be

$$Z_{m_i w_i} = w_i n(\alpha_i) Z\left[\frac{p(\alpha_i)x_m}{w_i}, x_f\right], \tag{3.6}$$

where he spends $p(\alpha_i)x_m/w_i \equiv x_m^*$ on each of his wives. An increase in the number of wives must reduce the output per wife, regardless of any economies of scale in the production of Z, because less of his resources is spent on each wife.[10] This explains why the number of children per wife declines as the number of wives increases (see note 5), and also implies that other outputs per wife decline as the number of wives increases.

Although men with fewer wives spend a larger fraction of their resources on each wife, women nevertheless might prefer to marry men with a larger number of wives if these men have sufficiently greater resources and sufficiently more efficient production functions. That is, women might prefer only part of the attention of "successful" men to the full attention of "failures." In George Bernard Shaw's colorful words, "the maternal instinct leads a woman to prefer a tenth

---

9. The discussion of polygynous Mormon households in Young (1954) indicates considerable autonomy. The polygynous Moslem households in a small Iraqi village in Fernea (1965) are interrelated. See also the discussion of land cultivation by women in different polygynous societies in Boserup (1970).

10. Since the output with each wife is

$$AP_{m_i w_i} = \frac{Z_{m_i w_i}}{w_i} = n(\alpha_i) Z\left[\frac{p(\alpha_i)x_m}{w_i}, x_f\right],$$

then

$$\frac{\partial AP_{m_i w_i}}{\partial w_i} = n(\alpha_i) \frac{\partial Z}{\partial x_m^*}\left[\frac{-p(\alpha_i)x_m}{w_i^2}\right] < 0.$$

share in a first rate man to the exclusive possession of a third rate one''
(1930, p. 220).

Since identical participants in efficient marriage markets receive the
same income regardless of whom they marry or the number of their
mates, and since participants receive their marginal products, the equilibrium marginal product of identical women would be the same in different marriages. Therefore, if all women in the marriage market are
identical, their equilibrium income in each marriage would be

$$Z^f = MP_{m_i w_i} = \frac{\partial Z_{m_i w_i}}{\partial w_i} = n(\alpha_i)Z - n(\alpha_i)\frac{\partial Z}{\partial x_m^*} x_m^*. \tag{3.7}$$

Here w_i is the equilibrium number of wives of the ith male, with

$$w_i > 0 \text{ and } \sum_{i=1}^{x_m'} w_i \le N_f, \tag{3.8}$$

where N_m' is the number of men who marry, and N_f is the number of
women in the marriage market. Equilibrium requires that the marginal
product of wives diminish as their number increases; otherwise, the
most efficient man would marry all the women. The marginal product
of wives diminishes if, and only if, the marginal product of *male*
resources spent on any wife diminishes.[11] If returns to scale in household production are not strongly increasing, complementarity between
men and women in the production of children and other commodities
implies that the marginal product of male resources, and hence also the
marginal product of wives, would diminish.[12]

---

11. By differentiation of Eq. (3.7) with respect to w_i,

$$\frac{\partial MP_{m_i w_i}}{\partial w_i} = \frac{\partial^2 Z_{m_i w_i}}{\partial w_i^2} = n(\alpha_i)\frac{\partial^2 Z}{\partial (x_m^*)^2}\frac{(x_m^*)^2}{w_i}.$$

Hence

$$\frac{\partial MP_{m_i w_i}}{\partial w_i} \gtreqless 0 \text{ as } \frac{\partial^2 Z}{\partial (x_m^*)^2} \gtreqless 0.$$

12. If Z is homogeneous of the tth degree,

$$tZ = \frac{\partial Z}{\partial x_m^*} x_m^* + \frac{\partial Z}{\partial x_f} x_f = Z_m x_m^* + Z_f x_f.$$

Then differentiating with respect to x_m^*,

$$tZ_m = Z_{mm} x_m^* + Z_m + Z_{fm} x_f,$$

or

$$Z_{mm} x_m^* = (t - 1)Z_m - Z_{fm} x_f.$$

Since complementarity between men and women implies $Z_{fm} > 0$, then
$Z_{mm} < 0$ when $t \le 1$, and also when $t > 1$ if $t - 1$ is not large.

Although the conclusions would be similar if the number of wives were restricted to integers, to simplify the analysis I have assumed that they can vary continuously. For example, what I call the number of wives might refer to the number of days married, which can be changed continuously by changing either the age at marriage or the age at separation. However, the assumption in Eqs. (3.6) and (3.7) that male resources are entirely spent in cooperation with the resources of their wives is unrealistic for males who delay marriage or terminate their marriages early. Nevertheless, I shall maintain this assumption, and the implication that the income of single persons is nil, because such simplification does not significantly change the conclusions and could be easily modified.

Some men are unable to marry because the marginal product of their wives would be below the marginal product of women with other men (Z^f). Although the marginal product of wives increases when the number of wives decreases, it will reach an upper bound if at some point additional male resources do not add to output.[13] Then the equilibrium male resources spent on each wife will not exceed the amount with a zero marginal product, and the equilibrium number of wives will have a positive lower bound.[14] The efficiency of men with this minimum number of wives is determined from Eq. (3.7) by the condition that $\partial Z / \partial x_m^* = 0$:

$$n(\alpha_0) = \frac{Z^f}{Z_{\max}} = \frac{Z^f}{Z(\bar{x}_m^*, x_f)} \quad \text{and} \quad w_{\min} = \frac{p(\alpha_0)x_m}{\bar{x}_m^*}, \tag{3.9}$$

where $\bar{x}_m^*$ is the minimum x_m^* with $\partial Z / \partial x_m^* = 0$. All less efficient men would be unable to marry because the marginal product of their wives would be too low.

The marginal product of additional wives would be the same to men of different efficiencies only if the more efficient men were to have a larger number of wives.[15] Indeed, the least efficient men are often

---

13. According to Eq. (3.7), the marginal product of wives is maximized when $\partial Z / \partial x_m^* = 0$, or output per wife ($Z$) is maximized. Diminishing marginal product of wives implies that $\partial Z / \partial x_m^*$ can be zero only when $x_m^* \geq \bar{x}_m^*$, where $\bar{x}_m^*$ is determined by the household production function.

14. If $p(\alpha)x_m / w = \bar{x}_m^*$, then

$$w_{\min} = \frac{p(\alpha)x_m}{\bar{x}_m^*} > 0.$$

15. Equation (3.7) implies that $MP_{m_j w_j} > MP_{m_i w_i}$ if $\alpha_j > \alpha_i$ and $w_j \leq w_i$ because $n(\alpha_j) > n(\alpha_i)$ and $p(\alpha_j) > p(\alpha_i)$.

forced to remain bachelors because they cannot offer women as much as other men can. By differentiating Eq. (3.7) with respect to the index of efficiency, α—holding constant the income of women, Z^f, and the parameters x_m, x_f, p, and n—we can derive the exact relationship between wives and efficiency (see Mathematical Appendix, note A):

$$\epsilon(w,\alpha) \equiv \frac{dw}{d\alpha} \cdot \frac{\alpha}{w} = \epsilon(p,\alpha) + \epsilon(n,\alpha) \frac{[1/\epsilon(Z,x_m^*)] - 1}{\epsilon(Z_m,x_m^*)}, \qquad (3.10)$$

where $\epsilon(p,\alpha) = dp/d\alpha \cdot \alpha/p$, $\epsilon(n,\alpha) = dn/d\alpha \cdot \alpha/n$, $x_m^* = p(\alpha)x_m/w$, $Z_m = \partial Z/\partial x_m^*$, $\epsilon(Z,x_m^*) = Z_m x_m^*/Z$, and $\epsilon(Z_m,x_m^*) = -\partial Z_m/\partial x_m^* \cdot x_m^*/Z_m$.

Since a polygynous husband spends the same amount on each wife, an increase in his effective resources simply increases his wives by the same percentage. This explains why the coefficient of $\epsilon(p,\alpha)$ is unity in Eq. (3.10), with the powerful implication that the pure "wealth" elasticity of demand for wives is unity.

The effect of a pure change in efficiency—a change in the value of $n(\alpha)$—on the number of wives is more complicated and depends on the properties of the household production function. The elasticity of number of wives with respect to a change in efficiency tends to exceed unity, and is larger when the *marginal* contribution of men to output is smaller—that is, when $\epsilon(Z,x_m^*)$ is smaller—or when the *marginal* contribution of women to output is larger.[16]

The elasticity of number of wives with respect to a change in efficiency can be rewritten to depend positively on the marginal contribution of women to output relative to the contribution of men, and negatively on returns to scale in the household production function. For example, if the household production function is Cobb-Douglas:

$$Z = c(x_m^*)^a x_f^{ar}, \qquad (3.11)$$

where a and ar are constants, the coefficient of $\epsilon(n,\alpha)$ is a constant

$$\frac{\epsilon(Z,x_m^*)^{-1} - 1}{\epsilon(Z_m,x_m^*)} = \frac{1}{a} = \frac{1 + r}{g}, \qquad (3.12)$$

where r measures the relative marginal share of women in output; and $g = a + ar$ measures returns to scale. The coefficient of $\epsilon(n,\alpha)$ necessarily exceeds unity when $g \leq 1$, and increases as r increases or g decreases.

---

16. Note that if the production function has constant returns to scale,

$$\epsilon(Z,x_m^*) + \epsilon(Z,x_f) = 1 \quad \text{and} \quad \epsilon(Z_m,x_m^*) = \epsilon(Z_f,x_f)\frac{Z_f x_f}{Z_m x_m}.$$

If the production function has a constant elasticity of substitution, σ, between the inputs of men and women, and constant returns to scale ($g = 1$), then (see Mathematical Appendix, note B):

$$\frac{\epsilon(Z,x_m^*)^{-1} - 1}{\epsilon(Z_m,x_m^*)} = \left[1 + r'\left(\frac{x_f}{x_m^*}\right)^{-\beta}\right]\sigma = (1 + r)\sigma, \qquad (3.13)$$

where the relative marginal share of women in output is

$$r'\left(\frac{x_f}{x_m^*}\right)^{-\beta} = \frac{x_f MP_f}{x_m^* MP_m} = r. \qquad (3.14)$$

This equation reduces to Eq. (3.12) when $g = \sigma = 1$. The elasticity of wives with respect to efficiency must exceed unity if $\sigma > 1$, and it increases as σ increases. Since x_f/x_m^* is greater for more efficient men, the elasticity of wives with respect to efficiency is smaller for more efficient men when $\sigma < 1$, because the equilibrium share of women in household production then decreases as efficiency increases.

If $\epsilon(p,\alpha)$ and $\epsilon(n,\alpha)$ are constants, and if the production function is Cobb-Douglas, Eq. (3.10) is a simple linear differential equation that can be solved explicitly for the number of wives:

$$w = \left(\frac{\alpha}{\bar{\alpha}}\right)^{\epsilon(p,\alpha) + \frac{1+r}{g}\epsilon(n,\alpha)}, \qquad (3.15)$$

where $\bar{\alpha}$ is the efficiency of men with one wife (see Mathematical Appendix, note C). The equilibrium number of wives is proportional to a man's total resources and increases much more rapidly than his efficiency if the marginal contribution of women to output is not less than that of men ($r \geq 1$) and if returns to scale are not increasing ($g \leq 1$). For example, a 10-percent increase in efficiency increases the number of wives by at least 30 percent if $r = 2$, $g \leq 1$, and $\epsilon(n,\alpha) = 1$! The inequality in the number of wives of married men then greatly exceeds the inequality in the efficiency of husbands, and the distribution of wives would be considerably skewed to the right even when the efficiency of husbands was symmetrically distributed.

The marginal contribution of men to the production of children is much less than the contribution of women, because women biologically house and feed the fetus. Moreover, in primitive and less developed societies women also contribute much more to the care of children in that they provide their own milk and care for older children while producing additional ones. Consequently, our analysis implies that polygyny is common and wives are unequally distributed in many of these societies because the marginal contribution of women is larger than the marginal contribution of men to the production and care of many children, the principal output of marriage in these societies.

As societies have become more urbanized and developed over time, families have greatly reduced their demand for "quantity" of children and greatly raised their demands for education, health, and other aspects of the "quality" of children (see Chapter 5). Since the marginal contribution of men to quality is much greater than to quantity, our analysis predicts correctly that the incidence of polygyny has declined substantially over time.

Equilibrium Income, Investments, and Sex Ratio

Since the income of a man equals the difference between the output of his family and the income of his wives, his income can be written as

$$Z^{m_i} = Z_{m_i w_i} - w_i Z^f = w_i n(\alpha_i) \frac{\partial Z}{\partial x_m^*} x_m^*, \tag{3.16}$$

where Z^f is given by Eq. (3.7) and is the same for all the identical women in the marriage market. The term on the far right-hand side can be considered the marginal product of men with efficiency α_i. The distribution of male income depends on the distribution of wives and on the distribution of the marginal contributions of men to the output with each wife $[n(\alpha_i)(\partial Z/\partial x_m^*)x_m^*]$.

If the household production function is Cobb-Douglas and has constant returns to scale, these contributions are the same for all men when the marriage market is in equilibrium.[17] Then Eq. (3.16) becomes

$$Z^{m_i} = \frac{Z^f}{r} w_i, \tag{3.17}$$

---

17. Since

$$Z^f = n(\alpha_i) \left(Z - \frac{\partial Z}{\partial x_m^*} x_m^* \right) = n(\alpha_i) \frac{\partial Z}{\partial x_f} x_f = n(\alpha_i) a r Z,$$

where a and r are constants if Z is Cobb-Douglas, then

$$n(\alpha_i) \frac{\partial Z}{\partial x_m^*} x_m^* = n(\alpha_i) a Z = \frac{Z^f}{r}$$

would be the same for all men.

and the equilibrium income of men is proportional to the number of their wives.[18] If the production function were not Cobb-Douglas but had an elasticity of substitution equal to σ, r would increase along with efficiency if σ exceeded unity and would decrease if σ were less than unity. Hence the income of men would increase more or less rapidly than the number of their wives[19] as $\sigma \lessgtr 1$.

Let me emphasize that these results do not assume that men value wives for their own sake, but only consider the value of the output produced by husbands and wives. Equations (3.16) and (3.17) indicate that changes in the equilibrium number of wives may be a good *proxy* for changes in the output that is valued. Indeed, assuming that the number of wives is measured correctly, it may be a better proxy than changes in money income, the proxy commonly used.

Equation (3.17) implies that the average income of men is

$$\bar{Z}^m = \frac{Z^f}{r} \, \bar{w} \, (N'_m/N_m), \qquad (3.18)$$

where N'_m is the number of married men (those with $w > 0$), $\bar{w}$ is the average number of wives of married men, and N_m is the number of men in the marriage market.[20] Since

$$\bar{w} = N_f/N'_m, \qquad (3.19)$$

---

18. Lucas (1978) has a similar result with a model of entrepreneurship: he shows that the equilibrium income of entrepreneurs is proportional to the number of their employees when the firm's production function is Cobb-Douglas.

19. This analysis is applicable to the earnings of top managers if they are considered to be the polygynous men and the number of wives measures the size of the firms. Equation (3.17) then implies that the earnings of top managers would increase more or less slowly than firm size as the elasticity of substitution between the time (and other resources) of managers and various inputs exceeded or was less than unity. Therefore, Herbert Simon (1979) must be mistaken in his assertion that an apparently concave relation between the earnings of top managers and the logarithm of firm size cannot be simply explained with neoclassical maximizing theory.

20. No men would remain single if the production function were Cobb-Douglas, because the marginal product of wives would always be positive and output per wife would increase indefinitely as the number of wives became smaller.

where N_f is the number of women in the marriage market,[21] the average income of men relative to the income of each identical woman is

$$R = \frac{\bar{Z}^m}{\bar{Z}^f} = \frac{Z^f \bar{w} N'_m}{Z^f r N_m} = \frac{\bar{w} N'_m}{r N_m} = \frac{N_f}{r N_m} = \frac{1}{rv}, \qquad (3.20)$$

where $v = N_m/N_f$ is the sex ratio of participants in the marriage market.

A decrease in the sex ratio of participants—an increase in the number of women relative to men—would reduce the income of women and raise the average income of men. The number of wives per married man would increase, since the marginal product of additional wives would exceed the reduced cost of wives. Consequently, a reduction in the sex ratio raises the incidence of polygyny as measured by the average number of wives of married men, or by the fraction of men with more than a fixed number of wives. However, the incidence of polygyny as measured by the fraction of men without wives would be reduced, because some men who would not have married earlier would now be able to offer women enough to entice them into marriage. Moreover, the inequality in the number of wives of married men is determined by the variables in Eq. (3.10) and is entirely independent of the sex ratio.

An increase in the marginal contribution to output of women relative to the marginal contribution of men (that is, an increase in r) raises the marginal product of wives and lowers the marginal product of husbands, which raises the income of women and lowers the average income of men. As a result, the number of men who marry decreases and the number of wives per married man increases. Since Eqs. (3.13) and (3.15) imply that the inequality in the number of wives of married men also would become greater, all measures of the incidence of polygyny increase when women become more important in the marginal production of output. An increase in the contribution of women also raises the inequality and skewness in male incomes, inasmuch as the distribution of their incomes is approximately proportional to the distribution of wives. The increase in equality and skewness implies that the most efficient men could be made better off even though the average income of men would be reduced.

---

21. All N_f women marry, because we have assumed that Z^f is positive and that the output of single women is negligible.

Groups opposing polygyny claim to be opposed to the degradation and exploitation of women.[22] My analysis of efficient, competitive marriage markets indicates, however, that the income of women and the competition by men for wives would be greater when polygyny is greater if the incidence of polygyny had been determined mainly by the relative marginal contribution of women to output. This view is supported by the fact that bride prices are more common and generally higher in societies with a greater incidence of polygyny (see Goode, 1963; Goldschmidt, 1973, p. 80; Whiting, 1977; and Grossbard, 1978).

An increase in polygyny due to an increase in the contribution of women induces men to postpone their entry into the marriage market until they have become more efficient with age and experience; for efficiency is more beneficial in the marriage market when the incidence of polygyny is greater. Similarly, an increase in polygyny probably induces women to enter the marriage market at younger ages because the demand for wives is greater, although the burden on young women is raised by marriage. Men do marry later and women appear to marry earlier in more polygynous societies.[23]

A decrease in the average income of men relative to women—$\bar{Z}^m/Z^f$ in Eq. (3.20)—because of an increase in the relative marginal contribution of women also reduces the sex ratio by inducing men to emigrate

---

22. David Hume wrote, "this sovereignty [that is, polygyny] of the male is a real usurpation, and destroys that nearness of rank, not to say equality, which nature has established between the sexes" (1854, pt. 1, essay 19). Young (1954) also discusses the opposition of various groups to polygyny among the Mormons. However, the Ayatollah Ruhollah Khomeini of Iran expressed a traditional Islamic view when he said in a 1979 interview with Oriana Fallaci: "The law of the four wives is a very progressive law and was written for the good of women since there are more women than men . . . Even under the difficult conditions which Islam imposes on a man with two or three or four wives, there is equal treatment, equal affection, and equal time. This law is better than monogamy."

23. In discussing the polygynous Sebei of Uganda, Goldschmidt said: "Although the men generally feel that plural wives are desirable, only a few of them actually have more than one wife. Yet this very fact makes women scarce. Significantly there is no such thing as an old maid in Sebei" (1973, p. 80).

The Mormons may be an exception in that the average age at first marriage in the late 1800s was 20–23 for women and 25 for men (see Smith and Kunz, 1976, pp. 469–470). However, the influx of many female converts probably significantly raised the average age at marriage of women, for girls with Mormon parents apparently married young: "By the age of 16 many girls were being courted, and certainly a girl beyond her 20th year who was not wed was already likely to be regarded as a potential spinster" (Young, 1954, p. 246).

and women to immigrate;[24] by increasing parental concern about the survival of daughters and decreasing their concern about the survival of sons; and by other responses as well. Since an increase in the contribution of women raises the incidence of polygyny, fewer men would be available when polygyny was more common, but the causation would be *from* polygyny *to* the shortage of men.

If these responses continued to reduce the sex ratio whenever the average income of men relative to women dropped below some income ratio R^*, and if they continued to raise the sex ratio whenever the relative income of men rose above R^*, the sex ratio would be stationary only at a relative income equal to R^*. We must remember that R^* does not necessarily equal unity; the net cost of raising sons and daughters may differ, and parents, especially elderly parents, may benefit differently from sons and daughters. We shall return to this point in Chapter 6. Since Eq. (3.20) shows that a change in the relative number of men changes their relative income in the opposite direction, the stationary sex ratio v^* would be a stable equilibrium ratio: starting from any initial position, over time the relative income of men would approach R^* as the sex ratio approached its equilibrium value. This value is determined from (3.20) to be

$$v^* = 1/(rR^*). \qquad (3.20')$$

The equilibrium ratio of men to women would be inversely related to the equilibrium ratio of the incomes of men and women and directly related to the ratio of the *marginal* contributions to output of men and women $(1/r)$. More generally, the sex ratio would depend positively on the income ratio but would not have a stationary value.[25]

Efficiency is not just exogenously given but is partly determined by education, training, and other investments in human capital. Men are willing to bear the sizable costs and risks of becoming efficient to attract more wives. Our analysis implies that the effect of increased efficiency on the number of wives and income, and thus the incentive to become efficient, is greater when the contribution of women is greater.

---

24. For example, the Mormons recruited female converts from abroad (Young, 1954, pp. 124–125). The highly polygynous Kapsirika herders import wives from the less polygynous Sasur farmers (Goldschmidt, 1973), and males migrated out of polygynous villages of the Ottoman Empire in the nineteenth century (McCarthy, 1979).

25. See the analysis and empirical evidence for primitive societies in Becker and Posner (1981).

To show this, let efficiency (α) be determined additively by produced skills (h) and "inherited" abilities (μ):

$$\alpha = \mu + h. \tag{3.21}$$

The production function for h is

$$h = \psi(x_m^0, \mu), \quad \text{with } \partial\psi/\partial x_m^0 > 0 \text{ and } \partial\psi/\partial\mu > 0, \tag{3.22}$$

and, presumably, $\partial^2\psi/\partial(x_m^0)^2 < 0$ and $\partial^2\psi/\partial\mu\partial x_m^0 > 0$, where x_m^0 are the resources spent on producing h. Total resources

$$x_m + x_m^0 = \bar{x}_m \tag{3.23}$$

are allocated between direct and indirect production of male income, and the equilibrium condition for an allocation that maximizes income, if Z is Cobb-Douglas and $p(\alpha) \equiv 1$, is as follows (see Mathematical Appendix, note D):

$$\frac{\partial\psi}{\partial x_m^0} = \frac{\alpha g}{(\bar{x}_m - x_m^0)(1 + r)}. \tag{3.24}$$

Therefore, an increase in the marginal contribution of women to the production of output (r) induces greater expenditure on efficiency until $\partial\psi/\partial x_m^0$ is lowered sufficiently. An increase in the contribution also raises the inequality among men by inducing abler men to increase their investments relative to other men.[26] Since an increase in the contribution of women to output also encourages polygyny, the average man would invest more and would be more efficient when polygyny is more common. Moreover, an increase in contribution not only raises the inequality in number of wives directly, from Eq. (3.15), but indirectly does so by raising the inequality among men.

As men invest more, they increase the competition for wives and thereby induce an increase in the incomes of women. Since the total number of wives is fixed—aside from any induced decline in the sex ratio—the effect on the demand for wives of a general increase in effi-

---

26. By differentiating the equilibrium condition (3.24) with respect to ability, we obtain

$$\frac{\partial x_m^0}{\partial\mu} = \frac{\partial^2\psi}{\partial x\partial\mu} \bigg/ \left[\frac{g}{1 + r}(\bar{x}_m - x_m^0)^2 - \frac{\partial^2\psi}{\partial(x_m^0)^2}\right] > 0.$$

An increase in r raises the right-hand side and thereby raises the effect of ability (μ) on the amount invested in produced skills (x_m^0). Hence an increase in r raises the differences in produced skills between abler and less able men.

ciency must be offset by higher incomes of women. Indeed, Eq. (3.20) shows that the ratio of the income of women to the average income of men would be independent of the distribution of efficiency among men if the production function were Cobb-Douglas.

I have been assuming that women are identical in terms of production and that men differ, but the analysis would be symmetrical if men were identical and women differed. The distribution of men among polyandrous families would be determined by the requirement that husbands have the same marginal product in all marriages. More efficient women would have more husbands because men are more productive with such women.

If production with each husband were independent of the production with each other husband (but see the subsequent discussion), the total output of the ith woman with h_i husbands would be

$$Z_{h_i,f_i} = h_i n(\alpha,\beta_i) Z(x_m, x_{f_i}^*) \tag{3.25}$$

where $x_{f_i}^* = \ell(\beta_i) x_f / h_i$, α is the efficiency of each husband, β_i is the efficiency of the ith woman, $\partial n / \partial \beta_i > 0$, and $d\ell / d\beta_i > 0$. If Z has constant returns to scale, the effect of a change in β_i on the equilibrium number of husbands is determined from Eqs. (3.10) and (3.13) to be

$$\epsilon(h,\beta) = \frac{dh}{d\beta} \cdot \frac{\beta}{h} = \epsilon(\ell,\beta) + \left(1 + \frac{1}{r}\right) \sigma \, \epsilon(n,\beta), \tag{3.26}$$

where $1/r$ is the relative marginal contribution of men to output. From Eq. (3.17) the equilibrium income of the ith woman would be approximately

$$Z^{f_i} \cong r Z^m h_i, \tag{3.27}$$

where Z^m is the equilibrium income of men, and the equation is exact when the production function is Cobb-Douglas.

An increase in the marginal contribution of women increases the incidence of polygyny, by Eq. (3.13), and reduces the incidence of polyandry, by Eq. (3.26). Therefore polygyny has been much more common than polyandry mainly because the *marginal* contribution of women to output has significantly exceeded that of men. Moreover, polyandry has been negligible when polygyny has been important and vice versa, because a change in the contribution of women changes the incidence of polygyny and polyandry in opposite directions.

The assumption that production with each mate is independent of production with other mates may be appropriate for polygynous families, but not for polyandrous families. Since own children are strongly preferred to children produced by others, and since the father of a child is not readily known when a mother has several husbands, each husband would lower the productivity of other husbands. This means that polyandrous marriages have diminishing returns to scale, which helps explain why polyandry has been rare[27] and also why husbands of polyandrous women have usually been brothers or other relatives (the children of relatives are preferred to those of strangers).

An argument similar to that leading to Eq. (3.24) shows that the average investment by women and the inequality in their investments would be positively related to the marginal contribution of men to married output (that is, negatively related to the marginal contribution of women). Since the marginal contribution of women exceeds that of men when number of children is the major output of marriage, the average investment and the inequality in investments would be lower for women when number of children is important.

Table 3.1 gives average and standard deviation[28] of years of schooling for men and women in various countries. As expected, both tend to be significantly lower for women than for men in poor countries, where number of children is the major output; they are only slightly lower for women in rich countries where quality of children is important.[29]

An increase in the marginal contribution of women to output directly raises the income inequality among men and lowers the income inequality among women, and from Eqs. (3.15) and (3.22) indirectly does so by raising the inequality in investments among men and lowering them among women. The inequality in male incomes is generally greater in poorer countries (Lydall, 1968, pp. 152–153).[30]

Polygamy could be "disguised" when both men and women differ, because a more efficient mate could substitute for several less efficient mates. The analysis in the next chapter implies that an efficient mar-

---

27. For evidence on polyandry see Rivers (1906), Saksena (1962), and Prince Peter (1963).

28. The theory of human capital implies that inequality in years of schooling should be measured by the standard deviation or by a similar *absolute* measure of dispersion (see Becker, 1975).

29. Although few countries in Table 3.1 have explicit polygamy, I show shortly that "implicit" polygamy of positive assortative mating has similar implications for investments by men and women.

30. The inequality in female incomes is difficult to measure because most of the income of women is not obtained through market transactions.

TABLE 3.1   Estimates of educational attainment by years of schooling of men and women, ages 25–34, in various countries.

Country and year sampled	Average		Standard deviation	
	Men	Women	Men	Women
Iran, 1966	2.1	0.7	3.9	2.4
India, 1971	2.6	0.8	4.0	2.4
Kenya,[a] 1969	3.4	1.2	3.4	2.4
Zambia, 1969	3.6	1.3	3.2	2.3
Malaysia, 1970	3.7	2.7	3.3	3.1
Ecuador, 1962	5.0	4.8	3.2	2.9
Mexico, 1976	5.5	4.5	4.5	3.7
Argentina, 1970	6.5	6.2	4.1	4.0
Hong Kong, 1971	7.6	6.8	3.5	3.5
Sweden, 1970	8.3	8.2	4.7	4.6
United States, 1970	12.4	11.9	3.5	2.8

SOURCES: India Office of the Registrar General, 1976; Iran Statistical Centre, 1968; Malaysia Department of Statistics, 1977; Mexico Direccion General de Estadistica, 1976; United Nations, 1972, table 19, and 1974, table 34; U. S. Bureau of the Census, 1973c, table 1.

[a] Ages 25–29.

riage market would have positive sorting of mates—for example, more efficient men would marry more efficient women—if, as is plausible, the efficiencies of men and women are reinforcing. They would, in fact, be reinforcing in the household production functions considered in this chapter if

$$\frac{\partial^2 n(\alpha,\beta)}{(\partial\alpha)(\partial\beta)} = \frac{\partial^2 n}{(\partial\beta)(\partial\alpha)} > 0, \tag{3.28}$$

or if an increase in the efficiency of one sex raises the contribution of an increase in the efficiency of the other sex. Consequently, the degree of effective polygyny or polyandry and the inequality in the distribution of income is understated even by distributions of continuous variables such as wife-days and husband-days, because the efficiency of each wife (or husband) tends to increase as the number of wife-days (or husband-days) increases.

When both men and women differ, more efficient persons have the additional option of choosing the full attention of several less efficient mates instead of part of the attention of one more efficient mate. In light of the previous analysis, it should not be surprising that efficient women are more likely to prefer part of the attention of efficient men when the marginal contribution of women to output is greater (see Mathematical Appendix, note E). Therefore, *explicit* polyandry has been rare partly because of the attraction of *implicit* polyandry.

We have shown that polygynous men have more incentive to invest in superior skills when the marginal contribution of women to output is greater, and that polyandrous women have more incentive to invest when men contribute more. The same conclusions apply to the implicit polygamy of assortative mating. An increase in the marginal contribution of women raises investments by men, lowers investments by women, and raises the average efficiency and the inequality in efficiency of men relative to women (see Mathematical Appendix, note F). Both average and standard deviation of years of schooling are usually much lower for women than men in poor countries with monogamous marriages (see Table 3.1), where presumably the marginal contribution of women to output is greater than the marginal contribution of men because of the value of having many children.

Mathematical Appendix

A. Differentiation of Eq. (3.7) gives

$$0 = n'(\alpha)(Z - Z_m x_m^*) + n\left[Z_m\left(\frac{-x_m^*}{w}\right)w'(\alpha) + Z_m\left(\frac{x_m^*}{w}\right)w'(\alpha)\right]$$

$$+ n\left[Z_m\frac{x_m^*}{p}p'(\alpha) - Z_m\frac{x_m^*}{p}p'(\alpha)\right]$$

$$+ n\left[Z_{mm}\frac{(x_m^*)^2}{w}w'(\alpha) - Z_{mm}\frac{(x_m^*)^2}{p}p'(\alpha)\right],$$

where $n'(\alpha) = dn/d\alpha$, $Z_m = \partial Z/\partial x_m^*$, $w'(\alpha) = dw/d\alpha$, $p'(\alpha) = dp/d\alpha$, and $Z_{mm} = \partial Z_m/\partial x_m^*$. Therefore

$$\frac{w'(\alpha)}{w} = \frac{p'(\alpha)}{p} + \frac{n'(\alpha)}{n}\left[\frac{(Z - Z_m x_m^*)}{-Z_{mm}(x_m^*)^2}\right]. \qquad (3.10')$$

Since

$$\frac{Z - Z_m x_m^*}{-Z_{mm}(x_m^*)^2} = \frac{\dfrac{Z}{Z_m x_m^*} - 1}{-Z_{mm} x_m^* \dfrac{1}{Z_m}} = \frac{\epsilon(Z, x_m^*)^{-1} - 1}{\epsilon(Z_m, x_m^*)},$$

Eq. (3.10) follows from Eq. (3.10′).

B. If the production function has a constant elasticity of substitution and constant returns to scale,

$$Z = [a (x_m^*)^{-\beta} + r' a (x_f)^{-\beta}]^{-1/\beta}.$$

Then it is readily shown that

$$\frac{\epsilon(Z, x_m^*)^{-1} - 1}{\epsilon(Z_m, x_m^*)} = \frac{\sigma(Z/x_m^*)^{-\beta}}{a}.$$

Substitution into the production function yields

$$\left(\frac{Z}{x_m^*}\right)^{-\beta} = a \left[1 + r' \left(\frac{x_f}{x_m^*}\right)^{-\beta}\right].$$

C. We can find $\bar{\alpha}$ by solving Eq. (3.7) for α when $w = 1$:

$$Z^f = n(\bar{\alpha}) \left(Z - \frac{\partial Z}{\partial x_m^*} x_m^*\right).$$

If Z is Cobb-Douglas,

$$Z - \frac{\partial Z}{\partial x_m^*} x_m^* = (1 - a)Z,$$

and therefore

$$(1 - a)n(\bar{\alpha})[p(\bar{\alpha})] = Z^f/(c x_m^a x_f^{ar}).$$

D. If r is a constant (Cobb-Douglas production), the income of a male is maximized if

$$\frac{dZ^m}{dx_m^0} = 0 = \frac{Z^f}{r} \left[\left(\frac{\partial w}{\partial \alpha}\right)\left(\frac{\partial \psi}{\partial x_m^0}\right) + \left(\frac{\partial w}{\partial x_m}\right)\left(\frac{\partial x_m}{\partial x_m^0}\right)\right].$$

Since

$$\frac{\partial w}{\partial \alpha} = \left(\frac{w}{\alpha}\right)\left(\frac{1 + r}{g}\right) \quad \text{and} \quad \frac{\partial w}{\partial x_m} = \frac{w}{x_m},$$

then

$$\left(\frac{w}{\alpha}\right)\left(\frac{\partial \psi}{\partial x_m^0}\right) = \left(\frac{g}{1 + r}\right)\left(\frac{w}{\bar{x} - x_m^0}\right).$$

E. A woman prefers a man with several wives if her marginal product with him exceeds her marginal product with several husbands of lesser efficiency. That is, she prefers a polygynous man with w_i wives and efficiency α_i to h_j husbands of efficiency $\alpha_k < \alpha_i$ if

$$MP_{iw_i} = n(\alpha_i, \beta_j)(Z - Z_m x_m^*) > MP_{h_j j} = n(\alpha_k, \beta_j) Z_f x_f^*,$$

where I have assumed for simplicity only (see Chapter 4) that all mates in a polygamous family have the same efficiency, and that a change in efficiency only has factor-neutral effects on output. That is, a change in efficiency affects only the value of n because $p(\alpha) \equiv \ell(\beta) \equiv 1$. If Z has constant returns to scale, this inequality becomes

$$n(\alpha_i, \beta_j)\frac{\partial Z}{\partial x_f}\left(\frac{x_m}{w_i}, x_f\right) > n(\alpha_k, \beta_j)\frac{\partial Z}{\partial(x_f/h_j)}\left(x_m, \frac{x_f}{h_j}\right)\frac{1}{h_j}.$$

If Z is also Cobb-Douglas, this becomes

$$\frac{n(\alpha_i, \beta_j)}{n(\alpha_k, \beta_j)}\frac{h_j^{1-ar}}{w_i^{-a}} = (h_j w_i)^{\frac{1}{1+r}},$$

where r is the relative marginal share of women in output. Hence the polygynous family is more likely to be preferred when r is larger, h_j and w_i are smaller, and α_i is larger relative to α_k.

F. To sketch out a proof (note D above gives a more complete treatment), each man is assumed to maximize his income (Z^m) by choosing an optimal allocation of his total resources ($\bar{x}_m$) between the production of skills and the direct production of income. Let the output Z of a monogamous marriage be

$$Z_{\alpha\beta} = n(\alpha, \beta) Z(x_m, x_f),$$

where α and β measure the skills of men and women, and x_m and x_f measure the resources they spend on output. The man's optimal allocation of $\bar{x}_m$ is determined by

$$\frac{dZ^m}{dx_m^0} = 0 = \left(\frac{\partial Z^m}{\partial \alpha}\right)\left(\frac{\partial \alpha}{\partial x_m^0}\right) + \left(\frac{\partial Z^m}{\partial x_m}\right)\left(\frac{\partial x_m}{\partial x_m^0}\right),$$

where x_m^0 are the resources he spends on raising his skills and $\partial x_m / \partial x_m^0 = -1$. Since

$$\frac{\partial Z^m}{\partial \alpha} = \frac{\partial Z_{\alpha\beta}}{\partial \alpha} - \frac{\partial Z^f}{\partial \alpha} = \frac{\partial Z_{\alpha\beta}}{\partial \alpha} \quad \text{because} \quad \frac{\partial Z^f}{\partial \alpha} = 0,$$

then

$$\frac{\partial \alpha}{\partial x_m^0} = \frac{n \dfrac{\partial Z}{\partial x_m}}{\dfrac{\partial n}{\partial \alpha} Z} = \frac{g}{\dfrac{\alpha \log n}{\partial \alpha}(1 + r)x_m},$$

where r is the relative marginal contribution of women to output, and g is the degree of homogeneity of Z (compare Eq. 3.24). Hence an increase in r raises the optimal investment in skills because the equilibrium value of $\partial \alpha / \partial x_m^0$ is reduced.

CHAPTER 4

Assortative Mating in Marriage Markets

Chapter 3 argued that an efficient marriage market assigns imputed incomes or "prices" to all participants that attract them to suitable polygamous or monogamous marriages. Imputed prices are also used to match men and women of different qualities: some participants, we have seen, choose to be matched with "inferior" persons because they feel "superior" persons are too expensive. Obstacles to the efficient pricing of participants arise when the gains from marriage cannot readily be divided or when one spouse (usually the husband) is given more power than the other. Bride prices, dowries, divorce settlements and other capital transfers evolved partly to overcome such obstacles.

This chapter shows that an efficient marriage market usually has positive assortative mating, where high-quality men are matched with high-quality women and low-quality men with low-quality women, although negative assortative mating is sometimes important. An efficient market also tends to maximize the aggregate output of household commodities, so that no person can improve his marriage without making others worse off.

As we have seen, the mating of superior men and women is an implicit form of polygamy, which can substitute for explicit polygamy.

This chapter proves the converse, that explicit polygamy is an implicit form of positive assortative mating, which can substitute for the mating of superior persons. Consequently, the mates of polygynous males tend to be of a lower average quality than the mates of equally superior monogamous males.

Equilibrium Conditions for Assortative Mating with Monogamy

Identical men receive the same income in an efficient marriage market regardless of whom they marry or whether they choose to remain single. Since marriages with superior women produce larger outputs, superior women receive higher incomes in efficient markets. If all marriages were monogamous, an assumption maintained in this section, the difference between the incomes of the jth woman and the ith woman would be:

$$Z_j^f - Z_i^f = (Z_{mj} - Z^m) - (Z_{mi} - Z^m) = Z_{mj} - Z_{mi}, \qquad (4.1)$$

where Z_k^f is the equilibrium income of the kth woman, Z^m is the equilibrium income of men, and Z_{mk} is the marital output of the kth woman and any man. Superior women receive a premium that is determined by their additional productivity as wives.

The analysis is considerably more complicated when both men and women differ; incomes then depend on how they are sorted into different marriages. Moreover, the optimal sorting in turn is determined by the set of equilibrium incomes. This appearance of circularity is resolved by recognizing that both are determined simultaneously in the marriage market. In an efficient marriage market superior persons tend to marry one another and are compensated for their higher productivity.[1]

The commodity outputs produced by single persons and by all possible monogamous matings between an equal number of men and women (unequal numbers are considered later in this chapter) are shown by the following matrix:

---

1. The discussion in the remainder of this section is based on Becker, 1973 and 1974a.

$$F_1 \cdot \cdot \cdot \cdot \cdot \cdot F_N$$

$$
\begin{array}{c}
M_1 \\
\cdot \\
\cdot \\
\cdot \\
\cdot \\
\cdot \\
\cdot \\
M_N
\end{array}
\left[
\begin{array}{cccccc}
& Z_{s1} & \cdot \cdot \cdot \cdot \cdot \cdot & Z_{sN} \\
Z_{1s} & Z_{11} & \cdot \cdot \cdot \cdot \cdot \cdot & Z_{1N} \\
\cdot & \cdot & \cdot & & \cdot \\
\cdot & \cdot & \cdot & & \cdot \\
\cdot & \cdot & \cdot & & \cdot \\
\cdot & \cdot & \cdot & & \cdot \\
\cdot & \cdot & \cdot & & \cdot \\
Z_{Ns} & Z_{N1} & \cdot \cdot \cdot \cdot \cdot \cdot & Z_{NN}
\end{array}
\right]
\qquad (4.2)
$$

where $F_1, \ldots, F_N$ and $M_1, \ldots, M_N$ refer to women and men of different qualities. Since the complementarity between men and women and the differences between their comparative advantages imply that both men and women are better off married, the row and column giving single outputs can be ignored and attention focused on the $N \times N$ matrix of marital outputs.

There are $N!$ ways to select one entry in each row and column, or $N!$ different sortings that permit each man to marry one woman and vice versa. The aggregate marital output produced by any sorting can be written as

$$Z^k = \sum_{i_k \in M, j_k \in F} Z_{ij}, \qquad k = 1, \ldots, N! \qquad (4.3)$$

If a sorting that maximizes total output is numbered so that its entries lie along the diagonal, the maximum total output can be written as

$$Z^* = \sum_{i=1}^{N} Z_{ii} = \max Z^k \geq Z^k \quad \text{for all } k. \qquad (4.4)$$

If each person is a utility maximizer and chooses the mate who maximizes his utility, the optimal sorting must have the property that persons not married to each other could not marry without making at least one of them worse off. In game theoretic language, the optimal sorting is in the core, since no (monogamous) coalition outside the core could make either of its members better off without making the other worse off.

Utility is monotonically related to commodity income; therefore a noncore marriage cannot produce more than the sum of the incomes that its two mates would receive in the core. If it could produce more, and if any division of output were feasible,[2] a division could be found that would make each better off, thereby contradicting the optimality of the core. If the sorting along the diagonal were in the core, this condition states that

$$Z_i^m + Z_j^f \geq Z_{ij} \quad \text{for all } i \text{ and } j, \tag{4.5}$$

where the accounting identity between output and income implies that

$$Z_i^m + Z_i^f = Z_{ii}, \quad i = 1, \ldots, N. \tag{4.6}$$

Condition (4.5) immediately excludes any sorting from the core that does not maximize aggregate commodity output, for otherwise at least one man and one woman would be better off with each other than with their mates assigned by the core. Conversely, any sorting that does maximize aggregate output must be part of the core.[3] Moreover, the theory of optimal assignments, which has the same mathematical structure as the sorting of persons by marriage, implies that generally more than one set of incomes satisfies conditions (4.5) and (4.6) for a sorting that maximizes aggregate output (for a proof see Koopmans and Beckmann, 1957, p. 60).

The solution can be illustrated with the following 2×2 matrix of outputs:

$$\begin{array}{c} \\ M_1 \\ M_2 \end{array} \begin{array}{cc} F_1 & F_2 \\ \begin{bmatrix} 8 & 4 \\ 9 & 7 \end{bmatrix} \end{array}. \tag{4.7}$$

Although the maximum output of a marriage is produced by a marriage between M_2 and F_1, the optimal sorting is (M_1, F_1) and (M_2, F_2). For if $Z_1^m = 3, Z_1^f = 5, Z_2^m = 5$, and $Z_2^f = 2$, then M_2 and F_1 have no incentive

---

2. Bride prices and dowries introduce considerable flexibility into the effective division of output, even when the apparent division is inflexible. I shall discuss this point later in the chapter.

3. If M_i married F_j and M_p married F_i in an optimal sorting k that does not maximize total output, condition (4.5) requires that $Z_i^m + Z_i^f \geq Z_{ii}$, for all i. Hence, by summation,

$$Z^k = \sum_{\text{all marriages in } k} Z_i^m + Z_i^f \geq \sum_i Z_{ii} = Z^*,$$

where Z^*, the maximum total output, must exceed Z^k because Z^k is less than the maximum by assumption. Thus we have contradicted the assumption that an optimal sorting can produce less than the maximum total output. It is easily shown in the same way that all sortings that maximize total output must be part of the optimal sortings.

to marry, since $Z_2^m + Z_1^f = 10 > 9$; neither do M_1 and F_2, since $Z_1^m + Z_2^f = 5 > 4$.

This example illustrates that the marriage market chooses not the maximum output of any single marriage but the maximum sum of the outputs over all marriages, just as competitive product markets maximize the sum of the outputs over all firms. Put another way, the marriage market acts as if it maximizes not the gain from marriage compared to remaining single for any particular marriage, but the total gain over all marriages.[4] Of course, the commodity output maximized by households is not to be identified with national output as usually measured, but includes the quantity and quality of children, sexual satisfaction, and other commodities that never enter into measures of national output.

The process of discovering optimal sortings is greatly simplified by this conclusion that aggregate output is maximized, because any sorting that maximizes aggregate output is an optimal sorting and must be able to satisfy condition (4.5), a condition that would be difficult to verify directly. I should emphasize, moreover, that the optimality of maximizing aggregate output is a theorem, not an assumption about behavior.[5] Each man and woman is assumed to be concerned only about his or her own "selfish" welfare, not about social welfare. In pursuing their selfish interests, however, they are unknowingly led by the "invisible hand" of competition in the marriage market to maximize aggregate output.

Mating of Likes

Psychologists and sociologists have frequently discussed whether persons with like or unlike traits mate, and biologists have occasionally assumed positive or negative assortative mating instead of random mating for nonhuman species. However, none of these disciplines have developed a systematic analysis that predicts for different traits

---

4. Clearly, $\Sigma_{i=1}^N [Z_{ii} - (Z_{si} + Z_{is})]$ is maximized when $Z^k = \Sigma Z_{ii}$ is maximized, because Z_{si} and Z_{is} (single commodity outputs) are given and are independent of marital sortings.

5. Goode (1974) confuses theorem with assumption in his comment on an earlier paper of mine.

whether likes or unlikes tend to mate.[6] My analysis implies that the mating of likes (or unlikes) takes place when such pairings maximize aggregate commodity output over all marriages, regardless of whether the trait is financial (wage rates, property income), biological (height, race, age, physique), or psychological (aggressiveness, passiveness). This analysis is also applicable to matching workers with firms, students with schools,[7] farms with farmers, customers with shopkeepers, and worker preferences for different kinds of working conditions with firms supplying these conditions.

Assume that men and women differ only in the quantitative traits A_m and A_f respectively, and that each trait has a positive marginal productivity:

$$\frac{\partial Z(A_m, A_f)}{\partial A_m} > 0 \quad \text{and} \quad \frac{\partial Z(A_m, A_f)}{\partial A_f} > 0. \tag{4.8}$$

The major theorem on assortative mating is that a positive sorting of large A_m with large A_f and small A_m with small A_f maximizes aggregate output if, and only if, increasing both A_m and A_f adds more to output than the sum of the effects of separate increases in A_m and A_f. For an increase in A_m would reinforce and raise the effect of an increase in A_f. Similarly, a negative sorting of large A_m with small A_f and small A_m with large A_f maximizes output when increasing both adds less to output than the sum of the effects of separate increases. All sortings have the same aggregate output when increasing both has the same effect as separate increases. This can be formally stated as the following theorem, which is proved in note A of the appendix to this chapter.

---

6. In an interesting discussion Winch (1958, pp. 88–89) assumes that each person tries to maximize utility ("In mate selection each individual seeks within his or her field of eligibles for that person who gives the greatest promise of providing him or her with maximum need gratification") and, especially in chap. 4, stresses complementary needs as a determinant of mating. However, he brings in "eligibles" as a deus ex machina and, more importantly, nowhere shows how mating by complementary needs produces equilibrium in the marriage market.

7. This sorting is analyzed for Japanese firms by Kuratani (1973). Hicks (1957, chap. 2) asserts, without offering any proof, that more able workers are employed by more able firms. Black and Black (1929, pp. 178 ff.) discuss the sorting of merchants and locations with a few numerical examples. Rosen (1978) gives a valuable, more recent discussion.

Theorem   Positive assortative mating—mating of likes—is optimal when

$$\frac{\partial^2 Z(A_m, A_f)}{\partial A_m \partial A_f} > 0, \qquad (4.9)$$

because aggregate output is then maximized. Negative assortative mating—mating of unlikes—is optimal when the inequality is reversed.

Consider, as an example, the matrix of outputs between two men and two women:

$$
\begin{array}{c}
 \\
M_1 \\
M_2
\end{array}
\begin{array}{cc}
F_1 & F_2 \\
\left[\begin{array}{cc} Z_{11} & Z_{12} \\ Z_{21} & Z_{22} \end{array} \right], & \text{with } A_{m_2} > A_{m_1} \text{ and } A_{f_2} > A_{f_1}.
\end{array} \qquad (4.10)
$$

If $Z_{22} - Z_{12} > Z_{21} - Z_{11}$ because A_m and A_f are complements, then $Z_{11} + Z_{22} > Z_{12} + Z_{21}$. A positive sorting between A_m and A_f would maximize aggregate output, because increasing both A_m and A_f adds more to output than do separate increases in A_m and A_f.

This theorem indicates that higher-quality men and women marry each other rather than selecting lower-quality mates when these qualities are complements: a superior woman raises the productivity of a superior man and vice versa. The mating of likes or unlikes is optimal as traits are complements or substitutes, because superior persons reinforce each other when traits are complements and offset each other when traits are substitutes. This theorem also implies that the gain from marriage to a woman of a given quality is greater for a superior man when traits are complements, and is greater for an inferior man when traits are substitutes.[8] I shall use this implication later to determine who remains unmarried when the total number of men and women of different qualities is equal.

The theorem can be used to analyze the optimal sorting of particular

---

8. The gain to M_i from marrying F_j rather than remaining single is

$$G_i = (Z_{ij} - Z_{is}) - Z_j^f,$$

where Z_j^f is the given income of F_j, and Z_{is} is the income of M_i if he remains single. The term in parentheses increases (or decreases) with the quality of M_i when A_m and A_f are complements (or substitutes); see note 16.

financial, biological, or other traits. For example, if men and women differ only in given market wage rates — each man and each woman is assumed to be identical in all other market and household traits — aggregate output is maximized by a perfect negative assortative mating of these wage rates, which maximizes the gain from the division of labor. Low-wage women should spend more time in household production than high-wage women because the time of low-wage women is less valuable, and low-wage men should spend more time in household production than high-wage men. By mating low-wage women with high-wage men and low-wage men with high-wage women, men and women with cheaper time are used more extensively in household production, and those with expensive time are used more extensively in market production.[9]

All differences in the output of commodities that are not related to differences in money incomes must be related to differences in nonmarket productivity — to differences in intelligence, education, health, strength, fecundity, height, personality, religion, or other traits. Consider now optimal sortings when men and women differ only in nonmarket productivity. Since an increase in productivity increases output by reducing the cost of production, the optimal sorting of most nonmarket traits tends to be positive because of the inverse or "harmonic" relation between commodity output and its cost of production:

$$Z = \frac{S}{\pi(w_m, w_f, p, A_m, A_f)},$$ (4.11)

where S is money full income; π is the average cost of producing the household commodity Z; w_m and w_f are the given wage rates; p is the price of goods; and A_m and A_f are traits of men and women respectively.

Since changes in A_m and A_f do not affect S because money income is given, then

---

9. The proof of this proposition (Appendix; note B) assumes that all men and women are in the labor force, and that an increase in the husband's wage rate does not increase the hours worked by his working wife. The second assumption is consistent with the available evidence (see for example Cain, 1966), but the first is not, since some women never participate in the labor force after they marry (Heckman, 1981). A perfect negative sorting might not be the only optimal sorting when some married women do not participate (see the discussion in Becker, 1973, pp. 827–829).

$$\frac{\partial^2 Z}{\partial A_m \partial A_f} > 0 \quad \text{if } 2\pi^{-1}\pi_{a_m}\pi_{a_f} > \pi_{a_m,a_f}, \quad \text{where } \frac{\partial \pi}{\partial A_i} = \pi_{a_i} < 0,$$

$$\text{for } i = m, f. \quad (4.12)$$

Condition (4.12) necessarily holds if A_m and A_f have either independent or reinforcing effects on average costs, for then $\pi_{a_m,a_f} \leq 0$; moreover, (4.12) might hold even if they have offsetting effects. Therefore, positive assortative mating is optimal not only when nonmarket traits have reinforcing effects on costs, but a less obvious and more impressive conclusion is that it is also optimal when the traits have independent effects on costs and may be optimal even when they have offsetting effects, because of the harmonic relation between output and cost of production.

This tendency toward complementarity between traits that affect nonmarket productivity can be seen more transparently by considering a couple of special cases. The cost function would be multiplicative and separable if the elasticity of output with respect to either trait were independent of goods and time:

$$\pi = b(A_m, A_f) K(w_m, w_f, p). \quad (4.13)$$

Hence,

$$\frac{\partial^2 Z}{\partial A_m \partial A_f} > 0 \quad \text{as } 2b^{-1}b_m b_f > b_{mf}, \quad (4.14)$$

which must hold if $b_{mf} \leq 0$ and might hold even if $b_{mf} > 0$. This is the same as condition (4.12) except that b does not depend on wage rates or on the substitutability between the household time of husbands and wives. Positive assortative mating is optimal even when the traits of husbands and wives have independent effects on b ($b_{mf} = 0$) because output is harmonically related to b.

The separability assumption embodied in Eq. (4.13) is too strong; most traits affect output partly by raising the efficiency of the time supplied to a household. A simple, if extreme, way to incorporate this relation is to assume each trait affects output only by augmenting the effective amount of household time. Appendix note C proves the plausible result that positive assortative mating is still optimal as long as the elasticity of substitution between the household time of men and women is not very high. Negative assortative mating is optimal for traits augmenting kinds of time that are easily substitutable between men and women.[10] Consequently, positive assortative mating is to be expected when the effective amount of time is augmented; the time of men and the time of women have generally not been close substitutes because of women's investments in and other orientation toward child rearing and men's investments in and other orientation toward market activities. Note, however, that the substitutability between the time of men and women increases as demand shifts away from the quantity of children to the quality of children (Chapter 5).

Does our analysis justify the popular belief that more beautiful, charming, and talented women tend to marry wealthier and more successful men? Note D of the appendix shows that it does: a positive sorting of nonmarket traits with property income always, and with earnings usually,[11] maximizes aggregate commodity output. Higher values of nonmarket traits tend to have larger absolute effects on output when combined with higher money incomes, because from Eq. (4.11) the optimal commodity output depends on the ratio of money (full) income to costs.

The simple correlations between intelligence, education, age, race, nonhuman wealth, religion, ethnic origin, height, place of origin, and many other traits of spouses are positive and strong (see Winch, 1958, chap. 1; Vandenberg, 1972). A small amount of evidence suggests that simple correlations between some psychological traits, such as propensities toward dominance, nurturance, or hostility, may be negative (Winch, 1958, chap. 5; Vandenberg, 1972). The correlation between spouses by intelligence is especially interesting, since it is as high as that between siblings (Alström, 1961). Apparently the marriage market, aided by coeducational schools and other devices, is more efficient at sorting than is commonly believed.

The evidence of positive simple correlations for most traits, and of negative correlations for some, is certainly consistent with my theory of sorting. A more powerful test of the theory, however, requires evidence on partial correlations when other traits are held constant. Even

---

10. Perhaps, therefore, dominant and deferential persons tend to marry (Winch, 1958, p. 215) because the dominant person's time can be used when the household encounters situations calling for dominance, and the deferential person's time can be used when deference is needed.

11. By "usually" I mean that a positive sorting with earnings always maximizes aggregate output when an increase in the nonmarket trait does not reduce the hours worked by the *spouse*, and that a positive sorting might maximize output even when the hours are reduced. I return to this point in note D of the appendix.

when age and wage rates are held constant, the correlation between years of schooling is high: $+0.53$ for white families and virtually the same $(+0.56)$ for black families.[12] Moreover, persons who marry out of their race, religion, age cohort, or education class have relatively high probabilities of divorce, even when other traits are held constant (see Becker et al., 1977). This is additional evidence that a positive sorting by education and by these other traits is optimal, because the analysis in Chapter 10 implies that divorce is more likely when mates are mismatched.

The evidence on divorce cited above also supports the somewhat surprising implication of the theory derived earlier, that a negative sorting by wage rates is optimal. Divorce is more likely when the wife's wage rate is high relative to that of her husband (again several other variables are held constant). The optimality of a negative sorting is also implied by the larger fraction of women who are married in American states that have higher wages of males and *lower* wages of females (age, years of schooling, the sex ratio, the fraction Catholic, and other variables are held constant—see Freiden, 1974; Preston and Richards, 1975; Santos, 1975) or by the larger fraction of households headed by unmarried women in metropolitan areas where women have higher earnings relative to men (Honig, 1974).[13]

Although the direct evidence on the correlation between the wage rates of spouses is less comforting because it is significantly positive even when age and education are held constant: $+0.32$ for whites and $+0.24$ for blacks (calculated from the 1967 Survey of Economic Opportunity mentioned in note 12), this evidence is seriously biased in that marriages are excluded if the wife did not participate in the labor force. Since a woman is more likely to participate when her wage rate is high relative to her husband's, a positive correlation between wage rates for those marriages where both participate is consistent with a negative correlation for all marriages. Indeed, estimates by H. Gregg Lewis (unpublished) and by Smith (1979) indicate that a positive "observed" correlation implies either a negative "actual" correlation (about -0.25

---

12. A 20-percent random sample of the approximately 18,000 married persons in the 1967 Survey of Economic Opportunity was analyzed. Families were excluded if the husband or the wife was either older than 65 or unemployed, or if the wife was employed for less than 20 hours in the survey week.

13. However, the causation may run the other way, from marital status to labor force participation to wage rates, because wage rates *become* higher when women participate more continuously in the labor force.

according to Lewis' estimate) or a much weaker actual correlation (about $+0.04$, according to Smith) for all marriages, because a relatively small fraction of married women have participated.[14] Consequently, when the evidence on the wage rates of husbands and wives is suitably interpreted, it also is not grossly inconsistent with a negative sorting.

Sorting with Unequal Numbers of Men and Women

A person enters the marriage market if he expects his marital income to exceed his single income. Therefore, the incomes imputed by the marriage market determine not only the sorting of persons marrying, but also determine who remains single because they cannot do as well by marrying. For example, men and women delay marriage until the complementarity between the sexes and the differences in their comparative advantages in producing children and other household commodities become sufficiently important that they would be better off married. The reason for the typical early marriages of women is that their biology, experiences, and other investments in human capital have been more specialized than those of men to the production of children and other commodities requiring marriage or its equivalent (Chapters 2 and 3).

Some men are forced to remain single if the number of men, N_m, exceeds the number of women, N_f, and if polygamy is not permitted. Those men remain single who cannot compete against other men for the scarce women because they gain less from marriage than the other men do. The equilibrium sorting of the men and women marrying must still maximize aggregate commodity income, for all other sortings violate the equilibrium condition of Eq. (4.5).

If men and women differ in the traits A_m and A_f respectively, positive

---

14. These adjusted correlations may also be misleading in view of the fact that wages are determined partially by investments in human capital. Women who spend less time in the labor force invest less in market-oriented human capital and thereby reduce their earning power. On the other hand, the positive correlation between the wage rates of husbands and wives who are both participating may really be measuring the predicted positive correlation between a husband's wage rate (or his nonmarket productivity) and his wife's nonmarket productivity. Many unobserved variables, like intelligence, raise both wage rates and nonmarket productivity.

or negative sorting is optimal, as these traits are complements or substitutes. The $N_m - N_f$ men with the lowest qualities remain single when A_m and A_f are complements, because lower-quality men then tend to gain less from marriage and would be outbid for wives by higher-quality men.[15] Similarly, the $N_m - N_f$ highest-quality men remain single when A_m and A_f are substitutes because they tend to be outbid for wives by lower-quality men. This analysis generalizes the Ricardian theory of the extensive margin by permitting idle land (the analogue of single persons) to be productive.

Consequently, the lowest-quality members of the redundant sex remain single when there is positive assortative mating of those marrying, and the highest-quality members remain single when there is negative sorting. Since positive sorting is more likely, lower-quality persons are more likely to remain single. For example, if A_m refers to the property income of men and A_f to the nonmarket productivity of women, and if men are redundant, lower-income men remain single because they gain less from marriage to these women than higher-income men do.

Consider men of three different qualities: M_k, M_j, M_g (ordered from highest to lowest), and women of three different qualities: F_k, F_j, F_g (similarly ordered), when the traits of men and women are complements. If M_k and F_k, M_j and F_j, and M_g and F_g were to marry each other in the equilibrium sorting, the following equilibrium conditions would have to hold:

$$Z_k^m + Z_j^f > Z_{kj}, \qquad Z_j^m + Z_g^f > Z_{jg}, \qquad (4.15)$$

where Z_k^m and Z_j^m are the equilibrium incomes of M_k and M_j when married to F_k and F_j respectively, and Z_j^f and Z_g^f are the equilibrium in-

---

15. To show that none of the $N_m - N_f$ lowest-quality men could marry if A_m and A_f were complements, assume the contrary: that M_i marries F_j and that M_k remains single, $A_{m_k} > A_{m_i}$. If this sorting were optimal,

$$Z_{ij} + Z_{ks} > Z_{kj} + Z_{is}, \quad \text{or} \quad Z_{ij} - Z_{is} > Z_{kj} - Z_{ks}.$$

By the definition of complementarity,

$$Z_{ij} - Z_{ig} < Z_{kj} - Z_{kg}, \quad \text{when } A_{m_k} > A_{m_i} \text{ and } A_{f_j} > A_{f_g}.$$

It seems plausible that the same inequality would tend to hold if remaining single is substituted for marrying the lower-quality women: if Z_{is} and Z_{ks} replace Z_{ig} and Z_{kg} respectively. If so, the first inequality above would contradict the assumption of complementarity between A_m and A_f, and M_i could not replace M_k in the optimal sorting if $A_{m_k} > A_{m_i}$. A similar argument shows that none of the highest-quality men could marry if A_m and A_f were substitutes.

comes of F_j and F_g when married to M_j and M_g respectively. If M_k and F_k were the only kinds of persons in the marriage market, an increase in the number of M_k would lower the income of married M_k to his single level, Z_{ks}, in order to induce the redundant men to remain single. When these other kinds of persons are also in the marriage market, however, Z_k^m could not be lowered to Z_{ks} without violating the first inequality[16] in (4.15). Some of the lower-quality F_j would be induced to marry the redundant M_k, and the new equilibrium income[17] of M_k would exceed Z_{ks}. The redundant M_k bump lower-quality M_j, since the traits of men and women are complements. Some M_j become redundant when they are bumped out of their marriages, their incomes fall, and some F_g are induced to marry these redundant M_j.

The bumping of lower-quality men out of their marriages through competitive reductions in the incomes of higher-quality men continues until the incomes of the lowest-quality men are reduced to their single levels. Since these men no longer gain from marriage, some are willing to remain single.

Thus an increase in the number of men of a particular quality tends to lower the incomes of all men and raise those of all women because of the competition in the marriage market between men and women of different qualities. Moreover, if the optimal sorting were positive because the traits of men and women were complements, some low-quality men

---

16. The left-hand side of the first inequality in (4.15) is maximized (given Z_k^m) when $Z_j^m = Z_{js}$, or when $Z_j^f = Z_{jj} - Z_{js}$. If also $Z_k^m = Z_{ks}$, that first inequality would become

$$Z_k^m + Z_j^f = Z_{ks} + Z_{jj} - Z_{js} > Z_{kj},$$

which can be written as

$$Z_{ks} - Z_{js} > Z_{kj} - Z_{jj}.$$

If positive assortative mating were optimal, the traits of men and women would be complements, and this last inequality could not be satisfied if M_j were of lower quality than M_k. Hence $Z_k^m > Z_{ks}$. Similarly, if negative assortative mating were optimal, these traits would be substitutes, and the inequality could not be satisfied if M_j were of higher quality than M_k.

17. If some M_k marry F_k and some marry F_j, the income of an M_k must be the same whether he marries an F_k or an F_j:

$$Z_k^m + Z_k^f = Z_{kk}, \qquad Z_k^m + Z_j^f = Z_{kj}.$$

The incomes of M_k, F_k, and F_j are not uniquely determined by these two equations (see the more extensive discussion in Becker, 1973), but the premium to F_k must equal her marginal productivity:

$$Z_k^f - Z_j^f = Z_{kk} - Z_{kj}.$$

would be bumped out of the marriage market and other men would be bumped into "inferior" marriages—that is, into marriages with lower-quality women.

This analysis shows that the equilibrium income and mate assigned to any person by the optimal sorting depend not only on his traits but also on the traits of everyone else in the marriage market (that is, they depend on the *relative* as well as the *absolute* level of traits). For example, an increase in the number of male college graduates would reduce the incomes of male high-school graduates and the education of mates assigned to them. On the other hand, even a significant increase in the education of any particular man might have little effect on the mate assigned to him if the education of all other men also significantly increased. To take an actual example, this analysis explains why higher-income men in the United States have married at younger ages and have had more stable marriages than lower-income men, yet sizable secular increases in average incomes have not had such strong effects on the average age at marriage or on the average stability of marriages (see Keeley, 1974; Becker et al., 1977, p. 1173).

Differences in Preferences, Love, and the Optimal Sorting

When there is a single homogeneous household commodity, as I have assumed so far in this chapter, each person could be said to have the same utility "function," defined most simply by the quantity of that commodity. However, the utility functions or preferences of different persons could differ vastly when there are many separate commodities. Would the preferences of men and women in the marriage market then be an additional, perhaps even a crucial, variable determining the equilibrium sorting—along with income, education, race, and other traits—or would preferences have no effect on the equilibrium sorting, no matter how much they differed?

The answer depends entirely on the cost of production in different households. If each commodity were produced at a constant relative cost that was the same in all households, the total output produced by a marriage of M_i and F_j could be measured unambiguously by

$$Z_{ij} = {}_1Z_{ij} + {}_2v\,{}_2Z_{ij} + \ldots + {}_nv\,{}_nZ_{ij}, \qquad (4.16)$$

where Z_{ij} is their total output measured in units of the commodity ${}_1Z$, ${}_kZ_{ij}$ is their output of the kth commodity, ${}_kv$ is the cost of producing a unit of $_kZ$ relative to the cost of producing a unit of $_1Z$, and this relative cost is assumed to be the same for all households. Since the output of each commodity is consumed by the mates, then

$$
\begin{aligned}
Z_{ij} &= \sum_{k=1}^{n} {}_kv \, ({}_kZ_i^m + {}_kZ_j^f) \\
&= \sum {}_kv \, {}_kZ_i^m + \sum {}_kv \, {}_kZ_j^f \\
&= Z_i^m + Z_j^f,
\end{aligned}
\tag{4.17}
$$

where $_kZ_i^m$ and $_kZ_j^f$ are the quantities of the kth commodity consumed by M_i and F_j respectively.

Since Eq. (4.16) can be used to convert any given total output into the commodity mix best suited to particular preferences, each person would maximize utility—that is, consume more of each commodity—by choosing the mate who helped maximize his aggregate income, regardless of his preferences or those of different possible mates.[18] In particular, M_i and F_j would marry each other if their total output exceeded their combined aggregate incomes from marrying other persons or from remaining single, no matter how radically their preferences differed.[19]

On the other hand, preferences could well affect the equilibrium sorting if costs were not the same in all households. In particular, persons with similar preferences have an incentive to marry each other if costs are lower when the consumption patterns of mates are more similar, as they would be when some commodities are jointly consumed, when production of commodities is more efficient at a larger scale, or when specialized consumption capital lowers the costs of particular commodities.[20] Conversely, persons with different preferences have an incentive to marry each other if there are decreasing returns to scale. *Therefore, preferences are more likely to be positively than neg-*

---

18. Robert Michael has reminded me of the nursery rhyme:

Jack Sprat could eat no fat,
His wife could eat no lean;
And so, betwixt them both, you see,
They licked the platter clean.

19. For example, if M_i only wanted to consume $_2Z$ and F_j only wanted to consume $_1Z$,

$$
Z_i^m + Z_j^f = {}_2v \, {}_2Z_i^m + {}_1Z_j^f = {}_2v \, {}_2Z_{ij} + {}_1Z_{ij} = Z_{ij}.
$$

20. The gain from investments in the consumption capital of a particular commodity is greater when more of that commodity is consumed (Chapter 2).

atively sorted—as are most other traits—because both joint consumption and specialized consumption capital encourage the matching of persons with similar preferences.

Many readers may be wondering whether romantic attachments have any place in my analysis, or is "love" too emotional or irrational to be analyzed by the economic approach? Although marriage for love has been much less important in other societies than in contemporary Western societies, love marriages do not have to be ignored; aspects of such marriages can be analyzed by the economic approach. Marriage for love is discussed more extensively in Chapters 8 and 11; here I show only that the effect of love on the equilibrium sorting is analytically a special case of the effect of differences in preferences.

It can be said that M_i loves F_j if her welfare enters his utility function, and perhaps also if M_i values emotional and physical contact with F_j. Clearly, M_i can benefit from a match with F_j, because he could then have a more favorable effect on her welfare—and thereby on his own utility—and because the commodities measuring "contact" with F_j can be produced more cheaply when they are matched than when M_i has to seek an "illicit" relationship with F_j. Even if F_j were "selfish" and did not return M_i's love, she would benefit from a match with someone who loves her, because he would transfer resources to her to increase his own utility. Moreover, a marriage involving love is more efficient than other marriages, even when one of the mates is selfish, and increased efficiency benefits the selfish mate also. These results and other aspects of altruism and love are discussed in Chapter 8, where it is shown that marriages involving love are likely to be part of the equilibrium sorting because in market terms they are more productive than other marriages.

Assortative Mating with Polygamy

The model of household production developed in Chapter 3 assumes that the output of the ith male married to the jth female is

$$Z_{ij} = n(\alpha_i,\beta_j)Z[p(\alpha_i)x_m,\ell(\beta_j)x_f], \qquad (4.18)$$

with $\partial n/\partial\alpha > 0$, $\partial n/\partial\beta > 0$, $dp/d\alpha > 0$, and $d\ell/d\beta > 0$, where the effective resources of men and women with efficiencies α_i and β_j are $p(\alpha_i)x_m$ and $\ell(\beta_j)x_f$ respectively. The basic theorem in this chapter states that superior men are mated with superior women and inferior men with inferior women if

$$\frac{\partial Z}{\partial \alpha \partial \beta} = \frac{\partial^2 n}{\partial \alpha \partial \beta} Z + \left(\frac{\partial n}{\partial \alpha}\right)\left(\frac{\partial Z}{\partial x_f}\right) x_f \frac{d\ell}{d\beta} + \left(\frac{\partial n}{\partial \beta}\right)\left(\frac{\partial Z}{\partial x_m}\right) x_m \frac{dp}{d\alpha}$$

$$+ n \frac{\partial^2 Z}{\partial x_m \partial x_f} x_m \cdot x_f \left(\frac{dp}{d\alpha}\right)\left(\frac{d\ell}{d\beta}\right) > 0. \tag{4.19}$$

Sufficient conditions for this inequality are that $\partial^2 n/\partial \alpha \partial \beta > 0$ and $\partial^2 Z/\partial x_m \partial x_f > 0$.

A given quantity of spouse resources can be obtained by marrying either one superior person—that is, a person with relatively large ℓ or p—or several inferior persons. Hence less assortative mating would be expected with polygamy than with monogamy, because polygamy can match the total resources of a superior man or woman by substituting several inferior for one superior mate. One small piece of evidence indicating that positive sorting is weaker with polygyny is that the simple correlation coefficient between the education of husbands and wives is only $+0.37$ for the polygynous men of Maiduguri, whereas it is more than 0.5 in the United States (Grossbard, 1978, p. 30).

The effect of polygamy on the degree of assortative mating is more complicated when an improvement in efficiency mainly raises the output from given inputs of male and female resources (given by the function n). To begin an analysis of this case, assume that all men and all women have the same resources ($p = \ell = 1$), and that only men can have several mates. More efficient men probably tend to marry more efficient women even if efficient men are polygynous, because $\partial^2 n/\partial \alpha \partial \beta > 0$ implies that the effect on output of a more efficient wife is greater when her husband is also more efficient.

Although positive assortative mating is a substitute for explicit polygyny, superior men still are more likely to be polygynous. They would be inclined to marry several women who might differ in quality.[21] The most inferior men cannot attract wives when superior men

---

21. The marginal product of β_1-women with α_1-men is reduced when β_2-women marry α_1-men, in that fewer resources remain to spend on β_1-wives. An α_1-man with w_{11} β_1-wives and w_{12} β_2-wives maximizes

$$Z_{1,w_1,w_2} = w_{11} n(\alpha_1,\beta_1) Z\left(\frac{x_m^1}{w_{11}}, x_f\right) + w_{12} n(\alpha_1,\beta_2) Z\left(\frac{x_m^2}{w_{12}}, x_f\right),$$

subject to $x_m^1 + x_m^2 = x_m$. The equilibrium condition is

$$\frac{\partial Z_{1,w_1,w_2}}{\partial x_m^1} = n(\alpha_1,\beta_1) \frac{\partial Z}{\partial x_m^1} = n(\alpha_1,\beta_2) \frac{\partial Z}{\partial x_m^2}.$$

Therefore the marginal product of x_m is the same with β_2-wives as with β_1-wives.

attract several in marriage markets with the same number of men and women. Since all women tend to marry, the average woman would marry a man "above" her in ability and skill if men and women in the marriage market are of equal average ability and skill. Of course, the average woman would marry above her even with monogamy, and even when all men and women marry, if the average man has invested more than the average woman has (see Table 3.1). Therefore, our analysis readily explains why women have typically married "up" and men have typically married "down" in both monogamous and polygamous societies.[22]

Inflexible Prices, Dowries, and Bride Prices

The analysis of equilibrium sorting developed in this chapter has assumed that all divisions of outputs between mates are feasible. The equilibrium division in any marriage, possibly not unique, is determined from conditions (4.5) and (4.6) and results from efforts by all participants in the marriage market to maximize their own commodity income. An important property of these equilibrium conditions is that each person prefers to be matched with the mate assigned by the equilibrium sorting than with any other person, for the reason that he would receive a lower income with anyone else. Moreover, the equilibrium sorting, and hence these preferences for mates, are not fixed but depend on the number of persons with particular traits and other variables.

If the division of output in any marriage were determined not in the marriage market but in other ways, and if a person would receive the same fraction of the output of all possible matches, then

$$Z_i^m = e_i Z_{ij} \quad \text{for all } j, \qquad Z_j^f = d_j Z_{ij} \quad \text{for all } i, \qquad (4.20)$$

where $e_i + d_j \neq 1$ if joint consumption or monitoring costs are significant, and e_i and e_j or d_j and d_k may not be equal because the shares of different men or women may differ. Appendix note E shows that a per-

---

22. For example, Hindu women were not permitted to marry mates of lower status, whereas Hindu men could (Mandelbaum, 1970); also, Islamic women are not supposed to marry mates of lower status (the doctrine of *kafā'a*), while Islamic men can (Coulson, 1964, pp. 49, 94).

fect positive assortative mating would maximize aggregate output and would be an equilibrium sorting because persons not assigned to each other would be made worse off if they married. This chapter has shown that a perfect positive assortative mating also tends to be the equilibrium sorting and to maximize output when the division of each output is determined by market equilibrium. Therefore, permitting the marriage market to determine the division of output and imposing that division by Eq. (4.20) frequently give the same sorting.

My approach to the marriage market contrasts sharply with other formal models of marital sorting (see Gale and Shapley, 1962; Stoffaës, 1974). These models, like the model given by Eq. (4.20), assume that each person has a *given* ranking of potential mates that determines rather than is determined by the equilibrium sorting. Unlike the rankings implied by (4.20), however, in these models different persons may not rank potential mates in the same way—for example, M_i may prefer F_j, who prefers M_k, who prefers F_i. If rankings were not the same, an "optimal" sorting could only try to minimize the overall conflict between feasible and preferred matches.[23]

These models can be said to assume implicitly, while the model given by (4.20) assumes explicitly, that the division of output in any marriage is not determined by the marriage market and is completely rigid. An individual usually would not prefer the mate assigned him by the optimal sorting, because marital prices are not permitted to eliminate the inconsistencies among the preferred choices of different persons. If the division of marital output were determined by the marriage market, the ranking of potential mates would not be given; it would depend on how the outputs produced with different mates were divided. That is to say, if marital prices were flexible, the problem formulated and solved by these models would be irrelevant to actual marital sortings.[24]

The division of marital output may seem to be inflexible, however, in

---

23. Gale and Shapley (1962) require optimal assignments to be "stable"; that is, persons not assigned to each other could not be made better off by marrying each other, a requirement that is closely related to condition (4.5).

24. It might be relevant, however, to markets that do not use prices to determine assignments. For example, Gale and Shapley (1962) also discuss the assignment of applicants to different universities, and Chapter 9 considers the mating of nonhuman species where each entity maximizes the survival of its genes.

that commodities like housing space, children, conversation, and love are jointly consumed (they are "family commodities"). Consumption by one person does not reduce by an equal amount the quantity available to other household members. Moreover, some mates may be able to obtain more than their equilibrium share of output by shirking their duties as a result of the division of labor between mates and the cost of monitoring behavior (Chapters 2 and 8). In addition, men have sometimes been given legal control over the assignment of shares (see Weitzman, 1974, pp. 1182 ff.).

Consider the marriage market represented in Figure 3.1, which contains homogeneous women and homogeneous men. If the number of men exceeds the number of women, $N'_m > N_f$, the equilibrium income of men and women would equal $Z^{*m} = Z_{ms}$ and $Z^{*f} = Z_{mf} - Z_{ms}$ respectively. Suppose, however, that the division of output is inflexible for the reasons just given, and, in particular, that the marital income of women cannot exceed $\bar{Z}^f < Z^{*f}$; hence the marital income of men would equal $\bar{Z}^m = Z_{mf} - \bar{Z}^f > Z^{*m}$. Since all the available men want to marry at that income, the scarce women must be distributed among the more numerous men. The distribution of wives among men is not likely to be purely random, for men would try to raise their chances of getting married. They could try to guarantee prospective wives more than $\bar{Z}^f$, but such guarantees might not be easily enforced.

One alternative would be to give a capital or lump-sum transfer to a woman as an inducement to marriage. Since men offering larger transfers would obtain wives more easily, competition among men for the scarce women would bid up the transfers until all men again were indifferent between marriage and remaining single. They would be indifferent when the transfer equaled the present value of the difference between Z^{*f} and $\bar{Z}^f$, the difference between the equilibrium and the actual income of married women. The same reasoning shows that transfers would be from women to men if married men received less than their equilibrium incomes. Transfers to women are called "bride prices," and those to men are called "dowries."

The analysis would be basically the same if payments went to parents (not to the children marrying) because parents "owned" their children and transferred them to other families through marriage (Cheung, 1972). The capital value of children transferred to other families would still equal the present value of the difference between their equilibrium marital income and their actual income. Bride prices then not only compensate parents for the transfer of their "property," but also induce them to invest optimally in daughters if girls with appropriate accumulations of human capital command sufficiently high prices.

The difference between actual and equilibrium income of wives is probably greater when their equilibrium income is a larger share of marital output (a larger share may not be as readily appropriated by wives). Therefore, the frequency and magnitude of bride prices should be greater when the equilibrium share of wives is greater, as in the following situations: in societies with a larger supply of men relative to women; for never married as opposed to divorced women;[25] in societies with a higher incidence of polygyny; and in patrilineal societies (Schneider, 1969) because husbands have more control over the division of marital output, especially over children, in such societies.

This analysis also implies that bride prices would have to be returned, at least in part, when a wife divorces without cause or when a husband divorces with cause—say, because his wife is unfaithful or barren (see the evidence in Goode, 1963, pp. 155 ff.). A husband divorcing without cause, however, would forfeit most of the bride price, especially if he had been married for a number of years.[26]

Consequently, even when the actual division of marital output diverges greatly from the equilibrium division, bride prices and dowries raise or lower marital incomes to the levels mandated by the equilibrium sorting. My assumption that marital *incomes* are flexible appears highly reasonable, therefore, when the purpose of bride prices and other capital transfers contingent on marriage is understood. Models that assume a rigid division of income greatly underestimate human ingenuity and experience in making the terms of marriage flexible and responsive to market conditions.

---

25. Divorced women would command lower prices because they tend to be older than single women, and because they may have been divorced as a result of their deficiencies as wives, including sterility (see Chapter 10). The evidence in Goldschmidt (1973) and in Papps (1980) indicates that bride prices in Uganda and Palestine have been lower for divorced women.

26. Goode has shown that Moslem men usually forfeit most of the bride price when they divorce without cause. In this way bride prices and other capital transfers insure divorced women against losses on their specialized investments in children; see the further discussion of divorce and divorce settlements in Chapter 10.

A Treatise on the Family
Mathematical Appendix

A. *Optimal Sorting*[27]
Given a function $f(x,y)$, I first show that if $\partial^2 f/\partial x \partial y < 0$,

$$\frac{\partial[f(x_2,y) - f(x_1,y)]}{\partial y} \equiv \frac{\partial Q(x_2,x_1,y)}{\partial y} < 0 \quad \text{for } x_1 < x_2. \qquad \text{(A.1)}$$

Since $\partial Q/\partial y = (\partial f/\partial y)(x_2,y) - (\partial f/\partial y)(x_1,y)$, then $\partial Q/\partial y = 0$ for $x_2 = x_1$. By assumption $(\partial/\partial x_2)(\partial Q/\partial y) = (\partial^2 f/\partial x \partial y)(x_2,y) < 0$. Since $\partial Q/\partial y = 0$ for $x_2 = x_1$ and $\partial Q/\partial y$ decreases in x_2, $\partial Q/\partial y < 0$ for $x_2 > x_1$; hence inequality (A.1) is proved. It follows immediately that if $y_2 > y_1$,

$$f(x_2,y_1) - f(x_1,y_1) > f(x_2,y_2) - f(x_1,y_2). \qquad \text{(A.2)}$$

A similar proof shows that if $\partial^2 f/\partial x \partial y > 0$,

$$f(x_2,y_1) - f(x_1,y_1) < f(x_2,y_2) - f(x_1,y_2). \qquad \text{(A.3)}$$

Theorem Let $f(x,y)$ satisfy

$$\partial^2 f/\partial x \partial y > 0.$$

Suppose $x_1 < x_2 < \ldots < x_n$ and $y_1 < y_2 < \ldots < y_n$. Then

$$\sum_{j=1}^{n} f(x_j, y_{i_j}) < \sum_{i=1}^{n} f(x_i, y_i) \qquad \text{(A.4)}$$

for all permutations $(i_1, i_2, \ldots, i_n) \neq (1, 2, \ldots, n)$.

Proof: Assume the contrary—namely, that the maximizing sum is for a permutation $i_1, \ldots, i_n$ not satisfying $i_1 < i_2 < \ldots < i_n$. Then there is (at least) one j_0 with the property $i_{j_0} > i_{j_0+1}$. Therefore, by (A.3),

$$f(x_{j_0}, y_{i_{j_0}}) + f(x_{j_0+1}, y_{i_{j_0}+1}) < f(x_{j_0}, y_{i_{j_0}+1}) + f(x_{j_0+1}, y_{i_{j_0}}), \qquad \text{(A.5)}$$

since $y_{i_{j_0}+1} < y_{i_{j_0}}$. But this contradicts the optimality of $i_1, \ldots, i_n$, and the theorem is proved.

A similar proof shows that if $\partial^2 f/\partial x \partial y < 0$, then

---

27. I owe the proofs in this section to William Brock. Since they were developed, simpler proofs in which the quality of men and women varies continuously have been given by Sattinger (1975).

$$\sum_{j=1}^{n} f(x_j, y_{i_j}) < \sum_{i=1}^{n} f(x_i, y_{n+1-i}) \tag{A.6}$$

for all permutations $(i_1, i_2, \ldots, i_n) \neq (n, n-1, \ldots, 1)$.

B. *Sorting by Wage Rates*
By differentiation of $Z = S/\pi(w_m, w_f, p)$, where S is money full income, π the average cost of producing a unit of Z, w_m and w_f are wage rates, and p the price of goods, we get

$$\left. \begin{aligned} \frac{\partial Z}{\partial w_i} &= Z_i = \frac{\partial S}{\partial w_i} \pi^{-1} - S\pi^{-2}\pi_i \\ &= T\pi^{-1} - S\pi^{-2}\pi_i, \end{aligned} \right\} \quad \text{for } i = m \text{ or } f, \tag{A.7}$$

where $T = \partial S/\partial w_i$ is the total time allocated between the market and nonmarket sectors. Since a basic result of duality theory is that

$$\pi_i = t_i Z^{-1}, \tag{A.8}$$

where t_i equals the time spent in the nonmarket sector by the ith person, then

$$Z_i = l_i \pi^{-1} \geq 0, \tag{A.9}$$

where $l_i = T - t_i$ is the time spent at work.

Positive or negative sorting by wage rates is optimal as

$$\frac{\partial^2 Z}{\partial w_m \partial w_f} = Z_{mf} \equiv Z_{fm} \gtrless 0. \tag{A.10}$$

Differentiate Z_f with respect to w_m to get

$$Z_{fm} = -\pi^{-2}\pi_m l_f + \pi^{-1}\partial l_f/\partial w_m. \tag{A.11}$$

The first term on the right is clearly negative, if $l_f > 0$; hence Z_{fm} will also be negative if $\partial l_f/\partial w_m \leq 0$, that is, if t_m and t_f are not gross complements as these terms are usually defined. The evidence does support the assumption that $\partial l_f/\partial w_m \leq 0$, since the hours worked by married women tend to decline, not rise, when their husband's wage rate increases. Moreover, a negative sorting between w_m and w_f would maximize commodity output even when the time of men and women were gross complements if the complementarity were not sufficiently large to dominate the first term in (A.11).

C. Own-Time–Augmenting Effects

Own-time augmenting means that the household production function can be written as $Z = f(x,t_f',t_m')$, where $t_f' = g_f(A_f)t_f$ and $t_m' = g_m(A_m)t_m$ are the household time inputs of women and men in "efficiency" units, and

$$\frac{dg_f}{dA_f} = g_f' > 0, \quad \text{and} \quad \frac{dg_m}{dA_m} = g_m' > 0 \qquad (A.12)$$

because an increase in each trait raises the number of efficiency units. The optimal Z can be written as $Z = S/\pi(p,w_m',w_f')$, where $w_m' = w_m/g_m$ and $w_f' = w_f/g_f$ are the wage rates in efficiency units. Therefore

$$\frac{\partial Z}{\partial A_m} = - t_m' \pi^{-1} \frac{\partial w_m'}{\partial A_m} > 0, \qquad (A.13)$$

since $\partial w_m'/\partial A_m < 0$. Hence

$$\frac{\partial^2 Z}{\partial A_m \partial A_f} = - \frac{\partial w_m'}{\partial A_m} \pi^{-1} \left[\frac{\partial t_m'}{\partial A_f} + \left(\frac{\partial w_f'}{\partial A_f} t_m' t_f' S^{-1} \right) \right]. \qquad (A.14)$$

The term outside the brackets and the second term in them are positive. The first term inside the brackets might well be negative; but H. Gregg Lewis has shown in an unpublished memorandum that $\partial^2 Z/\partial A_m \partial A_f$ is necessarily positive and that the second term would dominate the first if the elasticity of substitution between the time of men and women were less than 2.

D. Sorting by Income and Nonmarket Productivity

If men differed only in their nonhuman capital, K_m, and women only in a nonmarket trait, A_f, and if all men and women participated in the labor force, $\partial Z/\partial K_m = r\pi^{-1} > 0$, and

$$\frac{\partial^2 Z}{\partial K_m \partial A_f} = - r\pi^{-2}\pi_{a_f} > 0 \quad \text{since } \pi_{a_f} < 0, \qquad (A.15)$$

where r is the rate of return. If men differed only in their wage rate, w_m, $\partial Z/\partial w_m = \pi^{-1}l_m > 0$, and

$$\frac{\partial^2 Z}{\partial w_m \partial A_f} = - \pi^{-2}\pi_{a_f}l_m + \pi^{-1}\frac{\partial l_m}{\partial A_f}. \qquad (A.16)$$

The first term on the right is positive, and the second would be also if $\partial l_m/\partial A_f \geq 0$, that is, if an increase in A_f does not reduce the time men spend in the market sector. Even if it does, the cross-derivative is still positive if the first term dominates. In particular, Eq. (A.16) is necessarily positive if the elasticity of output with respect to A_f is independent of the input of goods and time. For then $\pi = b(A_f)\psi(p,w_m,w_f)$, and $l_m = (\partial\pi/\partial w_m)Z = (\partial\psi/\partial w_m)S\psi^{-1}$. Hence $\partial l_m/\partial A_f = 0$.

E. *Rigid Distribution of Outputs*
Given Eq. (4.20), the matrix showing the incomes of men and women for all marital combinations would be

	F_1 . . . . F_j . . . . F_N	
M_1	e_1Z_{11}, d_1Z_{11} . . . . e_1Z_{1N}, d_NZ_{1N}	
.	. .	
.	. .	
.	. .	
M_i	e_iZ_{ij}, d_jZ_{ij} .	(A.17)
.	. .	
.	. .	
.	. .	
M_N	e_NZ_{N1}, d_1Z_{N1} . . . . e_NZ_{NN}, d_NZ_{NN}	

If

$$\hat{Z}_1 \equiv Z_{st} > Z_{ij}, \quad \text{for all } i \neq s \text{ and for all } j \neq t, \qquad (A.18)$$

were the maximum output in any marriage, and if each person tried to maximize his or her commodity income, M_s would marry F_t because they could not do as well in any other marriage.[28] Exclude M_s and F_t from consideration, and if

$$\hat{Z}_2 = Z_{uv} > Z_{ij}, \quad \text{for all } i \neq u \text{ or } s \text{ and for all } j \neq v \text{ or } t, \qquad (A.19)$$

were the maximum output in all other marriages, M_u would marry F_v. The process can be continued through $\hat{Z}_3, \ldots, \hat{Z}_N$ until all the men

---

28. Clearly, by condition (A.18), $e_sZ_{st} > e_sZ_{sj}$, all $j \neq t$, and $d_tZ_{st} > d_tZ_{it}$, all $i \neq s$.

and women are sorted. This sorting combines the various maxima, and it need not be the same as the sorting that maximizes aggregate output. In the example provided by matrix (4.7), combining the maxima sorts M_2 with F_1 and M_1 with F_2, whereas maximizing aggregate output sorts M_1 with F_1 and M_2 with F_2. Yet these sortings are the same in perhaps the most important instances, which means that the sum of the maxima equals the maximum of the sums in those instances.

If men and women were numbered from lowest to highest values of their traits, and if an increase in each trait always increased output, then $\hat{Z}_1$ is obviously the output of M_N with F_N, $\hat{Z}_2$ is that of M_{N-1} with F_{N-1}, and $\hat{Z}_N$ that of M_1 with F_1. Consequently, combining the various maxima implies perfect positive assortative mating when traits have monotonic effects on output.

CHAPTER 5

The Demand for Children

Chapters 2 to 4 have argued that the main purpose of marriage and families is the production and rearing of own children, but they have not considered explicitly the demand for children. This chapter uses the price of children and real income to explain, among other things, why rural fertility has traditionally exceeded urban fertility, why a rise in the wage rate of working women reduces their fertility, why various government programs (such as aid to mothers with dependent children) have significantly affected the demand for children, and why families with higher incomes have had more children, except during the past 150 years in Western and developing countries.

The analysis is then extended to consider the interaction between quantity and quality of children, probably the major contribution of the economic analysis of fertility. This interaction explains why the quantity of children often changes rapidly over time even though there are no close substitutes for children and the income elasticity of quantity is not large. The interaction between quantity and quality also explains why education per child tends to be lower in families having more children, why rural fertility has approached and may even be less than urban fertility in advanced countries, and why blacks in the United States have had relatively many children and invested relatively little in each child.

Price and Income Effects

The most famous and influential theory of population change is that of Malthus, who assumed that populations grow at a rapid rate unless checked by limited supplies of food and other "subsistence" goods. When incomes fall because the growth in population exceeds the growth in subsistence goods, marriages are delayed, the frequency of coition within marriage is reduced, and fewer children survive to adulthood. The first two factors are "moral restraints" and the last produces "misery" (Malthus, 1933, bk. I, chap. II). Moral restraint would be the main check on excessive population growth if the demand for births had a high income elasticity, whereas misery would be the main check if the number of births were insensitive to income.

Darwin stated[1] that the Malthusian theory greatly influenced his own theory of evolution by natural selection, which brilliantly extends Malthus in the following way. The children of fertile parents will constitute a larger fraction of their own generation than their parents do of the earlier generation. The grandchildren and subsequent descendants of fertile parents will constitute a still larger fraction of their own generations *if fertility is strongly "inherited" from parents,* because the children of fertile parents would then also be fertile. It follows from Darwin's argument—that is, from natural selection—that populations tend to become dominated by the highly fertile.

Although the Darwinian theory is highly relevant to nonhuman populations, it appears less applicable to human populations. Most families have controlled their fertility and have had fewer children than their capacities permit. For example, seventeenth-century Italian village women marrying at age twenty-five averaged only six children, whereas their biological capacity probably exceeded eight children (Livi-Bacci, 1977, table 1.2). Even the Malthusian theory of a highly

---

1. Darwin (1958, pp. 42–43) wrote:

In October 1838, that is, fifteen months after I had begun my systematic enquiry, I happened to read for amusement Malthus on *Population,* and being well prepared to appreciate the struggle for existence which everywhere goes on from long-continued observation of the habits of animals and plants, it at once struck me that under these circumstances favourable variations would tend to be preserved and unfavourable ones to be destroyed. The result of this would be the formation of new species. Here, then, I had at last got a theory by which to work.

Alfred R. Wallace (1905, p. 361), codiscoverer of the theory of natural selection, also stated that he was influenced by Malthus.

The Demand for Children

elastic demand for children is unable to explain the large ▟
Western countries during the last hundred years in the average ▟
of children per family as family incomes rose dramatically.

However, any discrepancy between these and related facts and t▟
Malthusian or Darwinian theories is not so apparent if the number of
children is distinguished from parental expenditures on each child. A
reduction in the number of children born to a couple can *increase* the
representation of their children in the next generation if this enables the
couple to invest sufficiently more in the education, training, and
"attractiveness" of each child to increase markedly their probability of
survival to reproductive ages and the reproduction of each survivor.
Therefore, these theories can be combined and generalized by assuming that each family maximizes a utility function of the quantity of children, n; the expenditure on each child, called the quality of children, q;
and the quantities of other commodities:

$$U = U(n, q, Z_1, \ldots, Z_m). \tag{5.1}$$

The Malthusian theory ignores quality and assumes that the demand
for births (or number of children) is highly responsive to changes in income (hence, the demand for other commodities may be negatively related to income). The Darwinian theory, on the other hand, ignores
these other commodities and assumes that quantity and quality are
chosen to maximize the number of descendants in subsequent generations. The analysis developed in this and the next two chapters combines aspects of both these theories into a more general one. To be
sure, the Darwinian theory is highly relevant to nonhuman species and,
modified to include cultural selection, may also be relevant to some
primitive human societies (see the argument in Blurton Jones and
Sibly, 1978), while the Malthusian theory can explain changes in
human populations during much of recorded history. However, the
analysis developed here is far more suited to explaining fertility
changes in Western countries during the last few centuries and in
developing countries during this century.

The various other commodities will be combined into a single aggregate commodity, Z, because there are no good substitutes for children. Although the interaction between quantity and quality is a major
theme of this chapter, the demand for children is first discussed by ignoring their quality. The utility function in Eq. (5.1) then becomes

$$U = U(n,Z). \tag{5.2}$$

without a great loss in relevance, the utility
and (5.2) and the discussion throughout this
changes in the ages of children and in the
ths.

ot purchased but are self-produced by each
ds and services and the own time of parents,
nce the cost of own time and household pro-
among families, the total cost of producing
differs. If this cost is denoted by p_n and the
cost of Z by π_z, the budget constraint of a family equals

$$p_n n + \pi_z Z = I, \qquad (5.3)$$

where I is full income. Given p_n, π_z, and I, the optimal quantities of n
and Z are determined by the budget constraint and the usual marginal
utility condition:

$$\frac{\partial U}{\partial n} \Big/ \frac{\partial U}{\partial Z} = \frac{MU_n}{MU_Z} = \frac{p_n}{\pi_z}. \qquad (5.4)$$

The demand for children would depend on the relative price of children and full income. An increase in the relative price of children, in p_n
relative to π_z, reduces the demand for children and increases the demand for other commodities (if real income is held constant). The relative price of children is affected by many variables, some unique to
children, and several of the more important are now considered.

The evidence over hundreds of years indicates that farm families
have been larger than urban families. For example, the average household in the city of Florence was about 20 percent smaller in 1427 than
the average household in the surrounding countryside (Herlihy, 1977,
table 2); the number of live births per 1,000 women aged 15–49 was
about 45 percent higher in small than in large Italian *comuni* in 1901
(Livi-Bacci, 1977, table 3.8); and in 1800 the reproduction rate in rural
areas of the United States was about one and one-half times that in
urban areas (Jaffe, 1940, p. 410). Part of the explanation is that food
and housing, important inputs in the rearing of children, have been
cheaper on farms.

The net cost of children is reduced if they contribute to family income by performing household chores, working in the family business,
or working in the marketplace. Then an increase in the "earning" potential of children would increase the demand for children. Indeed, I
believe that farm families have had more children mainly because chil-

dren have been considerably more productive on farms than in cities. For example, children in rural India and Brazil begin to contribute to farm work by age five or six and are sizable contributors by age twelve.[2]

The contribution of farm children has declined as agriculture has become more mechanized and complex in the course of economic development. Both of these elements have encouraged farm families to extend their children's schooling.[3] Since rural schools are too small to be efficient, and since the cost in time and transportation of attending school is greater to farm children (Kenny, 1977, p. 32), the cost advantage of raising children on farms has narrowed, and possibly has been reversed, as farm children have increased the time they spend in school. Not surprisingly, therefore, urban-rural fertility differentials have narrowed greatly in developed countries during this century and rural fertility is now slightly *less* than urban fertility in some countries. (See the evidence for the United States, Italy, Japan, and Taiwan respectively in Gardner, 1973; Livi-Bacci, 1977; Hashimoto, 1974; and Schultz, 1973.)

Programs providing aid to mothers with dependent children have reduced the cost of children; aid increases as the number of children increases, and the decline in the labor force participation of mothers induced by these programs (Honig, 1974) reduces the opportunity cost of time spent on children. Since mothers without mates have more readily qualified for aid, the growth of these programs in recent years has contributed heavily to the sharp growth in the ratio of illegitimate to legitimate birth rates since the 1960s. The illegitimate birth rate has remained constant[4] (while the legitimate rate has fallen substantially),

---

2. See Makhija (1978); Singh et al. (1978). Adam Smith said about colonial America, ''Labour is there so well rewarded that a numerous family of children, instead of being a burthen is a source of opulence and prosperity to the parents. The labour of each child, before it can leave their house, is computed to be worth a hundred pounds clear gain to them'' (1937, pp. 70–71). For a recent study of the contribution of farm children in the United States, see Rosenzweig (1977).

3. The substitution between schooling and farm work in rural India and in Brazil is analyzed by Makhija (1978) and Singh et al. (1978). Compulsory-schooling laws may also have contributed to the increased school enrollments of farm children (but see Landes and Solmon, 1972).

4. For example, in California in 1966 and 1974 the illegitimate birth rate per 1,000 unmarried women aged 15–44 was 18 and 19 respectively for white women, and 69 and 66 for black women (Berkov and Sklar, 1976).

even though abortions have become more accessible and birth control techniques have improved.

The relative cost of children is significantly affected by changes in the value of the time of married women, because the cost of the mother's time is a major part of the total cost of producing and rearing children (it contributes about two-thirds of the total cost in the United States; see Espenshade, 1977). Indeed, I believe that the growth in the earning power of women during the last hundred years in developed countries is a major cause of both the large increase in labor force participation of married women and the large decline in fertility. Since fathers have spent relatively little time on children, the growth in their earning power has not significantly affected the cost of children and in fact would have reduced the relative cost if children used relatively less time of fathers than other commodities used.

Household surveys provide direct evidence on the relation between the demand for children and the value of time of husbands and wives. The number of children is strongly negatively related to the wage rate or other measures of the value of time of wives, and is more often positively rather than negatively related to the wage rate or earnings of husbands (see, for example, Mincer, 1963; De Tray, 1973; Willis, 1973; and Ben-Porath, 1973). Part of the causation, however, is from children to wage rates, because women invest less in market skills and more in household skills and men do the reverse when families have more children. However, there does appear to be significant causation from the value of time of wives to their demand for children (Lazear, 1972).

Apparently households have preferred their own children to those available from others, for practically all households choose to have their own. The explanation may be that humans and other species are biologically selected to propagate their own genes (Wilson, 1975). However, Chapter 2 develops several reasons why persons prefer their own children even when cultural as well as genetic factors influence the demand for children. One reason is that own children can reduce the uncertainty of parents, who have more information about the genetic constitutions and early environmental experiences of their own children than of those obtainable from others.

On the other hand, parents have less prior information about the sex, color, physical condition, and other noticeable characteristics of children they self-produce than of those that could be seen in a "child market." Yet the scope of such a market would be limited because parents would be more likely to put their inferior rather than their superior children up for sale or adoption if buyers were not readily able to determine quality. (See Akerlof, 1970, for a discussion of the market for "lemons.")

Reliance on own children implies that some families might not be able to satisfy their demand for children because they are wholly or partially sterile, and that other families would exceed their demands because they are too fertile. In this statement, "demand" means the number of children desired when there are no obstacles to the production or prevention of children. Husbands with sterile wives have terminated their marriages or have married additional wives in societies permitting polygyny, and some women have had more children than they desired or had them at inopportune times.

But have major changes in average fertility been caused by changes in sterility and in knowledge of birth control methods? Although I once gave an affirmative answer (Becker, 1960), I now believe that the major changes have been caused primarily by other changes in the demand for children. The various forces discussed in this chapter appear sufficient to explain major declines in fertility, and simple and sufficiently effective birth control methods have been available to produce these declines.

To demonstrate the effectiveness of simple methods, consider the basic relation between the average number of live births (n), the period of vulnerability or "exposure" to births (E), the average time required to produce a conception resulting in a live birth (C), and the average period of sterility during and after the production of a live birth (S):

$$n = E/(C + S), \qquad (5.5)$$

where $C + S$ is the average duration between live births. Since C is a "waiting time" to conception, it depends on the probability of conception during any coition (p) and the frequency of coition (f):[5]

$$C \cong 1/(fp). \qquad (5.6)$$

Women marrying at age twenty and not using any birth control methods average about eleven live births (see the evidence for the Hutterites in Eaton and Mayer, 1953, p. 233). Since they would be fertile until an average age of about forty-four, or for 288 months, the average interval between live births is 26 months. The number of births could

---

5. See Becker (1956) for an early derivation of this formula; an extensive discussion may be found in Sheps and Menken (1973).

A Treatise on the Family

be reduced by almost 25 percent without mechanical methods of birth control simply by delaying marriage (and coition) for 3 years, reducing the frequency of coition during marriage by 10 percent, and extending breast feeding for 3 months. Moreover, the number could be reduced much further by coitus interruptus, a birth control method known even in many primitive societies.[6]

Perhaps Malthus considered changes in age at marriage to be a major method of birth control because it is much more effective than equal percentage changes in the frequency of coition during marriage when birth rates are as high as they were in the eighteenth century. For example, if women married at age twenty and produced eleven births, a 10-percent increase in age at marriage, which is about a 9-percent decrease in exposure to births, would reduce the number of births by almost three times as much as a 10-percent decrease in coital frequency. On the other hand, if women marrying at age twenty produced only two births because of effective birth control methods, a decrease in coital frequency would have almost as large an effect as an equal percentage increase in age at marriage.[7]

Prior to the nineteenth century, even in advanced countries no more than about half of all live births survived to age ten. Therefore modest changes in age at marriage, frequency of coition, and breast feeding—combined with coitus interruptus—would have reduced the

---

6. From Eq. (5.5) and the observation of about 11 births in 288 months' exposure, we infer $C + S = 26$ months. If S, infertility during and after pregnancy, is about 17 months (Menken and Bongaarts, 1978), then C is about 9 months. A 10-percent reduction in f would raise C by 10 percent to about 10 months, and a 3-month extension of breast feeding would extend S by about 2 months. Then $C + S$ would be increased from 26 to 29 months. If, in addition, marriage is delayed to age twenty-three, E is reduced to 252 months. So $n' = 252/29 \cong 8.7$.

Coitus interruptus reduces the probability of conception by more than 90 percent (Michael, 1973). If used during half the coitions,

$$C'' = \frac{1}{p\dfrac{(0.9f)}{2} + 0.1p\dfrac{(0.9f)}{2}} = 2\left(\frac{1}{fp}\right) = 2C \cong 18.$$

Then $n'' = 252/(18 + 20) = 6.6$.

7. An increase in age at marriage from twenty to twenty-two—a decrease in E from 288 to 264—always reduces n by 8.3 percent if $C + S$ is unaffected by the decrease in E. The effect of a decrease in f, however, depends on the ratio of C to S. If, say, $S = 17$ and $C = 9$ ($n = 11$), a 10-percent decrease in f reduces n by only 3 percent, whereas if $S = 17$ and $C = 127$ ($n = 2$), a 10-percent decrease in f reduces n by 8 percent.

average number of surviving children to only three or less. However, without significant declines in the number of births per family, the number of survivors would have greatly increased during the nineteenth and twentieth centuries owing to the dramatic increase in the probability of surviving to age ten. Surely improvements in older methods of birth control, such as the diaphragm (Himes, 1963, pp. 321, 391), and the development of new methods, such as the pill, permitted births to decline sharply during the last 150 years even though age at marriage also declined and frequency of coition may have increased.[8] But I believe that these improvements in birth control methods are mainly an induced response to other decreases in the demand for children rather than an important cause of the decreased demand.

Evidence that more effective birth control methods are not sufficient to reduce fertility is provided by societies that have maintained high levels of fertility even when they have had the means to reduce their fertility substantially. For example, the ruling families of Europe averaged more than 5.5 births from the beginning of the sixteenth to the end of the eighteenth centuries (Peller, 1965, p. 90), although they could have had considerably fewer births with methods known at that time (Himes, 1963, chap. 8) and presumably available to these families. Or poor Indian families stubbornly maintain their fertility levels until economic and other conditions change (Makhija, 1977, 1980), despite the resources spent to encourage—and even force!—them to use effective methods of control.

Moreover, many societies managed large reductions in their fertility long before modern methods of birth control were developed. More than two thousand years ago the Greeks and Romans had very small families through delayed marriage, infanticide, reduced coition during marriage, abortion, primitive contraceptives, and nonproductive modes of sex (Wilkinson, 1978). The Jews in Florence and Leghorn reduced their birth rates by 50 percent between 1670 and 1840 only partly by raising their average age at marriage (Livi-Bacci, 1977, pp. 40–44). These Jews can hardly be said to have had access to the best information on contraception, since they were forced to live in ghettos and were excluded from many schools. Even the "contraceptive revolution," to use the term of Westoff and Ryder (1977), ushered in by the

---

8. Reliable historical evidence obviously is lacking, but apparently the frequency of coition increased in the United States during the 1960s, whereas birth rates fell rapidly (Westoff, 1974).

pill has probably not been a major cause of the sharp drop in fertility in recent decades. The decline began in the 1950s in countries like the United States and Japan, although the pill is illegal in Japan and was not extensively used in the United States until the 1960s. Moreover, women in the United States born between 1900 and 1910 had quite small families without the pill by using other contraceptives, abstinence, and induced abortions (Dawson et al., 1980).

The demand for children is affected not only by the price of children but also by real income. An increase in real income generally increases the demand for different commodities, and some of the evidence proves the relation between children and income to be no exception. In polygynous societies wealthier men tend to have many more children, chiefly because they are far more likely to be polygynous than poor men (Grossbard, 1978). Wealthier men also tended to have more children in monogamous societies prior to the nineteenth century; see the data relating wealth to children in fifteenth-century Tuscany (Klapisch, 1972, table 10.2; Herlihy, 1977, pp. 147–149) and in other parts of Italy during the fifteenth and eighteenth centuries (Livi-Bacci, 1977, tables 6.1 to 6.4). This positive relation between wealth and fertility in monogamous societies generally continued in rural communities throughout the nineteenth century; see the evidence for Canada in 1861 (McInnis, 1977, table 5), for the United States in 1865 (Bash, 1955, especially table 12), and for Germany in the late nineteenth and early twentieth centuries (Knodel, 1974, table 3.13).

Sometime during the nineteenth century, however, fertility and wealth became partially or wholly negatively related among urban families; evidence for German cities around 1900 can be found in Knodel, 1974, tables 3.14 and 3.15. The evidence for advanced countries during the twentieth century has been rather mixed, although income and fertility have generally been negatively related at lower income levels and unrelated or positively related at upper levels; the documentation is reviewed in Simon (1974, pp. 42–69). The economic approach suggests that a negative relation between income and fertility is an indication that the effective price of children increases with income, perhaps because the wives of men with higher incomes tend to have greater potential earnings from market activity (Mincer, 1963) or higher values of their time (Willis, 1973). I believe, however, that the interaction between the quantity and quality of children is the most important reason why the effective price of children rises with income.

The Interaction between Quantity and Quality

Let us return to the utility function, Eq. (5.1), that distinguishes the quality of children from other commodities. I assume here that all children in the same family have the same quality and that quality is fully produced by each family with its own time and market goods (these assumptions are dropped in Chapter 6). If p_c is the constant cost of a unit of quality, q the total quality of each child, and p_cqn the total amount spent on children, the budget constraint would be

$$p_cqn + \pi_z Z = I. \tag{5.7}$$

This budget constraint is not linear in the commodities entering the utility function, but depends multiplicatively on n and q. The nonlinearity is responsible for the interaction between quantity and quality in the following analysis.

Maximizing utility subject to the budget constraint gives the equilibrium conditions

$$\left. \begin{array}{l} \dfrac{\partial U}{\partial n} = MU_n = \lambda p_c q = \lambda \pi_n \\[2mm] \dfrac{\partial U}{\partial q} = MU_q = \lambda p_c n = \lambda \pi_q \\[2mm] \dfrac{\partial U}{\partial Z} = MU_z = \lambda \pi_z \end{array} \right\} . \tag{5.8}$$

The relevant shadow prices of n and q are π_n and π_q. Of course, each depends on p_c, the cost of a unit of quality, but what may appear surprising is that π_n depends on q and π_q depends on n. Since an increase in q raises the amount spent on each child, it raises the relevant cost of each child. Similarly, an increase in n raises the cost of adding to the quality of each child because a larger number of children would be affected.

Equations (5.7) and (5.8) can be solved for the equilibrium values of n, q, and Z as functions of these shadow prices and of income:

$$\left. \begin{array}{l} n = d_n(\pi_n, \pi_q, \pi_z, R) \\[2mm] q = d_q(\pi_n, \pi_q, \pi_z, R) \\[2mm] Z = d_z(\pi_n, \pi_q, \pi_z, R) \end{array} \right\} , \tag{5.9}$$

where shadow income, R, equals the sum of the *shadow* amounts spent on different commodities.[9] These demand functions have the usual substitution and income effects; for example, an increase in the shadow price of n, q, or Z, holding other shadow prices and shadow income constant, would reduce own quantity demanded. Note, however, that these demand functions depend on the quantities n and q through the shadow prices π_q and π_n respectively, and even on the interaction term nq through shadow income R (see the extensive discussion in Tomes, 1978).

Quantity and quality do not interact explicitly in demand functions that depend on shadow prices and income, but they do in demand functions that depend on "market" prices and income. If p_c, π_z, and I were held constant, an exogenous increase in n would raise the shadow price of q, π_q ($= np_c$), and thereby wo.ild reduce the demand for q. The reduction in q lowers the shadow price of n because it depends on q, which further increases the demand for n. But this raises π_q and lowers q still further, which lowers π_n and raises n still further, and so on. The interaction between n and q continues until a new equilibrium position is established.

Even a small exogenous increase in n (or q) could be responsible for a large decrease in q (or n) if the interaction between n and q were sufficiently strong. The interaction is determined by the substitution between n and q in the utility function: if they were sufficiently close substitutes, they would continue to interact until either n or q were negligible. In particular, if the elasticity of substitution between n and q, n and Z, and q and Z were the same, both n and q would be positive only if this elasticity were less than unity.[10] Consequently, the "spe-

---

9. Equation (5.7) can be written as

$$(p_c n)q + (p_c q)n + \pi_z Z = I + p_c nq \equiv R,$$

or as

$$\pi_q q + \pi_n n + \pi_z Z = R.$$

10. For proofs see Becker and Lewis (1973) and Tomes (1978). More generally, both n and q would be consumed only if

$$\sigma_{nq} < \frac{1 - k_z \sigma_z}{1 - k_z},$$

where σ_{nq} is the elasticity of substitution between n and q, σ_z is the elasticity of substitution between both Z and n and Z and q, and k_z is the share of Z in R. Therefore, $\sigma_{nq} < 1$ if $\sigma_z \geq 1$, and the maximum feasible σ_{nq} is negatively related to σ_z. That is, quantity and quality of children could not be close substitutes if other commodities were close substitutes for children.

cial'' relation between the quantity and quality of children that derives from their interaction does not presume that they are close substitutes; on the contrary, equilibrium would not be possible if they were close substitutes! Therefore, the interaction between quantity and quality explains why the education of children, for instance, depends closely on the number of children—even though we have no reason to believe that education per child and number of children are close substitutes.

The interaction between n and q is shown graphically in Figure 5.1, where U_0 and U_1 are convex indifference curves between n and q (Z is ignored or held constant), and AB and CD represent the budget equation. The interaction between n and q implies that the budget curve is not a straight line but is also convex to the origin.[11] Equilibrium would be at an internal position (like points e_0 and e_1) only if the curvature of the indifference curves exceeded the curvature of the budget curve. Since the curvature of these indifference curves is smaller when n and

FIGURE 5.1   Interaction between quantity and quality: indifference curves and budget curves of a typical family.

---

11. If $p_c nq = S'$, then

$$p_c n + p_c q(dn/dp) = dS' = 0,$$

and

$$p_c(dn/dq) + p_c(dn/dq) + p_c q(d^2n/dq^2) = 0,$$

or

$$d^2n/dq^2 = (-2\,dn/dq)/q > 0.$$

A Treatise on the Family

q are closer substitutes, internal equilibria are possible only when they are not close substitutes.

The quantity and quality of other commodities are also related (see Theil, 1952, and Houthakker, 1952, and the application to firms by Hirshleifer, 1955), but may not interact so strongly because the qualities of different physical units are not so closely related as the qualities of different children. For example, a rich person might well plan to own both expensive and inexpensive cars, but is unlikely to plan on having both expensive and inexpensive children. Still, the analysis developed in this section can be usefully applied to other commodities.

Fertility in many countries has changed greatly during short spans of time. Table 5.1 shows that the birth rate in the United States declined by 38 percent between 1960 and 1972, and by 24 percent during the 1920s. The total fertility rate in Japan dropped by 45 percent between 1950 and 1960, and the total fertility rate in Taiwan declined by 51 percent between 1960 and 1975. Or, to take an early episode, the birth rate in England and Wales decreased by 26 percent between 1871 and 1901. Commodities like children, which are presumed to have modest price elasticities because they do not have close substitutes, generally do not change by large amounts except during severe business cycles.

Several alternative explanations for large changes in fertility have been suggested, including the contraceptive revolution ushered in by the pill (see Westoff and Ryder, 1977, pp. 302–309), but this cannot explain the large decline in births in the United States during the twenties

TABLE 5.1   Changes in birth rates in various countries and time periods.

	Country and period	Percent change in birth rate
(1)	United States, 1920–1930	−24
(2)	United States, 1960–1972	−38
(3)	Japan, 1950–1960	−45
(4)	Taiwan, 1960–1975	−51
(5)	England and Wales, 1871–1901	−26

SOURCES: U.S. Bureau of the Census, 1975c, 1977b; Japan Bureau of Statistics, 1962; Taiwan Ministry of the Interior, 1974, 1976; Great Britain Registrar General, 1957.

(1) and (2) Birth rate for women ages 15–44.
(3) and (4) Total fertility rate for women ages 15–49.
(5) Birth rate for women ages 15–44.

or in Japan during the fifties. I am convinced that the most promising explanation is found in the interaction between the quantity and quality of children, for it implies that the demand for children is highly responsive to price and perhaps to income, even when children have no close substitutes.[12]

The demand for children can be better discussed after adding a fixed cost of each child, p_n, that includes the time, expenditure, discomfort, and risk spent in pregnancy and delivery, governmental child allowances (a negative cost), the costs of avoiding pregnancies and deliveries, and all other psychic and monetary expenditures on children that are largely independent of quality. In addition, let p_q refer to expenditures on children that are largely independent of the number of children because of joint consumption by different children (items like hand-me-down clothes and learning from parents), and let marginal and average variable costs of quality differ, perhaps because of public subsidies to schooling. The budget equation can then be written as

$$p_n n + p_q q + p_c(q)qn + \pi_z Z = I. \tag{5.10}$$

Maximizing utility subject to this constraint gives the following equilibrium conditions for n and q:

$$MU_n = \lambda(p_n + p_c q) = \lambda p_c q(1 + r_n) = \lambda \pi_n$$

$$MU_q = \lambda \left(p_q + p_c n + \frac{\partial p_c}{\partial q} nq \right) = \lambda p_c n(1 + r_q + \epsilon_{pq}) = \lambda \pi_q, \tag{5.11}$$

where $r_n = p_n/p_c q$ and $r_q = p_q/p_c n$ are the ratios of fixed to variable costs for quantity and quality respectively, and $1 + \epsilon_{pq}$ is the ratio of marginal variable cost to average variable costs of quality. Hence

$$\frac{MU_n}{MU_q} = \frac{\pi_n}{\pi_q} = \frac{q}{n} \frac{(1 + r_n)}{(1 + r_q + \epsilon_{pq})}. \tag{5.12}$$

The ratio of the shadow prices of n and q now depend not only on the ratio of q to n, but also on the ratios of fixed to variable costs, and on the ratio of marginal to average variable cost of quality.

Therefore, an increase in, say, the fixed cost of n, perhaps because

---

12. I did not fully appreciate the significance of the interaction between quantity and quality in my first paper on fertility. I claimed that economic theory had "little to say about the quantitative relationship between price and amount. There are no good substitutes for children, but there may be many poor ones" (Becker, 1960, p. 215).

of reduced child allowances or reduced costs of contraception, would induce a substitution away from n and toward q as well as Z, because π_n would increase relative to π_q as well as π_z. The interaction between n and q implies that the increase in q raises π_n further, while the decrease in n lowers π_q further, which encourages still more substitution away from n and toward q. The decrease in n and increase in q could be sizable even if the increase in the fixed cost of n were modest and the elasticity of substitution between n and q were not large.

A compensated increase in p_n rotates the budget line of Figure 5.1 through the initial equilibrium position, from AB to CD. Revealed preference shows that the new equilibrium must be to the left of e_0, as is e_1. Since the interaction between n and q implies that the slope of CD at e_1 increases when n decreases, the decrease in n must be sufficient to raise the slope of the equilibrium indifference curve to equality with the increased slope of CD.

To illustrate, assume that p_n is 25 percent of π_n, p_q and ϵ_{pq} are negligible, expenditures on n equal $10/27$ of R, and expenditures on q equal $8/27$ of R. If n and q did not interact, a compensated 1-percent increase in the price of n would reduce the demand for n only by 0.01 $(17/27)$ σ, where σ is the elasticity of substitution (for example, by 0.5 percent if $\sigma = 0.8$). The interaction with q, however, magnifies the response, for then a compensated 1-percent initial increase in π_n due to a 4-percent increase in p_n would reduce the demand for n by about 1.1 percent if $\sigma = 0.8$ and by about 2.3 percent if $\sigma = 1.0$.[13] These are $2\frac{1}{4}$ and $3\frac{2}{3}$ times as large as the reductions in n when n and q do not interact. Therefore, a moderate increase in the fixed cost of children (perhaps caused by an exogenous improvement in contraceptive knowledge) or a moderate decrease in the ratio of marginal to average costs of quality that raised the initial shadow price of quantity relative to quality by only 10 to 20 percent would reduce the demand for quantity and increase the demand for quality by significantly larger percentages.

Moderate initial increases in relative price could explain both the large declines in fertility in Table 5.1 and the large increases in quality in Table 5.2. For example, while the fertility rate in Taiwan declined by 51 percent, the fraction of persons aged 25–34 with a high-school education rose by 100 percent, or while the birth rate in the United States

---

13. See Becker and Lewis, 1973, eq. (A19). I am indebted to H. Gregg Lewis for correcting an error in earlier calculations.

TABLE 5.2 Changes in level of schooling in various countries and time periods.

Country and period	Percent change in schooling
(1) United States, 1920–1930	+81
(2) United States, 1960–1972	+33
(3) Japan, 1950–1960	+37
(4) Taiwan, 1960–1975	+100
(5) Great Britain, 1871–1900	+21

SOURCES: U.S. Department of Commerce, 1932; U.S. Bureau of the Census, 1963a, 1972; Japan Bureau of Statistics, 1961; Taiwan Ministry of the Interior, 1976; West, 1970, p. 134.

(1) Fraction of persons ages 14–17 enrolled in secondary school.
(2) Fraction of persons ages 25–34 who completed high school.
(3) Fraction of persons ages 25–34 who completed senior high school (current system) or middle school (old system); excludes youth training (old system).
(4) Fraction of persons ages 25–34 who completed high school.
(5) Fraction of males who were literate.

declined by 38 percent, the fraction of persons aged 25–34 who graduated from high school rose by 33 percent.

Further Empirical Implications of the Quality-Quantity Interaction

This analysis also can reconcile to some extent the view that family planning programs are necessary before fertility will fall significantly with the view that the value of children must be reduced before fertility falls significantly (see the discussion between Demeny, 1979a and b, and Bogue and Tsui, 1979). Suppose that an effective family planning program could be expected to reduce births by 10 percent because that many births are "unwanted." However, births would actually fall by a much larger percent; the interaction between quantity and quality implies that a 10-percent fall in births raises the demand for quality of children, which raises the cost of (lowers the value of) quantity and further lowers the demand for births. Although family planning might take credit for the whole decline in births because it is the initiating force, the induced increase in the demand for higher-quality children and the induced decrease in the demand for quantity of children are responsible for more than half of the decline in births.

Economic theory implies that a change in the price of any commodity changes in opposite directions the demands for that commodity and for substitute commodities. The interaction between the quantity and quality of children implies that an increase in, say, the price of quantity would increase quality by more than other commodities even if quality and these commodities were equally good substitutes for quantity. (Indeed, an increase in the price of quantity could *reduce* other commodities along with quantity and increase only quality even if the elasticity of substitution were the *same* for all commodities; see the proof in Tomes, 1978, section A2d.) This prediction of a strong negative relation between the quantity and quality of children is confirmed by Tables 5.1 and 5.2 and by various other evidence.

For example, over the last 150 years Jews have invested more in human capital (see the evidence in Schmelz, 1971, on the relatively low child mortality of Jews in the nineteenth and twentieth centuries in Europe and the United States) and in recent decades have had higher incomes. It is less well known, however, that Jewish families have been smaller than average. The Jewish birth rate was 47 percent below the average birth rate in Florence at the beginning of the nineteenth century (Livi-Bacci, 1977, table 1.23); Jewish marital fertility was 20 percent below Catholic fertility in Munich in 1875 (Knodel, 1974, table 3.18). I believe that the high achievement and low fertility of Jewish families are explained by high marginal rates of return—low values of ϵ_{pq} in Eq. (5.12)—to investments in the education, health, and other human capital of their children (see also Brenner, 1979) that lower the price of quality relative to quantity.

Blacks have invested less in training because rates of return on investments in education, health, and other training have been lower for blacks than for whites (Becker, 1975, sec. IV.3). The quantity-quality interaction implies that blacks would respond to poorer investment opportunities with higher fertility. As opportunities for blacks have improved in recent years, they have invested more in their training (Freeman, 1981) and at the same time reduced their fertility relative to whites (Sweet, 1974).

Not only are farm families in traditional agriculture larger than urban families because, as we have seen, children are cheaper on farms, but traditional farmers also invest less in each child (Schultz, 1963; Barichello, 1979). The early stages of economic development raise rates of return on investments in the education and other training of *urban* children, which lower the marginal cost of quality to urban families and shift them further toward quality and away from quantity.[14] As devel-

---

14. For example, urban fertility declined relative to rural fertility in Italy and Germany (Prussia) during the latter part of the nineteenth and the beginning of the twentieth centuries (Knodel, 1974, table 3.2; Livi-Bacci, 1977, table 3.8).

opment proceeds, however, rates of return on human capital are also raised in farming because farming becomes more mechanized and complicated. Farm families then also shift toward quality and away from quantity (see the recent evidence for rural India in Makhija, 1980); indeed, rural fertility today has dropped below urban fertility in many advanced countries as children have become *more* expensive on farms than in cities.

Since educated women have a lower demand for quantity of children (Michael, 1973), the interaction with quality implies that they would invest more in the education and other training of their children. Therefore, the many regressions showing a positive relation between children's education and mother's education may not be evidence that the causation is directly from mother's to children's education. This example illustrates why the interaction between quantity and quality implies that the demand functions for both should be estimated in a way that takes account of the interaction between them. One could use reduced forms or simultaneous equations; for example, the education (or other measure of quality) of a child could be related to the education of his parents, the number of his siblings, and other variables, while the number of children is related to the education of parents, the education of children, and other variables. Several empirical studies have taken account of the interaction, and have found a negative effect of quality on quantity, and usually also a negative effect of quantity on quality.[15]

If changes in child mortality are exogenous, the effect on fertility of a change in mortality could be determined simply by including child mortality among the independent variables in a fertility demand function. However, if the mortality of children is partly determined by their parents,[16] the demand for childhood survivors would interact with the demand for fertility. For example, an exogenous improvement in con-

---

15. See Makhija (1978) on rural India; Singh et al. (1978) on rural Brazil; Castañeda (1979) on urban Colombia; Gomez (1980) on Mexico; Barichello (1979) on Canada; and Tomes (1978), De Tray (1978), and Rosenzweig and Wolpin (1980) on the United States. Makhija and Castañeda find a positive or zero effect of quantity on quality.

16. The substantial evidence suggesting parental control is ably reviewed in Scrimshaw (1978). In addition, note that two-thirds of the children born to ruling families of Europe during the eighteenth century survived to age fifteen, compared to about one-third of those born to the general population of Vienna (Peller, 1965, p. 94), or that in 1931 life expectancy at birth in India was 53 years for the relatively high income Parsis, compared to 32 years for the general population (United Nations, 1953, p. 63). See also Gomez (1980) on endogenous Mexican mortality in recent decades.

traceptive knowledge would reduce the quantity of children, raise the probability they survive childhood, and also improve other aspects of the quality of children. The decline in fertility is not "caused" by the decline in child mortality nor is the decline in mortality "caused" by the decline in fertility, but both of these result from a rise in the price of quantity and the interaction between quantity and quality (Gomez, 1980).

Even an exogenous decline in child mortality would induce a quantity-quality interaction. Parents might reduce their own efforts to prevent child deaths when, say, a public health program is introduced,[17] but they would increase their expenditures on other aspects of child quality because the rate of return on these expenditures would be raised by a decline in mortality. If total parental expenditures increased, the effective price of quantity could be *increased* by an exogenous decline in child mortality, and the demand for child survivors would then *decrease* (see also O'Hara, 1972). An exogenous increase of a given percent in the probability that children survive childhood would then reduce births by a larger percentage.

Economic development affects fertility and the quality of children not only because incomes increase but also because rates of return on investments in education and other human capital increase. Since even a "pure" rise in income can reduce fertility through the interaction with quality, a rise in income combined with higher rates of return on quality could reduce fertility significantly. Consequently, economic development can have significant negative effects on fertility even when the "true" income elasticity of demand for fertility is positive and sizable. A similar analysis that incorporates systematic differences in rates of return to different families in developed countries implies that richer families can have fewer children than poorer families, even though richer families in less developed countries have more children than poorer families.

---

17. Chapters 6 and 11 analyze the effects on parental efforts of changes in public and other "endowments"; Scrimshaw (1978, pp. 391, 395) provides empirical evidence on parental reactions to public health programs.

A Reformulation of the Economic Theory of Fertility

The economic approach to fertility emphasizes the effects of parents' income and the cost of rearing children. With the exception of work by Easterlin (1973) and a few others (see Chapter 7), this approach has neglected the analytical links between decisions by different generations of the same family. Moreover, despite Malthus' famous precedent, fertility has not been integrated with the determination of wage rates, interest rates, capital accumulation, and other macroeconomic variables (exceptions include Razin and Ben-Zion, 1975, and Willis, 1985).

Our model in this supplement is based on the assumption that parents are altruistic toward their children. The utility of parents depends not only on their own consumption, but also on the utility of each child

This supplement was written with Robert J. Barro and originally appeared in the *Quarterly Journal of Economics* 103 (1988): 1–25. Reprinted here, in slightly amended form, by permission.

and the number of children. By relating the utility of children to their own consumption and to the utility of their children, we obtain a *dynastic* utility function that depends on the consumption and number of descendants in all generations. We venture to use the word "reformulation" in the supplement title because of the emphasis on dynastic utility functions and descendants in different generations. The reformulated approach provides a new way of looking at the determination of fertility.

In the next section we set out the model of altruism toward children and derive the budget constraint and utility function of a dynastic family. The first-order conditions to maximize utility imply that fertility in any generation depends positively on the real interest rate and the degree of altruism, and negatively on the rate of growth in per capita consumption from one generation to the next. Consumption of each descendant depends positively on the net cost of rearing a descendant.

The effects on fertility of child mortality, subsidies to (or taxes on) children, and social security and other transfer payments to adults are considered. Although the demand for surviving children rises during the transition to low child mortality, demand for survivors returns to its prior level once mortality stabilizes at a low level.

In economies fully linked to an international capital market but not to an international labor market, fertility falls in response to declines in international real interest rates and increases in an economy's rate of technological progress. This analysis of fertility in open economies may contribute to the explanation of low fertility in Western countries during the past couple of decades.

We extend the analysis to include life-cycle variations in consumption, earnings, and utility. Fertility is a function of expenditures on the subsistence and human capital of children, but not of expenditures that simply raise the consumption of children. The path of aggregate consumption in demographic steady states does not depend on interest rates, time preference, or other determinants of life-cycle variations in consumption.

A Model of Fertility and Population Change

We assume at the beginning of this supplement that each person has two periods of life: childhood and adulthood. Later we will show how to combine a full life-cycle analysis with intergenerational forces. We pretend that each adult has children without "marriage" because we believe that the incorporation of marriage between men and women would complicate but not affect the essence of the analysis (although see Bernheim and Bagwell, 1988). We also bypass issues related to the spacing of children by assuming that parents have all of their children at the beginning of adulthood.

Economic analyses of fertility have assumed that the utility of parents depends on the number and "quality" of children. These analyses usually do not specify how or why children affect utility. Although agnosticism about preferences is common among economists, a more powerful analysis of fertility results by building on recent discussions of altruism toward children.

The importance of altruism within families began to be recognized systematically by economists during the 1970s (two early studies are Barro, 1974, and Becker, 1974b). Obviously, many parents are altruistic toward children in the sense that the utility of parents depends positively on the utility of their children. Also, many children care about the welfare of their parents and siblings (and other relatives). Here we rely heavily on the assumption of altruism toward children to generate a dynamic analysis of fertility and population change.

If the utility (U_0) of an adult is an additively separable function of his own consumption (c_0) and the utility of each child ($U_{1,i}$), then

$$U_0 = v(c_0, n_0) + \sum_{i=1}^{n_0} \psi_i(U_{1,i}, n_0), \qquad (5S.1)$$

where v is a standard current-period utility function (with $v_c > 0$ and $v_{ii} < 0$ for $i = c_0, n_0$). Since reactions by parents to differences among their children are not important for the issues discussed in this Supplement,[1] we simplify by assuming that siblings are identical; hence the function $\psi_i = \psi$ is the same for all children. If this function is increasing and concave in the utility of each child, the parent's utility is maximized when all children attain the same level of utility: $U_{1,i} = U_{1,j}$ for all i and j. Then the parent's utility function becomes

$$U_0 = v(c_0, n_0) + n_0\psi(U_1, n_0). \qquad (5S.2)$$

With the additional assumption that U_0 depends linearly on U_1, so that $\psi(U_1, n_0) = U_1 a(n_0)$, the parent's utility would be given by

---

1. See the discussion in Chapter 6 and in Sheshinski and Weiss (1982) and Behrman et al. (1982).

A Treatise on the Family

$$U_0 = v(c_0, n_0) + a(n_0)n_0U_1. \tag{5S.3}$$

The term $a(n_0)$ measures the degree of altruism toward each child, and converts the utility of children into that of parents. We assume that, for given utility per child U_1, parental utility is increasing and concave in the number of children n_0. This property, together with Eq. (5S.3), requires the altruism function to satisfy the conditions

$$v_n + a(n_0) + n_0a'(n_0) > 0, \quad \text{and} \quad v_{nn} + 2a'(n_0) + n_0a''(n_0) < 0, \tag{5S.4}$$

where we neglect integer restrictions on the number of children. Notice that v_n could be negative—children could provide consumption disutility.

The utility of each child, U_1, depends as in Eq. (5S.3) on own consumption (c_1), and the number (n_1) and utility (U_2) of own children. The utility of great-grandchildren appears if U_2 is replaced by a function of c_2, n_2, and U_3. If the parameters of the utility function are the same for all generations of a dynastic family, and if utility during childhood is neglected for the present, then by continuing to substitute later consumption and fertility, we arrive at a *dynastic* utility function that depends on the consumption and number of children of all descendants of the same family line. This dynastic utility function is

$$U_0 = \sum_{i=0}^{\infty} A_i N_i v(c_i, n_i), \tag{5S.5}$$

where n_i is the number of children and c_i is the consumption per adult in generation i. The term A_i is the implied degree of altruism of the dynastic head toward each descendant in the ith generation, as given by

$$A_0 = 1, \quad A_i = \prod_{j=0}^{i-1} a(n_j), \quad i = 1, 2, \ldots \tag{5S.6}$$

The term N_i is the number of descendants in the ith generation:

$$N_0 = 1, \quad N_j = \prod_{j=0}^{i-1} n_j, \quad i = 1, 2, \ldots \tag{5S.7}$$

If children are also altruistic to parents, dynastic utility would depend on the consumption and fertility of all ancestors as well as the consumption and fertility of all descendants (see Kimball, 1987).

A parent is "selfish" if the marginal utility of own consumption exceeds the marginal utility derived from his child's consumption when the parent has one child ($n = 1$). This definition implies that $a(1) < 1$ for selfish parents. We assume that parents are "selfish" because the utility of a dynastic family with stationary consumption per person ($c_i = c$) and a stationary number of descendants ($N_i = 1$) would be bounded only if $a(1) < 1$.

Instead of starting with the linear altruism function in Eq. (5S.3) and deriving the dynastic utility function in Eq. (5S.5), we could have started with a dynastic utility function. If we assume that dynastic utility is time consistent and additively separable in the per capita consumptions of different generations,[2] then the dynastic utility function must have essentially the form of Eq. (5S.5) (see Becker and Barro, 1986).[3] In this sense, Eq. (5S.5) is more general than might appear from our derivation. Of course, preferences do not have to be additively separable and time consistent. Nonetheless, these assumptions are a good starting point for an economic theory of fertility, especially since convincing theoretical or empirical arguments have not been advanced for radical changes in either assumption when analyzing family decisionmaking. Furthermore, the social-preference functions used in many discussions of the intergenerational allocation of resources (such as Arrow and Kurz, 1970) are special cases of the dynastic utility function in Eq. (5S.5).

Each adult supplies one unit of labor to the market[4] and earns the wage w_i. Parents leave a bequest of nondepreciable capital, k_{i+1}, to each child at the beginning of the child's adulthood. Capital k_i earns rent at the rate r_i. An adult in generation i spends his earnings and inheritance, $w_i + (1 + r_i)k_i$, on own consumption, c_i, on bequests to

---

2. Time consistency means that each generation will be led to implement the fertility and consumption decisions desired by previous generations. Note that time consistency does not rule out conflict between parents and children, because children may want larger bequests than parents are willing to make. We are indebted to Kevin M. Murphy for helpful discussion of the properties of dynastic utility functions.

3. Abel (1986) generalizes our analysis by assuming that a parent's utility is a concave rather than a linear function of children's utility. His formulation amounts to the assumption that the consumption of future generations enters the dynastic utility function in a particular nonadditive way.

4. The labor-leisure choice is readily incorporated by including leisure along with consumption in the v function, and by considering a "full-income" budget equation (see Tamura, 1985).

A Treatise on the Family

children, $n_i k_{i+1}$, and on costs of raising children. We assume that each child costs β_i, so that $n_i \beta_i$ is the total cost of raising children to adulthood. Therefore, the overall budget condition for an adult in generation i is

$$w_i + (1 + r_i)k_i = c_i + n_i(\beta_i + k_{i+1}). \tag{5S.8}$$

The parameter β_i represents a cost of raising children that is independent of the "quality" of children (as measured by their consumption c_{i+1}, wage rate w_{i+1}, or inheritance k_{i+1}). To capture the emphasis in the fertility literature on the value of parents' time, we sometimes assume that β_i is positively related to the parent's wage rate w_i. We also assume that debt can be left to children—that is, bequests k_i can be negative as well as positive[5]—although parents cannot leave negative levels of human capital.

The optimization problem as seen by the dynastic head is to maximize utility U_0 in Eq. (5S.5), subject to the budget constraints in Eq. (5S.8), and to initial assets k_0. In carrying out this maximization, each head takes as given the path of wage rates w_i, interest rates r_i, and child-rearing costs β_i. The chosen path of consumption per adult, c_0, c_1, c_2, . . . ; capital stock per adult, k_1, k_2, . . . ; and number of descendants, N_1, N_2, . . . , must be consistent with this maximization problem.[6]

The analysis of the first-order conditions simplifies if fertility does not affect current-period utility v, and if the degree of altruism toward children has a constant elasticity with respect to the number of children; that is, if

$$a(n_i) = \alpha(n_i)^{-\varepsilon}. \tag{5S.9}$$

In this case, the degree of altruism toward descendants, A_i in Eq. (5S.6), depends only on the number of descendants in generation i, $N_i = \Pi_{j=0}^{i-1} n_j$. Specifically, $A_i = \alpha^i(N_i)^{-\varepsilon}$. Conversely, Eq. (5S.9) must be true if we assume that A_i depends only on N_i (and not on N_j, $j \neq i$), so that dynastic utility in generation i depends only on the

---

5. Ponzi games, in which the debt grows forever as fast as or faster than the interest rate, are ruled out by an assumption that the present value of debt must approach zero asymptotically. If all the capital stocks k_i are positive, then obviously bequests from parents to children are also positive.

6. We pretend that the dynastic head can pick the entire time path. Since the objective function is time consistent, however, the descendants face a problem of the same form, and they have no incentive to deviate from the choices made initially.

number of descendants and consumption per descendant in generation i.

The condition $0 < a(1) < 1$ requires that $0 < \alpha < 1$, and the condition that parents' utility is increasing and concave in the number of children for given utility per child (as ensured by the inequalities in expression (5S.4) corresponds to $0 < \varepsilon < 1$. By substituting the altruism function from Eq. (5S.9) into the expression for dynastic utility in Eq. (5S.5), we get

$$U_0 = \sum_{i=0}^{\infty} \alpha^i (N_i)^{1-\varepsilon} v(c_i). \qquad (5S.10)$$

Suppose that we change the number of descendants in generation i, N_i, while holding fixed the *total* consumption, $C_i = N_i c_i$, for generation i, as well as the number of persons and consumption per person in other generations (N_j and c_j for $j \neq i$). Then the change in U_0 measures the benefit or loss from having more people in generation i to consume a given aggregate quantity of goods. Since the production of children is costly, an increase in N_i in this manner must raise U_0 near a utility-maximizing position (if children are to be produced). Otherwise, people would do better with fewer children. The derivative of U_0 in Eq. (5S.10) with respect to N_i—holding fixed C_i and the values of c_j and N_j for all other generations—is positive only if

$$\sigma(c_i) < 1 - \varepsilon, \qquad (5S.11)$$

where $\sigma(c_i) = v'(c_i)c_i/v(c_i)$ is the elasticity of $v(c_i)$ with respect to c_i. The inequality in (5S.11) is important for the subsequent discussion.

The first-order conditions obtain in the usual manner, with allowance for a Lagrange multiplier for each of the budget constraints in Eq. (5S.8). (We continue to neglect integer restrictions on the number of children.) One set of first-order conditions is

$$\frac{v'(c_i)}{v'(c_{i+1})} = a(n_i)(1 + r_{i+1}) = \alpha \frac{(1 + r_{i+1})}{(n_i)^\varepsilon}, \qquad i = 0, 1, \ldots \quad (5S.12)$$

This condition holds for an arbitrary form of $a(n_i)$ that satisfies the inequalities in (5S.4), although we focus on the constant-elasticity specification in Eq. (5S.9).

The other set of first-order conditions[7] is

---

7. The second-order condition is $\varepsilon + (1 - \varepsilon)vv''/(v')^2 < 0$ (see the appendix to Becker and Barro, 1986). If $\sigma(c_i)$ is the constant σ, then this condition reduces to $\sigma + \varepsilon < 1$, which is expression (5S.11). We assume that the

A Treatise on the Family

$$v(c_i)[1 - \varepsilon - \sigma(c_i)] = v'(c_i)[\beta_{i-1}(1 + r_i) - w_i], \quad i = 1, 2, \ldots,$$
$$(5S.13)$$

where $\sigma(c_i)$ is again the elasticity of $v(c_i)$ with respect to c_i. There is also the dynastic budget constraint, which equates the present value of all resources to the present value of all expenditures:[8]

$$k_0 + \sum_{i=0}^{\infty} d_i N_i w_i = \sum_{i=0}^{\infty} d_i (N_i c_i + N_{i+1} \beta_i), \quad (5S.14)$$

where

$$d_i = \prod_{j=0}^{i} (1 + r_j)^{-1}.$$

Equation (5S.12) is an arbitrage condition for shifting consumption from one generation to the next. Aside from the term that depends on fertility, n_i, this equation expresses the familiar result that the utility rate of substitution between consumption in periods $i + 1$ and i, $v'(c_i)/v'(c_{i+1})$, depends directly on the time-preference factor α and on the interest-rate factor $1 + r_{i+1}$. The standard conclusion is that a rise in α or in the interest rate r_{i+1} increases c_{i+1} relative to c_i. In our modified arbitrage condition, an increase in fertility n_i lowers altruism per child, given by $a(n_i)$, and increases the discount on future consumption. Therefore, higher fertility is associated with a reduction in c_{i+1} relative to c_i, for given values of α and r_{i+1}.

Equation (5S.13) says that the marginal benefit of an additional child (or equivalently of an additional adult descendant for the next period) must balance the marginal cost. The right side of the equation is the

---

parameters of the utility function and budget constraint lead to a finite level of utility. For a steady state with constant values of β, w, r, c, and n, this outcome requires $(1 + r) > n$, which is the standard condition that the interest rate exceed the growth rate (of population). From Eqs. (5S.12) and (5S.9), a constant c implies that $n = [\alpha(1 + r)]^{1/\varepsilon}$, so that $(1 + r) > n$ requires that $(1 + r)^{1-\varepsilon} < 1/\alpha$. Hence, utility would be unbounded if the interest rate were too high. The reason that n exceeds $1 + r$ when r is sufficiently large is that an increase in $1 + r$ raises n more than equiproportionately. A closed economy restricts steady-state values of r to regions where $1 + r > n$ (see Barro and Becker, 1985).

8. The dynastic budget equation follows from the constraints for each period as shown in Eq. (5S.8), as long as the transversality condition is satisfied: that the present value of the future capital stock approach zero asymptotically. We also use the constraint on borrowing that is discussed in note 5 above.

net cost of an additional adult in generation i. The left side is essentially the effect on utility from adding another adult descendant in generation i, while holding fixed the total consumption C_i of that generation.[9] As discussed earlier, this marginal utility must be positive near an optimal position, which implies that $1 - \varepsilon - \sigma(c_i) > 0$ (see expression (5S.11)).

Equation (5S.13) appears to imply that consumption is positive only when children are a financial burden; that is, when the cost of rearing a child exceeds the present value of his *lifetime* earnings. Since this condition may not hold in many countries, especially modern ones, our approach seems to have a serious flaw. The apparent difficulty arises from the neglect of investments in human capital.

To see this, interpret k as the amount invested in children to raise their earnings, so that

$$w = e + (1 + r)k, \qquad (5S.15)$$

where r is the rate of return on investments in human capital (assumed constant for simplicity), and e represents earnings that are independent of these investments. The entire analysis goes through as before except that Eq. (5S.13) becomes

$$v(c_i)[1 - \varepsilon - \sigma(c_i)] = v'(c_i)[\overline{\beta}_{i-1}(1 + r_i) - e], \qquad (5S.13')$$

where $\overline{\beta}$ represents the child-rearing costs that do not involve human capital. The fixed component of earnings, e, is likely to be a small fraction of total earnings, especially in modern countries. Then it would be reasonable to suppose that the right side of Eq. (5S.13') is positive; that fixed costs of rearing children exceed the fixed component of earnings.

Practically all families invest in the human capital of children—a form of "bequest" that is far more common than transfers of assets. Discussions that consider capital accumulations over the life cycle to be much more important than capital bequests usually neglect the sizable "bequests" to children through investments in their human capital (see for example Modigliani, 1986).

When we use the definition of σ_i, Eq. (5S.13) becomes

$$\frac{c_i[1 - \varepsilon - \sigma(c_i)]}{\sigma(c_i)} = \beta_{i-1}(1 + r_i) - w_i, \qquad i = 1, 2, \ldots \quad (5S.16)$$

---

9. Differentiate the appropriate term in Eq. (5S.10) with respect to N_i while holding fixed C_i. Aside from the factor $\alpha^i(N_i)^{-\varepsilon}$, the result is the left side of Eq. (5S.13).

The left side would be proportional to c_i if $\sigma(c_i)$ were constant. Otherwise, we assume that $\sigma(c_i)$ either falls or increases slowly enough with c_i that the left side is increasing in c_i. Then Eq. (5S.16) implies that c_i is a positive function of the net cost of producing another descendant in generation i. That is, each person is endowed with a higher level of consumption when people are more costly to produce. In effect, it pays to raise the "utilization rate" of each descendant (in the sense of a higher c_i) when their costs of production are greater.

The results imply that consumption per person, c_i, would rise across generations only if the net cost of creating descendants also rose. In contrast, the usual models of optimal consumption over time imply that consumption grows (or falls) over time if the real interest rate exceeds (or is less than) the rate of time preference. In our analysis the rate of growth across generations of consumption per person is essentially independent of the level of interest rates, and also does not depend on pure altruism or time preference.

Changes in the level of interest rates or in the degree of altruism mainly affect fertility, n_i. We can rewrite Eq. (5S.12) to solve for the fertility rate:

$$n_i = \left[\frac{\alpha(1 + r_{i+1})v'(c_{i+1})}{v'(c_i)} \right]^{1/\varepsilon}, \qquad i = 0, 1, \ldots \qquad (5S.17)$$

Equation (5S.16) pegs the intertemporal-substitution term, $v'(c_{i+1})/v'(c_i)$, for $i = 1, 2, \ldots$, because c_i in each future generation depends only on the net cost of producing descendants. With substitution in consumption pegged, the fertility rate n_i for $i = 1, 2, \ldots$, rises with increases in the interest rate, r_{i+1}, or the pure rate of altruism, α.

In life-cycle analyses, higher interest rates raise the rate of growth over time in consumption. Our analysis implies that higher interest rates raise the level but not the rate of growth of consumption per descendant; see Eq. (5S.13). But since steady-state fertility increases from Eq. (5S.12), the rate of growth across generations in the total consumption of descendants does increase when interest rates rise.

The increase in fertility may seem surprising, in that one might have expected "investment demand" n_i to vary inversely with the cost of capital, r_{i+1}. The utility of each child (U_{i+1}), however, and hence the marginal utility of an additional child rise when consumption per descendant increases. In the steady state this rise in marginal utility dominates the increase in the cost of capital.[10]

Another important property of the model concerns the effects of changes in wealth, which we represent by shifts in the initial assets k_0. Equation (5S.16) implies that future consumption per person, c_i, is unaffected if a shift in wealth does not change the net cost of raising children. Then Eq. (5S.17) implies that future fertility n_i for $i = 1$, $2, \ldots$, also does not change. With future consumption per capita and future fertility unchanged, the dynastic budget equation (5S.14) requires either initial consumption c_0 or fertility n_0 to change. Using Eq. (5S.17) for $i = 0$, we can see that an increase (or decrease) in c_0 must be accompanied by an increase (or decrease) in n_0. Therefore, wealthier persons would consume more and also would have larger families.

These results imply that an increase in inherited wealth increases only the scale of a dynastic family. The number of descendants N_i and aggregate consumption C_i in each future generation would increase only because of the increase in initial fertility n_0. To see the effect on N_i directly, recall that $N_i = n_0 n_1 \ldots n_{i-1}$ for $i = 1, 2, \ldots$ Substitution for each fertility rate from Eq. (5S.17) leads to

$$N_i = \left\{ \alpha^i \left[\frac{v'(c_i)}{v'(c_0)} \right]^i \prod_{j=1}^{i} (1 + r_j) \right\}^{1/\varepsilon}, \qquad i = 1, 2, \ldots \qquad (5S.18)$$

An increase in wealth raises c_0 and thereby lowers $v'(c_0)$. Since all future values of c_i are unchanged, Eq. (5S.18) implies that all values of N_i, $i \geq 1$, rise by an equal proportion.

---

10. If the cost of raising a child, β_i, is increasing in the number n_i, then the first-order condition associated with optimization over the number of children (that is, a modified form of Eq. 5S.13) does imply the usual investment-demand function. For a given value of c, an increase in r implies that a *lower* value of n satisfies this first-order condition (in the steady state). However, since c_i is constant in the steady state—or, more generally, if $v(\cdot)$ were homothetic and c_i grew at an exogenous rate in the steady state—the consumption arbitrage condition in Eq. (5S.12) still implies a positive steady-state relation between r and n. An increase in r implies enough of an increase in c that the increase in n is consistent with the downward-sloping investment-demand function (for a given c). These results do not change greatly if parents get direct service value from children, in the form $v(c_i, n_i)$. The first-order condition analogous to Eq. (5S.12) still ensures that r and n are positively related in the steady state. As long as parents and children are linked altruistically, this result tends to follow.

A somewhat surprising result (brought to our attention by Sanford Grossman) is that future capital per person, k_i for $i = 1, 2, \ldots$, is not affected by a change in wealth. This result follows from the dynastic budget constraint in Eq. (5S.14) because future consumption per person c_i and fertility n_i are unchanged. Put differently, bequests to *each* child are unaffected by a change in parent's wealth.

Wealth completely regresses to the mean between parents and each child because wealthier parents spend all of their additional resources on their own consumption and on raising larger families. A positive relation between wealth and fertility would help to explain why per capita wealth regresses to the mean across generations in the United States and other countries. Fortunately, the unrealistic implication of complete regression to the mean over one generation no longer holds when we drop some special assumptions about preferences and the cost of children (see below).

Our model also has surprising implications about the effects of changes in the cost of producing children on the demand for children. Consider a tax on raising children in generation j that raises β_j but does not change β_i, for $i \neq j$. Furthermore, to abstract from wealth effects, assume a compensating increase in initial assets, k_0, that leaves the marginal utility of wealth, $v'(c_0)$, unchanged. Equation (5S.16) indicates that c_{j+1} rises, whereas all other c_i do not change. Equation (5S.17) implies that n_j falls; after all, children are now more costly to produce in that generation. The surprising result is that n_{j+1} increases, and by an amount that exactly offsets the fall in n_j. The tax in generation j would not change the number of descendants after the $(j + 1)$st generation. The reason is that dynastic utility in Eq. (5S.10) is a time-separable function of the number of descendants and consumption in each generation. Dynastic utility does not depend explicitly on the fertility of any generation. As is well known, time-separable utility functions imply that the demand for a variable at time i depends only on the marginal utility of wealth and the prices of variables at time i. Consequently, for a given marginal utility of wealth, the number of descendants and consumption in the ith generation would not be affected by price changes in other generations.

Consider now a compensated, permanent increase in the cost of children that raises the net cost of children, $\beta_i(1 + r_{i+1}) - w_{i+1}$, by the same proportion for each generation $i \geq j$. Equation (5S.16) implies that consumption per person rises in generation $j + 1$ and in each subsequent generation. Further, if we now assume as an approximation that the elasticity of $v(c_i)$ with respect to c_i is the constant σ, then the increases in c_{j+1}, c_{j+2}, . . . are equiproportional. The arbitrage condition for consumption over time in Eq. (5S.12) simplifies in this case to

$$\left(\frac{c_{i+1}}{c_i}\right)^{1-\sigma} = \frac{\alpha(1 + r_{i+1})}{(n_i)^\varepsilon}, \qquad i = 0, 1, \ldots \qquad (5S.19)$$

Equiproportional increases in c_i for $i = j + 1$, . . . , imply that fertility in generation j falls (because c_{j+1}/c_j rises), while fertility in all subsequent generations is unchanged.

Consequently, given interest rates, even a permanent (compensated) tax on children reduces fertility only in the generation where the tax is first enacted. However, the decline in fertility in one generation alone has lasting effects on descendants—the relevant decision variable—because the number of descendants in all later generations also declines. Fertility, which is the rate of investment in the stock of descendants, is only temporarily affected by a permanent change in the cost of children.

A permanent increase in β_i also permanently raises consumption per person, c_i. With c_i and β_i higher, and with n_i unchanged (for $i > j$), expenditures by each descendant are higher in all generations after j. Higher levels of capital and bequests per person, k_i for $i > j$, are needed to support these higher expenditures.

If β, r, and w are stationary over time, and if σ and ε are constants, there exist unique steady-state values of n, c, and k equal to

$$n^* = \alpha^{1/\varepsilon}(1 + r)^{1/\varepsilon}, \qquad (5S.20)$$

$$c^* = [\sigma/(1 - \varepsilon - \sigma)] [\beta(1 + r) - w], \qquad (5S.21)$$

and
$$k^* = \frac{c^* + \beta n^* - w}{1 + r - n^*}. \qquad (5S.22)$$

These unique steady states are globally stable, and the steady state is reached in only one generation from any initial capital stock. The steady-state value of fertility depends positively on the interest rate and the degree of altruism and is independent of the cost of children and other parameters.

The steady-state level of consumption per descendant is positively related to the net cost of children, $\beta(1 + r) - w$. By contrast, in the usual life-cycle models the rate of growth over time in consumption is positively related to the interest rate. There is no steady-state level of consumption in these models except when the interest rate equals the rate of time preference.

Our results on steady states and one-generation dynamics are so striking that many readers of earlier versions have concluded that they depend critically on several assumptions: that the altruism function and the current period utility function have constant elasticities (ε and σ, respectively), that children do not provide consumption utility to parents (that $v_n = 0$), that children are not concerned about parents, and that the marginal cost of children is constant. Some of these assumptions are crucial for the one-generation dynamics, but they are *not* the source of the main properties of steady states. The crucial assumption is that the rate of altruism–time preference depends negatively on the number of children.[11] Given that assumption, it is sufficient to have the utility of children enter linearly in the parents' utility function (see the proof in Becker and Barro, 1986, pp. 20–22). We have seen that this specification amounts to the assumption that dynastic utility functions are time consistent and additively separable in the consumption of different generations.

Even in the general case, the steady-state value of n is unique if $a(n)$ is monotonic. We have not proved convergence to the steady state in the general case. But if $v_n = 0$ and $a(n) = \alpha n^{-\varepsilon}$, we can readily prove convergence when the marginal cost of children depends positively on the number of children (see the proof in section 2 of the appendix to Becker and Barro, 1986). Although steady states remain stable even when marginal costs are increasing, transitions between steady states now take several generations.

As an example of the dynamic effects that arise, consider an increase in initial assets k_0. When the marginal cost of children is constant, an increase in k_0 increases c_0 and n_0, but it does not change future values of c_i and n_i. If marginal costs are rising, an increase in n_0 increases c_1. Then an increase in c_1 raises n_1 (by Eq. 5S.12), which implies that c_2 increases, and so on. In this way the increase in wealth would raise consumption per person and fertility in several subsequent genera-

---

11. Uzawa (1968) and Epstein and Hynes (1983) also develop models where the rate of time preference is variable. In their cases the rate depends on the level of future consumption. In contrast to models with constant time preference, their models typically generate a steady-state level of consumption even when the interest rate is constant.

tions. These effects become smaller over time as the steady state is approached. Although consumption per person and assets per person still regress to the mean from parents to children, the process is no longer completed in a single generation. Clearly, this gradual process is more consistent with the empirical evidence.

The Great Depression, World War II, and the Baby Boom

The Great Depression featured a sharp decline in real incomes and wage rates. The cost of rearing children (β) may not have declined greatly, since few married women participated in the labor force (see Butz and Ward, 1979a). Indeed, if people perceived the depression as long-lasting, the net cost of rearing children, $\beta_i(1 + r_{i+1}) - w_{i+1}$, would have increased, since w_{i+1} declined and β_i changed little. Therefore, income and substitution effects would have reduced fertility during the Great Depression.

The diversion of resources to the military during World War II implied a reduction in wealth, which lowered fertility. The cost of rearing children, $\beta_i(1 + r_{i+1})$, increased relative to the prospective wage rate, w_{i+1}. This increase reflected the sharply higher labor force participation of women at relatively high current wages, the temporary absence of many young men who served in the armed forces, and perhaps also a high real rate of discount, r_{i+1}. The resulting temporary increase in net child-rearing costs also reduced fertility.

The same approach explains the baby boom after the protracted fertility decline during the Great Depression and World War II. If the increases in net child-rearing costs during these episodes were temporary, fertility would rise in the postwar period to make up for the births lost while fertility declined. We do not mean only that birth rates at older ages make up for lower birth rates at younger ages, as the literature on cohort fertility emphasizes. Our previous analysis shows that dynastic families replace in subsequent generations the births lost earlier when child-rearing costs were high.

Child Mortality and Social Security

The decline in fertility observed since the mid-nineteenth century in most Western countries has sometimes been explained partly by the

A Treatise on the Family

secular decline in child mortality that continued to reduce the number of births required to produce a target number of surviving children. Our analysis has novel implications about the effects of declines in child mortality on birth rates and the demand for surviving children.

Assume that wage rates and interest rates are stationary over time, and that parents ignore the uncertainty about child deaths and respond only to changes in the fraction p of offspring that survive childhood. Let β_s be the constant marginal cost of rearing a child to adulthood, and β_m be the cost of a child who dies prior to becoming an adult. The expected cost of n_b births is $[p\beta_s + (1 - p)\beta_m]n_b$. The ratio of this expected cost to the expected number of survivors ($n = pn_b$)—which corresponds to our previous cost per (surviving) child—is

$$\beta = \beta_s + \beta_m(1 - p)/p. \tag{5S.23}$$

As before, parents choose own consumption, the expected number of surviving children, and bequests to surviving children, but these choices are now subject to a budget constraint that depends on the expected cost β.

A permanent decline in the level of child mortality lowers the cost of raising surviving children in all generations. Our prior analysis implies that the demand for surviving children per adult (n_i) rises in the initial generation, but that it is no higher in later generations.[12] Since the demand for surviving children increases in the initial generation, birth rates may also rise then, although the higher probability of survival, p, reduces the number of births, n_b, needed to produce a given number of survivors. Birth rates definitely fall in later generations because the demand for surviving children in these generations would not be affected by the increase in p.

If child mortality continues to fall over time, the cost of rearing surviving children would continue to fall over time, and hence the demand for surviving children per adult would increase for more than one generation. The rate of decline in child mortality, however, must slow down once it approaches zero, as it has in the West during the past 50 years. As the rate of decline slows, the rate of decline in the cost of producing survivors also slows and eventually more or less

---

12. If the marginal cost of a child increases with the number of children, fertility increases for more than one generation when mortality rates fall permanently. Eventually, however, the demand for surviving children returns to its previous value.

ceases. Thereafter the *cumulative* increase in the child survival probability does not affect the demand for surviving children.

Our analysis explains why transitions to regimes of low child mortality have only temporary positive effects on rates of population growth. It can also explain why birth rates often rise before they decline (see the evidence in Dyson and Murphy, 1985), and why declines in birth rates initially lag behind declines in child mortality. Eventually the decline in birth rates must accelerate until the percentage decline from prior levels equals the percentage increase in the probability of surviving to adulthood.

Some of the secular decline in fertility has also been attributed to the growth in social security and other transfer payments to the elderly. Our model of altruistic families implies that *growing* public transfer payments to the elderly reduce the demand for children even when children do not support elderly parents.

The model is not set up to incorporate social security precisely, because we have only one period of adulthood. Therefore, a pay-as-you-go system of taxes on young working adults cannot finance payments to old adults. However, similar results obtain if we imagine (unrealistically) that levies on children finance transfers to adults.

Let s_i be the transfer received by the representative adult in generation i, and τ_{i+1} be the tax paid during generation i by each child (or by parents on behalf of their children). The government's budget is balanced if $s_i N_i = \tau_{i+1} N_{i+1}$, which implies that

$$\tau_{i+1} = s_i/n_i. \tag{5S.24}$$

For given values of fertility, the benefits from social security and the taxes to finance them have exactly offsetting effects on the dynastic wealth of the representative family. Therefore, if fertility were unchanged, a change in the scale of the social security program would not affect intergenerational patterns of consumption. Parents would use their social security benefits to pay their children's taxes; in a more general context, parents would raise their bequests sufficiently so that their children could pay these taxes without cutting back on their consumption (see Barro, 1974).

But the endogeneity of fertility modifies this so-called Ricardian Equivalence Theorem. An extra child in generation i pays the tax $\tau_{i+1} = s_i/n_i$ and receives the transfer s_{i+1} when he becomes an adult. Thus, the social security program imposes the lifetime cost per child of

$$\frac{s_i}{n_i} - \frac{s_{i+1}}{(1 + r_{i+1})}, \tag{5S.25}$$

where $s_{i+1}/(1 + r_{i+1})$ is the present value of the future transfer. The net tax is positive[13] with constant benefits per person ($s_{i+1} = s_i = s$) if $1 + r_{i+1} > n_i$. With a positive net tax, an increase in the scale of the social security program (an increase in s) raises the cost of children. This increase has the same substitution effect as an increase in the cost of raising a child, β. Therefore, our previous analysis of the effects of changes in the cost of children applies to social security.

For example, a permanent increase in the level of social security benefits is analogous to a permanent increase in β. Holding fixed the marginal utility of wealth, $v'(c_0)$, and the interest rate, we found that fertility declines in the initial generation while fertility in later generations does not change. Therefore, a permanent increase in social security benefits tends to reduce fertility temporarily even when children do not support their elderly parents.[14]

We also found before that a permanent increase in child-rearing costs would raise consumption and wealth per person in all future generations. In the same way, the positive effect of higher social security benefits on the cost of rearing children would raise "capital intensity." This conclusion is the opposite of the usual conclusion from life-cycle models, where social security lowers capital intensity (see for example Feldstein, 1974). That conclusion treats fertility as exogenous and neglects the interplay between consumption and intergenerational transfers.

Open Economies and Western Fertility

Our analysis applies to the determinants of fertility in an open economy, defined as an economy connected to an international capital market with a single real interest rate. Wages are determined separately

---

13. More generally, we need total social security payments to grow more slowly than the interest rate; that is, $n_i s_{i+1}/s_i < 1 + r_{i+1}$.

14. For discussions of the initial impact of social security on fertility, see Becker and Tomes (1976, note 15), Wildasin (1986), and Willis (1986). Mosher (1983, p. 241) notes that the Chinese government in recent years has encouraged rural collectives to establish social security programs, apparently for the purpose of reducing fertility.

in each economy because labor is assumed to be immobile across national boundaries. Wage rates would differ between economies with the same interest rate if production functions differed, if returns to scale were not constant, or if wages were taxed at different rates.

If the elasticity of the current period utility function is the constant σ and ε is the elasticity of the altruism function, then

$$\rho_i^j \approx \frac{\log(\alpha^j)}{\varepsilon^j} + \frac{r_{i+1}}{\varepsilon^j} - \left(\frac{1 - \sigma^j}{\varepsilon^j}\right)g_i^j, \qquad (5S.26)$$

where j refers to country j, r_{i+1} is the long-term real interest rate in generation $i + 1$, $n_i^j = 1 + \rho_i^j$, where ρ_i^j is the (natural) growth rate of the adult population in country j between generations i and $i + 1$, and g_i^j is the growth rate of consumption per person in country j between generations i and $i + 1$. The first term on the right side of (5S.26) indicates that population grows more rapidly in economies where parents are more altruistic (α^j). The second term shows that population growth is more rapid when the long-term world real interest rate is higher. The change in population growth exceeds the change in interest rates because $\varepsilon^j < 1$. For small values of ε^j, even moderate changes in long-term interest rates induce large changes in population growth rates. The term on the far right indicates that population grows more rapidly when consumption per person grows more slowly. Differences in population growth exceed differences in consumption growth because $(1 - \sigma^j)/\varepsilon^j > 1$ (see expression 5S.11).

The growth in consumption per person between generations equals the growth in the net cost of producing descendants. The latter is negatively related to growth in the probability of child survival, and it is positively related to the growth in social security benefits and other taxes on children. Presumably, faster technical progress raises the growth of consumption per person. Therefore, population growth should be lower in open economies that have more rapid technological progress, more rapid increases in social security benefits, and slower declines in child mortality.

These implications seem relevant to understanding the low fertility in Western countries since the late 1950s. Economic growth was rapid until the mid-1970s; specifically, the annual rate of growth in per capita real GDP averaged 3.7 percent per year from 1950 to 1980 in nine industrialized countries that include the United States (Barro, 1987, chap. 11). Child mortality in the West was already quite low by 1950 and did not improve much further. Social security payments and other transfers to adults expanded dramatically over the past 40 years. For example, per capita real social security payments in the United States and Great Britain grew by 7.5 and 5.0 percent per year, respectively, from 1950 to 1982 (see Hemming, 1984, and U.S. Bureau of the Census, 1965, 1984). Moreover, international real interest rates were low until the 1980s; real interest rates on short-term U.S. government securities averaged 1.8 percent per year from 1948 to 1980 after adjusting for anticipated inflation (see Barro, 1987, chap. 7).

All of these forces lowered fertility, especially since even small changes in their values are magnified into larger changes in fertility. Note too the implication that Western fertility will rise during the next decade if the higher real interest rates of the 1980s continue into the 1990s, if social security and other transfer payments grow more slowly—as eventually they must—and if the slowdown in economic growth that began in the 1980s continues.

Life Cycle and Aggregate Consumption

In this section we incorporate a full life cycle into the model to compare the determinants of consumption over the life cycle and between generations. We also show how aggregate consumption relates to life-cycle and generational consumption.

We continue to neglect uncertainty about age of death, but now assume that everyone lives for l years. A parent has all his children when h years old, where the value of h determines the length of a generation. Preferences are additive over the life cycle, with $v_j(c_{ij})$ being the utility from consumption, c_{ij}, at age j in generation i. These current-period utilities over the life cycle are discounted by the constant time-preference factor δ. Therefore, the utility generated by lifetime consumption in generation i is

$$v_i = \sum_{j=1}^{l} \delta^{j-i} v_j(c_{ij}).$$
(5S.27)

As before, the degree of altruism toward each child varies inversely with the number of children. Specifically, we again assume a constant elasticity function of the form $\tilde{\alpha}(n_i)^{-\varepsilon}$. Then the weight A_i attached to the utility of generation i in the dynastic utility function is

$$A_i = (\bar{\alpha}\delta^h)^i (N_i)^{-\varepsilon} = \alpha^i (N_i)^{-\varepsilon}. \qquad (5S.28)$$

The parameter α includes both altruism ($\bar{\alpha}$) and time preference (δ^h). Life-cycle utilities in Eq. (5S.27) are discounted only by time preference δ, whereas generational utilities in the dynastic utility function are discounted also by the degree of altruism toward descendants, $\bar{\alpha}$. Even if fully rational people do not discount the future ($\delta = 1$), the weight A_i need not equal unity because rational individuals might prefer their children's consumption to their own, or vice versa. They prefer their own consumption, for example, in biological models of gene maximization when a parent has only some genes in common with each offspring. Generational utilities—but not necessarily life-cycle utilities—must be discounted to bound dynastic utilities in the stationary state (where $n_i = 1$ and $c_{ij} = c_{kj}$, for all i,k).

When dynastic utility is maximized subject to dynastic resources with a full life cycle, the first-order conditions give the usual arbitrage relation for consumption over the life cycle and an arbitrage relation across generations; the latter is essentially the same as Eq. (5S.12). We can solve the arbitrage relations explicitly for the rates of growth of consumption between ages and generations if we again assume that the elasticity of utility with respect to consumption is the constant σ. Then the life-cycle arbitrage condition is

$$\frac{\gamma_{j+1}}{\gamma_j} \left(\frac{c_{ij}}{c_{i,j+1}} \right)^{i-\sigma} = \frac{1}{\delta(1+r)}, \quad \text{for all } i,j, \qquad (5S.29)$$

where γ_j is the utility weight assigned to consumption—that is, to $(c_{ij})^\sigma / \sigma$—at age j. (The value of γ would, for example, be small for young children.) The intergenerational condition is

$$\left(\frac{c_{ij}}{c_{i+1,j}} \right)^{1-\sigma} = \frac{n_i^\varepsilon}{\alpha(1+r)^h}, \quad \text{for all } i,j. \qquad (5S.30)$$

Equation (5S.16) now becomes

$$[(1 - \varepsilon - \sigma)/\sigma]\bar{c}_i = (1 + r)^h \beta_{i-1} - \bar{w}_i, \quad \text{for } i = 1, 2, \ldots \qquad (5S.31)$$

The present value of lifetime consumption and earnings in generation i ($\bar{c}_i$ and $\bar{w}_i$) replace consumption and earnings during adulthood in Eq. (5S.16). Equation (5S.31) implies that at each age, the rate of growth in consumption per descendant across generations equals the rate of growth between generations in the net cost of children. Notice that the equilibrium growth of consumption per descendant does not depend on time preference δ, the degree of altruism $\bar{\alpha}$, or the interest rate. By contrast, Eq. (5S.29) shows that the growth of consumption over the life cycle does not depend on the cost of children, but it does depend in the usual way on the interest rate and time preference. Therefore, even when parents are not "selfish" (say $\bar{\alpha} = 1$), the growth in consumption over the life cycle and the growth between generations are equal only by accident. We see again that models with reproducing generations have very different implications from models with infinitely lived individuals who do not reproduce.

The fertility rate in the ith generation is still given by Eq. (5S.17) except that now $\alpha = \bar{\alpha}\delta^h$. Fertility is positively related to the extent of altruism $\bar{\alpha}$, the time-preference factor δ, and the interest rate r. Fertility is also affected negatively by the growth between generations in the net cost of producing children. Note that expenditures by parents on the consumption of children are not part of the costs that determine the demand for children by altruistic parents, and that no distinction exists between the earnings of children while under the authority of their parents and their earnings while on their own.[15]

The change in per capita consumption between two time periods is the sum of the changes for individuals of different ages:

$$\frac{\Delta c_t}{c_t} = \sum_{j=0}^{l} \left| \left(\frac{c_{jt}}{c_t} \right) \Delta \theta_{jt} + v_{jt} \left(\frac{\Delta c_{jt}}{c_{jt}} \right) \right| . \qquad (5S.32)$$

The term c_t is consumption per capita at time t, c_{jt} is the consumption of a person aged j at time t, $\theta_{jt} = N_{jt}/N_t$, with N_{jt} the number of persons aged j at time t and N_t the total population, and $v_{jt} = \theta_{jt}c_{jt}/c_t$ is the proportion of total consumption accounted for by persons of age j. The symbol Δ denotes the change in a variable between the two time periods, and we assume that all persons of a given age are identical.

The first term on the right side of this equation depends on the change over time in the age distribution of the population. This term is zero in a demographic steady state (where $\Delta \theta_{jt} = 0$ for all j). A basic theorem of demography states that a closed population with constant age-specific birth and death rates eventually approaches a demographic steady state (see for example Coale et al., 1983).

---

15. Empirical studies of the cost of children typically include all expenditures on their consumption to a particular age, such as age eighteen, net of their earnings to that age (see for instance Espenshade, 1984), without much discussion of why this is the appropriate measure when studying the demand for children.

The second term on the right side of Eq. (5S.32) depends on the growth of consumption between generations, which is determined by the growth in the cost of children. If the net cost of children grows at the constant rate g, then Eq. (5S.32) implies that steady-state per capita consumption also grows at that rate. The rate of growth of steady-state per capita consumption would then be independent of time preference, the degree of altruism, and the interest rate, and it would depend only on the rate of growth of the cost of children.

Many have recognized that when the age distribution is constant, changes over time in per capita consumption are independent of changes in consumption over a finite life cycle (see Modigliani, 1986). Some studies model the representative person as if he lives forever to justify life-cycle interpretations of the determinants of aggregate consumption. The procedure has been rationalized by the assumption that parents are altruistic toward children (Summers, 1981, p. 537). But we do not know of studies that have found the strong relation between long-term real interest rates and long-term rates of growth in per capita consumption implied by life-cycle models.

Altruism can justify the assumption that heads of dynastic families effectively have infinite lives. But endogenous fertility greatly alters the implications of parental altruism. In our model the path of steady-state consumption per descendant is independent of time preference and long-term real interest rates because fertility fully absorbs the effects of these variables. As a result, long-term changes of per capita consumption do not depend on long-term real interest rates or on time preference, even though each dynastic family effectively lives forever.

This supplement develops the implications of parental altruism toward children, where the utility of parents depends on their own consumption, their fertility, and the utility of each child. Altruism toward children implies that the welfare of all generations of a family are linked through a dynastic utility function that depends on the consumption, fertility, and number of descendants in all generations. The head of a dynastic family acts as if he maximizes dynastic utility subject to a dynastic resource constraint that depends on the wealth inherited by the head, the cost of rearing children, and earnings in all generations.

Utility maximization requires equality between the marginal benefit of an additional descendant and the net cost of producing that descendant. Costs depend negatively on lifetime earnings of children and positively on the costs of rearing children and of investing in their human capital. This optimization condition implies a positive relation between consumption per descendant and the net cost of creating a descendant.

Utility maximization also implies an arbitrage condition for consumption over generations. According to this condition, fertility—not the growth of consumption per descendant—responds to variations in interest rates and the degree of altruism. If the cost of rearing descendants is constant over time, fertility depends *only* on interest rates (positively), the time-preference factor (positively), and the degree of altruism (positively). More generally, fertility also is negatively related to the growth in net costs between generations.

A permanent tax on children beginning in generation i lowers fertility in generation i because the tax raises the cost of rearing children then, relative to the cost in other generations. If interest rates are unchanged, fertility in all generations after i is unaffected because the cost of rearing children is equally higher in all these generations. For the same reason, a permanent reduction in the mortality rate initially raises population growth, and a permanent expansion of social security initially lowers fertility, but neither change has a permanent effect on fertility if interest rates are unchanged.

Real interest rates are given if an economy is linked to an international capital market. We show that fertility in such an open economy depends positively on the world's long-term real interest rate. Fertility also depends negatively on the rate of technological progress and the growth rate of transfer payments in this economy. We speculate that this analysis is relevant to understanding why fertility has declined in Western countries since the mid-fifties.

In our model the rate of change in consumption over the life cycle depends in the standard way on interest rates and time preference, whereas the rate of change in per capita consumption over a generation does not depend on interest rates or time preference. Therefore, the rate of change over time in an economy's steady-state per capita consumption would not depend on long-term interest rates.

We have neglected uncertainty, marriage, and the spacing of births. Especially important is the idea that parents are linked to children through operative intergenerational transfers. Nevertheless, even a highly simplified model of the behavior of dynastic families appears to capture important aspects of the long-term behavior of fertility and consumption. If it does, a new approach is warranted to the analysis of trends and long-term fluctuations in fertility, population growth, and consumption.

CHAPTER 6

Family Background and the Opportunities of Children

Chapter 5 shows that expenditures on children are determined by the income and preferences of parents, the number of children, and the cost of child quality. The well-being of children is determined by these expenditures, the reputation and contacts of their family, their genetic inheritance, and the values and skills absorbed through membership in a particular family culture. Children from successful families are more likely to be successful themselves by virtue of the additional time spent on them and also their superior endowments of culture and genes.

This chapter systematically analyzes the influence of family expenditures and endowments on the income of children. A simple model first relates their income to the income and endowment of their parents, good or bad luck, and other variables. Investments in human capital are then distinguished from bequests and gifts of nonhuman capital, because human capital must be self-financed and rates of return on human capital are more sensitive to endowments and other personal variables.

Even children with the same parents often have quite different incomes because their luck differs and because the composition and level of parental investments depend on the abilities, handicaps, sex, and other characteristics of children. This neglected subject of inequality among siblings is discussed next, with the emphasis on whether parents prefer boys to girls and whether they magnify or narrow the differences between abler and less able children.

The effect of endowments on the interaction between the quantity and quality of children is considered, and we see that an increase in the endowment reduces the amount spent on each child and increases the number of children. I show why persons coming from prosperous families have fewer children, and why persons with many siblings appear to have more children than others with the same preferences, incomes, and prices.

Determination of Income

Each person is assumed to live for two "generations": he is a child during the first generation, when his parents invest time and other resources in his adult productivity; he is an adult during the second generation, when he produces income, consumes, and invests in his own children. The utility of parents is assumed to depend on their own consumption and the quality of their children, where quality is measured by the adult wealth of children. Wealth differs from expenditures on children, the measure of quality in the previous chapter, because some expenditures raise the consumption of children rather than their adult wealth, and because wealth is determined in part by endowments and other considerations. The quality of children so measured is not the same as the adult utility of children, which may depend on the quality of their own children, as we shall see in note H of the Mathematical Appendix to Chapter 7.

The utility function of parents in the tth generation would be

$$U_t = U(Z_t, I_{t+1}), \tag{6.1}$$

where Z_t is their consumption and I_{t+1} is the adult wealth of their children in the next generation. The interaction between quantity and quality of children is ignored for the moment by assuming that parents have only one child, and the distinction between human and nonhuman capital is temporarily neglected by assuming that all capital is homogeneous. If y_t is the investment in each child and π_t is the consumption foregone (Z_t) per unit of y_t acquired, the budget equation of parents would be

$$Z_t + \pi_t y_t = I_t, \tag{6.2}$$

where I_t is their wealth. If the value of each unit of capital in generation $t + 1$ is w_{t+1}, the rate of return on investments in the tth generation is defined by the equation

$$\pi_t y_t = \frac{w_{t+1} y_t}{1 + r_t}, \tag{6.3}$$

where r_t is the rate of return per generation, which may encompass 20 or more years.

The total capital of children equals the sum of the capital invested in them, their endowment, e_{t+1}, and their "capital gain" due to luck in the market sector, u_{t+1}. Since all capital is homogeneous, the wealth of children equals

$$I_{t+1} = w_{t+1} y_t + w_{t+1} e_{t+1} + w_{t+1} u_{t+1}. \tag{6.4}$$

Government taxation is ignored until Chapter 7, so no distinction need be made between before-tax and after-tax wealth. Since wealth can be converted into "permanent" income streams, I treat Z_t and I_t as stationary flows of consumption and income within a generation,[1] although the basic analysis applies more directly to wealth and present values of flows.

If Eqs. (6.3) and (6.4) are substituted into (6.2), the budget constraint can be written in terms of Z_t and I_{t+1}, the variables entering the utility function:

$$Z_t + \frac{I_{t+1}}{1 + r_t} = I_t + \frac{w_{t+1} e_{t+1}}{1 + r_t} + \frac{w_{t+1} u_{t+1}}{1 + r_t} = S_t. \tag{6.5}$$

Parental consumption and income of children are determined not by parental income alone, but also by discounted value of endowment and luck of children. The sum of these values, denoted by S_t, will be called "family income."[2]

---

1. For discussions of life-cycle decisions, here ignored, see Ghez and Becker (1975), Heckman (1976), or Blinder and Weiss (1976).
2. Family income is a special case of "social income" in the theory of social interactions; see Becker (1974b).

Parents maximize their utility with respect to Z_t and I_{t+1} subject to their expectations about family income. If they correctly anticipate both the endowment and the market luck of their child, the equilibrium conditions are given by Eq. (6.5) and by

$$\frac{\partial U}{\partial Z_t} \bigg/ \frac{\partial U}{\partial I_{t+1}} = 1 + r_t. \tag{6.6}$$

If the utility function is assumed to be homothetic so that Z_t and I_{t+1} both have unitary family income elasticities, these equilibrium conditions determine demand functions for Z_t, I_{t+1}, and y_t that are linear in S_t:

$$\frac{I_{t+1}}{1 + r_t} = \alpha(\delta, 1 + r)S_t,$$

$$Z_t = (1 - \alpha)S_t, \tag{6.7}$$

and $\quad \dfrac{1}{1 + r_t} w_{t+1}y_t = \alpha S_t - \dfrac{1}{1 + r_t} w_{t+1}e_{t+1} - \dfrac{1}{1 + r_t} w_{t+1}u_{t+1}.$

The parameter δ measures the preference for the income of children relative to own consumption, and $\partial\alpha/\partial(1 + r) \gtreqless 0$ as the elasticity of substitution between Z_t and I_{t+1} in the utility function exceeds, equals, or falls short of unity.

The equilibrium condition given by Eq. (6.6) assumes that the rate of return is independent of the amount invested in children, and that parents can consume more than their own income by leaving a debt to be paid by their children. Both assumptions are maintained until human capital is distinguished from nonhuman capital.

By substitution of the definition of family income into (6.7), the generating equation for the income of children can be written as

$$\begin{aligned}
I_{t+1} &= \alpha(1 + r_t)I_t + \alpha w_{t+1}e_{t+1} + \alpha w_{t+1}u_{t+1} \\
&= \beta_t I_t + \alpha w_{t+1}e_{t+1} + \alpha w_{t+1}u_{t+1}
\end{aligned} \tag{6.8}$$

where $\beta_t = \alpha(1 + r_t)$. Also,

$$w_{t+1}y_t = \beta_t I_t - (1 - \alpha)w_{t+1}e_{t+1} - (1 - \alpha)w_{t+1}u_{t+1}. \tag{6.8'}$$

If parents correctly anticipate their children's luck and endowment, an increase in either would not add an equal amount to the income of children, because part of the increase would be spent on parental consumption through reduced investment in children; this can be seen from the negative relation of y_t to e_{t+1} (or u_{t+1}). Equation (6.8) shows that the equilibrium relation between I_{t+1} and e_{t+1} (and u_{t+1}) depends on α, the fraction of S_t that is spent on children. This equation also shows that I_{t+1} is related to I_t through β_t, which can be called the "propensity to invest in children." This propensity links the incomes of parents and children and is one of the important building blocks in the analysis of inequality and intergenerational mobility in the next chapter.

The concept of the endowment is a fundamental part of the analysis. Children are assumed to receive endowments of capital that are determined by the reputation and "connections" of their families; the contribution of the genetic constitutions of parents to the ability, race, and other characteristics of children; and the learning, skills, and goals acquired through belonging to a particular family culture. Obviously, endowments depend on many characteristics of parents, grandparents, and other family members, and may also be "culturally" influenced by other families.

A linear endowment-generating equation can be written as

$$e^c_{t+1} = \sum_{j=0}^{m} f_j \bar{e}_{t-j} + h_p e^p_t + \sum_{k \in f} \sum_{j=0}^{m} h_{jk} e^k_{t-j} + q^c_p + \sum_{k \in f} q^c_k + v_{t+1}, \quad (6.9)$$

where e^c_{t+1} is the endowment of a child with a parental endowment equal to e^p_t, e^k_{t-j} is the endowment of the kth member of his family in generation $t - j$, h_p and h_{jk} measure the fractions of e^p_t and e^k_{t-j} respectively that are transmitted to ("inherited by") this child, $\bar{e}_{t-j}$ is the average endowment in generation $t - j$, and the term $f_j \bar{e}_{t-j}$ is a simple way to incorporate the influence of the culture, or social capital, of all families in generation $t - j$. (For a formulation of cultural transmission along these lines, see Cavalli-Sforza and Feldman, 1973.) The terms q^c_p and Σq^c_k represent expenditures by parents and by all other family members respectively that directly raise the child's endowment, and v_{t+1} is the stochastic determinant of his endowment. By substituting Eq. (6.9) into (6.8), we see that the income of children is greater, the greater the income and propensity to invest of parents, the endowments of parents and other family members, the inheritability of endowments, and the expenditures on endowments of children by different members of their family.

Expenditures on endowments enter the endowment-generating equation both directly (through q^c_p and Σq^c_k) and indirectly (as determinants of h_p and h_{jk}). These expenditures differ from other expenditures on children (the y_t) mainly because the latter are "private capital'' that benefits only the recipients, whereas expenditures on endowments are "family capital" that benefits all members. That is to say, only parents would be willing to contribute to the y_t, inasmuch as they alone are assumed to be directly concerned about the well-being of children, whereas uncles, aunts, cousins, and other relatives may be willing to contribute to endowments because these have external effects benefiting all members.

However, these relatives must be induced to contribute their appropriate shares because each may try to free-ride on the endowment expenditures of others. Fortunately, the optimal investment in family capital is more readily attained than is the optimal investment in public goods (Samuelson, 1955) because the value of family capital to any member is likely to be known by other members. Moreover, families often appoint a "head," who coordinates expenditures on family capital and other family projects.[3]

The endowment of children is more closely related to the endowments of parents than to the endowments of other relatives ($h_p > h_{jk}$). Parents are most closely related genetically to children and usually are also closer environmentally, although grandparents, uncles and aunts, and even great-grandparents had almost as large an influence in some kinship groups of earlier times. The differences between modern nuclear families and the more extended families of the past indicate that inheritability is not rigidly determined by intrinsic properties of the biological and cultural process, but is partly subject to the control of families.

Inheritability can be increased by supervising the upbringing, training, and occupational, marital, and other choices of children to ensure that their behavior is suited to the social standing of their parents, grandparents, uncles, aunts, and other relatives. Families have more incentive to engage in costly supervision if outsiders must rely heavily on family background in assessing skills and other characteristics of persons because direct information is not available (see Chapters 10 and 11). Relatives other than parents are willing to contribute to supervisory efforts because they and their kin benefit when a niece or nephew, for instance, enhances the reputation of the family.

Reliance on family background for information about individuals has significantly decreased during the last few centuries in light of examinations, enforceable contracts, and other direct methods developed to

---

3. Chapter 8 discusses the role of the head in organizing family decisions.

assess skills, trustworthiness, and other characteristics, and to protect against mistaken assessments. Since grandparents, uncles and aunts, and the like now have less incentive to invest in the endowments of their younger relatives, the decreasing importance of these relatives is not surprising.

Unusual ability, motivation, or handicaps are often revealed prior to the time when most investments in children are committed, so families may be able to anticipate fully the endowment luck of their children (v_{t+1} in Eq. 6.9). The market luck of children, however, is determined by fluctuations in production possibilities and the prices of goods and factors of production that are usually revealed only after children have received their educations and much of their other training and entered the labor force. Families usually must commit most of their investment before they know much about their children's market luck.

If families can fully anticipate the endowed luck but not the market luck of children, and if parents do not care about risk[4] and maximize a utility function that depends on their own consumption and the expected income of children, then the equilibrium expected income of children would be proportional to expected family income:

$$E_t(I_{t+1}) = \beta_t E_t(S_t) = \beta_t I_t + \alpha w_{t+1} e_{t+1};$$

hence

$$I_{t+1} = \beta_t I_t + \alpha w_{t+1} e_{t+1} + w_{t+1} u_{t+1}, \tag{6.8}$$

and

$$w_{t+1} y_t = \beta_t I_t - (1 - \alpha) w_{t+1} e_{t+1}, \tag{6.8'}$$

where E_t represents expectations on the basis of information available at time t. The only difference between Eqs. (6.8) and $\overline{(6.8)}$ is in the coefficient of market luck. Increased investment cannot partially offset bad luck and reduced investment cannot partially nullify good luck if luck cannot be anticipated. Hence the coefficient of market luck is raised from α in the equation for I_{t+1} in (6.8) to unity in $\overline{(6.8)}$, and from $-(1 - \alpha)$ in the equation for y_t in (6.8') to zero in $\overline{(6.8')}$.

Human and Nonhuman Capital

A constant rate of return on investments in children is not a bad first approximation for nonhuman capital. Its rate is determined in efficient

---

4. If parents care about risk, their investments are affected by the third derivative of their utility function; see Loury (1976).

markets and is largely independent of the personal characteristics of investors. The rate of return on human capital, however, is significantly influenced by the sex, race, ability, age, allocation of time, social background, and many other characteristics of children. Moreover, investments in human capital are usually financed by parents (or self-financed), because human capital is not good collateral for loans. Therefore, instead of a single efficient market, a separate market exists for the human capital invested in each person.

I continue to assume that the rate of return on nonhuman capital is the same for everyone, but I now assume that rates on human capital decline as more is invested in a person (rate dependence on personal and family characteristics will be considered shortly). Since even families having little attachment to children generally invest a nonnegligible amount in the nutrition, shelter, and other human capital of their surviving children (otherwise they would not survive)—but not in the nonhuman capital of these children—the rate of return on a small investment in human capital is presumably higher than the rate on nonhuman capital.

Families investing little in their children would then invest entirely in human capital. Since the marginal rate of return on human capital declines as more is invested, it would eventually equal the constant rate on nonhuman capital. Additional investments would be put into nonhuman capital, where the constant rate of return would exceed the marginal rate on human capital.

If we also assume that human capital is entirely financed by parents, and that no investments are made in endowments (family capital), then our analysis implies that the income-generating equation of children whose parents invest only in their human capital would be

$$I_{t+1} = \alpha(1 + r_t^h)I_t + \alpha w_{t+1}(e_{t+1} + u_{t+1}),$$

and $\quad w_{t+1}y_t^h = \alpha(1 + r_t^h)I_t - (1 - \alpha)w_{t+1}(e_{t+1} + u_{t+1}),$

(6.10)

where r_t^h is the average rate of return on y_t^h invested in human capital. Clearly, $dr_t^h/dy_t^h < 0$ and $r_t^h > r_t^n$, where r_t^n is the market rate on nonhuman capital. This equation is not linear in the income of parents because r_t^h declines as I_t increases, since y_t^h increases as I_t does.

The income-generating equation of parents investing in both the human and nonhuman capital of their children would be

$$I_{t+1} = \alpha(1 + r_t^n)I_t + \alpha w_{t+1}(e_{t+1} + u_{t+1})$$

$$+ \alpha w_{t+1}\bar{y}_t^h \frac{(\bar{r}_t^h - r_t^n)}{1 + \bar{r}_t^h},$$

(6.11)

where $\bar{r}_t^h$ is the average rate of return on human capital when the amount invested equals $\bar{y}_t^h$. The marginal rate of return on both kinds of capital is r_t^n. The income-generating equation is again linear in I_t because marginal investments are in nonhuman capital with a constant rate of return equal to r_t^n.

"Rich" families can be defined by whether they invest in both human and nonhuman capital. The dividing line is determined by parental preferences, the rate on nonhuman capital, the relation between the rate on human capital and the amount invested, and the correlation between the income of parents and the endowments of their children. Although practically all families in the United States invest in the health, education, and other human capital of children, Blinder (1973) estimates that less than 40 percent also invest significantly in their nonhuman capital.

The term "inheritance" is commonly restricted to gifts and bequests of nonhuman capital, although an analytically more satisfactory concept would also include the human capital invested in children. Figure 6.1 plots the relation between the inheritance of human and nonhuman capital and the income of parents implied by the analysis in this section. Children inherit both nonhuman and human capital when the incomes of parents exceed I^r and only human capital when incomes are less than I^r. Moreover, the inheritance of human capital is independent of incomes above I^r and is closely dependent on incomes below I^r,

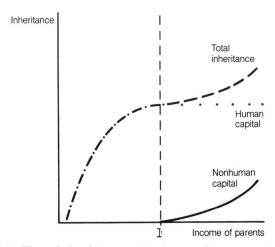

FIGURE 6.1   The relation between inheritance of human and nonhuman capital and income of parents; I^r represents the income when parents begin to invest in nonhuman capital.

A Treatise on the Family

whereas the inheritance of nonhuman capital is independent of incomes below I^r and closely dependent on incomes above I^r. The empirical evidence for the United States is consistent with these implications: the education of children is more dependent on the incomes of parents when nonhuman capital is not inherited than when it is inherited (Tomes, 1979), and the inequality in the earnings of children is greater among poorer than among richer families, whereas the inequality in inheritance as usually measured is much greater among richer families.

Marginal rates of return on human capital invested in children from poorer families exceed the market rate of return on nonhuman capital because poorer families cannot readily borrow to finance their investments. Public (or private) policies that improve access to the capital market by poorer families—perhaps a loan program to finance education and other training with repayments tied to the income tax system (Friedman, 1955; Shell et al., 1968)—would increase the efficiency of society's investments in human capital while equalizing opportunity and reducing inequality (Becker, 1967, 1975). Contrast these effects with those of a progressive income tax, considered in the next chapter.

Compensation and Reinforcement of Differences among Children

Although parents sometimes treat their children differently—for example, the eldest son inherits the entire landed estate under primogeniture, and daughters often have received less schooling than sons—children treated better may not be "preferred" to their siblings. To show this and to separate preferences from opportunities, I assume that parents are neutral among their children. That is, if their utility function is

$$U_t = U(Z_t, I_{t+1}^1, I_{t+1}^2, \ldots, I_{t+1}^n), \qquad (6.12)$$

where I_{t+1}^i is the adult income of the ith child, and the number of children (n) is given, the marginal rate of substitution between I_{t+1}^i and I_{t+1}^j is less than unity only when $I_{t+1}^i > I_{t+1}^j$, and equals unity only when $I_{t+1}^i = I_{t+1}^j$:

$$\frac{\partial U}{\partial I_{t+1}^i} \bigg/ \frac{\partial U}{\partial I_{t+1}^j} \lesseqqgtr 1 \quad \text{as } I_{t+1}^i \gtreqqless I_{t+1}^j. \qquad (6.13)$$

Clearly, so-called neutral parents favor their less fortunate children, regardless of their sex, birth order, or other characteristics, because the marginal utility from children with lower income always exceeds the marginal utility from children with higher income.

If r_t^i is the rate of return from additional investments in the ith child, utility is maximized when

$$\frac{\partial U}{\partial I_{t+1}^i} \bigg/ \frac{\partial U}{\partial I_{t+1}^j} = \frac{1 + r_t^j}{1 + r_t^i}. \tag{6.14}$$

Equations (6.13) and (6.14) together imply that the equilibrium income of the ith child exceeds the incomes of other children if, and only if, the marginal rate of return on the ith child exceeds the marginal rate on other children.

Even children with the same parents are born with different defects and abilities, and have different accidents, luck, and other experiences as they interact with their environment; stated formally, they have different values of market luck (u) and endowed luck (v) in Eqs. (6.8) and (6.9). Do neutral parents exacerbate the differences among their children by investing more in better endowed and luckier children, or do they compensate their less fortunate children? If parents invest in both the nonhuman and human capital of children, the marginal rate of return is the same for all children and equals the market rate on nonhuman capital. Equations (6.13) and (6.14) then imply that incomes also are the same for all children: neutral parents would fully compensate their less fortunate children.

Rates of return on human capital are likely to be higher for abler children because they benefit more from additional human capital; that is,

if $r_t^{*h} = f(y_t^h, e_{t+1})$,   then $\dfrac{\partial f}{\partial y_t^h} < 0$ and $\dfrac{\partial f}{\partial e_{t+1}} > 0$,   (6.15)

where r^{*h} is the marginal rate of return on human capital. Since r^{*h} must equal r^n (the market rate on nonhuman capital) when parents invest in both kinds of capital, additional human capital would be invested in better-endowed children to reduce their marginal rates to the lower rates on other children: $r_t^{*h_i} = r_t^{*h_j} = r_t^n$ implies $y_t^{h_i} > y_t^{h_j}$ if $e_{t+1}^i > e_{t+1}^j$. Therefore, differences in earnings would exceed differences in endowments because investments in human capital reinforce the differences in endowments. However, incomes tend to be equal because investments in nonhuman capital offset fully the differences in endowments and human capital.

Stated algebraically, if

$$I_{t+1}^i \equiv w_{t+1}(e_{t+1}^i + u_{t+1}^i) + w_{t+1}y_t^{h_i} + w_{t+1}y_t^{n_i} = I_{t+1}^i, \\ \text{where} \quad I_{t+1}^j \equiv w_{t+1}(e_{t+1}^j + u_{t+1}^j) + w_{t+1}y_t^{h_j} + w_{t+1}y_t^{n_j}, \quad \Bigg\} \quad (6.16)$$

then

$$y_t^{n_j} - y_t^{n_i} = (e_{t+1}^i - e_{t+1}^j) + (y_t^{h_i} - y_t^{h_j}) + (u_{t+1}^i - u_{t+1}^j). \quad (6.17)$$

Differences in nonhuman capital, given by the left-hand side of (6.17), fully offset differences in endowments and human capital, given by the right-hand side.

The conclusions are more ambiguous for poorer families, who invest only in the human capital of their children. If the same amount were invested in each child, marginal rates of return would be higher for better-endowed children, while marginal utilities would be higher for the worse-endowed. More human capital would be invested in the better-endowed only if differences in rates of return exceeded differences in marginal utilities as defined in Eq. (6.14). Poorer families have a conflict between equity and efficiency and invest more in abler children only if efficiency outweighs equity. Hence the inequality in earnings among siblings would tend to be smaller in poorer than in richer families at the same time that the inequality in total income would be larger in poorer families.

The conflict between efficiency and equity is reduced when abler children are altruistic and are concerned about the welfare of their siblings, a situation to be considered in Chapter 8. Poorer families then could also gain the efficiency of investing more human capital in abler children without sacrificing the interests of other children, for the abler would voluntarily transfer resources to the others when they became adults. Even if abler children were not altruistic, poorer families would invest more in them if they "agreed" to look after their siblings, agreements that could be enforced by the legal system or by social norms.

The presumption, then, is that poorer families also invest more human capital in abler children, although the relation would be weaker than in richer families. The empirical evidence for the United States does indicate that abler siblings are more educated and have higher earnings, especially in richer families (Griliches, 1979; Tomes, 1980a).

In (richer) families that contribute nonhuman capital to all children, the amount invested in human capital depends only on a child's own characteristics and is not directly dependent on either the number or the abilities of his siblings. Gifts and bequests of nonhuman capital,

however, are greater when siblings are abler because nonhuman capital is always compensating. In poorer families the amount invested
in human capital directly depends on the abilities (as well as the
number) of siblings, because poorer parents must choose between the
equity and the efficiency of their investments. A poorer child would be
better off with abler siblings if the incomes of different children were
not close substitutes in his parents' utility function, if abler children
were altruistic to siblings or would agree to compensate siblings, or if
less able children were to learn more from abler siblings.[5]

"Compensatory education has been tried and it apparently has
failed . . . The chief goal of compensatory education—to remedy the
educational lag of disadvantaged children and thereby narrow the
achievement gap between 'minority' and 'majority' pupils—has been
utterly unrealized in any of the large compensatory education programs that have been evaluated so far" (Jensen, 1969). So begins
Arthur Jensen's famous and controversial essay on compensatory education and intelligence. His assertion about the failure of compensatory
education has been less controversial than his linking the apparent failure of such programs to inferior intelligence of the children being compensated, primarily black children. My analysis has nothing to add
directly to the controversy about the relative intelligence of different
groups of children, but it is indirectly relevant because the supposed
failure of compensatory education can be explained even when the
children involved are as able as other children, *especially when the
control group contains siblings of participating children.*

Public compensatory education programs redistribute resources to
some children in poor families. An increase in the public resources
spent on these children would induce parents concerned with equity to
redistribute time and other expenditures away from these children
toward other children and themselves. That is, an induced "parental

---

5. Zvi Griliches (1979) suggests that differences between the amounts invested in the human capital of siblings are smaller than differences between the
investments in unrelated children with equal differences in ability. My analysis
implies, however, that the human capital invested in a richer child would depend only on his own characteristics and not on those of siblings. My analysis
supports Griliches' suggestion for poorer families only if equity dominates efficiency in these families. See the extended theoretical analysis of these issues in
Sheshinski and Weiss (1982) and Tomes (1980a). Equity does appear to dominate in the small sample of poorer families that Tomes analyzes. (I am grateful
to Griliches for helpful correspondence on the content of this note.)

compensatory program'' offsets these programs, as it also offsets public health programs (Scrimshaw, 1978, pp. 391, 395) and food supplements to pregnant women (Jacobson, 1980). If taxes to finance these programs were levied entirely on other families, the resources of families with children participating in the programs would rise by the full amount of the expenditures on their children. Yet the total expenditure on these children would rise by only a fraction of these expenditures as a result of the induced decline in parental expenditures. The increase in the total expenditure on these children depends on the increase in family resources and the income elasticity of demand for children's welfare.

Parents might not reduce, and could even raise, their expenditures on participating children if these programs raised rates of return on parental expenditures. Still, however, the main effect of the programs is probably a redistribution of family expenditures away from the children participating, with a small net increase in the *total* expenditure on these children. These programs could then be classified as failures, since redistribution of income is not supposed to be their main purpose.

Thus the failure of compensatory programs can be explained without assuming that compensated children are inferior in ability or motivation; they could be above average. Nor does it imply that these programs are badly planned or administered; they could be better run than more nominally successful programs. What Jensen and others failed to realize is that family time and other resources would be allocated away from participating children to siblings and parents.

There is a widespread belief that parents in most poor societies have traditionally preferred sons to daughters. Table 3.1 shows that parents in poorer countries usually do invest more in the education of boys, and female infanticide has been more common than male infanticide (Goode, 1963; Dickemann, 1979), although see Jaynes (1980) for evidence of male rather than female infanticide. Other evidence supporting this belief includes answers to questions about preferences (see Sun et al., 1978, for Taiwan); greater efforts to curtail additional births in families without daughters than in families without sons (ibid., table 18); larger propensities to become pregnant after the death of male than of female children (Schultz and DaVanzo, 1970); the negative effect of the number of boys surviving in a family on the mortality of girl children (Gomez, 1980); the positive effect of proportion of sons on family size and birth intervals (Ben-Porath and Welch, 1976); and accounts of different societies.[6]

A boy is produced when the male's Y sperm fertilizes the female's egg. Men are more prone to produce boys when they have a large fraction of Y sperm, and females are more prone to boys when their vaginas or eggs are more receptive to Y sperm (Barash, 1977, p. 178). If sons were preferred to daughters, persons known to be prone to produce boys would receive higher incomes or capital transfers in the marriage market,[7] and these would induce them to marry earlier and remarry faster if widowed or divorced.

Proneness to produce boys might be assessed from the ratio of boys among the children produced in a previous marriage, or among the children produced by parents, siblings, grandparents, and other close relatives. The marriage market does take account of proneness to produce boys, since women have been divorced when they did not produce sons—one prominent example is the former Queen Soraya of Iran—and men have taken additional wives when their first wives did not produce sons (Goode, 1963, p. 112; Goody, 1976, pp. 42, 48, 51, 90–92). I do not know whether many societies have had larger incomes and bride

---

6. For example, in discussing rural Taiwan, Margery Wolf said, "Until a woman bears a male child she is only a provisional member of her husband's household . . . With the birth of a son, she becomes the mother of one of its descendants, a position of prestige and respect" (1968, p. 45). Or in a small Iraqi village, "Boys are really the best . . . ; they can take care of their mother when she's old. What good are girls?" (Fernea, 1965, p. 292). Also see Goody (1976) on Africa and Asia.

7. The monetary value of the expected utility from a child is

$$V_c = \frac{EU_c}{\lambda} = \frac{U_b p_b + U_g (1 - p_b)}{\lambda} = p_b (V_b - V_g) + V_g,$$

where λ is the marginal utility of income, U_b and U_g are the utilities from sons and daughters respectively, V_b and V_g are the monetary values of these utilities, and p_b is the probability of a son. If the probability of sons is determined only by the characteristics of women, if all women have a single child, and if π_i is the premium to women with the probability p_b^i, then identical men marrying the ith and jth women would be equally well off if

$$\pi_i - \pi_j = V_c^i - V_c^j = (p_b^i - p_b^j)(V_b - V_g).$$

Therefore, $\pi_i > \pi_j$ if $p_b^i > p_b^j$ and $V_b > V_g$. Moreover,

$$\frac{d(\pi_i - \pi_j)}{d(V_b - V_g)} = p_b^i - p_b^j > 0 \quad \text{if } p_b^i > p_b^j.$$

prices (or dowries) for persons whose family backgrounds indicated that they were prone to produce boys.

Papps' investigation (1980) of bride prices in a Palestinian village does not detect any effect of the sex of children produced by mothers on the bride prices offered their daughters. Perhaps proneness is too difficult to assess with confidence, or perhaps enough sons can be obtained with normal propensities. If four children survive to adulthood, fewer than 10 percent of families would have no sons if sons and daughters are equally likely to survive. If one son were needed to continue the family name or business, the husband without sons could take a second wife, adopt the son of a relative or stranger, or have additional children (Goody, 1976, pp. 68 ff., 90–95).

Perhaps too the preference for boys has been exaggerated, since much of the evidence cited above shows only small differences by sex of children. Moreover, the evidence on "blood wealth" demanded to compensate for the killing of kin does not indicate that sons were more valuable than daughters in primitive societies: the blood wealth for killing females equaled or exceeded that for killing males in about 80 percent of the societies included in the study by Becker and Posner (1981). Furthermore, greater investments in sons, including lower male infanticide, do not imply that parents prefer sons, but only indicate that rates of return are higher on investments in sons. The discussion in Chapters 3 and 4 explains why investments in sons are more profitable in poor countries than investments in daughters (see also the evidence for India in Rosenzweig and Schultz, 1980). Males can be less valuable even when more is invested in them if the demand for children, and hence the value of females as mothers, is sufficiently important (see Chapter 3, especially Eq. 3.20).

England required the eldest son to inherit all land (primogeniture) for five or six centuries beginning in the eleventh century (Sayles, 1952).[8] Moslem law for more than a thousand years has specified the bequests to all children, with girls receiving less than boys (Anderson, 1976). The Romans, on the other hand, imposed few restrictions on the division of property among children (Goudy, 1911).

The effect on the wealth of children of different restrictions on bequests depends on whether these restrictions can be offset through

---

8. Adam Smith predicted that primogeniture is "still likely to endure for many centuries" (1937, p. 362).

expenditures on children believed to be neglected. That is, the effect depends, as does the effect of other public programs that benefit particular children, on whether parents can compensate their neglected children. If all land must pass to the eldest son while other assets are unregulated, a parent could mortgage his land (thereby reducing its value to the eldest son) and give the proceeds to younger children;[9] or daughters who inherit less could be given dowries[10] and other gifts, perhaps with funds raised by claims on the inheritances of sons. Regulations of inheritances have been avoided in these and other ways, so they are not strong evidence that utility functions of parents were biased toward eldest sons, against daughters, or in other ways.

Endowments and the Interaction between Quantity and Quality

In this section the effect of endowments on the interaction between the quantity and quality of children is analyzed. If siblings are assumed to have the same endowment and market luck, we have seen that all children of neutral parents would receive the same income. Then neutral parents could be said to maximize an indirect utility function of the number of children and the income of each child, as in

$$U_t = U(Z_t, I_{t+1}, n_t), \tag{6.18}$$

where n_t is the number of children.[11] The own-income and family-income equations would be

---

9. For example, the concept of the trust developed in England in the fourteenth century partly to evade primogeniture (oral communication from John Langbein). Moreover, many landed estates that passed to eldest sons were significantly reduced in value by mortgages and other encumbrances; see the discussion in Cooper (1976).

10. Moslem thinkers reversed this argument and maintained that sons should inherit larger shares *because* daughters received dowries.

11. Since all children have the same income, the equilibrium utility of their parents would be

$$U^* = U(Z_t^*, I_{t+1}^{*1}, I_{t+1}^{*2}, \ldots, I_{t+1}^{*n_t^*}) = U(Z^*, I_{t+1}^*, \ldots, I_{t+1}^*),$$

where the superscript * indicates equilibrium values. Then U_t^* would depend only on Z_t^*, I_{t+1}^*, and n_t^*, as in Eq. (6.18).

$$Z_t + \frac{n_t w_{t+1} y_t}{1 + r_t} = I_t$$

$$\text{and} \qquad Z_t + \frac{n_t I_{t+1}}{1 + r_t} = I_t + \frac{n_t w_{t+1} e_{t+1}}{1 + r_t} + \frac{n_t w_{t+1} u_{t+1}}{1 + r_t} = S_t,$$

(6.19)

where y_t is the identical investment in each child.

If the utility function given by Eq. (6.18) is maximized subject to family income, the equilibrium conditions are

$$\frac{\partial U_t}{\partial Z_t} = \lambda = \lambda \pi_z,$$

$$\frac{\partial U_t}{\partial n_t} = \lambda \left[\frac{I_{t+1} - w_{t+1}(e_{t+1} + u_{t+1})}{1 + r_t} \right] = \frac{\lambda w_{t+1} y_t}{1 + r_t} = \lambda \pi_n,$$

$$\frac{\partial U_t}{\partial I_{t+1}} = \frac{\lambda n_t}{1 + r_t} = \lambda \pi_I,$$

(6.20)

where r_t is assumed to be independent of y_t and n_t. The shadow price of quality (π_I) depends on the quantity of children for the reasons presented in Chapter 5; it is proportional to quantity because fixed costs of quality are neglected and rates of return are independent of quantity. Even though fixed costs of quantity are also neglected, the shadow price of quantity (π_n) is not proportional to total quality but to the amount spent on each child.

The effect on the interaction between quantity and quality of the distinction between total quality (I_{t+1}) and expenditures on children (y_t) can be seen from a rise in family income that does not change the endowment or market luck of children. Total quality and number of children would rise by the same percent if their true income elasticities were equal and if π_n and π_I were unaffected. Expenditures on children would rise by a larger percent, however, inasmuch as total quality can be increased only by increasing expenditures. Therefore, *expenditures* on children would be more responsive to income than quantity (an assumption made in chapter 5) even when total quality and quantity are equally responsive.

Moreover, the rise in y_t relative to n_t would increase π_n relative to π_I and induce a substitution away from n_t and toward I_{t+1} and y_t. Hence the equilibrium rise in I_{t+1} would exceed the rise in n_t even when they have the same true income elasticities. Indeed, the observed income elasticity of quantity could be negative (Simon, 1974) even when its true elasticity is positive and sizable, owing to the interaction between quantity and quality and the distinction between total quality and expenditures on children.

If family income rose because of an increase in the endowment or market luck of children, and if rates of return were unaffected, parents would spend less on each child because they want to spend more on themselves at higher family incomes. They would substitute away from total quality and toward quantity, because the shadow price of quantity is reduced when less is spent on children. Therefore, the observed elasticity of total quality could be weak and perhaps negative when the endowment or luck of children increases, even if the true elasticity of total quality were positive and substantial.

An increase in the expected rate of growth over time of the income produced by capital (w) would raise family income through an increased (expected) endowment of children. If rates of return were not affected, investment in each child would be reduced, and the interaction between quantity and quality could raise quantity substantially because its shadow price would be lowered. The reduced investment in each child would be in the form of reduced gifts and bequests of nonhuman capital as long as these were positive. Consequently, a sizable increase in the expected rate of growth that did not raise rates of return on nonhuman capital could greatly reduce the number of families that leave bequests to their children.

Increased growth might raise rates of return, however, especially on investments in education and other general training of children, for general training is more useful in dynamic economies (Schultz, 1975, 1980). Then the shadow prices of quantity and quality (π_n and π_I) would fall initially by the same percent, and parents would substitute toward n_t and I_{t+1} and away from Z_t. If n_t and I_{t+1} initially increased by the same percent, the equilibrium rise in I_{t+1} would exceed that in n_t because y_t and π_n would rise relative to n_t and π_I. Indeed, n_t could fall while I_{t+1} and y_t increased significantly. This provides some support for the argument in Chapter 5 that increased rates of return on urban human capital in Western countries during the nineteenth century reduced urban fertility and significantly raised investments in urban education and other human capital.

The last several paragraphs have discussed properties of the observed demand functions for quantity and quality of children:

$$\left.\begin{array}{l} n_t = d_n(I_t, e_{t+1} + u_{t+1}, r) \\ I_{t+1} = d_I(I_t, e_{t+1} + u_{t+1}, r) \end{array}\right\}. \tag{6.21}$$

To simplify further discussion of these functions, we assume income per unit of capital and rates of return to be constant over time, so that $w_t = 1$ and $r_t = r$, for all t. Taking linear approximations and assuming that the rate of return affects only the coefficients of other variables, as in Eq. (6.8), we can write these functions as[12]

$$n_t = c_0 + c_I I_t + c_e(e_{t+1} + u_{t+1}), \qquad (6.22)$$

$$I_{t+1} = b_0 + b_I I_t + b_e(e_{t+1} + u_{t+1}). \qquad (6.23)$$

The interaction between quantity and quality tends to raise the effect of $e_{t+1} + u_{t+1}$ on n_t (c_e) and of I_t on I_{t+1} (b_I), and lowers the effect of I_t on n_t (c_I) and of $e_{t+1} + u_{t+1}$ on I_{t+1} (b_e). Indeed, the interaction could make c_I and b_e negative even if an increase in family income would raise the demand for both quantity and quality of children when their *shadow* prices were held constant.

Unfortunately, these demand functions cannot be directly estimated. Endowments are difficult to measure, since little is known about the cultural and biological inheritance of many characteristics.[13] However, endowments can be eliminated, and the quantity and quality of children can be related only to own incomes, lagged quantities and qualities, and luck. To show this more readily, we simplify the endowment-generating equation in (6.9) to

$$e_{t+1} = a + he_t + v_{t+1}, \qquad (6.24)$$

where e_t is the endowment of parents and a is a constant.

By lagging Eq. (6.22) one period and using Eq. (6.24), the demand for quantity of children can be expressed entirely in terms of observables and a serially correlated residual (quality is considered in the next chapter):

$$n_t = c_0^* + c_I I_t - hc_I I_{t-1} + hn_{t-1} + u_{t+1}^*,$$

where

$$c_0^* = ac_e + c_0(1 - h),$$

and

$$u_{t+1}^* = c_e(u_{t+1} - hu_t + v_{t+1}). \qquad (6.25)$$

12. I have benefited here from an unpublished analysis by Nigel Tomes.
13. See, for example Goldberger's careful and critical review (1978) of the evidence on the biological inheritability of intelligence.

The endowment of children has been replaced by grandparents' income (I_{t-1}), the siblings of parents (n_{t-1}), and the market luck of parents (u_t).

The number of siblings has a positive coefficient equal to the inheritability of endowments (h). This coefficient indicates that persons with many siblings tend to have more children when preferences and the capacity to produce children are the same for everyone, and when the incomes of parents and grandparents are held constant. Therefore, the persistence of family differences in fertility (Fisher, 1958, chap. 9; Ben-Porath, 1973; Williams, 1979; and Tomes, 1980b) does not imply that family differences in preferences persist across generations, and it appears to go beyond the persistence of family differences in incomes.

R. A. Fisher explained family differences in fertility by the inheritance of biological differences in fecundity. My analysis also implies that family differences are explained by inheritance (holding I_t, I_{t-1}, and u_{t-1}^* constant), but the coefficient of the number of siblings in Eq. (6.25) equals the (average) inheritability of *all* cultural and *all* biological factors that contribute to family capital. Biological determinants of fertility presumably make only a small contribution to a family's aggregate biological capital and usually make a negligible contribution to total family capital, including cultural capital.

A fascinating implication of Eq. (6.25) is that changes in the incomes of parents and grandparents appear to have opposite effects: the ratio of their coefficients is less than zero and equals $-h$, where h (the degree of inheritability) is the coefficient of number of siblings. Income of parents would have a negative coefficient and income of grandparents a positive coefficient with a sufficiently strong interaction between quantity and quality of children ($c_I < 0$).

One would expect the number of children to depend, perhaps only indirectly, on the income of grandparents. Indeed, Richard Easterlin has stressed in a series of important and influential papers the significance of generational influences for understanding the determinants of fertility. In particular, he has argued that persons who grow up in prosperous families want *fewer* children than other persons with the same income; a prosperous childhood is said to increase the preference for own consumption and decrease the preference for children (Easterlin, 1973). Equation (6.25) can appear to support Easterlin because a prosperous childhood, as measured by the income of the grandparents, appears to reduce fertility if the *observed* parental income elasticity of demand for children is positive ($c_I > 0$). However, even such an apparent negative effect would not operate through induced changes in preferences, because Eq. (6.25) was derived without assuming that preferences are affected by childhood prosperity or poverty! Consequently, evidence of an apparent negative relation between childhood prosperity and fertility[14] does not imply that preferences toward children are adversely affected by childhood prosperity.

I intentionally have said "apparent" negative relation, as the coefficients of grandparents' income and of number of siblings in Eq. (6.25) are misleading. Without changing I_t and u_{t+1}^*, I_{t-1} could increase only if v_t (which does not appear in Eq. 6.25) decreased sufficiently to offset the effect on I_t of the increase in I_{t-1}. Since a decrease in v_t would decrease n_t, the compensatory change in v_t, rather than the change in I_{t-1}, is responsible for the apparent negative effect on n_t of I_{t-1}.

A correct analysis must recognize that an increase in the income of grandparents *with no change in endowments* would increase the income of their children (I_t), and may increase or decrease the number of their children (n_{t-1}). An increase in I_t would increase or decrease n_t as the observed income elasticity of demand for quantity was positive or negative (as $c_I \gtrless 0$).

---

14. Some studies have found a negative coefficient, while others (Williams, 1979; Tomes, 1980b) have found a positive or zero coefficient for grandparents' income. Equation (6.25) implies, however, that all of these estimates are biased in that the residual (u_{t+1}^*) is correlated with I_t and n_{t-1} through the effect of u_t on these variables (see Chapter 7).

CHAPTER 7

Inequality and Intergenerational Mobility

In an earlier study I wrote:

> How does one explain then that in spite of the rapid accumulation of empirical information and the persisting and even increasing interest in [the distribution of income], . . . economists have somewhat neglected the study of personal income distribution during the past generation? In my judgment the fundamental reason is the absence, despite ingenious and valiant efforts, of a theory that both articulates with general economic theory and is useful in explaining actual differences among regions, countries, and time periods (Becker, 1967, p. 1).

Although the so-called just distribution of income has since received an enormous amount of attention—see, for example, Rawls (1971) and Okun (1975)—a satisfactory theory of the actual distribution still has not been developed.

This chapter is derived primarily from joint work with Nigel Tomes. Portions of the study were published in 1979 in the *Journal of Political Economy* 87(6): 1153–1189 and appear here by permission of the University of Chicago Press.

201

A Treatise on the Family

A full analysis of the distribution of income should include both the inequality in income among different generations of the same family—what is usually called intergenerational social mobility—and the inequality in income among different families in the same generation. Because of their divergent views about the forces generating inequality, sociologists have been concerned chiefly with intergenerational mobility and economists with inequality within a generation. Sociologists have emphasized the role of an individual's forebears in the determination of his socioeconomic status through their influence on his background, class, or caste (Blau and Duncan, 1967; Boudon, 1974). On the other hand, most models of inequality by economists have neglected the transmission of inequality through the family because they have assumed that stochastic processes largely determine inequality through distributions of luck and abilities (see Roy, 1950; Champernowne, 1953).

Two recent analytical developments suggest that a unified approach to intergenerational mobility and inequality is possible. Human capital theory shows that inequality can result from maximizing behavior without major reliance on luck and other stochastic forces.[1] The economic approach to the family developed in this book views an individual not in isolation but as part of a family whose members span several generations. Members contribute to the production of family income and to the care of children who continue the family into the future.

The central decision makers are individual members of long-lived families. Those in the current generation can increase their consumption at the expense of future generations, but are discouraged from doing so by their concern for the interests of their children and perhaps of other future family members. This link between generations of the same family is buttressed by family endowments that are transferred from parents to children.

The analysis incorporates the human capital approach to inequality in that parents maximize their utility by choosing optimal investments in the human and nonhuman capital of children and other members. Moreover, the analysis recognizes that endowments and market rewards depend on luck, so that incomes are partly determined by the interaction between luck and maximizing behavior.

From any initial position, the inequality in family incomes and in-

---

1. See Mincer (1958) and Becker (1967, 1975); see also the "abilities" models of Roy (1950), Mandelbrot (1962), Houthakker (1975), and Rosen (1978).

tergenerational mobility over time approach equilibrium levels that depend on luck and various family parameters, especially the inheritability of endowments and the propensity to invest in children. They also depend, sometimes in surprising ways, on the rate of economic growth, taxes and subsidies, foresight about the incidence of "disturbances," discrimination against minorities, and family reputations. For example, even a progressive tax-subsidy system might raise the inequality in *disposable* incomes, and discrimination against minorities not only reduces their income but also the effect of their family background on income.

The Equilibrium Inequality in Income

Even if all families were basically identical, incomes would be unequally distributed because of the unequal incidence of endowment and market luck. The income inequality in any generation depends, of course, on the inequality of luck in that generation, but also in a decisive way on the luck in previous generations. Since lucky parents invest more in their children, the increase in the children's incomes would induce them to invest more in their own children in the succeeding generation, and so on until all descendants benefit from the initial luck. Since investments depend on the parameters β and h introduced in the previous chapter, which measure the propensity to invest in children and the degree of inheritability of endowments, the effect of luck in previous generations on the income inequality in a given generation also depends on these parameters.

Rates of return on capital (r) and the income per unit of capital (w) are assumed to be independent of the aggregate accumulation of capital and given to the community as well as to each family (I do not analyze equilibrium in factor markets). Temporarily I assume these parameters to be stationary over time, so that $r_t = r$ and $w_t = w = 1$ by the choice of units.

All families would maintain their separate identities indefinitely, and the fortunes of any family could be followed over as many generations as desired, if each person produced children without mating. Families also effectively maintain their separate identities when each person mates with someone having the same endowment, same parental income, and same luck (imperfect assortative mating is considered later in this chapter).

If each family has only one child and invests in a homogeneous human or nonhuman capital of their child at a constant rate of return—and if all families have the same utility function, rate of return, and degree of inheritability—the equilibrium income of the sole representative of the *i*th family in generation $t + 1$ can be written from Eq. (6.8) as:

$$I_{t+1}^i = \alpha(1 + r)I_t^i + \alpha e_{t+1}^i + \alpha u_{t+1}^i = \beta I_t^i + \alpha e_{t+1}^i + \alpha u_{t+1}^i, \quad (7.1)$$

where e_{t+1}^i is his endowment, u_{t+1}^i is his market luck, α is the fraction of family income spent on children, and β is the propensity to invest in children. If the average endowment ($\bar{e}$) does not change over time, the simplified endowment-generating equation, (6.24), becomes

$$e_{t+1}^i = a + he_t^i + v_{t+1}^i = (1 - h)\bar{e} + he_t^i + v_{t+1}^i, \quad (7.2)$$

where h is the degree of inheritability of endowments, e_t^i is the endowment of parents, and v_{t+1}^i is the endowed luck of children. By substituting this equation into (7.1), we can write the income-generating equation[2] as

$$I_{t+1}^i = \alpha a + \beta I_t^i + \alpha h e_t^i + \alpha v_{t+1}^i + \alpha u_{t+1}^i. \quad (7.3)$$

Since all families are assumed to be identical, they would have the same income in any generation if they have had the same luck in that and in all previous generations. Therefore, the income inequality in any generation would depend on the distribution of luck in all previous generations. This can be shown explicitly by repeatedly substituting Eqs. (7.2) and (7.3) into (7.3) to relate the income of the *i*th family in generation $t + 1$ to its income and endowment in the $(m + 1)$st prior generation and to its luck in all intervening generations:

$$I_{t+1}^i = \alpha a \sum_{j=0}^{m} \beta^j \sum_{k=0}^{m-j} h^k + \beta^{m+1} I_{t-m}^i + \alpha h \left(\sum_{j=0}^{m} \beta^{m-j} h^j \right) e_{t-m}^i$$

$$+ \alpha \sum_{j=0}^{m} \beta^j u_{t+1-j}^i + \alpha \sum_{k=0}^{m} \sum_{j=0}^{k} \beta^j h^{k-j} v_{t+1-k}^i. \quad (7.4)$$

---

2. In an interesting article on social mobility Conlisk (1974) assumes an equation system with a reduced form similar to Eq. (7.3); see his eq. (16), p. 84. However, his system is not derived from utility maximizing behavior and does not incorporate the relations between the coefficients of I_t^i, e_t^i, v_{t+1}^i, and u_{t+1}^i implied by maximizing behavior and found in Eq. (7.3), such as the effect on β of a change in α. Moreover, since the coefficients in his equations are not related to rates of return on investments, to the importance of children in parental preferences, or to other market and household characteristics, his equation cannot be used (without introducing assumptions about behavior) to determine the effects of these characteristics on the distribution of income.

Presumably $0 < h < 1$, or only some of the parents' endowment passes to children. The rate of return (r) has the units of percent per generation, and even a modest percent per year implies a sizable percent per generation because human generations are separated by 20 or more years. Therefore, r would exceed 0.5 and might even exceed unity; hence $\beta = \alpha(1 + r)$ also might exceed unity, because the fraction of family income spent on children (α) is far from negligible.

If, however, β as well as h is assumed for the present to be less than unity, the coefficients of both I^i_{t-m} and e^i_{t-m} approach zero as m becomes larger and larger, and the coefficient of αa approaches a constant. Since

$$\sum_{j=0}^{k} \beta^j h^{k-j} = \begin{cases} \dfrac{\beta^{k+1} - h^{k+1}}{\beta - h} & \text{for } \beta \neq h \\[2em] \beta^k(k + 1) & \text{for } \beta = h, \end{cases} \tag{7.5}$$

Eq. (7.4) could be extended back through infinitely many generations and written (for $\beta \neq h$) as

$$I^i_{t+1} = \frac{\alpha a}{(1 - \beta)(1 - h)} + \alpha \sum_{k=0}^{\infty} \beta^k u^i_{t+1-k}$$

$$+ \alpha \sum_{k=0}^{\infty} \left(\frac{\beta^{k+1} - h^{k+1}}{\beta - h} \right) v^i_{t+1-k}. \tag{7.6}$$

The income of the ith family in any generation is expressed solely in terms of its luck in that and in all previous generations; the family parameters α, β, and h; and the "social" parameter a. Starting from *any* initial distribution of income and endowment, the distribution of income would change over time and eventually approach the right-hand side of Eq. (7.6).

If u_t and v_t are identically distributed random variables with finite variances, the variance of income must approach a stationary level without any additional restrictions on the properties of u_t and v_t or on the utility function. If u_t and v_t are independently distributed, the stationary variance can be simply written (see Mathematical Appendix, note A) as:

$$\sigma_I^2 = \frac{\alpha^2}{1 - \beta^2} \sigma_u^2 + \frac{\alpha^2(1 + h\beta)\sigma_v^2}{(1 - h^2)(1 - \beta^2)(1 - h\beta)}, \tag{7.7}$$

where σ_I^2, σ_u^2, and σ_v^2 are the variances of I, u, and v respectively.

Since the expected value of both endowed and market luck equals zero, Eq. (7.6) implies that expected or average income in any generation must approach the stationary level

$$\bar{I} = \frac{\alpha a}{(1 - \beta)(1 - h)} = \frac{\alpha \bar{e}}{1 - \beta} \quad \text{since } a = \bar{e}(1 - h). \tag{7.8}$$

The equilibrium level of average income is a simple function of the family parameters (α and β) and of the social parameter ($\bar{e}$), and is independent of the inheritability of endowments (h). The fraction contributed by invested capital is

$$d = 1 - \frac{\bar{e}}{\bar{I}} = 1 - \frac{(1 - \beta)}{\alpha} = 2 + r - \frac{1}{\alpha}, \tag{7.9}$$

where $d > 0$ if $\alpha > 1/(2 + r)$. Not surprisingly, this fraction is positively related to the rate of return on investments and to the fraction of family income invested in children. Although the derivation of Eq. (7.1) assumes that parents can borrow by leaving a debt to be repaid by children, Eq. (7.9) shows that in equilibrium the average family would not borrow but would invest in its descendants as long as a sizable fraction of family income were spent on children. Clearly, $d > 0$ if $\alpha \geq 0.4$, since $r \geq 0.5$.

Writers on social justice and on the political process have usually been interested in relative measures of inequality, such as the Gini coefficient or the coefficient of variation. If the expression in Eq. (7.7) is divided by the square of the expression in (7.8), the square of the equilibrium coefficient of variation in income would be

$$\begin{aligned} CV_I^2 &= \frac{1 - \beta}{1 + \beta} CV_u^2 + \frac{(1 + h\beta)(1 - \beta)}{(1 - h^2)(1 - h\beta)(1 + \beta)} CV_v^2 \\ &= \frac{1 - \beta}{1 + \beta} CV_u^2 + \frac{(1 + h\beta)(1 - \beta)}{(1 - h\beta)(1 + \beta)} CV_e^2, \end{aligned} \tag{7.10}$$

since $\sigma_v^2 = (1 - h^2)\sigma_e^2$ (see Mathematical Appendix, note A). The inequality in both market and endowed luck are measured relative to the average endowment:

$$CV_u = \frac{\sigma_u}{\bar{e}}, \qquad CV_v = \frac{\sigma_v}{\bar{e}}.$$

Of course, the equilibrium inequality in income depends on, and indeed is proportional to, the inequality in market and endowed luck. The factors of proportionality, however, are determined by families through the inheritability of endowments and the propensity to invest in children. Since $\beta < 1$, the coefficient of market luck must be less than unity—probably less than one-third, because β almost certainly exceeds one-half. Therefore, the effect of market luck on inequality is greatly attenuated by the reactions of parents to its anticipated incidence.

The coefficient of endowed luck exceeds that of market luck, and the difference is large when both h and β are large; for example, the coefficient of CV_v^2 would be about 2.5 times, and the coefficient of CV_e^2 would be about 2.0 times, that of CV_u^2 when $\beta = 0.6$ and $h = 0.5$. Endowed luck, automatically inherited by children, has a much greater effect on income inequality. This explains why endowed luck has a larger effect on income inequality when h is larger.

Not only does the coefficient of endowed luck exceed the coefficient of market luck, but the inequality in endowed luck probably significantly exceeds the inequality in market luck. Endowed luck is a "fixed effect," determined by childhood experiences and genetic inheritance, that tends to last throughout a lifetime, whereas market luck is more transitory and fluctuates from year to year. Therefore, the "permanent" or lifetime inequality in endowed luck would be considerably greater than the lifetime inequality in market luck if the annual inequality in market and endowed luck were about the same. We shall see how the permanent inequality in both endowed and market luck can be estimated from data on the permanent incomes of different generations.

An increase in the rate of return raises the propensity to invest, $\beta = \alpha(1 + r)$, which according to Eq. (7.7) raises the equilibrium standard deviation of income. However, from Eq. (7.8) an increase in β also raises the equilibrium level of average income; indeed, the percentage increase in the average income exceeds the percentage increase in the standard deviation, so that an increase in the rate of return and the propensity to invest lowers the coefficient of variation in income of Eq. (7.10). A well-known result from human capital theory states the contrary, that an increase in rates of return on human capital raises inequality, but this result only considers the *impact* of changes in rates of return on income inequality and neglects longer-run effects on income through changes in the level and distribution of investments in human capital.[3] The negative relation between income inequality and

3. See Chiswick (1974) or Becker (1975). One analysis that incorporates the effect of changes in rates of return on the equilibrium distribution of investment does not find any relation between inequality and rates of return (Becker, 1967, 1975).

the rate of return in Eq. (7.10) is used later in this chapter to determine the effects of discrimination, taxation, and economic growth on inequality.

Perhaps the most interesting property of Eq. (7.10) is that h and β do not enter additively, but multiplicatively: an increase in h has a larger effect on income inequality when β is larger. This relationship reflects the interaction in the model between inheritability and investment in children through the covariance between income and endowment in any generation (see Eq. A.1 in Mathematical Appendix, note A).

The effect of utility maximization on the interaction between inheritability and investments as well as on other properties of the equation determining inequality can be seen from a comparison with the inequality when families do not maximize. Inheritability and investment would not interact if the amount invested in children were independent of rates of return, family income, endowments, and luck, and then the contribution of endowed inequality to income inequality would be greatly reduced.[4] For example, if $h = 0.5$ and $\beta = 0.6$, the coefficient of endowed inequality would be twice that of market luck with utility maximization, and only the same as that of market luck without maximization. Therefore, mechanical models of the intergenerational transmission of inequality that do not incorporate optimizing responses of parents to their own or to their children's circumstances greatly understate the contribution of endowed inequality and thereby understate the influence of family background on inequality.

If parents could not anticipate their children's market luck but were

---

4. The equilibrium variance of income would be

$$\sigma_I^2 = \sigma_y^2 + \sigma_e^2 + \sigma_u^2 = \sigma_y^2 + \frac{\sigma_v^2}{1 - h^2} + \sigma_u^2,$$

where σ_y^2 is the given variance in the amount invested in children. The equilibrium average income would be

$$\bar{I} = \bar{y} + \bar{e} = \frac{\bar{e}}{1 - d},$$

where $\bar{y}$ is the given average investment in children and d is defined in Eq. (7.9). Then

$$CV_I^2 = (1 - d)^2 CV_u^2 + (1 - d)^2 CV_e^2 + d^2 CV_y^2$$

$$= (1 - d)^2 CV_u^2 + \frac{(1 - d)^2}{1 - h^2} CV_v^2 + d^2 CV_y^2,$$

where $CV_y = \sigma_y/\bar{y}$.

not affected by risk and had unbiased expectations, the coefficient of CV_u^2 in Eq. (7.10) would simply be multiplied by $1/\alpha^2$ (see Chapter 6). Since α is below unity, imperfectly anticipated "disturbances" increase the variability in individual incomes as well as the cyclic variability in aggregate incomes (on the latter, see Sargent and Wallace, 1975). Moreover, the coefficient of market luck might then exceed the coefficient of endowed luck because parents could not offset the bad or good market luck of their children with larger or smaller investments.

Intergenerational Mobility

Variation in the income and status of a given family in different generations has usually been known as intergenerational mobility, the "circulation of the elites" (Pareto, 1971), or equality of opportunity. Little inequality among different families in the same generation is consistent with a highly stable ranking of families in different generations, and an unstable ranking is consistent with sizable inequality in the same generation. An enormous literature discusses each type of inequality, yet only rarely have they been brought together in a common analytic framework. My goal in this section is to analyze intergenerational mobility with the same framework used for intragenerational inequality and to show that the propensity to invest in children and the degree of inheritability are also important determinants of intergenerational mobility.

The influence of the family on the income of children can be measured by the correlation between the incomes of children and those of parents or grandparents. If the degree of inheritability (h) were negligible, the equilibrium correlation coefficient between the incomes of children and parents would equal the propensity to invest in children (β) regardless of the inequality in market and endowed luck.[5] If h were not negligible and if the inequality in market luck is small relative to the inequality in endowed luck (and I indicated earlier why this should be so), the equilibrium multiple correlation coefficient between the in-

---

5. Since $I_{t+1}^i = \beta I_t^i + \alpha e_{t+1}^i + \alpha u_{t+1}^i$,

$$R(I_{t+1},I_t) = \frac{\beta\sigma_{I_t}}{\sigma_{I_{t+1}}} = \beta$$

because e_{t+1} is independent of I_t if $h = 0$, and $\sigma_{I_t} = \sigma_{I_{t+1}}$ in equilibrium.

come of children and the income *and* endowment of parents would exceed β by an amount that depends only on β and h (see Mathematical Appendix, note B).

I want to consider now a different and in some ways more revealing measure of intergenerational mobility: the sequence of changes in the incomes of parents, children, grandchildren, and later descendants. If the degree of inheritability were negligible, an increase in the income of parents by δI_t because of favorable market or endowed luck would increase the income of children by $\beta \delta I_t$, the income of grandchildren by $\beta^2 \delta I_t$, and the income of the mth generation of descendants (see Eq. 7.4) by:

$$\delta I_{t+m} = \beta^m \delta I_t, \quad \text{for } m = 1, 2, \ldots, \tag{7.11}$$

when $h = 0$. These increases decline monotonically as long as $\beta < 1$, and are close to zero after a few generations if $\beta < 0.8$—"from shirtsleeves to shirtsleeves in four generations." Consequently, unless the propensity to invest is close to unity, intergenerational mobility would be considerable if utility-maximizing investments in children *alone* linked different generations of a family.

If investments did not depend on income or other variables and were simply given to each family, an increase in the endowment of parents by δv_t would increase the income of their children by $h \delta v_t$, the income of grandchildren by $h^2 \delta v_t$, and the income of the mth generation of descendants by

$$\delta I_{t+m} = h^m \delta v_t, \quad \text{for } m = 1, 2, \ldots, \tag{7.12}$$

when y_t is exogenous. These increases, which also decline monotonically if $h < 1$, would be close to zero after a few generations because usually $h < 0.75$. Unless the degree of inheritability is close to unity, intergenerational mobility would be considerable if cultural and biological inheritance *alone* linked different generations of a family.

If investments in children depend on family circumstances, and if the degree of inheritability is not negligible, an increase in the income of parents would not simply raise the incomes of their descendants by the sum of the increases given in Eqs. (7.11) and (7.12). Inheritances and investments interact. In particular, the incomes of descendants could continue to rise for several generations even though h and β were both less than unity, and many generations might elapse before the increases were below 25 percent of the initial increase. Consequently, the interaction between investments and inheritances can sharply increase the effect of the incomes and endowments of ancestors on current incomes.

Consider, for example, an increase in the endowed luck of the ith family in the tth generation (δv_t^i) that is compensated by a decline in market luck so that own income (I_t^i) remains the same. Since family income (S_t^i) increases because the endowment of children increases by $h\delta v_t^i$, parents in t want to increase their own consumption and reduce their investment in children. The own income of children (I_{t+1}^i), then, would increase only by a fraction (α) of their increased endowment; the rest is spent by parents on their own consumption. The own income of grandchildren (I_{t+2}^i) would also increase, partly because the own income of their parents increases and partly because these grandchildren inherit some of the increased endowment of their parents. The total increase in the income of grandchildren would be

$$\delta I_{t+2}^i = \beta \delta I_{t+1}^i + \alpha \delta e_{t+2}^i = \alpha h \beta \delta v_t^i + \alpha h^2 \delta v_t^i$$
$$= \alpha h(\beta + h)\delta v_t^i = (\beta + h)\delta I_{t+1}^i. \tag{7.13}$$

Therefore, if $\beta + h > 1$ (if the sum of the degree of inheritability and the propensity to invest in children exceeds unity), a compensated increase in the endowment of parents would increase the income of grandchildren by *more* than the income of children.

The effects on the incomes of great-grandchildren, great-great-grandchildren, and still more distant descendants can be derived in the same way. The increase in the income of, say, great-great-grandchildren would also exceed that of children if $\beta + h$ were *sufficiently* greater than unity. A general formula relating the change in the income of the mth generation of descendants to a compensated change in the endowment of parents is given by the coefficient of e_{t-m}^i in Eq. (7.4). This coefficient can be measured relative to the equilibrium level of average income and written as

$$\frac{\delta I_{t+m}^i}{\bar{I}} = h(1 - \beta) \sum_{j=0}^{m-1} \beta^{m-1-j} h^j \frac{\delta e_t^i}{\bar{e}}$$

$$= \begin{cases} h(1 - \beta) \dfrac{\beta^m - h^m}{\beta - h} \dfrac{\delta e_t^i}{\bar{e}} = h(1 - \beta)g_m \dfrac{\delta e_t^i}{\bar{e}} & \text{for } \beta \neq h \quad (7.14) \\[2ex] h(1 - \beta)m\beta^{m-1} \dfrac{\delta e_t^i}{\bar{e}} & \text{for } \beta = h. \end{cases}$$

The term g_m is a symmetric polynomial in β and h that has a maximum at the initial generation when $\beta + h < 1$; it rises to a peak and then declines monotonically when $\beta + h > 1$, where the peak is later the larger $\beta + h$ is (see Mathematical Appendix, note C). Figure 7.1 plots the path of g_m for three sets of values of β and h. In curve A both are "low," $h = 0.20$ and $\beta = 0.45$, and by the fourth generation g_m is only 16 percent of its initial value; in curve B, $h = 0.30$ and $\beta = 0.80$, and g_m rises for one generation, then declines to less than 25 percent of the initial value by the tenth generation; in curve C, $h = 0.70$ and $\beta = 0.90$, and g_m rises for five generations, then declines slowly, does not reach its initial value until the fifteenth generation, and is less than 25 percent of the initial value only after the twenty-ninth generation!

The income of a given family can be well above or below average for several consecutive generations because of a run of very good or bad luck; that is, because the u and v in Eq. (7.4) have the same sign and are not negligible for several consecutive generations. Since these random variables are assumed to be independently distributed, the probability is low that more than two consecutive generations have *unusually* good or bad luck. However, the income of a family with unusual luck in only one generation and average luck in all subsequent generations would also be significantly above or below average for several consecutive generations if the degree of inheritability and the propensity to invest in children were substantial.

Thus the welfare of several consecutive generations of the same family would be closely linked whenever inheritability and investments are

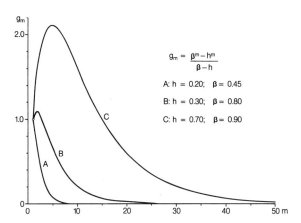

FIGURE 7.1 Generational pattern of changes in income with different values for the propensity to invest and the degree of inheritability, where m denotes the number of generations after a shock to family income and g_m measures the effect on subsequent incomes.

substantial. The degree of inheritability and the size of endowments are not rigidly determined by the biology of human inheritance, but are greatly influenced by social organization. Some societies rely heavily on family reputation in assessing various characteristics of individuals because there is no accurate method of assessing them directly. Families then have an incentive to maintain and enhance their reputations by controlling and guiding the characteristics of their members through investments in family endowments (see Chapters 6 and 11). As a result of these efforts, members of the same family become more similar than they are in "open" societies where families gain less from controlling their members. Therefore, if the propensity to invest were the same, the income of children would be more similar to the incomes of their parents, grandparents, and other relatives when cousins, uncles, nephews, grandparents, grandchildren, and other family members are more concerned about one another.

Since a run of successes or failures in the same family is more likely when the degree of inheritability is greater, perhaps the Adams family in the United States has received so much attention precisely because many generations of accomplishment are unusual in this open society. Successful families presumably are more common and less worthy of attention in a more closed society like traditional India or China.

Estimation of Family and Market Parameters

The concept of an endowment may seem to be another "empty box." Endowments cannot readily be measured, since little is known about the cultural and biological inheritance of many characteristics. Chapter 6 showed, nonetheless, how the demand for children could be related to more readily measured variables, and in the same manner endowments can be eliminated from the income-generating equation. (I am indebted to Sherwin Rosen for suggesting this approach.) If Eqs. (7.1) and (7.3) are combined, a second-order stochastic difference equation results, which depends only on the income of the same family in three consecutive generations and its market and endowed luck:

$$I_{t+1}^i = \alpha \bar{e}(1 - h) + (\beta + h)I_t^i - \beta h I_{t-1}^i + \alpha u_{t+1}^{*i}$$
$$= \alpha \bar{e}(1 - h) + (\beta + h - \beta h)I_t^i + \beta h(I_t^i - I_{t-1}^i) + \alpha u_{t+1}^{*i}, \quad (7.15)$$

where $u_{t+1}^{*i} = u_{t+1}^i - hu_t^i + v_{t+1}^i$ and $\beta + h - \beta h < 1$ if $\beta, h < 1$.

The effect of a change in the incomes of parents and grandparents on the income of children is determined by the propensity to invest and

A Treatise on the Family

the degree of inheritability. Both parameters must be less than unity if income is to converge to the equilibrium level $a\bar{e}/(1 - \beta)$. The positive coefficient of the difference in income between parents and grandparents measures the momentum that carries the growth in income between these generations into the children's generation.

The residual, u^*, is negatively correlated over time because u_t affects u_t^* positively and u_{t+1}^* negatively. Since the absolute value of the covariance between u_{t+1}^* and u_t^* is larger when h is larger, and since $h < 1$ and $E(u_{t+1}^*) = 0$, the residuals from Eq. (7.15) would have damped oscillations around the origin that would be more pronounced when h is larger.

An increase in the income of grandparents, I_{t-1}, would lower the income of grandchildren, I_{t+1}, if the income of parents, I_t, the market luck of parents and grandchildren, u_t and u_{t+1}, and the endowed luck of grandchildren, v_{t+1}, were held constant. This negative relation between the incomes of grandparents and grandchildren is surprising[6] in view of the fact that an increase in the income of grandparents would raise the income of parents, which in turn would raise the income of grandchildren. The negative relation in Eq. (7.15) assumes, however, that the income of parents and the stochastic terms u_{t+1}, u_t, and v_{t+1} are held constant. Since the income of grandparents can increase without changing these variables only if the endowed luck of parents, v_t, has decreased (see Eq. 7.3), and since a decrease in v_t would decrease I_{t+1} even when I_t is held constant (because endowments are partly inherited by children), an increase in I_{t-1} appears to decrease I_{t+1} only because of the implied decrease in v_t.

Many discussions of intergenerational mobility estimate Markov and related processes to generate income and wealth but fail to consider the underlying behavior (Hodge, 1966, and Singer and Spilerman, 1974, are examples). Our analysis shows that such estimates can give a misleading impression about causation. For example, the decrease in I_{t+1} in Eq. (7.15) is not caused by the increase in I_{t-1} but by the implied decrease in v_t.

Since both β and h could be determined if the two income coefficients in Eq. (7.15) were known,[7] the inheritability of endowments

---

6. However, see the Chapter 6 discussion of the negative relation between the number of grandchildren and the income of grandparents.

7. If $\beta + h = a_1$ and $\beta h = a_2$, then

$$(\beta - h)^2 = a_1^2 - 4a_2$$

and
$$\beta - h = \pm\sqrt{a_1^2 - 4a_2}.$$

could then be determined without any knowledge of endowment. The variance in endowed luck relative to the variance in market luck could also be determined without information on endowments if the variance and covariance of the residual u^* were known (see Mathematical Appendix, note D). Once β is determined, information on rates of return could be used to estimate the fraction of family income spent on children, α, because $\alpha = \beta/(1 + r)$. Finally, β, h, α, and σ_v^2/σ_u^2 could be inserted into Eq. (7.7) to determine the variances in endowed and market luck from information on the variance in income. Consequently, if the parameters in (7.15) could be estimated, all the information required to understand the determinants of inequality and intergenerational mobility would be available without information on endowments: the propensity to invest, the degree of inheritability, the fraction of income spent on children, and the inequality in market and endowed luck.

The income parameters in (7.15) could be estimated from information on three generations of incomes of homogeneous families faced with a stable environment. Since the residual u_{t+1}^* is negatively correlated with I_t (because u_t is positively correlated with I_t), I_t should be replaced by an "instrument" that is uncorrelated with u_{t+1}^*, such as the income of great-grandparents.[8] If a suitable instrument is not available and ordinary least squares are used, the coefficient of I_t ($\beta + h$) would be biased downward and that of I_{t-1} ($-\beta h$) would be biased upward. For example, if $\alpha = h = 0.5$, $\beta = 0.7$, $\sigma_u = 1$, and $\sigma_v = 2$ (earlier discussion has showed why σ_v would significantly exceed σ_u), the least-squares estimate of $\beta + h = 1.2$ from large samples would be 1.11, and that of $-\beta h = -0.35$ would be -0.27. The estimate of β derived from Eq. (*) in note 7 would then be slightly biased upward to 0.78, but the estimate of h would be biased downward by almost 30 percent to 0.36.

Unfortunately, few data sets contain good information on the income of parents and children, let alone on grandparents. If the income of children were related only to the income of parents, the least-squares estimate of $\beta + h$ would be bounded between β and $\beta + h$ if incomes were accurately measured (see Mathematical Appendix, note E). Actual estimates might be much lower because of the low quality of

---

Since presumably $\beta > h$,

$$\beta = \frac{a_1 + \sqrt{a_1^2 - 4a_2}}{2}, \qquad h = \frac{a_1 - \sqrt{a_1^2 - 4a_2}}{2}. \qquad (*)$$

8. Therefore, the parameters could be identified if information on four generations were available (identification of this system is discussed in Goldberger, 1979).

data on incomes of consecutive generations (see the estimates and discussion in Diamond, 1980).

Heterogeneous Families

Income would be more symmetrically distributed than the earnings due to market and endowed luck, because—from Eq. (7.6)—income is a weighted sum of the luck in different generations. This is not disturbing, however, even though actual income distributions invariably are skewed to the right. The distribution of earnings resulting from luck is likely to be quite skewed, even when the endowed and market abilities that determine luck are symmetrically distributed (see Chapter 3 and Rosen, 1978). More disturbing is the implication of Eq. (7.8) that all families have the same long-run equilibrium income; we know that blacks in the United States and other groups elsewhere have had lower than average incomes for many generations.

This implication can be altered without changing the basic approach and the linearity of the model by dropping the assumption that all families are identical. They may have different utility functions, rates of return, expected endowments, and degrees of inheritability because of market discrimination and favoritism or inherited differences in talents, abilities, and opportunities. If r, h, $\bar{e}$, and α differed among families but were the same for all generations of a given family—if parameter values were fully inherited by children—Eq. (7.6) would be modified only by introducing a superscript to indicate the parameters of the ith family.

If β and h were less than unity for all families, Eq. (7.8) implies that the long-run equilibrium income of the ith family would be

$$\bar{I}^i = \frac{\alpha^i \bar{e}^i}{1 - \beta^i}. \tag{7.16}$$

The equilibrium income of the ith family is independent of its degree of inheritability, but is positively related to average endowment, fraction spent on children, and propensity to invest in children.[9] For example,

---

9. A more reasonable assumption than full inheritability is that some parameters are only partially inherited. The fraction spent on children and the propensity to invest in generation $t + 1$ might be linearly related to the parameters in the tth generation:

$$\alpha^i_{t+1} = (1 - b^i)\bar{\alpha}^i + b^i\alpha^i_t + \epsilon^i_{t+1}, \qquad 0 \le b^i \le 1$$

and $\beta^i_{t+1} = (1 - c^i)\bar{\beta}^i + c^i\beta^i_t + \delta^i_{t+1}, \qquad 0 \le c^i \le 1,$

black families in the United States have had lower equilibrium incomes than white families partly as a result of their lower rates of return on investments in human capital (Becker, 1975).

Since the income of each family fluctuates around its own equilibrium level, the incomes of different generations of the same family would usually be below average if its equilibrium income were below average. Similarly, different generations of a family usually would be above average if its equilibrium income were above average. As a result, the distribution of equilibrium incomes would affect the degree of intergenerational mobility as measured by the correlation between the income of children and the incomes of parents and other ancestors, or by the effect of a change in current income on the incomes of descendants. In particular, the coefficients of I_t and I_{t-1} in Eq. (7.15) or the function g_m in Eq. (7.14) would differ among families if the propensity to invest and the degree of inheritability differed.

Since rates of return on human capital have been lower for blacks—some evidence in Freeman (1981) suggests that the differences may have narrowed in recent years—the propensity to invest would be lower for blacks if utility functions were the same in both black and white families.[10] Hence the effect on the income of children of a change in the income of parents would also be lower for blacks, as demonstrated in Diamond (1980) and Freeman (1981).

The equilibrium distribution of income depends on the distributions as well as the means of family parameters. Indeed, the distribution of income can be quite skewed and unequal even when market and endowed luck are negligible. For example, if the average endowment ($\bar{e}$) and fraction spent on children (α) were the same in all families, and if the degree of inheritability and market and endowed luck were negligible ($u = v = h = 0$), the income-generating equation would be

$$I_{t+1}^i = \alpha\bar{e} + \beta^i I_t^i. \tag{7.17}$$

If β^i were symmetrically distributed, and if $I_0^i = 1$ for all i, I_1^i would be

where ϵ^i and δ^i are disturbances, and $\bar{\alpha}^i$ and $\bar{\beta}^i$ are the equilibrium values of these parameters for the ith family. It is easy to show that the equilibrium income is independent of b^i and c^i and is proportional to $\bar{\alpha}^i$, $(1 - \bar{\beta}^i)^{-1}$, and $\bar{e}^i$, as in Eq. (7.16).

10. The propensity to invest in children, $\beta = \alpha(1 + r)$, is also *indirectly* affected by r because an increase in r lowers or raises α as the elasticity of substitution in the utility function between the consumption of parents and the income of children is less than or greater than unity. However, β must change in the same direction as r if the income of children is not an "inferior" commodity to parents.

symmetrically distributed with the same variance as β^i. The variance in I_2^i, however, would exceed that in I_1^i and the distribution of I_2^i would be skewed to the right because β^i and I_1^i are positively correlated. The skewness and inequality in I_3^i would exceed that in I_2^i, and both skewness and inequality would continue to increase until the equilibrium distribution of income was reached (see Mathematical Appendix, note F). The main cause of skewness in the distribution of income is the positive correlation between the equilibrium income of parents and their propensity to invest in children. Families with higher propensities to invest have higher incomes in that they spend a smaller fraction of their incomes on consumption and a larger fraction on investments in descendants.

Government Redistribution of Income

Taxation, subsidies, and other public expenditures have been ignored up to now, but can readily be incorporated into our analysis of income distribution. The difference between taxes paid and benefits received by the ith family in the tth generation can be approximated by the relation

$$T_t^i = b + sI_t^{gi} + \Omega_t^i, \qquad (7.18)$$

where I^g is "taxable" income, b and s are constants, and Ω has a zero mean and is assumed to be distributed independently of market and endowed luck. If $b < 0$ and $s > 0$, the tax-benefit system would tend to be "progressive," because net taxes would be a larger fraction of income at higher income levels; if s were constant, the system would, however, be "proportional" at the margin. The variable Ω partly measures the difficulty in defining taxable income (leisure, for instance, is excluded), and partly measures differences in the political power of persons with similar incomes. Farmers, teachers, and truck drivers, for example, have received greater political benefits than delicatessen owners, auto mechanics, and laborers because they have had greater political power.

Disposable family income can be defined as the sum of the income of parents net of their taxes and benefits (their disposable own income) and the value to parents of the disposable endowment and market luck of their children:

$$S_t^d = I_t^d + \frac{(1 - s)(e_{t+1} + u_{t+1}) - (b + \Omega_{t+1})}{1 + r_a}, \qquad (7.19)$$

where r_a is the after-tax rate of return on investments. If the effect on the family of all government programs were known to parents, they would maximize their utility subject to disposable family income, where utility depends on own consumption and the disposable income of children. The income- and investment-generating equations would be

$$I_{t+1}^d = \beta_a I_t^d + \alpha(1 - s)(e_{t+1} + u_{t+1}) - \alpha b - \alpha \Omega_{t+1}, \qquad (7.20)$$

$$y_t = \beta_a I_t^d - (1 - \alpha)(1 - s)(e_{t+1} + u_{t+1})$$
$$+ (1 - \alpha)b + (1 - \alpha)\Omega_{t+1}, \qquad (7.21)$$

where $\beta_a = \alpha(1 + r_a)$ is the after-tax propensity to invest.[11] Each dollar of taxes paid by children reduces their disposable income only by α dollars, because parents increase their investments by $(1 - \alpha)$ dollars.

Equation (7.19) implies that disposable family income is not affected by a subsidy to parents financed by a tax on children or by a subsidy to children financed by a tax on parents; that is,

$$dS_t^d = 0, \quad \text{if } dI_t^d = \frac{(db + d\Omega_{t+1})}{1 + r_a}. \qquad (7.22)$$

Furthermore, the disposable income of children would not change if disposable family income were unchanged. Parents would increase or decrease their expenditures on children (see Eq. 7.21) to offset the taxes on or benefits to children. Therefore, Eqs. (7.19) to (7.21) immediately show why a public debt financed by future taxes, or transfers to the elderly financed by taxes on the young, may not burden future generations or the young—nor will they benefit present generations or the elderly.[12] Similarly, public education and other programs to aid the young may not significantly benefit them because of compensating decreases in parental expenditures.[13]

---

11. Equation (7.21) implies that Ω_{t+1}^i would not be independent of before-tax income (I_{t+1}^i) if Ω_{t+1}^i were anticipated by parents, since their investments increase when Ω_{t+1} increases. This explains why I have assumed that Ω_t^i is independent of u_t^i and v_t^i, but not necessarily of taxable income (I_t^{gi}).

12. See the argument in Barro (1974) and subsequent discussions in his later work (1976, 1978) and that of Feldstein (1976); see also Chapter 11.

13. Some of these programs are discussed in Chapter 6. Peltzman (1973) and McPherson (1974) find rather small effects of subsidies to higher education on enrollments in higher education.

Therefore, little generality is lost by assuming that the budget is balanced in each generation:

$$\bar{T}_t = 0, \quad \text{for all } t,$$

which implies that

$$b = -s\bar{I}^g, \quad \text{and} \quad \bar{I}_t^d = \bar{I}_t - \bar{T}_t = \bar{I}_t, \tag{7.23}$$

where $\bar{I}_t$ is average before-tax income. If all families are identical, the equilibrium level of average income is immediately derived from Eq. (7.20):

$$\bar{I}^d = \bar{I} = \frac{\alpha(1 - s)\bar{e}}{1 - \beta_a - \alpha s\ell}, \tag{7.24}$$

where $\ell = \bar{I}^g/\bar{I}$. An increase in s reduces β_a by reducing the after-tax rate of return,[14] and an increase in s would also reduce the numerator of Eq. (7.24) if α were not significantly raised. Therefore, an increase in s is likely to reduce equilibrium incomes because investments in children are discouraged by the reduction in after-tax rates of return.

The equilibrium standard deviation of disposable income is also readily derived from Eq. (7.20). The equilibrium coefficient of variation is obtained by dividing the equilibrium standard deviation by equilibrium average income:

$$CV_{\bar{I}d}^2 = \frac{(1 - \beta_a - \alpha s\ell)^2}{1 - \beta_a^2} \left[CV_u^2 + \frac{(1 + h\beta_a)}{(1 - h\beta_a)} CV_e^2 + \frac{CV_\Omega^2}{(1 - s)^2} \right], \tag{7.25}$$

where $CV_\Omega = \sigma_\Omega/\bar{e}$. It is easily shown from Eqs. (7.24) and (7.25) that an increase in s would decrease the equilibrium standard deviation of disposable income if α and σ_Ω^2 were not significantly raised. The effect on the coefficient of variation, however, is less obvious because an increase in s tends also to reduce average income.

The effect on the coefficient of variation can be determined if the definition of taxable income is explicitly related to the definition of before-tax income. Taxable income depends on whether investments

---

14. A reduction in the after-tax rate of return would raise the fraction of disposable family income spent on children if the elasticity of substitution between parental consumption and the disposable income of children were less than unity. The after-tax propensity to invest, $\beta_a = \alpha(1 + r_a)$, would be reduced, however, because any rise in α would not completely offset the fall in r_a (see note 10). An increase in s could reduce the denominator of (7.24) if any increase in $\alpha s\ell$ exceeded the decrease in β_a.

in children can be written off, whether depreciation can be deducted from taxable income, whether interest is taxed as it accrues, and by similar issues. Consider two plausible definitions:

$$I_t^{g_1} = y_{t-1} + e_t + u_t = I_t$$

$$\text{and} \quad I_t^{g_2} = I_t^{g_1} - \frac{y_{t-1}}{1 + r} = I_t - \frac{y_{t-1}}{1 + r}.$$

(7.26)

The first is the before-tax income of previous sections, while the second permits investments in children to be depreciated. If we continue to assume that the before-tax rate of return, r, is unaffected by the accumulation of capital, the after-tax propensities to invest corresponding to these definitions of taxable income are

$$\alpha(1 + r_{a_1}) = \beta_{a_1} = \alpha(1 - s)(1 + r)$$

$$\text{and} \quad \alpha(1 + r_{a_2}) = \beta_{a_2} = \alpha[1 + (1 - s)r].$$

(7.27)

The term outside the brackets in Eq. (7.25) (since $\ell_1 = 1$) is

$$f_1 = \frac{(1 - \beta_{a_1} - \alpha s \ell_1)^2}{1 - \beta_{a_1}^2} = \frac{(1 - \beta_{a_2})^2}{1 - \beta_{a_1}^2}, \quad \text{for } I^g = I^{g_1}$$

$$\text{and} \quad f_2 = \frac{(1 - \beta_{a_2} - \alpha s \ell_2)^2}{1 - \beta_{a_2}^2}, \quad \text{for } I^g = I^{g_2}.$$

(7.28)

An increase in s necessarily increases f_1 if α is unaffected, if r exceeds 0.52, and if s exceeds $+0.1$. An increase in s also tends to increase f_2, especially if r is larger than ℓ_2.[15]

An increase in s lowers the coefficient of CV_e^2 and raises the coefficient of CV_Ω^2 in the bracketed term in Eq. (7.25) and may affect the variability of Ω itself. Since an increase in s also tends to raise the term outside the brackets, our analysis does not support the prevalent view that redistribution within a progressive tax/benefit system narrows the inequality in disposable incomes; indeed, such redistribution may well widen the inequality even in disposable income.

Most discussions of inequality ignore the relation between taxes or

---

15. By differentiation, $\partial f_1 / \partial s > 0$ if $r > (1 + r)^2(1 - s)\alpha(1 - \alpha)$. If $s \geq 0.1$, this inequality would be satisfied when $r > 0.225(1 + r)^2$—because $\alpha(1 - \alpha) \leq 1/4$—or when $r > 0.52$.

In the case of f_2, $\partial f_2 / \partial s > 0$ if $r - \ell_2 > r\beta_a(1 - \alpha s \ell_2) - \ell_2 \beta_{a_2}^2$. This inequality necessarily holds if $r > \ell_2$ and if $1 - \alpha s \ell_2 \leq \beta_{a_2}$, and it could hold when these inequalities are reversed.

benefits and variables other than income (represented by Ω in our formulation) and do not go beyond the initial impact to equilibrium distributions. Although progressive redistribution *initially* narrows inequality by reducing the variability in after-tax incomes (if the variability in Ω is small), the equilibrium level of inequality may well be raised, because families reduce their investments in descendants. Perhaps this conflict between initial and equilibrium effects explains why the large growth in redistribution during the last 50 years has had only modest effects on after-tax inequality.

Therefore, a progressive income tax system not only reduces efficiency by discouraging investment but may also widen the equilibrium inequality in disposable incomes. By contrast, policies that improve access of poor families to the capital market to finance their investments in human capital reduce inequality while raising efficiency (see the discussion in Chapter 6).

Economic Growth

The equilibrium level of income is stationary because I have assumed that β and h are less than unity, and that income per unit of capital (w), rates of return (r), and average endowments ($\bar{e}$) are constant over time. If, say, w grew over time because of autonomous technological progress, the income-generating equation (6.8) could be written as

$$I^*_{t+1} = \frac{\beta}{1+\gamma} I^*_t + \alpha w_{t+1} e_{t+1} + \alpha w_{t+1} u_{t+1}$$
$$= \beta^* I^*_t + \alpha w_{t+1} e_{t+1} + \alpha w_{t+1} u_{t+1}, \qquad (7.29)$$

where $I^*_t = (w_{t+1}/w_t)\, I_t = (1 + \gamma)I_t$ is the income in generation t valued in units of w_{t+1}, and γ is the given rate of growth per generation in w. The propensity to invest is reduced from β to β^* because parents invest less in children when the endowments of children increase.

If β^* and h were less than unity, Eq. (7.29) implies that the equilibrium level of average income in generation t would equal

$$\bar{I}_t = \frac{\alpha w_t \bar{e}}{1 - \beta^*}. \qquad (7.30)$$

Since w_t grows at the rate of γ per generation, $\bar{I}_t$ would not be stationary but would grow at the same rate. An increase in γ raises the equilibrium rate of growth in income, at the same time lowering the equilibrium level of income for any given w_t because an increase in γ reduces the propensity to invest in children.

The equilibrium coefficient of variation in income would still be stationary, inasmuch as both the standard deviation of income and average income grow at the rate of γ per generation. The only change from Eq. (7.10) is that β is replaced by β^*. Similarly, the relative degree of intergenerational mobility is unchanged from Eq. (7.14), except that again β is replaced by β^*.

Since intergenerational mobility and the coefficient of variation are negatively related to the propensity to invest, an increase in γ would raise intergenerational mobility and inequality within a generation. More rapid growth in incomes would be associated both with more equal opportunity between generations and with less equal outcomes within a generation. The absence of a clear-cut association between economic growth and "inequality" (Paukert, 1973, diagram 1), is not surprising, especially since growth might also be associated with higher rates of return on investments and lower degrees of inheritability.

Since the distribution of income converges to a stationary coefficient of variation even when β exceeds unity if β^* (and h) are less than unity, the assumption made throughout this chapter that $\beta < 1$ can be replaced by the weaker assumption that

$$\beta = \alpha(1 + r) < 1 + \gamma. \tag{7.31}$$

Therefore, the rate of return per generation could significantly exceed unity, and more than half of family income could be spent on children, yet the analysis in this chapter would be fully applicable as long as the rate of growth in income was sufficiently large.

The Quantity of Children

An easy way to generalize the assumption that each family has only one child is to assume that the number of children is determined exogenously. The utility function and family income of parents would then depend on the number as well as the income of children:

$$U_t^i = U(Z_t^i, I_{t+1}^i, n_t^i) \tag{7.32}$$

and
$$Z_t^i + \frac{n_t^i}{1 + r} I_{t+1}^i = I_t^i + \frac{n_t^i(e_{t+1}^i + u_{t+1}^i)}{1 + r}, \tag{7.33}$$

where $w_t = 1$ for all t, n_t^i is the number of children of the ith family in the tth generation, and all siblings are assumed to be identical. The shadow cost of investing in children is

$$\pi_{I_{t+1}}^i = \frac{n_t^i}{1 + r} \tag{7.34}$$

because an increase in the number of children raises the total cost of adding to the income of each child (as discussed in Chapters 5 and 6).

If U_t is maximized with respect to Z_t and I_{t+1}, subject to Eq. (7.33) and a given n_t, the income-generating equation for I_{t+1} would be

$$I_{t+1}^i = \frac{\alpha(\pi_{I_{t+1}}^i, n_t^i)(1 + r)I_t^i}{n_t^i} + \alpha(e_{t+1}^i + u_{t+1}^i)$$

$$= \hat{\beta}_t^i I_t^i + \alpha(e_{t+1}^i + u_{t+1}^i), \tag{7.35}$$

where $\hat{\beta}_t^i = [\alpha(\pi_{I_{t+1}}^i, n_t^i)(1 + r)]/n_t^i$ is the quantity-adjusted propensity to invest of the ith family in the tth generation. The fraction of family income spent on children (α) depends on the shadow cost of adding to the income of children (π_I), and also separately on the number of children (a change in numbers would usually change the ratio of the marginal utility of own consumption to the marginal utility of children's income).

An increase in numbers would lower the adjusted propensity to invest (β), because the fraction of family income spent on children would increase (if at all) by a smaller percent than the numbers. Therefore, families with more children invest less in each child and the effect of parents' income on the income of each child is weaker. Moreover, the distribution of income is more unequal and skewed when the distribution of children among families is more unequal and skewed, because the distribution of adjusted propensities to invest is then more unequal and skewed.

The trouble with this analysis is that the number of children is not exogenous; as we saw in Chapters 5 and 6, it is determined by the utility maximizing behavior of parents along with the quality of children and parental consumption. The simultaneously determined "observed" demand functions for quantity and quality of children (see Eq. 6.21) are as follows:

$$n_t = d_n(I_t, e_{t+1} + u_{t+1}) \tag{7.36}$$

$$I_{t+1} = d_I(I_t, e_{t+1} + u_{t+1}). \qquad (7.37)$$

The interaction between the demands for quantity and quality raises the effect of endowments or market luck and lowers the effect of own income on the quantity of children; indeed, an increase in own income could reduce the quantity of children even if an increase in own income would significantly raise quantity when the *shadow* prices of quantity and quality were held constant. Similarly, the interaction raises the effect of own income and lowers the effect of endowments or market luck on the demand for quality of children.

By repeated substitution for e_{t+1} from Eq. (7.2) and I_t from Eq. (7.37), n_t and I_{t+1} would become functions of the whole series of past and present values of market and endowed luck (u_{t+1}, u_t, . . . ; v_{t+1}, v_t, . . .), the degree of inheritability (h), and the parameters of Eqs. (7.36) and (7.37). These derived functions can be used to obtain the equilibrium distributions of income per person and number of children per family, and the equilibrium covariance between number of children and parental income (Tomes and Becker, 1981).

If the endowments or market luck of siblings differed, if human capital were distinguished from nonhuman capital, and if parental preferences were child neutral (see Eq. 6.12), richer families would invest more human capital and less nonhuman capital in abler children, whereas "poorer" families (that is, families who invest only in human capital) would invest more human capital in abler children only if efficiency dominated equity in these families. Parental responses in richer families to differences among their children would widen the inequality in earnings and narrow the inequality in total incomes of these children, while parental responses in poorer families would widen or narrow the inequality in earnings of their children as efficiency or equity dominated.

Assortative Mating

Chapters 3 and 4 assume that participants in marriage markets maximize their utility subject to the competition from other participants. If each has complete knowledge of the characteristics of all participants, efficient marriage markets combine persons with similar family background, intelligence, preferences, and other characteristics. If, however, the information about participants is imperfect, the degree of positive sorting can be substantially reduced (see Chapter 10).

Each family is easily followed over time in this analysis because marriage and sexual reproduction have been ignored. Fortunately, families can also be followed when persons marry to reproduce, even if the degree of assortative mating is quite weak. To simplify the discussion, assume that parents have two children who are identical except that only one (perhaps the elder or the son) carries the family name after he marries. All children marry when they become adults, and for the present, marriage is assumed to be unproductive in the sense that the income of each person is entirely determined by his endowment, market luck, and investments by parents. If children inherit a fraction (h) of the average endowment of their parents, the income-generating equation for a child of the ith family would be

$$I_{t+1}^i = \frac{\beta}{2}(I_t^i + I_t^{ki}) + \frac{\alpha h}{2}(e_t^i + e_t^{ki}) + \alpha(1 - h)\bar{e} + \alpha(v_{t+1}^i + u_{t+1}^i), \quad (7.38)$$

where $e_t^i = (1 - h)\bar{e} + (h/2)(e_{t-1}^i + e_{t-1}^{ki}) + v_t^i$, $I_t^i + I_t^{ki}$ is the total income of his parents, the person carrying the name of the ith family in the tth generation marries someone from the k_tth family, and I assume that $w_t = 1$ for all t.

The similarity between the incomes and endowments of mates depends on the information in marriage markets. We assume that these characteristics of mates are determined through the following linear stochastic sorting equations:

$$I_t^{ki} = \bar{I}_t(1 - R_I) + R_I I_t^i + \phi_t^i$$
$$\text{and} \quad e_t^{ki} = \bar{e}(1 - R_e) + R_e e_t^i + \psi_t^i. \quad (7.39)$$

The stochastic variables ϕ_t and ψ_t are assumed to be uncorrelated with I_t and e_t but tend to be correlated with each other. The coefficients R_I and R_e measure the degree of assortative mating of each characteristic and assumed to be stationary over time. An increase in the information in marriage markets would raise R_I and R_e and lower the variability in ϕ and ψ.[16] Although persons with similar family backgrounds tend to

---

16. Since all persons are assumed to marry, $\sigma_{I^k}^2 = \sigma_{I^i}^2$ and $\sigma_{e^k}^2 = \sigma_{e^i}^2$. Therefore

$$\sigma_{\phi_t}^2 = (1 - R_I^2)\sigma_{I_t}^2 \text{ and } \sigma_{\psi_t}^2 = (1 - R_e^2)\sigma_{e_t}^2,$$

and increases in R_I and R_e decrease σ_ϕ^2 and σ_ψ^2 respectively.

marry (R_I and R_e would be greater than zero), different generations of the same family usually marry into different families (that is, k depends on t as well as i).

By substituting these equations into (7.38), one obtains the income-generating equation

$$I_{t+1}^i = \tilde{\beta}I_t^i + \alpha\tilde{h}e_t^i + z_{t+1}^i, \tag{7.40}$$

where $\tilde{\beta} = (\beta/2)(1 + R_I)$, $\tilde{h} = (h/2)(1 + R_e)$, and

$$z_{t+1}^i = \alpha(1 - h)\bar{e} + \frac{\beta}{2}(1 - R_I)\bar{I}_t + \frac{\alpha h}{2}(1 - R_e)\bar{e}$$
$$+ \alpha(v_{t+1}^i + u_{t+1}^i) + \frac{\beta}{2}\phi_t^i + \frac{\alpha h}{2}\psi_t^i. \tag{7.41}$$

Endowments can be eliminated from Eq. (7.40) (by the method used earlier) to obtain an equation linking the incomes of three consecutive generations:

$$I_{t+1}^i = (\tilde{\beta} + \tilde{h})I_t^i - \tilde{\beta}\tilde{h}I_{t-1}^i + \alpha z_{t+1}^{*i}, \tag{7.42}$$

where z_{t+1}^{*i} depends on z_{t+1}, h, and lagged values of some of the stochastic variables.

Equations (7.40) and (7.42) are the same as Eqs. (7.3) and (7.15) except that β and h are replaced by $\tilde{\beta}$ and $\tilde{h}$ (see Mathematical Appendix, note G), and ϕ and ψ are part of the stochastic terms. Since (7.40) and (7.42) are identical to these earlier equations when $R_I = R_e = 1$, the previous analysis is equivalent to assuming perfect assortative mating in incomes and endowments. Perfect sorting of both characteristics may not be feasible, however, partly because each participant in a marriage market has a given "bundle" of income and endowments (see Wessels, 1976; Goldberger, 1979; and note G), but mainly because of imperfect information about these characteristics. The family backgrounds and other characteristics of prospects can be readily assessed, but not their endowments and market luck. Imperfect information reduces the degree of positive sorting and raises the importance of stochastic determinants of marriages.

Improved information in marriage markets raises the degree of positive sorting by income and endowments, and hence also raises $\tilde{\beta}$ and $\tilde{h}$. Since an increase in β or h increases the equilibrium variance in incomes, improved information and more positive sorting also increases the equilibrium variance in incomes,[17] although the effect would be tempered by a reduced variability in the stochastic determinants of sorting (ϕ and ψ).

I have shown that if β and h are sufficiently large—that is, if ($\beta + h$) is sufficiently greater than unity—the incomes of descendants would remain well above or below average for many generations, simply because one ancestor had been rich or poor. Equation (7.42) indicates that ($\tilde{\beta} + \tilde{h}$) is the relevant determinant of intergenerational mobility when assortative mating is not perfect. Then if β and h are both less than unity, intergenerational mobility would *necessarily* be quite large without strong assortative mating by income and endowments. For example, the incomes of descendants return monotonically and rapidly to normal for all values of β and h less than unity when one ancestor has been rich or poor, if mating is randomly related to income and endowments. This is so because

$$\tilde{\beta} + \tilde{h} < 1, \quad \text{if } R_I = R_e = 0 \text{ and } \beta, h < 1. \tag{7.43}$$

Aside from repeated good or bad luck, families would not remain rich or poor for many generations unless mates by and large have similar characteristics.

I have been assuming that a person's income does not depend on the characteristics of his mate, which is equivalent to assuming that

---

17. Others have also concluded that inequality is raised by an increase in assortative mating (see for instance Blinder, 1973, 1976, and Atkinson, 1975). Indeed, Plato argued for negative sorting by temperament and family background because he believed that positive sorting increased inequality:

We will say to him who is born of good parents,—O my son, you ought to make such a marriage as wise men would approve . . . always to honour inferiors, and with them to form connexions;—this will be for the benefit of the city and of the families which are united . . . he who is conscious of being too headstrong . . . ought to desire to become the relation of orderly parents; and he who is of the opposite temper ought to seek the opposite alliance . . . everyone is by nature prone to that which is likest to himself, and in this way the whole city becomes unequal in property and in disposition; and hence there arise in most states the very results which we least desire to happen . . . the rich man shall not marry into the rich family, nor the powerful into the family of the powerful . . . we should try . . . to charm the spirits of men into believing the equability of their children's disposition to be of more importance than equality of excessive fortune when they marry (Plato, 1953, pp. 340–341).

average income is independent of the degree of sorting.[18] Yet the analysis of marriage markets in Chapters 3, 4, and 10 indicates that the degree of sorting is important precisely because the output of married households depends on the characteristics of *both* mates. An increase in R_I and R_e due to improved information in marriage markets raises the output of the average marriage because mates would be better matched. Therefore, an increase in R_I and R_e might well lower the equilibrium coefficient of variation in incomes even though the standard deviation of incomes would increase (average income could increase by a greater percent). Other discussions of the effect of assortative mating on income inequality, which have concluded that an increase in the degree of positive sorting must raise inequality, ignore the effect of sorting on marital productivity. See, for example, Blinder (1973, 1976) or Atkinson (1975, pp. 150–151).

If the rate of growth in income per unit of capital (w) equals γ per generation, the adjusted propensity to invest and the degree of inheritability become:

$$\tilde{\beta} = \frac{\beta(1 + R_I)}{2(1 + \gamma)} \quad \text{and} \quad \tilde{h} = \frac{h(1 + R_e)}{2}. \tag{7.44}$$

If $R_I \cong 0.6$ (approximately the correlation between the education of spouses), $R_e = +0.5$, and $\gamma \cong +0.4$ (about a 1.2-percent growth in w per year compounded for 25 years), then $\tilde{\beta} = 0.57\beta$ and $\tilde{h} = 0.75h$. Hence sizable growth and far-from-perfect sorting substantially reduce both the propensity to invest and the degree of inheritability, and thereby significantly lower both the absolute variability of income and the degree of intergenerational *im*mobility (as measured by the function g_m in Figure 7.1). The relative variability of income, however, is

---

18. Equation (7.40) implies that average income is independent of R_I and R_e, for by taking expectations:

$$E(I_{t+1}) = \tilde{\beta}E(I_t) + \alpha\tilde{h}\bar{e} + \frac{\beta}{2}(1 - R_I)E(I_t) + \frac{\alpha h}{2}(1 - R_e)\bar{e} + \alpha\bar{e}(1 - h)$$

$$= \beta E(I_t) + \alpha\bar{e}.$$

Hence, in stationary equilibrium,

$$E(I) = \frac{\alpha\bar{e}}{1 - \beta},$$

which is the same as Eq. (7.8) and is independent of R_I and R_e.

raised by growth and might also be raised by imperfect sorting because sorting has a sizable effect on marital output.

Summary and Conclusions

The crucial assumption in the theory of inequality and intergenerational mobility presented in this chapter is that each family maximizes a utility function spanning two generations—an assumption I use throughout the book. Utility depends on the consumption of parents and the quality of children, where quality is measured by the income of children when they become adults. Note H of the Mathematical Appendix shows that the implications are similar when quality is measured by the utility of children when they become adults.

The income of children is raised when they receive human and nonhuman capital from their parents. Their income is also raised by endowments of family reputation and connections; knowledge, skills, and goals provided by their family environment; and genetically determined race and other characteristics. The fortunes of children are linked to their parents not only through investments but also through these endowments.

The income of children also depends on stochastic terms measuring their luck in the endowment "lottery" and in the market for income. The distribution of luck is the foundation of many models of the distribution of income that ignore utility maximization. Luck and utility maximization interact in our analysis because the optimal investment in children depends on both their market luck and their endowed luck.

Parents maximize their utility subject to their own income, the inherited endowments of children, and any anticipated endowed and market luck of children. The optimal investment in children depends on the propensity to invest in children, an important parameter of the analysis. This propensity is positively related to the fraction of family income spent on children, rates of return on investments in children, and the degree of assortative mating; it is negatively related to the rate of growth in income.

The equilibrium income of children is determined by their market and endowed luck, the income and endowment of parents, and the two basic parameters—the degree of inheritability of endowments and the propensity to invest in children. If these parameters are both less than unity, the distribution of income between families approaches a stationary distribution. The stationary coefficient of variation of income is greater, the larger the inequality in the distribution of market and endowed luck, the larger the degree of inheritability, and the smaller the propensity to invest in children. The propensity to invest is increased by a fall in the rate of growth in incomes over time or by a rise in rates of return.

Differences among families in rates of return, average endowments, or other parameters raise the inequality in income and stretch out the income distribution by interacting with income and luck. For example, families with higher propensities to invest have higher incomes, an interaction that raises inequality and skews the distribution of income to the right, even if luck and all parameters are symmetrically distributed.

A progressive system of government redistribution is usually said to narrow the inequality in disposable income. One of the more surprising implications of our analysis is that progressive taxes and expenditures may well widen the inequality in the long-run equilibrium distribution of disposable income, essentially because parents are discouraged from investing in their children by lower after-tax rates of return.

The incomes and endowments of parents and other family members have a more significant effect on the incomes of children and later descendants when the degree of inheritability and the propensity to invest are larger. Although a higher income in one generation has negligible effects on the incomes of much later descendants if both these parameters are less than unity, the incomes of children, grandchildren, and other early descendants can be significantly increased. Indeed, if the sum of these parameters were to exceed unity, incomes would rise for several generations before falling, and the maximum increase in income could exceed the initial increase. These effects do not always decline continuously because of the interaction between the degree of inheritability and the propensity to invest: an increase, say, in the degree of inheritability raises the effect on incomes of a change in the propensity to invest.

The influence of family background on the relative economic position of children is greater when propensities to invest and other parameters differ more among families. For example, all generations of a family with a lower-than-average propensity to invest tend to have lower than average incomes by virtue of investing less in their descendants.

The analysis in this chapter firmly demonstrates that a theory of the distribution of income need not be a mixture of Pareto distributions, ad hoc probability mechanisms, and arbitrary assumptions about inheritance, but can be based on the same principles of maximizing behavior and equilibrium that form the core of microeconomics. The theory readily incorporates the effects of luck, family background, assortative mating, and cultural, biological, and financial inheritance on the distribution of income. Furthermore, inequality within a generation and inequality across generations do not require separate economic and sociological approaches; both can be analyzed with a unified theory of the determination of the incomes of different families in different generations.

Mathematical Appendix

A. From Eq. (7.6),

$$\sigma_I^2 = \alpha^2\sigma_u^2 \sum_{k=0}^{\infty} \beta^{2k} + \alpha^2\sigma_v^2 \sum_{k=0}^{\infty} \left(\frac{\beta^{k+1} - h^{k+1}}{\beta - h}\right)^2$$

$$= \frac{\alpha^2\sigma_u^2}{1 - \beta^2} + \alpha^2\sigma_v^2 \sum_{k=0}^{\infty} \frac{\beta^{2(k+1)} + h^{2(k+1)} - 2h^{k+1}\beta^{k+1}}{(\beta - h)^2} \quad \text{if } \beta, h < 1.$$

The summation in the second term can be written as

$$\left(\frac{\beta^2}{1 - \beta^2} + \frac{h^2}{1 - h^2} - \frac{2h\beta}{1 - h\beta}\right) \frac{1}{(\beta - h)^2},$$

or as

$$\frac{\beta^2(1 - h^2)(1 - h\beta) + h^2(1 - \beta^2)(1 - h\beta) - 2h\beta(1 - h^2)(1 - \beta^2)}{(\beta - h)^2(1 - h^2)(1 - \beta^2)(1 - h\beta)},$$

which equals

$$\frac{(\beta - h)^2(1 + h\beta)}{(\beta - h)^2(1 - h^2)(1 - \beta^2)(1 - h\beta)}.$$

A simpler and more transparent derivation of the equilibrium variance follows from taking the variance of both sides of Eq. (7.6):

$$\sigma_{I_{t+1}}^2 = \beta^2\sigma_{I_t}^2 + \alpha^2h^2\sigma_{e_t}^2 + 2\alpha\beta h \, \text{Cov}_{I_t e_t} + \alpha^2\sigma_v^2 + \alpha^2\sigma_u^2. \quad \text{(A.1)}$$

Since $e_t^i = a + he_{t-1}^i + v_t$,

$$\text{Cov}_{I_t e_t} = \beta h \, \text{Cov}_{I_{t-1} e_{t-1}} + \alpha \sigma_e^2.$$

If variances and covariances are in stationary equilibrium,

$$\text{Cov}_{I_t e_t} = \text{Cov}_{I_{t-1} e_{t-1}}, \qquad \sigma_{I_{t+1}}^2 = \sigma_{I_t}^2 = \sigma_I^2 \text{ and } \sigma_{e_{t+1}}^2 = \sigma_{e_t}^2 = \frac{\sigma_v^2}{1 - h^2}.$$

Then Eq. (A.1) can be written as

$$(1 - \beta^2)\sigma_I^2 = \frac{\alpha^2 \sigma_v^2}{1 - h^2} + \frac{2\alpha^2 \beta h \sigma_v^2}{(1 - \beta h)(1 - h^2)} + \alpha^2 \sigma_u^2.$$

Hence

$$\sigma_I^2 = \frac{\alpha^2}{1 - \beta^2} \sigma_u^2 + \frac{\alpha^2(1 + \beta h)}{(1 - h^2)(1 - \beta h)(1 - \beta^2)} \sigma_v^2.$$

B. Since $I_{t+1}^i = \beta I_t^i + \alpha h e_t^i + \alpha u_{t+1}^i + \alpha v_{t+1}^i + a$ constant, then by definition of the multiple correlation coefficient:

$$R^2(I_{t+1}; I_t, e_t) = \frac{\beta^2 \sigma_{I_t}^2 + \alpha^2 h^2 \sigma_{e_t}^2 + 2\alpha h \beta \, \text{Cov}_{I_t e_t}}{\sigma_{I_{t+1}}^2}$$

$$= \beta^2 + \frac{\alpha^2 \sigma_{e_t}^2}{\sigma_I^2}\left(h^2 + \frac{2h\beta}{1 - h\beta}\right) > \beta^2$$

since in equilibrium $\text{Cov}_{I_t e_t} = (\alpha \sigma_e^2)/(1 - h\beta)$ and $\sigma_{I_{t+1}}^2 = \sigma_{I_t}^2 = \sigma_I^2$. If $\sigma_u^2/\sigma_e^2 \cong 0$, from Eq. (7.7) $\sigma_I^2 \cong (1 + h\beta)\alpha^2 \sigma_e^2/(1 - h\beta)(1 - \beta^2)$ if we recall that $\sigma_v^2 = (1 - h^2)\sigma_e^2$. Then

$$R^2 \cong \beta^2 + \frac{(1 - \beta^2)h(2\beta + h - \beta h^2)}{1 + h\beta}.$$

(Note that $\partial R^2/\partial h > 0$.)

C.

$$\dot{g}_m = \frac{\partial g_m}{\partial m} = \frac{\beta^m \log \beta - h^m \log h}{\beta - h}.$$

If $\beta > h$, $\dot{g}_m \lesseqgtr 0$ as $(\beta/h)^m \gtreqless \log h/\log \beta$, since $\beta < 1$.

The right-hand side is a constant and the left-hand side increases indefinitely as m increases, so g_m must reach a single peak at a finite m

and then decline monotonically. Therefore, since $g_1 = 1$ and $g_2 = \beta + h$, g_m falls for all m when $\beta + h < 1$ and reaches a peak at $m > 1$ when $\beta + h > 1$. The maximizing value of m is found from

$$\dot{g}_m = 0 = \beta^m \log \beta - h^m \log h,$$

$$\text{or} \quad \hat{m} = \frac{\log \left(\dfrac{\log h}{\log \beta} \right)}{\log \beta - \log h}.$$

If $\beta = kh$, $1 < k < 1/h$, then

$$\frac{\partial \hat{m}}{\partial h} = \frac{1}{h \log h} \frac{1}{\log kh} > 0,$$

or increases in β and h that keep their ratio constant would increase $\hat{m}$.

D. Since

$$\sigma_{u_*}^2 = \alpha^2 [\sigma_u^2 (1 + h^2) + \sigma_v^2]$$

and

$$\text{Cov}_{u_t^* u_{t+1}^*} = \alpha^2 (-h\sigma_u^2),$$

then

$$\sigma_v^2 / \sigma_u^2 = (-h\sigma_{u_*}^2 / \text{Cov}_{u_t^* u_{t+1}^*}) - (1 + h)^2.$$

Consequently, σ_v^2 / σ_u^2 could be determined from h, $\sigma_{u_*}^2$, and $\text{Cov}_{u_t^* u_{t+1}^*}$.

E. A regression of I_{t+1} on I_t would omit I_{t-1} and u_t from Eq. (7.15). The least-squares estimate of the regression coefficient would be

$$b_{I_{t+1} I_t} = \beta + h - \beta h b_{I_{t-1} I_t} - \alpha h b_{u_t I_t},$$

where b_{yx} is the coefficient in a simple regression of y on x. Since $b_{I_{t-1} I_t}$ and $b_{u_t I_t}$ are both positive, and since $b_{I_{t+1} I_t} = b_{I_{t-1} I_t} = R_{I_{t+1} I_t} \leq 1$, where $R_{I_{t+1} I_t}$ is the correlation coefficient between I_{t+1} and I_t,

$$b_{I_{t+1} I_t} = \frac{\beta + h - \alpha h b_{u_t I_t}}{1 + \beta h} \leq \min(1, \beta + h),$$

and the difference might not be negligible.

A regression of I_{t+1} on I_t also omits the endowment of parents (e_t) from Eq. (7.3). Then

$$b_{I_{t+1} I_t} = \beta + \alpha h b_{e_t I_t} > \beta.$$

Hence

$$\beta < b_{I_{t+1}I_t} < \min(\beta + h, 1).$$

F. Since the equilibrium income of the ith family is $\bar{I}^i = \alpha\bar{e}/(1 - \beta^i)$, the distribution of these incomes would be skewed to the right when β^i is symmetrically distributed, because the inverse of a positive symmetrically distributed variable like $1 - \beta^i$ is skewed to the right.

To prove this, let $1 - \beta^i = x_i$, $y_i = 1/x_i$, and x_p and y_p be the pth percentile point in the distribution of x and y respectively. Then a (nonparametric) measure of skewness for the distribution of x is

$$s_x = \frac{x_p - x_{50}}{x_{50} - x_{100-p}} = 1$$

by the assumption that x is symmetrically distributed. Since $y_p = 1/(x_{100-p})$ for all p, because the ordering of the inverse is reversed, then

$$s_y = \frac{y_p - y_{50}}{y_{50} - y_{100-p}} = \frac{\dfrac{1}{x_{100-p}} - \dfrac{1}{x_{50}}}{\dfrac{1}{x_{50}} - \dfrac{1}{x_p}} = \frac{x_p}{x_{100-p}} > 1$$

where $p > 50$.

The distribution of income would be skewed even when all families have the same equilibrium propensity to invest, if temporarily high or low propensities are partly inherited. If

$$\beta_{t+1}^i = (1 - c)\bar{\beta} + c\beta_t^i + \delta_{t+1}^i, \qquad 0 < c \le 1,$$

then Eq. (7.17) becomes

$$I_{t+1}^i = \alpha\bar{e} + (1 - c)\bar{\beta}I_t^i + c\beta_{t-1}^i I_t^i + \delta_t^i I_t^i.$$

The distribution of $\beta_{t-1}^i I_t^i$ would be skewed to the right because β_{t-1}^i and I_t^i would be positively correlated.

G. Equation (7.39) can readily be generalized to include e_t^i in the determination of I_t^{ki} and I_t^i in the determination of e_t^{ki}:

$$I_t^{ki} = c_I + R_{II}I_t^i + R_{Ie}e_t^i + \phi_t^i$$

$$\text{and} \quad e_t^{ki} = c_e + R_{eI}I_t^i + R_{ee}e_t^i + \psi_t^i.$$

With this generalization the adjusted degree of inheritability ($\bar{h}$) depends on the rate of return (r) and on the effect of e^i on $I^{ki}(R_{Ie})$; similarly, the adjusted propensity to invest depends on h, r, and on the effect of I^i on $e^{ki}(R_{el})$:

$$\tilde{\beta} = \frac{\beta}{2} \left(1 + R_{II} + \frac{h}{1 + r} R_{el} \right)$$

and $\quad \tilde{h} = \frac{h}{2} \left(1 + R_{ee} + \frac{1 + r}{h} R_{Ie} \right).$

Otherwise, Eqs. (7.40) and (7.42) are not basically changed.

H. This appendix replaces the assumption that the utility function of parents depends on the income of children with the assumption that it depends on the utility or welfare of children (see also Chapter 8). Fortunately, the implications with respect to inequality and intergenerational mobility are similar.

If the utility function of parents in generation t depends on their own consumption and the welfare of children, as measured by a monotonic transformation of the children's utility function, then

$$U_t = V[Z_t, \psi(U_{t+1})], \tag{A.2}$$

where $(d\psi/dU_{t+1}) > 0$. Since the children's utility function, in turn, depends on their own consumption and a transformation of the utility function of their children—the grandchildren of the parents in the tth generation—and since the utility functions of different generations are assumed to be the same, Eq. (A.2) can be written as

$$U_t = V(Z_t, \psi\{V[Z_{t+1}, \psi(U_{t+2})]\}) = V^*[Z_t, Z_{t+1}, \phi(U_{t+2})]. \tag{A.3}$$

The utility function of grandchildren depends also on their own consumption and the utility function of their children, and so on for all generations. By substituting each of these successively later utility functions into the utility function of the tth generation, we can write the latter as a function of their own consumption and that of all descendants:

$$U_t = U(Z_t, Z_{t+1}, Z_{t+2}, \ldots). \tag{A.4}$$

Each generation either consumes or invests in children (investments in later generations are unnecessary). If the investment by the tth generation, y_t, is replaced using the budget equation of generation $t + 1$, the budget equation of the tth generation becomes:

$$Z_t + \frac{1}{1 + r} Z_{t+1} + \frac{1}{(1 + r)^2} y_{t+1} = I_t + \frac{1}{1 + r} e_{t+1} + \frac{1}{1 + r} u_{t+1}, \tag{A.5}$$

where y_{t+1} is the investment by generation $t + 1$ in generation $t + 2$. Replacing y_{t+1} by means of the budget equation of generation $t + 2$, and so on for all the subsequent y_{t+i}, the budget equation of the tth generation can be written in the following fundamental form:

$$Z_t + \frac{1}{1 + r} Z_{t+1} + \frac{1}{(1 + r)^2} Z_{t+2} + \ldots$$

$$= I_t + \frac{1}{(1 + r)} (e_{t+1} + u_{t+1}) + \frac{1}{(1 + r)^2} (e_{t+2} + u_{t+2}) + \ldots$$

(A.6)

The right-hand side gives "family wealth" at generation t, or the sum of own income at t and the present value of all subsequent endowments and market luck. The left-hand side shows that family wealth is spent on present consumption and the consumption of all descendants.

Family wealth at t is known only when there is perfect knowledge at t of the market and endowed luck of all descendants into the indefinite future, a task that exceeds the capacities of the most prescient. A more reasonable approach is to go to the opposite extreme and assume that the luck of descendants cannot be anticipated at all. If each family were unconcerned about risk, a utility function that depends on the expected consumption of different generations would be maximized subject to expected family wealth. The equilibrium conditions imply that expected family wealth in generation t depends on expected family wealth in $t - 1$, the propensity to invest (β), and realized market and endowed luck.

More important is the equilibrium relation among incomes in three consecutive generations:

$$I_{t+1} = k + (\beta + h)I_t - \beta h I_{t-1} + (u_{t+1} - hu_t) + (v_{t+1} - hv_t)$$

$$+ \frac{h(\beta - h)}{1 + r - h} v_t.$$

(A.7)

The coefficients of I_t and I_{t-1}—$(\beta + h)$ and $(-\beta h)$—are the same as in Eq. (7.15). The coefficients of current and lagged market luck and current endowed luck are similar to those in (7.15), while lagged endowed luck has a negative coefficient in (A.7) and does not enter (7.15). Since the coefficients of I_t and I_{t-1} in (A.7) and (7.15) are identical, utility functions that depend on the welfare of children and those that depend on the income of children have identical implications for the influence of family background on the incomes of children. Moreover, they have similar implications for the determination of the equilibrium distribution of income.

Human Capital and the Rise and Fall of Families

Ever since Pareto discovered that the distribution of larger incomes and wealth is reasonably well approximated by a particular skewed distribution, since then called the Pareto distribution, economists have continued to discuss inequality in the distribution of earnings, income, and wealth among individuals and families. However, they have paid little attention to the inequality within families over generations as determined by the relation between the incomes or wealth of parents, children, and later descendants. Schumpeter is the only major economist who systematically considered intergenerational mobility with empirical evidence as well as with theoretical analysis (see Schumpeter, 1951).

Sociologists and other social scientists, on the other hand, have

This supplement was written with Nigel Tomes and originally appeared in the *Journal of Labor Economics* 4 (1986): S1–S39. Reprinted here, in slightly amended form, by permission.

presented considerable empirical evidence on the occupations, education, and other characteristics of children and parents. Blau and Duncan (1967), in their influential book *The American Occupational Structure,* consider the effect of family background on the achievements of children. As long ago as 1889 John Dewey wrote, "Upon the average, children of parents who are exceptional, or who deviate from the mean, will themselves deviate from the mean only one third of their parents' deviation . . . It is not likely that children of the poor would be better off, and children of the wealthier poorer in anything like the ratio of 2/3" (Dewey, 1889, pp. 333–334; this statement was brought to our attention by O. D. Duncan).

Although discussions of inequality among families have been almost entirely separate from discussions of inequality among generations of the same family, analytically these inequalities are closely related. In particular, regression away from the mean in the relation between, say, the incomes of parents and children implies large and growing inequality of income over time, while regression toward the mean implies a smaller and more stable degree of inequality. These statements are obvious in a simple Markov model of the relation between parents and children:

$$I_{t+1} = a + bI_t + \varepsilon_{t+1}, \tag{7S.1}$$

where I_t is the income of parents, I_{t+1} is the income of children, a and b are constants, and the stochastic forces affecting the income of children (ε_{t+1}) are assumed to be independent of the income of parents.

Inequality in income will continue to grow over time if b is greater than or equal to unity, whereas inequality in income will approach a constant level if b is smaller than unity in absolute value. Clearly, the size of b also measures whether children of richer parents tend to be less rich than their parents and whether children of poorer parents tend to be better off than their parents. This example implies that, even in rigid and caste-dominated societies, many of the elite and underprivileged families would change places over generations unless inequality continued to grow over time ($b \geq 1$).

The degree of regression toward or away from the mean in the achievements of children compared to those of their parents is a measure of the degree of equality of opportunity in a society. This supplement analyzes the determinants of unequal opportunities, sometimes called intergenerational mobility or, as in our title, the rise and fall of families. We use these terms interchangeably.

A Treatise on the Family

The many empirical studies of mobility by sociologists have lacked a framework or model to interpret their findings. We try to remedy this defect and to fill a more general lacuna in the literature by developing a systematic model that relies on utility-maximizing behavior by all participants, equilibrium in different markets, and stochastic forces with unequal incidence among participants.

An analysis that is adequate to cope with the many aspects of the rise and fall of families must incorporate concern by parents for children as expressed in altruism toward children, investments in the human capital of children, assortative mating in marriage markets, the demand for children, the treatment by parents of exceptionally able or handicapped children, and expectations about events in the next or in even later generations. Although these and other aspects of behavior are incorporated in a consistent framework based on maximizing behavior, we do not pretend to handle them all in a satisfactory manner. But our approach indicates how a more complete analysis can be developed in the future.

Much of our analysis of human capital is based on the model developed in my Woytinsky Lecture (Becker, 1967) to explain different investments among families. That lecture, however, was mainly concerned with inequality and skewness in earnings and wealth and did not derive relations between the earnings and assets of parents and children. The approach here is also based on a series of papers by us that analyze marriage, fertility, altruism of parents, and long-run equilibrium relations between parents and children (see especially Becker, 1974b and this volume; Becker and Tomes, 1976, 1979; Tomes, 1981).

This supplement is closest in spirit to Becker and Tomes (1979), but there are important differences. We believe that the present discussion is a considerable improvement. We now distinguish human capital and earnings from other wealth, and we incorporate restrictions on the intergenerational transfer of debt. We assume that the utility of parents depends on the utility of children instead of on the permanent income of children. We also consider the effect of endogenous fertility on the relation between the wealth and the consumption of parents and children. These improvements explain why the implications of this supplement are sometimes quite different from those of the previous paper. In an essay devoted to critiquing parts of this book, Becker and Tomes (1984), and an early draft of this supplement, Goldberger (1985) sometimes fails to see these differences.

Since inequality over generations and inequality among families are closely related (as implied by Eq. 7S.1), any adequate analysis of inequality must also consider marital patterns, fertility, expectations about future generations, and investments in human capital. It is hardly surprising that a growing literature has tried to integrate more realistic models of family behavior into models of the distribution of income and wealth.[1] Although this literature and our work have many similarities, we are virtually alone in relating the rise and fall of families to investments in human capital that interact with the accumulation of assets, the evolution of consumption, and the demand for children.

Earnings and Human Capital

Perfect Capital Markets

Some children have an advantage because they are born into families with substantial ability, a strong emphasis on childhood learning, and other favorable cultural and genetic attributes. Both biology and culture are transmitted from parents to children, one encoded in the DNA and the other in a family's heritage. Much less is known about the transmission of cultural attributes than of biological ones, and even less is known about the relative contributions of biology and culture to the distinctive endowment of each family. We do not need to separate cultural from genetic endowments, and we will not try to specify the exact mechanism of cultural transmission. We follow our previous paper (Becker and Tomes, 1979; see also Bevan, 1979) in assuming as a first approximation that both are transmitted by a stochastic-linear or Markov equation:

$$E_t^i = \alpha_t + hE_{t-1}^i + v_t^i, \qquad (7S.2)$$

where E_t^i is the endowment (or vector of endowments) of the ith family in the tth generation, h is the degree (or vector of degrees) of "inheritability" of these endowments, and v_t^i measures unsystematic components or luck in the transmission process. We assume that parents cannot invest in their children's endowment.

---

1. Among the important contributors to this literature are Stiglitz (1969), Blinder (1974), Conlisk (1974), Behrman and Taubman (1976), Meade (1976), Bevan (1979), Laitner (1979), Menchik (1979), Shorrocks (1979), Loury (1981), and Atkinson (1983).

A priori restrictions on the magnitude or even on the sign of the inheritability of endowments are unnecessary, because the degree of inheritability can be estimated from accurate information on the earnings of parents and children (and perhaps also grandparents). Yet the assumption that endowments are only partially inherited, that h is less than unity and greater than zero, is a plausible generalization to cultural endowments of what is known about the inheritance of genetic traits. This assumption implies that endowments regress to the mean: children with well-endowed parents tend also to have endowments that are above average but smaller relative to the mean than those of their parents, whereas children with poorly endowed parents tend also to have below-average endowments but larger relative to the mean than those of their parents.

The term α_t can be interpreted as the social endowment common to all members of a given cohort in the same society. If the social endowment were constant over time, and if $h < 1$, the average endowment would eventually equal $1/(1 - h)$ times the social endowment (that is, $\lim \bar{E}_t = \alpha/[1 - h]$). However, α may not be constant because, for example, governments invest in the social endowment.

Practically all formal models of the distribution of income that consider wages and abilities assume that abilities automatically translate into earnings, mediated sometimes by demands for different kinds of abilities (see for example Roy, 1950; Mandelbrot, 1962; Tinbergen, 1970; Bevan and Stiglitz, 1979). This assumption is useful in understanding certain gross features of the distribution of earnings, such as its skewness, but it is hardly satisfactory for analyzing the effect of parents on their children's earnings. Not only do parents pass on some of their endowments to children, they also influence the adult earnings of their children by expenditures on their skills, health, learning, motivation, "credentials," and many other characteristics. These expenditures are determined by the abilities of children and also by the incomes, preferences, and fertility of parents as well as by the public expenditures on education and other human capital of children and other variables. Since earnings are practically the sole income for most persons, parents influence the economic welfare of their children primarily by influencing their potential earnings.

To analyze these influences in a simple way, assume two periods of life, childhood and adulthood, and assume that adult earnings depend on human capital (H), partly perhaps as a measure of credentials, and market luck (ℓ):

$$Y_t = \gamma(T_t, f_t)H_t + \ell_t. \tag{7S.3}$$

The earnings of one unit of human capital (γ) is determined by equilibrium in factor markets. It depends positively on technological knowledge (T) and negatively on the ratio of human capital to nonhuman capital in the economy (f). Since we are concerned with differences among families, the exact value of γ is not usually important because it is common to all families. Therefore we assume that the measurement of H is chosen so that $\gamma = 1$.

Although human capital takes many forms, including skills and abilities, personality, appearance, reputation, and appropriate credentials, we further simplify by assuming that it is homogeneous and the same "stuff" in different families. Since research demonstrates that investments during childhood are crucial to later development (see for instance Bloom, 1976), we assume also that the total amount of human capital accumulated, including on-the-job training, is proportional to the amount accumulated during childhood. Then adult human capital and expected earnings are determined by endowments inherited from parents and by parental (x) and public (s) expenditures on the child's development:

$$H_t = \Psi(x_{t-1}, s_{t-1}, E_t), \quad \text{with} \quad \Psi_j > 0, \quad j = x, s, E. \tag{7S.4}$$

Ability, early learning, and other aspects of a family's cultural and genetic "infrastructure" usually raise the marginal effect of family and public expenditures on the production of human capital; that is,

$$\frac{\partial^2 H_t}{\partial j_{t-1} \partial E_t} = \Psi_{jE} > 0, \quad j = x, s. \tag{7S.5}$$

The marginal rate of return on parental expenditures (r_m) is defined by the equation

$$\frac{\partial Y_t}{\partial x_{t-1}} = \frac{\partial H_t}{\partial x_{t-1}} = \Psi_x = 1 + r_m(x_{t-1}, s_{t-1}, E_t), \tag{7S.6}$$

where $\partial r_m/\partial E > 0$ by inequality (7S.5).

Although the human capital of different persons may be close substitutes in production, each person forms a separate human-capital "market." Rates of return to him depend on the amount invested in him as well as on aggregate stocks of human capital. Marginal rates of return eventually decline as more is invested in a person, because investment costs eventually rise as his forgone earnings increase. Also, benefits decline ever more rapidly as his residual working life shortens (see the more extended discussion in Becker, 1975).

Nonhuman capital or assets can usually be purchased and sold in relatively efficient markets. Presumably, therefore, returns on assets are less sensitive to the amount owned by any person than are returns on human capital. Little is known about the effect of abilities, other endowments, and wealth on returns from different assets, although some theory suggests a positive relation (see Ehrlich and Ben-Zion, 1976, and the evidence in Yitzhaki, 1984). Our analysis requires only the reasonable assumption that returns on assets are much less sensitive to endowments and accumulations by any individual than are returns on human capital (a similar assumption is made in Becker, 1967, 1975). A simple special case of this assumption is that the rate of return on assets is the same to all persons.

Much of the endowed luck of children (v_t) is revealed to parents prior to most of their investment in children. Therefore, we assume that rates of return on these investments are fully known to parents (as long as the social environment, α_t, and public expenditures, s_{t-1}, are known). Parents must decide how to allocate their total "bequest" to children between human capital and assets. We assume initially that parents can borrow at the asset interest rate to finance expenditures on children and that this debt can become the obligation of children when they are adults.

Parents are assumed to maximize the welfare of children when no reduction in their own consumption or leisure is entailed. Then parents borrow whatever is necessary to maximize the net income (earnings minus debt) of their children, which requires that expenditures on the human capital of children equate the marginal rate of return to the interest rate:

$$r_m = r_t, \quad \text{or} \quad \hat{x}_{t-1} = g(E_t, s_{t-1}, r_t), \tag{7S.7}$$

with $g_E > 0$ (by Eq. 7S.6), $g_r < 0$, and also with $g_s < 0$ (7S.8)

if public and private expenditures are substitutes. Parents can separate investments in children (an example of the separation theorem) from their own resources and altruism toward children because borrowed funds can be made the children's obligation.

The optimal investment is given in Figure 7S.1 by the intersection of the horizontal "supply curve of funds," rr, with a negatively inclined demand curve (HH or $H'H'$). This figure clearly shows that better-

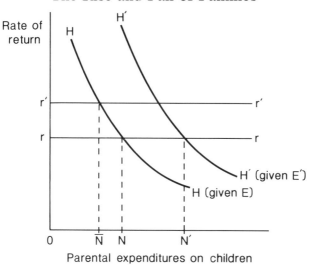

FIGURE 7S.1   Rates of return on parental expenditures on children.

endowed children accumulate more human capital; those with the endowment E accumulate ON units of expenditure, while those with $E' > E$ accumulate $ON' > ON$. Therefore, better-endowed children would have higher expected earnings because Eq. (7S.3) converts human capital into expected adult earnings. The total effect of endowments on earnings, and the inequality and skewness in earnings relative to that in endowments, is raised by the positive relation between endowments and expenditures.

An increase in the rate of interest reduces the investment in human capital, and hence earnings. Compare ON and $O\bar{N}$ in Figure 7S.1. The effect of an increase in public expenditures is less clear. If public expenditures are perfect substitutes dollar for dollar for private expenditures, the production of human capital would be determined by their sum, $x + s$, and by E; an increase in public expenditures would then induce an equal decrease in private (parental) expenditures, and the accumulation of human capital would be unchanged. Even then, a sufficiently large increase in public expenditures would raise the accumulation of human capital because private expenditures cannot be negative.

Note that the human capital and earnings of children would not depend on their parents' assets and earnings, because poor parents can borrow what is needed to finance the optimal investment in their children. But the income of children would depend on parents, because gifts and bequests of assets and debt would be sensitive to the earnings and wealth of parents. Indeed, wealthy parents would tend to self-finance the whole accumulation of human capital and to add a sizable gift of assets as well.

Although the earnings and human capital of children would not be directly related to parents' earnings and wealth, they would be indirectly related through the inheritability of endowments. The greater the degree of inheritability, the more closely related would be the human capital and earnings of parents and children. To derive the relation between the earnings of parents and children, substitute the optimal level of x given by Eq. (7S.7) into the earnings-generating equation (7S.3) to get

$$Y_t = \Psi[g(E_t, s_{t-1}, r_t), s_{t-1}, E_t] + \ell_t = \phi(E_t, s_{t-1}, r_t) + \ell_t,$$

(7S.9)

where

$$\phi_E = \Psi_g g_E + \Psi_E = \left(\frac{\partial Y}{\partial x}\right)\left(\frac{\partial x}{\partial E}\right) + \frac{\partial Y}{\partial E} > 0.$$

Since this equation relates E to Y, ℓ, g, and r, E_t can be replaced by E_{t-1} from (7S.2) and then Y_t can be related to Y_{t-1}, ℓ_t, v_t, ℓ_{t-1}, and other variables:

$$Y_t = F(Y_{t-1}, \ell_{t-1}, v_t, h, s_{t-1}, s_{t-2}, r_t, r_{t-1}, \alpha_t) + \ell_t.$$ (7S.10)

Not surprisingly, the earnings of parents and children are more closely related when endowments are more inheritable (h). The relation between their earnings also depends on the total effect of endowments on earnings (ϕ_E). If this effect is independent of the level of endowments ($\phi_{EE} = 0$), then

$$Y_t = c_t + \alpha_t \phi_E + h Y_{t-1} + \ell_t^*,$$ (7S.11)

where

$$\ell_t^* = \ell_t - h\ell_{t-1} + \phi_E v_t$$

and

$$c_t = c(s_{t-1}, s_{t-2}, h, r_t, r_{t-1}).$$

The intercept c_t would differ among families if government expenditures (s_{t-1}, s_{t-2}) differed among them. The stochastic term ℓ_t^* is negatively related to the market luck of parents.

If the luck of adults and children (ℓ^*) is held constant, the earnings of children would regress to the mean at the rate of $1 - h$. The coefficient is biased downward, however, by the "transitory" component of lifetime earnings of parents (ℓ_{t-1}) in OLS regressions of the actual lifetime earnings of children on the actual lifetime earnings of parents (Y_t on Y_{t-1}). If c_t is the same for all families, the expected value of the regression coefficient would equal

$$b_{t,t-1} = h\left(1 - \frac{\sigma_\ell^2}{\sigma_y^2}\right), \qquad (7S.12)$$

where σ_ℓ^2 and σ_y^2 are the variances of ℓ_t and Y_t. This coefficient is closer to the degree of inheritability when the inequality in the transitory component of lifetime earnings is a smaller fraction of the total inequality in lifetime earnings.

Families of particular races, religions, castes, or other characteristics who suffer from market discrimination earn less than do families without these characteristics. Persons with characteristics that are subject to discrimination earn less than do persons not subject to discrimination even when their parents' earnings are equal. Persons subject to discrimination would earn less—given the degree of inheritability—as long as discrimination reduces the earnings from given endowments, for discrimination then reduces the intercept in the equation that relates the earnings of parents and children ($c_t + \alpha_t \phi_E$ in Eq. 7S.11).

Imperfect Access to Capital

Access to capital markets to finance investments in children separates the transmission of earnings from the generosity and resources of parents. Economists have long argued, however, that human capital is poor collateral to lenders. Children can "default" on the market debt contracted for them by working less energetically or by entering occupations with lower earnings and higher psychic income. Such "moral hazard" from the private nature of information about work effort and employment opportunities can greatly affect the earnings realized from human capital. Moreover, most societies are reluctant to collect from children debts that were contracted by their parents, perhaps because the minority of parents who do not care much about the welfare of their children would raise their own consumption by leaving large debts to children.

To bring out sharply the effect of imperfect access to debt contracted for children, we assume that parents must finance investments in children by selling assets, by reducing their own consumption, by reducing the consumption by children, or by raising the labor force activities of children. Consider parents without assets[2] who would have to finance the efficient investment in human capital (say, ON in Figure 7S.1) partly by reducing their own consumption because they cannot contract debt for their children. A reduction in their own consumption would raise its marginal utility relative to the marginal utility of resources invested in children and thereby discourage some expenditure on children. Consequently, both the amount invested in children and parental consumption are reduced by limitations on the debt that can be left to children. Richer parents would tend to have both higher consumption and greater investments in children.

Therefore, expenditures on children by parents without assets depend not only on endowments of children and public expenditures, as in Eq. (7S.7), but also on earnings of parents (Y_{t-1}), their generosity toward children (w), and perhaps also on the uncertainty (ε_{t-1}) about the luck of children and later descendants, as in

$$\hat{x}_{t-1} = g^*(E_t, s_{t-1}, Y_{t-1}, \varepsilon_{t-1}, w), \quad \text{with} \quad g_Y^* > 0. \tag{7S.13}$$

Public and private expenditures would not be perfect substitutes if public expenditures affected rates of return on private expenditures, as when tuition is subsidized. However, if they are perfect substitutes, g^* would depend simply on the sum of s_{t-1} and Y_{t-1}: an increase in public expenditures is then equivalent to an equal increase in parental earnings. The effect of children's endowments on investments is now ambiguous ($g_E^* \gtreqless 0$), in that an increase in their endowments raises the resources of children as well as the productivity of investments in their human capital. Expenditures on children are discouraged when children are expected to be richer, because that lowers the marginal utility to parents of additional expenditures on children.

The demand curves for expenditures in Figure 7S.2 are similar to those in Figure 7S.1 and are higher in families with better-endowed children. The cost of funds to a family is no longer constant or the same to all families. Increased expenditures on children lower the consumption by parents, which raises their subjective discount rates (the shadow cost of funds). These discount rates are smaller to parents with higher earnings or more poorly endowed children. Expenditures

---

2. Even parents who accumulate assets over their lifetime may lack assets while investing in children.

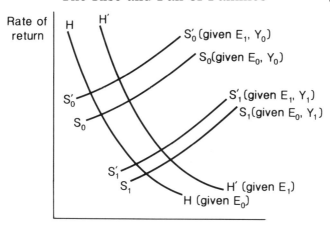

Parental expenditures on children

FIGURE 7S.2   Parental expenditures on children, with capital constraints.

on children in each family are determined by the intersection of supply and demand curves. An increase in parental earnings shifts the supply curve to the right and induces greater expenditures on children (compare S_1 and S_1' in Figure 7S.2). The distribution of intersection points determines the distribution of investments and rates of return and hence, as shown in Becker (1967, 1975), the inequality and skewness in the distribution of earnings.

By substituting Eq. (7S.13) into the earnings-generating equations (7S.3) and (7S.4), we get

$$Y_t = \Psi[g^*(E_t, Y_{t-1}, k_{t-1}), s_{t-1}, E_t] + \ell_t$$
$$= \phi^*(E_t, Y_{t-1}, k_{t-1}) + \ell_t,$$

$$(7S.14)$$

where k_{t-1} includes w, s_{t-1}, and ε_{t-1}. Earnings of children now depend on the earnings of parents directly, as well as indirectly through the transmission of endowments. Some authors (Bowles, 1972; Meade, 1976; Atkinson, 1983) argue for a direct effect because "contacts" of parents are said to raise the opportunities of children; others argue for a direct effect because parents are said to receive utility directly from the human capital of children. Fortunately, the effects of parent earnings on access to capital can be distinguished analytically from their effects on "contacts" and "utility."

The indirect effect of parents' earnings on the earnings of children operates through the transmission of endowments and can be found by substituting E_{t-1} for E_t and then using Eq. (7S.14) for E_{t-1}:

$$Y_t = F(Y_{t-1}, Y_{t-2}, \ell_{t-1}, v_t, h, \alpha_t, k_{t-1}, k_{t-2}) + \ell_t. \qquad (7S.15)$$

The sum of both the direct and the indirect effects of parents' earnings is

$$\frac{\partial Y_t}{\partial Y_{t-1}} = \phi^*_{Y_{t-1}} + \frac{h\phi^*_{E_t}}{\phi^*_{E_{t-1}}} > 0. \qquad (7S.16)$$

The indirect effect of grandparents' earnings, holding parents' earnings constant, is

$$\frac{\partial Y_t}{\partial Y_{t-2}} = -h\phi^*_{Y_{t-2}} \left(\frac{\phi^*_{E_t}}{\phi^*_{E_{t-1}}} \right) < 0. \qquad (7S.17)$$

Earnings of grandparents and grandchildren are indirectly linked through the constraints on financing investments in children. That is, the earnings of parents are not sufficient to describe the effects on children of both the resources and the endowments of parents. Equation (7S.17) shows that an increase in the earnings of grandparents lowers the earnings of grandchildren when parents' earnings and grandchildren's luck are held constant. Constraints on financing investments in children introduce a negative relation between the earnings of grandparents and grandchildren and raise the positive effect of parents' earnings on children's earnings.[3]

If Y_t were approximately linearly related to E_t and Y_{t-1}, then[4]

---

3. Goldberger (1985, pp. 16–17) perhaps properly takes us to task for expressing too much surprise about a negative coefficient for grandparents' wealth (or income), inasmuch as such a coefficient is implied by our model. (Becker and Tomes, 1979, say on p. 1171 that a negative coefficient "may seem surprising"; on p. 148 of the first edition of this book, I say "it is surprising"). We never claimed, however, that an increase in grandparents' wealth would lower the wealth of grandchildren; Goldberger's discussion (1985, p. 2) is misleading in that respect. We asked how persons who *start* with a presumed relation among the wealth of grandchildren, parents, and grandparents would interpret a negative coefficient for grandparents' wealth such as is found in Wahl's study (1985), reported later in Table 7S.2.

4. A similar equation is derived in Becker and Tomes (1979, eq. 25). But the coefficient there called β refers to the propensity to bequeath all capital, including debt, to children, not the propensity to invest in the human capital of children by parents who cannot leave debt.

The approximation in Eq. (7S.18) would be linear in the logs of the earn-

$$Y_t \cong c'_t + (\beta^* + h)Y_{t-1} - \beta^* h Y_{t-2} + \ell^*_t, \quad \text{with} \quad \beta^* = \phi^*_Y. \quad (7S.18)$$

The coefficient of parents' earnings exceeds the degree of inheritability by the marginal propensity to invest in the human capital of children (β^*). As in Eq. (7S.12), OLS estimates of the coefficient of Y_{t-1} are biased downward by the transitory component of lifetime earnings. Ordinary least-squares estimates of the relation between Y_t and Y_{t-1} tend toward[5]

$$\beta^* < b^*_{t,t-1} = \frac{b^*_{t,t-1 \cdot t-2}}{1 + h\beta^*} \le \min(1, \beta^* + h, b^*_{t,t-1 \cdot t-2}), \quad (7S.19)$$

where $b^*_{t,t-1 \cdot t-2}$ is the partial regression coefficient between Y_t and Y_{t-1}. Therefore, both partial and simple regression coefficients between the lifetime earnings of parents and children provide upper limits of the effect of capital market constraints on the propensity to invest in children. The biases in these OLS estimates can sometimes be overcome by the use of instruments for the lifetime earnings of parents, such as the lifetime earnings of uncles or of greatgrandparents (see Goldberger, 1979; Behrman and Taubman, 1985).

The direct relation between the earnings of parents and children in Eq. (7S.14) is likely to be concave rather than linear, because obstacles to the self-financing investments in children decline as parents' earnings increase. When investments in the human capital of children are sufficient to lower marginal rates of return to the market rate on assets, further increases in parents' earnings raise the assets bequeathed to children but have no effect on the amount invested in the human capital of children (if rates on assets are independent of parents' earnings). Presumably, "contacts" of parents and the direct utility to parents

---

ings of children, parents, and grandparents if the endowment and earnings-generating equations were linear in logs. Then $\beta^* + h$ would give the percentage increase in the earnings of children per 1 percent increase in the earnings of fathers, and similarly for $-\beta^* h$.

5. Equation (7S.18) implies that

$$b_{t,t-1} \cong \beta^* + h - h[b^*_{(\beta^* y_{t-2} + l_{t-1}) \cdot y_{t-1}}]$$

$$\cong \beta^* + h - \frac{h\sigma_l^2}{\sigma_y^2} - h\beta^* b^*_{t-1,t}.$$

If the economy is in long-run equilibrium (see Becker and Tomes, 1979), then $b^*_{t,t-1} = b^*_{t-1,t}, \sigma^2_{y_{t-1}} = \sigma^2_{y_t}$, and the equality in Eq. (7S.19) follows. The relation between $b^*_{t,t-1}$ and the right-hand side of Eq. (7S.19) is derived in Becker and Tomes (1979, appendix E).

from the human capital of children are more important in richer families. Hence, capital constraints have different implications for the curvature of the relation between the earnings of parents and children than do these alternative explanations.

The discussion in Becker and Tomes (1979) implies that, because β^* and h enter symmetrically, even knowledge of the true values of the coefficients attached to parents' and grandparents' incomes in an equation such as (7S.18) could not identify β^* and h without other information, such as which coefficient is larger. Earnings in rich families not subject to capital constraints are related by the simple equation (7S.11), which does not include β^*. Therefore, h would be known if the coefficient on parents' earnings in rich families is known. Then β^* and h could be distinguished in Eq. (7S.18) by using this information on h.

Since the coefficient β^* measures the marginal propensity to invest in the human capital of children by capital-constrained parents who are prevented from making the wealth-maximizing investment in their children, β^* does not enter the earnings-generating equation for richer families (Eq. 7S.11) who are not so constrained. Put differently, β^* is zero in richer families. There is no general presumption about the size of β^* relative to h even in low-income families, because β^* depends on public transfers to children, incomes, and other variables.

The coefficient β in our earlier work (see for example Becker and Tomes, 1979) measures the marginal propensity to bequeath wealth to children when parents can leave debt to children and when human wealth is not distinguished from other wealth. Our earlier work and a later section of the present supplement show that this propensity depends on the generosity of parents toward children and may not be sensitive to the level of income. It is likely to be large in most families. Such a presumption motivated the assumption in our earlier work that $\beta > h$, an assumption used to identify β and h from the coefficients in an equation such as (7S.18).

Goldberger (1985, pp. 19–20) correctly states that we did not provide an independent way to evaluate this assumption. This supplement makes progress toward the goal of identification in that h can be determined from knowledge of the coefficients in the equation for the earnings of parents and children in (richer) families who leave positive bequests to children. Given h, β^* (or a more general relation between β^* and parents' earnings) can be determined from knowledge of the coefficients on parents' or on grandparents' earnings in the earnings equation for poorer families who are capital constrained. Even β—the marginal propensity of parents to bequeath wealth to children—might be determined from information on the relation between the consumption of parents and children in richer families.

Rich families can more readily self-finance a given investment in children than can poor and middle-level families. Richer families also have better than average endowments, which raises the wealth-maximizing investment in human capital by richer families above that by poorer families. Empirical observations strongly indicate that richer families come closer to financing the optimal investment in the human capital of children than do poorer families. The implication is that the wealth effect on investments in children dominates the endowment effect. The wealth effect would dominate if endowments regressed strongly to the mean, for then the endowments of richer children would be much below those of their parents and the endowments of poorer children would be much above those of their parents. Our evidence suggests that endowments relevant to earnings do regress strongly to the mean.

If returns on assets are not highly sensitive to earnings and endowments, the greater resources available to rich families to finance wealth-maximizing investments in children imply that equilibrium marginal rates of return on investments in children are lower in richer families than they are in more capital-constrained poor and middle-level families, even though endowments and average rates of return are higher in richer families. Equilibrium marginal rates then tend to decline, perhaps not monotonically, as earnings of parents rise. Eventually, marginal rates on human capital would equal the rate of return on assets, and then marginal rates would be relatively constant as parents' earnings rose. Poorer children are at a disadvantage both because they inherit lower endowments and because capital constraints on their parents limit the market value of the endowments they do inherit.

If marginal rates are lower in richer families, a small redistribution of human capital away from these families and toward children from poorer families would raise the average marginal rate of return across different families. This redistribution would raise efficiency, even though endowments and the average productivity of investments in children are greater in richer families (see also Becker, 1967, 1975). The usual conflict between "equity," as measured by inequality, and efficiency is absent; a redistribution of investments toward less advantaged children is equivalent to an improvement in the efficiency of capital markets.

Larger public expenditures on the human capital of children in families subject to capital constraints raise the total amount invested in these children even when public and private expenditures are perfect substitutes. The reason is that public expenditures increase the total resources of a family if taxes are imposed on other families. An increase in family resources in capital-constrained families is shared between parents and investments in children in a ratio determined by the marginal propensity to invest (β^*). If public and private expenditures are perfect substitutes, the fraction $1 - \beta^*$ of government expenditures on children is offset by compensatory responses of their parents. That is, to further equity toward other family members, even constrained parents redistribute some time and expenditures away from children, who benefit from government expenditures to siblings and themselves. Compensatory responses of parents apparently greatly weaken the effects of public health programs, food supplements to poorer pregnant women, some head-start programs, and social security programs (see the discussion in Chapters 6 and 11 of this book).

We have seen that the total investment in children in families with positive bequests to children is unaffected by public expenditures on children that are perfect substitutes for parents' expenditures. Parents reduce their own expenditures to offset fully such public expenditures. Yet public and private expenditures may not be perfect substitutes. If, for example, public expenditures raise rates of return on family expenditures, increased public expenditures could even raise family expenditures because a "substitution effect" works against the "redistribution effect."

Goldberger criticizes us (1985, pp. 9–10; and Simon, 1986, repeats Goldberger's criticism) because we emphasize redistribution or income effects at the expense of substitution effects when discussing various public programs. Since our first joint paper we have explicitly noted that government programs may have substitution effects by changing rates of return on parental investments in children (see Becker and Tomes, 1976, p. S156). We have emphasized the redistribution effects of many programs—including head-start programs, welfare, aid to pregnant women, and social security—because the redistribution effects are clear, whereas substitution effects are not clear, even in direction. For example, what is the substitution effect of a social security program? Or is there evidence that head-start programs raise rather than lower marginal rates of return on parents' expenditures? (See Chapter 6.) Although tuition subsidies to education may appear to raise rates of return on parents' expenditures on education, actually they may lower marginal rates of return when combined with rationing of places (see Peltzman, 1973).

Redistribution of expenditures within families induced by government subsidies can explain why many programs appear to have weak effects on participants (see the discussion in Chapters 6 and 11). Of course, weak effects on participants do not imply that substitution effects are negligible or that they reinforce redistribution effects, but weak effects do imply that these programs do not have strong offsetting substitution effects.

Capital-constrained parents could finance expenditures on children by reducing their life-cycle savings if children could be counted on to care for elderly parents. In many societies, poorer and middle-income parents are supported during old age by children instead of by the sale of gold, jewelry, rugs, land, houses, or other assets that could be accumulated by parents at younger ages. Our analysis suggests that these parents choose to rely on children instead of on assets, because rates of return on investments in children are higher than they are on other assets.

In effect, poorer and middle-level parents and children often have an implicit contract, enforced imperfectly by social sanctions, that parents invest in children in return for support during old age. Both parents and children would be made better off by such contracts if investments in children were to yield a high return, where included in the yield would be any insurance provided by children against an unusually long old age.

Assets and Consumption

Our analysis implies that bequests and gifts of assets to children do not rise rapidly until marginal rates of return on investments in children are reduced to the rate on assets. Further increases in contributions from parents then mainly take the form of assets rather than of human capital, because returns on assets are less sensitive to the amount accumulated. These conclusions imply that most bequests to children are found in a relatively small number of richer families and that the ratio of assets to human capital of children rises as parents' wealth rises. The empirical evidence clearly indicates that assets and income from nonhuman capital are much more important in richer than in poorer families.

Empirical studies also indicate that the proportion of income saved remains reasonably constant or that it rises as income, including "permanent" income, increases (see the studies reviewed in Mayer, 1972). Yet these studies provide flawed measures of savings, because investments in human capital and "capital gains or losses" from intergenerational increases or decreases in endowments are not considered savings. Lower- and middle-income families invest primarily in their children's human capital. Endowments tend to increase from parents to children at lower income levels and to decrease from parents to children at higher levels owing to regression to the mean in endowments. Therefore, empirical studies understate relative savings by lower- and middle-income families because both intergenerational capital gains and investments in human capital are relatively larger in these families. We believe that an appropriate concept of savings may well show that the fraction saved declines as permanent income rises. After all, this would be expected if equilibrium marginal rates of return on investments in children decline as income increases.

Our conclusion that most bequests of assets are found in a relatively small number of richer families does not presuppose "class" differences in altruism or other class differences in the propensity to save, as in Kaldor (1956) and Pasinetti (1962), or as used in Atkinson (1983). In our analysis all families have the same intrinsic tendency to save and leave estates, because they are assumed to have the same altruism toward children. Still, apparent "class" differences in savings would exist; poorer families save mainly in the human capital of children, which is not recorded as savings or bequests.

The assets of a person are determined by bequests from parents and by the individual's own life-cycle accumulations. We assume that parents choose bequests by maximizing their expected utility, subject to the expected earnings and life-cycle asset accumulation of children. To develop further our analysis of bequests, we must turn to an explicit treatment of utility maximization by parents. We continue to assume for the moment that each adult has no marriage and one child.

Suppose that the utility function of parents is additively separable in their own consumption and in various characteristics of children. Most of our analysis does not depend on a specific measure of these characteristics as long as they are positively related to the total resources of children. But we can simplify the relation between the consumption by parents and children by assuming that parents' utility depends on the utility of children (U_c), as in

$$U_t = u(Z_t) + \delta U_{t+1}, \qquad (7S.20)$$

where Z_t is the consumption of parents and δ is a constant that measures the altruism of parents.

If the preference function given by Eq. (7S.20) is the same for all generations and if consumption during childhood is ignored, then the utility of the parents indirectly would equal the discounted sum of the utilities from the consumption of all descendants:

$$U_t = \sum_{i=0}^{\infty} \delta^i u(Z_{t+1}). \qquad (7S.21)$$

The utility of parents depends directly only on the utility of children, but it depends indirectly on all descendants because children are concerned about their descendants.

We assume that parents succeed in maximizing their "dynastic" utility, as represented by Eq. (7S.21). This assumption rules out bargaining by children to obtain larger transfers than those that maximize parents' utility. A more general assumption is that parents maximize a weighted average of their own and their children's utility, with weights determined by bargaining power (see the normative use of this assumption in Nerlove et al., 1986); however, this generalization would not change any major conclusions.

With perfect certainty about rates of return and incomes in all generations, the first-order conditions to maximize utility are the usual ones. For example, with a constant elasticity of substitution in consumption,

$$u'(Z) = Z^{-\sigma}, \quad \sigma > 0, \qquad (7S.22)$$

and

$$\ln Z_{t+1} = \frac{1}{\sigma} \ln(1 + r_{t+1})\delta + \ln Z_t, \qquad (7S.23)$$

where r_{t+1} measures the marginal rate of return to investments in children in period t. With an exponential utility function,

$$u'(Z) = e^{-pZ}, \quad p > 0, \qquad (7S.24)$$

and

$$Z_{t+1} = \frac{1}{p} \ln(1 + r_{t+1})\delta + Z_t. \qquad (7S.25)$$

A Treatise on the Family

If parents could finance expenditures on their children with debt that becomes the obligation of children, the marginal cost of funds would equal the rate on assets in all families. Then Eq. (7S.23) or Eq. (7S.25) implies that the relative or absolute change in consumption between generations would be the same in all families that are equally altruistic (δ) and that have equal degrees of substitution (σ or p). Each family would maintain its relative or absolute consumption position over generations, and consumption would not regress to the mean. Stated differently, any degree of relative or absolute inequality in consumption in the parents' generation would then be fully transmitted to the children's generation.

Nevertheless, the earnings of children would still regress to the mean, regardless of the altruism of parents, as long as endowments are not fully inherited by children. Consumption does not automatically regress to the mean when earnings do, because parents can anticipate that their children will tend to earn less or more than they do. They can use debt and assets to offset the effect on wealth of the expected regression in earnings.

Therefore, although earnings may regress to the mean, well-being as measured by consumption will not regress at all if parents have full access to capital markets to finance investments in their children's human capital. The assets bequeathed to children will rise and the debt bequeathed will fall as parents' earnings rise. This crucial distinction between regression across generations in earnings and consumption appears to have been ignored in the extensive literature on the mobility of families.

Still, the main implication of equations such as (7S.23) and (7S.25) is disquieting, namely, that all initial differences among families in consumption and total resources are fully transmitted to future descendants. Surely the resources of the current generation are essentially independent of the resources of their distant ancestors. Several forces are responsible for the decay over time in the influence of the past on consumption and total resources. These include difficulties in transmitting debt to children, uncertainty about the future, the effect of parents' wealth on fertility, and imperfect assortative mating. We consider these variables in turn.

Consumption is fully separated from earnings only when children can be obligated for debts created by parents. If debt cannot be created for children, parents without assets cannot offset any upward regression in the endowments and earnings of their children. Parents face a complicated maximization problem because capital constraints may be binding only for some descendants. The results of utility maximization can be summarized by endogenously determined subjective discount rates and marginal rates of return for each generation of a family, which guide as well as reflect the decisions for that generation. These shadow prices exceed the rate on assets whenever constraints on access to debt prevent borrowing from children. Discount rates of (richer) parents with sufficient assets to raise or lower their bequests to children equal the rate on assets.

We argue that equilibrium marginal rates of return of constrained parents tend to decline as their earnings become larger. Then Eq. (7S.23) or Eq. (7S.25) implies that the relative or absolute growth in consumption between generations would also decline as the earnings of parents rose. The relative or absolute growth in consumption between generations, however, would be constant among richer families, who receive a marginal rate of return equal to the rate on assets. Therefore, the consumption of children would regress more rapidly upward to the mean in poor families than downward to the mean in rich families. The result is a convex relation between the consumption of parents and children. At the same time, earnings regress more slowly upward in poor families than they regress downward in rich families.

Assets bequeathed to children in richer families act as a buffer to offset any regression to the mean in the earnings of children. The richest families can maintain their consumption over time compared to less rich families only by increasing their bequests sufficiently to offset the stronger downward regression in the earnings of the richest children. As a result, bequests may regress away from the mean.

Our analysis of consumption has assumed perfect certainty, although uncertainty about much of the luck of future generations is not fully insurable or diversifiable. If each generation knows the yields on investments in the human capital of children and in bequests to children, but does not have perfect certainty about the earnings of children and is still more uncertain about subsequent generations, then the first-order condition for maximization of expected utility is

$$\varepsilon_t u'(Z_{t+1}) = \left(\frac{\delta^{-1}}{1 + r_{t+1}}\right) u'(Z_t), \qquad (7S.26)$$

where ε_t refers to expectations taken at generation t before any new information about earnings and other wealth of descendants is acquired between t and $t + 1$.

With the exponential function, this first-order condition becomes

$$Z_{t+1} = c + \frac{1}{p}\ln(1 + r_{t+1})\delta + Z_t + n_{t+1}, \qquad (7S.27)$$

where c is a positive constant and where n_{t+1}, the distribution of fluctuations in Z_{t+1} around $\hat{Z}_{t+1}$, does not depend on Z_t. If the capital market permitted all families to finance the wealth-maximizing investments in their children, $r_{t+1} = r_a$ in all families, where r_a is the asset rate. Then Eq. (7S.27) implies that the growth in consumption follows a random walk with drift. (Kotlikoff et al., 1986, derive a similar result when the length of life is uncertain.) More generally, Eq. (7S.27) shows that, if the utility function is exponential, uncertainty adds a random term to consumption but does not basically change the implications of our analysis concerning the degree of regression to the mean in consumption.

A second-order approximation to the left-hand side of Eq. (7S.26) readily shows that the effect of uncertainty on the degree of regression toward the mean with general utility functions depends on the signs and magnitudes of second- and higher-order derivatives of the utility function.[6] Uncertainty could induce regression toward the mean in consumption even when there would be none with certainty. Uncertainty could also induce regression away from the mean, or greater rates of regression toward the mean at higher rather than at lower levels of consumption, with utility functions that otherwise seem as empirically relevant as those having opposite implications. Consequently, we cannot make any strong statement concerning the effect of uncertainty on the degree of regression toward the mean in the consumption of parents and children.

---

6. If r_{t+1} is constant, a second-order approximation to u'_{t+1} in Eq. (7S.26) gives

$$\frac{d\hat{Z}_{t+1}}{dZ_t} = v\frac{u''_t}{u'_t}\varphi \left[\frac{u'_{t+1} + \dfrac{v(u_{t+1})^3}{2}}{u''_{t+1} + \dfrac{v(u_{t+1})^4}{2}} \right],$$

where $(u_{t+1})^j, j = 3, 4$ is the jth derivative of utility from consumption in the $t + 1$ generation, and v is the given variance of n_{t+1} around $\hat{Z}_{t+1}$. The term on the left-hand side is more likely to be less than 1 (regression toward the mean) when $(u)^4$ is large relative to $(u)^3$.

Fertility and Marriage

Regression toward the mean in marriage and the positive effect of wealth on fertility help explain why differences in consumption and total resources among richer families do not persist indefinitely into future generations. Here we only sketch out an analysis. The implications of fertility and marriage for consumption and bequests are also discussed in Becker and Tomes (1984), Becker and Barro (1988), and the supplement to Chapter 11 of this volume.

Let us first drop the assumption that all parents have only one child and generalize the utility function in Eq. (7S.20) to

$$U_p = u(Z_p) + a(n)nU_c, \qquad (7S.28)$$

with $a' < 0$, where U_c is the utility of each of the n identical children and $a(n)$ is the degree of altruism per child. The first-order condition for the optimal number of children is that the marginal utility and the marginal cost of children are equal. The marginal cost of children to parents equals net expenditures on children, including any bequests and other gifts. The marginal costs are determined by the circumstances and decisions of parents.

The previous section showed that the consumption and total resources of wealthy families may not regress down, because these families can offset the downward regression in the earnings of their children by sufficiently large gifts and bequests. Fortunately, this unrealistic implication does not hold when the number of children can vary. Richer families tend to spend some of their greater resources on additional children. This likelihood reduces the bequest to each child below what it would be if the number of children did not increase (see the proofs in Becker and Barro, 1985). A positive response of fertility to increases in wealth causes consumption and wealth per child to regress down, perhaps rapidly.

Poor and middle-income families without assets who are prevented from leaving debt to their children must trade off between earnings of each child, number of children, and parent consumption. The human capital invested in each child, and hence the earnings of each child, would then be negatively related to the number of children, as found in many studies (see for instance Blake 1981). The degree of regression to the mean in earnings among these families would be lower if fertility and parents' earnings were negatively related than if they were unrelated.

We do not have much to add to our previous analysis of responses to differences between children (see Becker and Tomes, 1976; Tomes, 1981; and Chapter 6). This analysis implies that richer families invest more human capital in better-endowed children and that they compensate other children with larger gifts and bequests. Poorer families who primarily invest in human capital face a conflict between the efficiency of greater investments in better-endowed children and the equity of greater investments in less well endowed children.

Despite the claim that observed differences in earnings between siblings is helpful in determining the degree of intergenerational mobility in earnings (see for example Brittain, 1977, pp. 36–37), there is no necessary connection between the relation among siblings and the degree of intergenerational mobility. The reason is that differences in earnings between siblings are determined by characteristics within a single generation, such as the substitution between siblings in the utility function of parents, whereas intergenerational mobility in earnings is determined by differences across generations, such as the regression toward the mean of endowments (for a further discussion see Tomes, 1984).

Regression to the mean in marriage—called imperfect positive assortative mating—also increases the degree of regression to the mean in earnings, consumption, and assets. Still, the effect of marriage is less obvious than it may appear, because parents often can anticipate the marital sorting of children. For example, wealthy parents would use gifts and bequests to offset some of the effects on the well-being of their children of the tendency for rich children to marry down, just as they use gifts and bequests to offset the effect of the regression downward in endowments. Although a full analysis of the interaction between the behavior of parents and expectations about the marriages of children is complicated by bargaining between in-laws on the gifts to be made to their children (some issues are discussed in Chapter 7 and in Becker and Tomes, 1984), one cannot be satisfied with the many models that simply ignore expectations about children's marriages (see Stiglitz, 1969; Pryor, 1973; Blinder, 1976; Atkinson, 1983).

Fertility and marriage have not been fully integrated into our analysis of intergenerational mobility—we would insert "fully" into Goldberger's statement that "it's fair to say that [fertility and marriage are] not integrated into his intergenerational system" (1985, p. 13).

Nevertheless, the discussion in this section, the discussion of fertility in Becker and Barro (1988) and in the supplement to Chapter 11, and the discussion of marriage in Becker and Tomes (1984) indicate to us that a utility-maximizing approach can integrate fertility, marriage, and intergenerational mobility into a common framework with useful implications.

Empirical Studies[7]

Only a few empirical studies link the earnings or wealth of different generations, because of difficulties in gathering such information and because of insufficient interest by social scientists. Tables 7S.1 and 7S.2 present estimates from several studies of the degree of regression to the mean in earnings, income, and wealth, with coefficients of determination (when available), number of observations, and notes about other variables (if any) included in each regression.

Table 7S.1 has evidence on the earnings or incomes of sons and fathers from three studies based on separate data sets for the United States and one study each for England, Sweden, Switzerland, and Norway.[8] Although the average age of fathers and sons is quite different except in the Geneva study, both Atkinson (1981) and Behrman and Taubman (1983) present evidence that such differences in age do not greatly affect the estimated degree of regression to the mean.

The point estimates for most of the studies indicate that a 10 percent increase in father's earnings (or income) raises son's earnings by less than 2 percent. The highest point estimate is for York, England, where son's hourly earnings appear to be raised by 4.4 percent. The confidence intervals are sizable in all studies except Malmö, because fathers' earnings "explain" a small fraction of the variation in earnings

---

7. We are indebted to Robert Hauser for bringing to our attention several studies of intergenerational mobility that use the data on Wisconsin high school graduates, and for guiding us through various adjustments that correct for response and measurement errors in these studies.

8. These studies have various limitations. Hauser et al. (1975) sample families in one state only (Wisconsin) and include only sons who graduated from high school; all fathers in the Behrman and Taubman (1983) sample are twins; fathers in the Atkinson (1981) sample had modest earnings in the city of York; fathers in the de Wolff and van Slijpe (1973) study are from the city of Malmö; Girod (1984) surveys students in the canton of Geneva; and Soltow (1965) uses a very small sample from one city in Norway.

TABLE 7S.1 Regressions of son's income or earnings on father's income or earnings in linear, semilog, and log-linear form.

Location and son's year	Father's year	Variables Dependent	Variables Independent	Variables Other	Coefficient	t	R^2	N	ε	Author
Wisconsin										
1965–1967 [a]	1957–1960	E	IP	None	.15	8.5	.03	2,069	.13	Hauser et al. (1975)
	1957–1960	Log E	IP	None	.0006	10.6	.05	N.A.	.09	Hauser (in press)[b]
1974	1957–1960	Log E	Log IP	None	.28[c]	15.7	.09	2,493	.28	Tsai (1983)[b]
United States										
1981–1982	1981–1982	Log E[d]	Log E[d]	None	.18	3.7	.02	722	.18	Behrman and Taubman (1983)
United States										
1969 (young white)	When son was 14	Log H	Log $I3$	e	.16	3.2	—	1,607	.16	Freeman (1981)
1966 (older white)	When son was 14	Log H	Log $I3$	e	.22	7.3	—	2,131	.22	Freeman (1981)
1969 (young black)	When son was 14	Log H	Log $I3$	e	.17	1.9	—	634	.17	Freeman (1981)
1969 (older black)	When son was 14	Log H	Log $I3$	e	.02	0.4	—	947	.02	Freeman (1981)

York, England										
1975–1978	1950	Log H	Log W	None	.44	3.4	.06	198	.44	Atkinson (1981)
1975–1978	1950	Log W	Log W	None	.36	3.3	.03	307	.36	Atkinson (1981)
Malmö, Sweden										
1963	1938	Log I	ICD	None	.08	1.8	.19	545	.17[f]	de Wolff and van Slijpe (1973)
					.12	2.4	.19	545	.13	
					.69	10.9	.19	545	.79	
Geneva, Switzerland										
1980	1950	IHH	IHH	None	.31	4.1	.02	801	.13	Girod (1984)
Sarpsborg, Norway										
1960	1960	Log I	Log I	None	.14	1.2	.01	115	.14	Soltow (1965)

NOTE: ε = elasticity of son's income or earnings with respect to father's income or earnings; E = earnings; H = hourly earnings; I = income; $I3$ = income in three-digit occupation; ICD = income-class dummy; IHH = household income; IP = parents' income; W = weekly earnings.

[a] First five years in labor force.
[b] Also Robert M. Hauser (personal communication, October 2, 1984).
[c] Adjusted for response variability.
[d] Adjusted for work experience. Sons with work experience of four years or less were excluded. The regression was weighted so that each father had equal weight.
[e] Work experience, three dummies for region of residence at age 14, five dummies for type of place of residence at age 14, and a dummy for living in one-parent or female home at age 14.
[f] The elasticities are values between pairs of income classes.

TABLE 7S.2   Regressions of son's wealth on father's and grandfather's wealth.

Location and son's year	Father's year	Notes	Coefficient for father's wealth	Coefficient for grandfather's wealth	R^2	N	Author
United States Prior to 1976	1930–1946	a,b	.69 (7.5)	—	.29	173	Menchik (1979)
	1860	b	.76	—	.25	199	Menchik (1979)
1860	1860	c,d	.21 (1.6)	.05 (2.0)	.46	45	Wahl (1985)
1860	1860	d,e	.26 (2.1)	−.008 (−1.6)	.14	106	Wahl (1985)
1870	1870	c,d	.30 (5.5)	.05 (2.4)	.27	46	Wahl (1985)
1870	1870	d,e	.46 (2.1)	−.03 (−1.6)	.10	125	Wahl (1985)

Great Britain								
1934, 1956–1957	1902, 1924–1926	[b]	.48 (3.7)	—	—	—	—	Harbury and Hitchens (1979)
1956–1957, 1965	1916, 1928	[b]	.48 (5.3)	—	—	—	—	Harbury and Hitchens (1979)
1973	1936	[b]	.59 (8.4)	—	—	—	—	Harbury and Hitchens (1979)

NOTE: *t*-statistics are in parentheses.

[a] Menchik also includes the following as explanatory variables: number of years between death of parents and child, number of child's siblings (plus one), and stepchild dummy.

[b] Log-linear regression.

[c] Wahl uses an instrument for parent's wealth. The following variables are used to create the instrument: age of household head (and age squared), occupational and regional dummies, residence farm or nonfarm, and whether parent is bloodline. Grandparent's wealth is actual wealth.

[d] Wahl uses data for parents and maternal grandparents instead of for fathers and grandfathers.

[e] Wahl uses instruments for both parent's and grandparent's wealth. She creates the instruments by using the list given in note c above.

of sons. Moreover, response errors and the transitory component in father's earnings (or income) may severely bias these regression coefficients.[9] Furthermore, the analysis earlier in this supplement indicates that transitory variations in lifetime earnings and the omission of the earnings of grandparents bias these regression coefficients downward. The error from omitting grandparents' earnings will be small if parents' earnings do not have a large effect (see Eq. 7S.18) and if the transitory component in lifetime earnings is not large.

Hauser et al. (1975) reduce response errors and the transitory component by using a four-year average of parents' income and a three-year average of son's earnings, whereas Hauser (1990) uses a four-year average of parents' income and a five-year average of son's earnings during his initial period of labor-force participation. Tsai (1983) not only averages incomes of parents over several years but also uses a retrospective report on their income in 1957. At Hauser's suggestion, we have corrected for the response errors in father's earnings by using the analysis in Bielby and Hauser (1977). Behrman and Taubman (1983) exclude sons who have less than four years of work experience, because their earnings do not appropriately represent their lifetime earnings. De Wolff and van Slijpe (1973) and Freeman (1981) reduce the importance of the transitory component by using the average income in father's occupation as an estimate of his lifetime earnings.

Despite these adjustments for response errors and transitory incomes, point estimates of the regression coefficients for earnings and incomes are rather low in all the studies (except for large incomes in Sweden). Moreover, a study by Peters (1985) that uses data from the National Longitudinal Survey (the same survey used by Freeman, 1981) also finds a small coefficient (below .2) when a simple average of four years of son's earnings is regressed on a simple average of five years of father's earnings.

Some indirect evidence of sizable regression toward the mean in lifetime earnings is provided by life-cycle variations in earnings. By definition, endowments are fixed over a lifetime. Therefore, earnings should be more closely related over the life cycle than across generations because endowments are imperfectly transmitted from parent to

---

9. These estimates may also be biased (the direction is not clear) because information is not available on hours worked and nonpecuniary income from employment (see the discussion in Becker and Tomes, 1984, note 13).

child (endowments are not a "fixed effect" across generations). Stated differently, relative to other members of his cohort, a person is usually much more similar to himself at different ages than a father is similar to his son when they are of the same age. The correlation coefficient between the "permanent" component of male earnings at different ages has been estimated from a seven-year panel to be about .7 in the United States (see Lillard and Willis, 1978, table 1). The inheritability of endowments from fathers to sons is surely less, probably much less, than is the correlation between the permanent component of earnings at different ages.

The evidence in Table 7S.1 suggests that neither the inheritability of endowments by sons (h) nor the propensity to invest in children's human capital because of capital constraints (β^*) is large. For example, if the regression coefficient between the lifetime earnings of fathers and sons is ≤.4 and if the transitory variance in lifetime earnings is less than one-third of the variance in total lifetime earnings, then both h and β^* would be less than .28 if $h = \beta^*$; moreover, $h \leq .6$ if $\beta^* = 0$, and $h \leq 0$ if $\beta^* \geq .4$ (see note 4).

If capital constraints completely disappeared, would the same families dominate the best-paid and most prestigious occupations? (For this fear, see the often-cited article by Herrnstein, 1971.) The answer is no: families in the best occupations would change frequently even in "meritocracies," because endowments relevant to earnings are not highly inheritable—h is less than .6 and may be much less. Another way to see this is to note that if the relation between the lifetime earnings of fathers and sons is no larger than .4, practically all the advantages or disadvantages of ancestors tend to disappear in only three generations: "from shirtsleeves to shirtsleeves in three generations." Parents in such "open" societies have little effect on the earnings of grandchildren and later descendants. Therefore, they have little incentive to try to affect the earnings of descendants through family reputation and other means.

In particular, any lifetime "culture of poverty" tends to disappear between generations, because characteristics that determine earnings are variable between generations. For example, children of parents who earn only half the mean can expect to earn above 80 percent of the mean in their generation, and their own children can expect to earn only slightly below the mean.

Yet family background is important. For example, even if the degree of regression to the mean is 80 percent, children of parents whose earnings are twice the mean tend to earn 30 percent more than the children of parents whose earnings are only 50 percent of the mean. A 30 percent premium is large relative to the 10 percent–15 percent premium from union membership (Lewis, 1986) or to the 16 percent premium from two additional years of schooling (Mincer, 1974). Children from successful families do have a significant economic advantage.

Families who are poor partly because of discrimination against their race, caste, or other "permanent" characteristics may advance more slowly. Obviously, blacks in the United States have advanced much more slowly than have immigrants, partly because of public and private discrimination against blacks. Although many have studied changes over time in the average position of blacks relative to whites (see for instance the excellent study by Smith, 1984), few have studied the relation between earnings of sons and fathers in black families. The evidence in Table 7S.1 suggests that older blacks regress more rapidly to the mean than do older whites, although the evidence may be spurious because response errors are higher and apparently more complicated for blacks (see Bielby et al., 1977). Opportunities for younger blacks clearly have improved during the last 20 years. The evidence in Table 7S.1 that younger blacks regress more slowly suggests that discrimination raises the regression toward the mean in earnings (see the theoretical discussion earlier in this supplement).

Goldberger points out (1985, pp. 29–30) that our previous work uses much higher illustrative values for β than the values of β^* suggested by the empirical evidence in this section. But β and β^* are different: to repeat, β refers to the propensity to bequeath wealth to children by families who are not capital constrained. Therefore, low β^*'s are not inconsistent with high β's. A low β^* combined with a low h does imply sizable intergenerational mobility in earnings, whereas a high β implies low intergenerational mobility in wealth and consumption among families that bequeath wealth to their children (we ignore the distinction between the wealth and consumption of children and the wealth and consumption per child).

We readily admit that the distinction in this supplement between earnings, wealth, and consumption, as well as our attention to intergenerational capital constraints and fertility behavior, have greatly clarified our thinking about intergenerational mobility. But since a low β^* is not inconsistent with a high β, we see no reason why the empirical evidence of a low β^* "would occasion the tearing of [our] hair and the gnashing of [our] teeth'' (Goldberger, 1985, pp. 29–30). Moreover, aside from fertility and marriage, we still expect high values for β.

Table 7S.2 presents evidence from three studies for the United States and Great Britain on the relation between the wealth of parents and children. Harbury and Hitchens (1979) and Menchik (1979) use probates of wealthy estates, while Wahl (1985) uses data on wealth from the 1860 and 1870 censuses. The estimated elasticity between the assets of fathers and sons is about .7 in the United States for probated assets in relatively recent years but is less both for assets of living persons in the nineteenth century and for probated assets in Britain.

Wahl finds a small negative coefficient for grandparents' wealth when instruments are used for both parents' and grandparents' wealth, but a positive coefficient for grandparents' wealth when their actual wealth is used. The theoretical analysis incorporated into Eq. (7S.18) does imply a small negative coefficient for grandparents' wealth when the effect of parents' wealth is not large, as is the case in her study. Behrman and Taubman (1985) usually find small positive (but not statistically significant) coefficients on grandparents' schooling in their study of years of schooling for three generations. Their findings may be inconsistent with our theory, although Eq. (7S.18) does imply a negligible coefficient for grandfathers' schooling when the coefficient on parents' schooling is small—it is less than .25 in their study.

The data in Tables 7S.1 and 7S.2 are too limited to determine with confidence whether wealth or earnings regress less rapidly to the mean, although wealth appears to do so. Wealth will regress slowly if parents bequeath assets to children to buffer the total wealth and consumption of children against regression in their earnings. Wealth will regress rapidly, however, if wealthier parents have sufficiently more children than do poorer parents. Wahl (1985) does find a strong positive relation in the nineteenth century between the fertility and the wealth of parents.

Capital constraints on investments in children probably declined during the twentieth century in the United States and in many other countries because fertility declined, incomes rose, and government subsidies to education and to social security grew rapidly. Evidence in Goldin and Parsons (1984) is consistent with sizable capital constraints on poor families in the United States during the latter part of the nineteenth century. These families withdrew their children from school at early ages in order to raise the contribution of teenage children to family earnings. A weakening of capital constraints in the

United States is also indicated by the decline over time in the inequality in years of schooling and by the declining influence of family background on the educational attainments of children (Featherman and Hauser, 1976).

There is evidence that the influence of family background on the achievements of children is greater in less-developed countries than it is in the United States. For example, father's education has a greater effect on son's education in both Bolivia and Panama than in the United States. Moreover, the influence of father's education apparently declined over time in Panama as well as in the United States (see Kelley et al., 1981, pp. 27–66; Heckman and Hotz, 1985).

We have developed a model of the transmission of earnings, assets, and consumption from parents to children and later descendants. The model is based on utility maximization by parents concerned about the welfare of their children. The degree of intergenerational mobility, or the rise and fall of families, is determined by the interaction of utility-maximizing behavior with investment and consumption opportunities in different generations and with different kinds of luck.

We assume that cultural and genetic endowments are automatically transmitted from parents to children, with the relation between the endowments of parents and children determined by the degree of "inheritability." The intergenerational mobility of earnings depends on the inheritability of endowments. Indeed, if all parents can readily borrow to finance the optimal investments in children, the degree of intergenerational mobility in earnings essentially would equal the inheritability of endowments.

Poor families often have difficulty financing investments in children, because loans to supplement their limited resources are not readily available when human capital is the collateral. Such capital-market restrictions lower investments in children from poorer families. Intergenerational mobility in earnings then depends not only on the inheritability of endowments but also on the willingness of poor families to self-finance investments in their children.

The degree of intergenerational mobility in earnings is also determined by the number of children in different families. Additional children in a family reduce the amount invested in each one when investments must be financed by the family. Consequently, a negative relation between family size and the earnings of parents also reduces the intergenerational mobility of earnings.

Assets act as a buffer to offset regression to the mean in the endowments and hence in the earnings of children. In particular, successful families bequeath assets to children to offset the expected downward regression in earnings.

Parents with ready access to capital markets can transfer assets or debt to nullify any effect of regression to the mean in earnings on the consumption of children. This access effectively separates the relation between the consumption by parents and children from inheritability of endowments and regression to the mean in earnings. Consumption in poorer and middle-level families who do not want to leave bequests tends to regress upward, because equilibrium marginal rates of return on investments in the human capital of children tend to be higher in families with low earnings. Consumption and total resources in richer families that do leave bequests to children regress down to the mean, mainly because fertility is positively related to parents' wealth. In this way larger families dilute the wealth bequeathed to each child. Imperfect assortative mating also tends to cause consumption and wealth to regress to the mean.

We have examined about a dozen empirical studies relating the earnings, income, and assets of parents and children. Aside from families victimized by discrimination, regression to the mean in earnings in the United States and other rich countries appears to be rapid, and the regression in assets is sizable. Almost all earnings advantages and disadvantages of ancestors are wiped out in three generations. Poverty would not seem to be a ''culture'' that persists for several generations.

Rapid regression to the mean in earnings implies that both the inheritability of endowments and the capital constraints on investments in children are not large. Presumably these constraints became less important as fertility declined over time and as incomes and subsidies to education grew.

In this supplement and in previous work we claim that a theory of family behavior is necessary to understand inequality and the rise and fall of families. In making the claim, however, we have not intended to downgrade the importance of empirically oriented studies. Indeed, we have always viewed them as a necessary complement to theoretical analysis. We apologize if our claims for maximizing theory can be interpreted as denying the value of empirical and statistical work that is not explicitly based on a model of maximizing behavior.

We still claim, however, that our model of family behavior is useful in understanding the effect of public policies and other events on inequality and the rise and fall of families. Here we part company with Goldberger (1985), who denies that our theory adds much to formulations not based on a model of maximizing behavior. He claims (see especially pp. 30–33) that our theory has few implications that differ from simple regressive models of the earnings or incomes of different generations of a family. Perhaps some perspective about the validity of his claim can be acquired through a brief summary of a few implications of our analysis.

1. Earnings regress more rapidly to the mean in richer than in poorer families. Even though endowments of children and earnings of parents are positively related, a small redistribution of investment in human capital from richer to poorer families tends to raise the overall efficiency of investments. The reason is that investments by poorer families are constrained by limited access to funds.

2. Unlike earnings, consumption regresses more rapidly to the mean in poorer than in richer families if fertility is not related to parents' wealth. Indeed, consumption does not tend to regress at all among rich families who leave gifts and bequests to their children.

3. Our analysis also implies that fertility is positively related to the wealth of parents. This relation dilutes the wealth that can be left to each child and induces a regression to the mean among rich families in the relation between consumption per child and consumption of parents.

We do not know of any other analysis of the family that has these implications, regardless of the approach used. The implications have not been tested empirically; but Goldberger (1985) mainly questions the novelty of the implications of our analysis, not their empirical validity. Additional implications are obtained by considering the effect of public programs.

Becker and Tomes (1979, pp. 1175–78) show that a progressive income tax could raise the long-run relative inequality in after-tax income. The standard deviation clearly falls, but average incomes also fall eventually because parents reduce their bequests to children. Goldberger's useful calculations (1985, pp. 24–25) support our analytical proof that an increase in the degree of progressivity could actually lead to an increase in after-tax inequality. His calculations suggest, however, that a couple of generations would elapse before relative inequality might even begin to increase. He overstates the delay before inequality might begin to increase, and he understates the likelihood of an eventual net increase, by not considering the effect of greater progressivity on the contribution to inequality of the unsystematic component of the tax system (see Becker and Tomes, 1979, pp. 1177–78).[10]

We are not here concerned with inequality, but we believe that the model developed also implies that after-tax inequality might increase when the degree of progressivity increases. Income taxes alter behavior in our analysis partly by affecting the coefficients in equations such as (7S.11), (7S.18), and (7S.27). Empirical or regressive models that start with such equations or with other equations not derived from an explicit model of behavior across generations would have difficulty analyzing the effects of income taxes on the coefficients in these equations, because such models usually provide insufficient guidance about how these coefficients are determined.

This conclusion applies to other policies as well, and to various changes in the environment faced by families. Indeed, the issues are not special to inequality and intergenerational mobility but apply to efforts to understand all social behavior.

To illustrate with a different public program, consider the effects of public debt and social security on the consumption of different generations of a family. Barro (1974) uses a model of parent altruism that is similar to our model of altruism when fertility is fixed, to question whether social security and public debt have significant effects on consumption. Parents who make positive bequests to children do not raise

---

10. Although Goldberger admits that we only claim a possible long-run increase in inequality, he criticizes the statement in Chapter 7 that "perhaps this conflict between initial and equilibrium effects explains why the large growth in redistribution during the last fifty years has had only modest effects on after-tax inequality." A similar statement appears in Becker and Tomes (1979, p. 1178). Goldberger omits the "perhaps" in our statement and says we "conjecture." He asks, "Is it true that over the past fifty years, the mean and variance of disposable income both fell? If not, what explanation has his model [that is, the Becker-Tomes model] provided?" (1985, pp. 26–27). These are strange questions. We were not foolish enough to contend that *only* the tax system affected the growth of incomes during the past 50 years, nor did we try to assess how other forces affected inequality. Since we could prove with our model that a progressive income tax need not lower inequality in the long run, and since inequality apparently did not decline significantly over the past 50 years, we speculated about whether progressive income taxes did lower inequality over this period. Surely that speculation could be highly relevant in forcing a reassessment of the common belief that progressive taxes lower inequality. Of course, other changes during this period might have masked a negative effect of income taxes on inequality, but this needs to be proven rather than simply assumed.

their consumption when they receive social security or revenue from public debt. Instead, they raise their bequests to offset the effect of these programs on the consumption of children. Yet the consumption of altruistic parents who are constrained from leaving debt to children is raised by social security and public debt, and the consumption of their children is lowered (see Drazen, 1978).

To avoid misunderstanding, we hasten to add that we do not claim that all public programs are neutralized through compensatory reductions within families. Such a hypothesis is not true for poorer families in this example or for all families when fertility can vary (see Becker and Barro, 1988, and the supplement to Chapter 11 of this volume). Moreover, we have shown that progressive income taxes reduce the incentive to invest in children. We claim not neutrality, but that our analysis of family behavior is helpful in understanding the effects of various public programs on the rise and fall of families.

Systematic empirical evidence is necessary before this and other claims can be evaluated. We close by reiterating our belief that such evidence will confirm that the analysis of family behavior within a utility-maximizing framework provides many insights into the rise and fall of families in modern societies.

CHAPTER 8

Altruism in the Family

Adam Smith argued in a famous passage that people are selfish in their market transactions: "It is not from the benevolence of the butcher, the brewer, or the baker, that we expect our dinner, but from their regard to their own interest. We address ourselves, not to their humanity but to their self-love, and never talk to them of our own necessities but of their advantages" (1937, p. 14). In an earlier study he said with irony, "We are not ready to suspect any person of being defective in selfishness" (1853, p. 446). Selfishness in market transactions has been assumed in virtually all subsequent discussions of the economic system. Objections were dismissed with vague allusions to "human nature" or with an assertion that altruism loses out to selfishness in the struggle to survive in the market sector.

Yet altruism is generally recognized to be important within a family. Again, Adam Smith said: "Every man feels his own pleasures and his own pains more sensibly than those of other people . . . After himself, the members of his own family, those who usually live in the same house with him, his parents, his children, his brothers and sisters, are naturally the objects of his warmest affections. They are naturally and usually the persons upon whose happiness or misery his conduct must

have the greatest influence'' (1853, p. 321; see the insightful discussion
of Smith by Coase, 1976).

Effects of Altruism

Initially, take as given that a person, h, is effectively altruistic toward
another member of his family, say his spouse, w. ''Altruistic'' means
that h's utility function depends positively on the well-being of w (see
note H in the Mathematical Appendix to Chapter 7), and ''effectively''
means that h's behavior is changed by his altruism. Stated formally,
altruism is defined by

$$U_h = U[Z_{1h}, \ldots, Z_{mh}, \psi(U_w)]$$
and $$\partial U_h / \partial U_w > 0,$$

(8.1)

where U_h and U_w are the utilities of the altruist and his beneficiary
respectively, ψ is a positive function of U_w, and Z_{jh} is the jth commodity consumed by h. His altruism is effective if the equilibrium levels of
Z_{jh}, for some $j = 1, \ldots, m$, would be different if U_w did not enter his
utility function.

If h is effectively altruistic and spends some of his income on w
rather than on his own consumption, and if h and w consume amounts
Z_h and Z_w of a single (aggregate) commodity, h's budget constraint is

$$Z_h + y = I_h,$$ (8.2)

where the price of Z is set equal to unity, y is the amount spent on w,
and I_h is h's own income imputed by the marriage market. The
spouse's total consumption equals the sum of her[1] income and the contribution from h:

$$Z_w = I_w + y,$$ (8.3)

where I_w is the income that would be imputed to w by the marriage
market if she had married a selfish person otherwise identical to h. By
replacing y in Eq. (8.2) with $Z_w - I_w$ from Eq. (8.3), the equation for
h's family income, S_h, is derived:

$$Z_h + Z_w = I_h + I_w = S_h.$$ (8.4)

---

1. To distinguish the altruist from the beneficiary, I use the masculine pronoun for the altruist and the feminine pronoun for the beneficiary.

Since an altruist maximizes his own utility (subject to his family income constraint), he might be called selfish, not altruistic, in terms of utility.[2] Perhaps—but note that h also raises w's utility through his transfers to w. I am giving a definition of altruism that is relevant to behavior—to consumption and production choices—rather than giving a philosophical discussion of what "really" motivates people.

The allocation of resources by an effective altruist like h is determined from the equilibrium condition

$$\frac{\partial U/\partial Z_h}{\partial U/\partial Z_w} = 1. \tag{8.5}$$

This equation (obtained by maximizing Eq. 8.1, subject to the family income equation) can be solved to derive h's demand functions for both Z_h and Z_w:

$$Z_h = Z_h(S_h) \quad \text{and} \quad Z_w = Z_w(S_h), \tag{8.6}$$

where $\partial Z_i/\partial S_h > 0$, for $i = h,w$ if h wants to increase both Z_h and Z_w when his family income increases and if $y > 0$.

The behavior of h is shown graphically in Figure 8.1, where Z_h is plotted along the horizontal axis, Z_w along the vertical axis, and U_0, U_1, and U_2 are indifference curves of h. If his budget line is $S_h S_h$, equilibrium is at point e, where the slope of an indifference curve, $(\partial U/\partial Z_h)/(\partial U/\partial Z_w)$, equals the slope of this line, which is -1. An increase in family income to $\bar{S}_h$ shifts the budget line out parallel to itself. The new equilibrium values of Z_h and Z_w are given by point $\bar{e}$, where both Z_h and Z_w are larger than at point e.

The altruism of h would be effective if the slope of his indifference curve at the "endowed" point E_0 were less (in absolute value) than the slope of the budget line. Effective altruism moves the equilibrium along the family income line from the endowed position (where $Z_h = I_h$ and $Z_w = I_w$) to a position like e. Contributions are given by y $(= Z_w - I_w)$, and the altruist's consumption is given by Z_h $(= I_h - y)$. Clearly, h not

---

2. Consider the following: "It's only you, the generous creatures, whom I envy . . . I envy you your power of doing what you do. It is what I should revel in, myself. I don't feel any vulgar gratitude to you. I almost feel as if *you* ought to be grateful to *me*, for giving you the opportunity of enjoying the luxury of generosity . . . I may have come into the world expressly for the purpose of increasing your stock of happiness. I may have been born to be a benefactor to you by sometimes giving you an opportunity of assisting me in my little perplexities" (Dickens, 1867, p. 41).

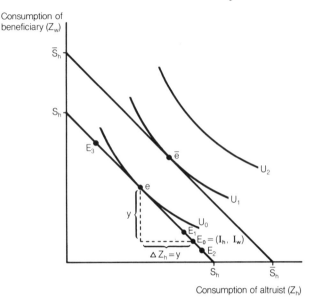

FIGURE 8.1   Contributions of an altruist to his beneficiary, as determined by his preferences and their consumption.

only allocates his own income between his consumption and contributions to w but also determines the *total* consumption of his beneficiary.

If w were selfish and her utility depended only on Z_w, the movement from the endowment E to the equilibrium position at e would raise the utility of both w and h. Any further movement along the budget line beyond e would raise w's utility but lower h's, which is why he stops at e. The utility-possibility boundary traced by the family income constraint[3] is given by the curve S_hS_h in Figure 8.2. The positively sloped section (S_he) is the result of h's altruism, and all movements along this section toward e are Pareto-optimal improvements for h and w.

The location of the budget line in Figure 8.1, and hence of the equilibrium consumption of Z_w and Z_h, is determined only by family income, the sum of own incomes of h and w. Therefore, a redistribution of own income between h and w would shift the endowment position but would not change the budget line. If the endowment still remained to the right of the equilibrium position, as E_1 and E_2 are to the right of e in Figure 8.1, the consumption of Z_h and Z_w would be unaffected, since

---

3. I am indebted to Sherwin Rosen for suggesting this figure; see also Collard (1978, p. 106).

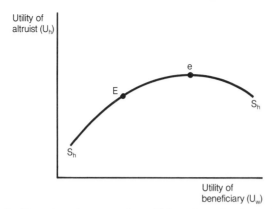

FIGURE 8.2   Boundary between the utilities of an altruist and his beneficiary when their incomes are given and the contribution from the altruist
varies.

e is still the equilibrium position. The change in the amount contributed
to *w* by *h* would fully offset any decrease (as at E_2) or increase (as at E_1)
in *w*'s income. Consequently, redistributions of income toward as well
as away from *w* have no effect on the consumption of either *w* or *h*, as
long as *h* remains effectively altruistic; his contributions contract or expand sufficiently to offset fully these redistributions.

If the redistributions to *w* were sufficiently great to push the endowment to the left of the initial equilibrium, *h* would cease being effectively altruistic because *w* would be "too" wealthy. Still, *h* offsets part
of the redistribution to *w* by eliminating his contributions to *w*. He
would like to offset more of it, but lacks the power to exact contributions from a selfish *w*.

If either *h* or *w* had a disaster that greatly reduced his or her own income, family income would decline by the same amount. The consumption of the person with the disaster would be reduced by a smaller
amount, however, because the decline in family income induces the
altruist to spread the consequences of the income reduction by lowering the consumption of himself and his beneficiary. For example, if I_w
fell, *h* would raise his contribution to his spouse and thereby reduce his
own consumption and offset part of her fall in income; conversely if I_h
fell, he would lower his contribution and reduce her consumption.

In this manner altruism helps families insure their members against
disasters and other consequences of uncertainty: each member of an
altruistic family is partly insured, inasmuch as all other members are

induced to bear some of the burden through changes in contributions from the altruist. As a result, they are more willing to take actions that raise the variability of their own incomes than are members of selfish families, because altruistic families have more insurance. However, *family* income might well be *less* variable in altruistic families; their members consider the interests of the whole family (see the following discussion) and try to reduce the covariance of the incomes of different members.

An altruist is made better off by actions that raise his family income and worse off by actions that lower it. Since family income is the sum of his own and his beneficiary's income, he would refrain from actions that raise his own income if they lower hers even more; and he would take actions that lower his own if they raise her income even more. To show this behavior geometrically, let E_0 in Figure 8.3 represent the initial endowments of h and w, $S_h S_h$ his budget line, and e_0 the initial equilibrium position. If an action lowers his income by less than it increases her income (new endowment point E_1), the new budget line $S_h^1 S_h^1$ is above $S_h S_h$, and he is better off at e_1 than at e_0. On the other hand, if an action raises his income by less than it lowers hers (new endowment point E_2), the new budget line, $S_h^2 S_h^2$ is below $S_h S_h$, and he is worse off at e_2 than at e_0.

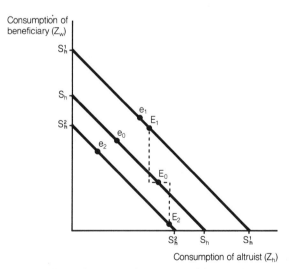

FIGURE 8.3   The effect of changes in opportunities on the consumptions of an altruist and his beneficiary.

In particular, an altruist would refrain from moving to another community where his earnings would be higher if his working wife's earnings would be lowered even more, and he would move when her earnings were lowered if his were raised even more. "Tied" stayers and "tied" movers—as he is in the first example and she is in the second—have become more important over time as the labor force participation of married women has risen. This not only implies that the migration of multiperson households is less frequent than that of single persons, but also that unemployment is positively related to migration (for analysis and evidence, see Mincer, 1978).

Would a selfish beneficiary try to raise her utility at the expense of her benefactor, or does his altruism affect her behavior toward him? If his contribution were beyond her control, a selfish beneficiary would maximize her own income because that would maximize her consumption and utility. She would take all actions that raise and refrain from all actions that lower her own income, regardless of the effects on his income. However, his contribution is not beyond her control. For example, if raising her own income has the effect of lowering his even more, he would reduce his contribution to her by more than the increase in her income (if his contribution had been larger than the increase in her income) because family income goes down; hence the optimal level of her consumption also goes down (see Eq. 8.6). But she as well as he would then be worse off, and she would be discouraged by her own selfish interest from actions that harmed him.

Since W maximizes

$$S_w = Z_w = I_w + y, \tag{8.7}$$

she refrains from actions that raise I_w if y is lowered even more, and she takes actions that lower I_w if y is raised even more. In particular, she would be willing to lower I_w if I_h were raised still higher, for then h would raise y by more than the fall in I_w, since family income and h's demand for Z_w would be raised. From Eq. (8.4) we know that

$$S_w = Z_w = S_h - Z_h. \tag{8.8}$$

Although S_w and S_h are not equal (they differ by Z_h), they would increase and decrease together if Z_w were a superior commodity to h. Then w would maximize her utility by maximizing family income. If Z_w were an inferior commodity to h, so that Z_w would be raised when S_h were lowered, reductions in I_w and hence S_h would make w better off because she would be *over*compensated by h. Since bad investments are plentiful, w could raise her utility by reducing I_w to zero or even less. Therefore, positive income for a beneficiary appears to *require* that her utility be a superior commodity to her benefactor.

Of course, the interests of altruistic benefactors and selfish beneficiaries are not identical. Selfish beneficiaries like larger contributions than their benefactors are willing to make. For example, the benefactor is unwilling to move beyond point e in Figure 8.2 into the negatively sloped section of the utility-possibility curve. However, this conflict between their interests does not imply, and should not be confused with, any conflict between the actions they choose.

Since a selfish beneficiary wants to maximize family income, she is led by the invisible hand of self-interest to act as if she is altruistic toward her benefactor. Put still differently, the scarce resource "love" is used economically,[4] because sufficient caring by an altruist induces even a selfish beneficiary to act as if she cares about her benefactor as much as she cares about herself. Although I have elsewhere called this the Rotten Kid Theorem (see Becker, 1974b and 1976a, and the discussion in the next section), it applies to the interaction between all types of altruists and beneficiaries. This simple, yet remarkable theorem has major implications for efficiency, the division of labor, and many other aspects of family behavior.

For example, both an altruist and his selfish beneficiary internalize all "externalities" affecting each other. They not only internalize any effects of their actions on the own income of the other, but also internalize the direct effects on consumption. For example, an altruist (or his selfish beneficiary) would eat with his fingers only when its value to him exceeds the value of the disgust suffered by the other, or would read in bed late at night only when its value exceeds the value of the loss of sleep suffered by the other (see Mathematical Appendix, note A). These examples illustrate how personal manners and other rules of behavior indicative of concern for the well-being of family members *automatically* develop in families with an effective altruist.

Perhaps a surprising implication of this analysis is that both are made better off when an altruist or his selfish beneficiary decides to eat with his fingers or read in bed. Since the utility of the altruist would be raised, he would increase his contribution to her by more than her ini-

---

4. According to D. H. Robertson, "We [economists] can . . . contribute mightily to the economizing, that is to the full but thrifty utilization, of that scarce resource Love—which *we* know, just as well as anybody else, to be the most precious thing in the world" (1956, p. 154).

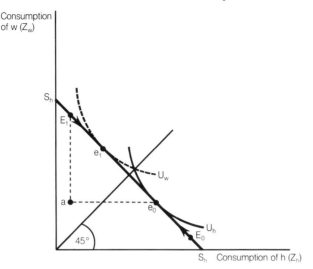

FIGURE 8.4 Reciprocal altruism between two persons, as determined by their preferences and consumption.

tial harm from his actions or reduce his contribution by more than his initial harm from her actions. In this way the person harmed is compensated by changes in contributions from the altruist that make him or her better off. These changes are positive if the beneficiary is harmed initially and negative if the altruist is harmed initially.

A selfish beneficiary would be willing to increase her own income at the expense of family income if the increase exceeds the contribution from her benefactor. He would be harmed because he is pushed to a "corner" where he stops contributing to her, but she is made better off because the increase in her income exceeds the reduction in his contribution. For example, if income were redistributed between h and w from the endowed point E_0 to E_1 in Figure 8.4, the consumption of a selfish w would be raised by aE_1, even though h no longer contributes to her. Although an altruist does not maximize family income when he is at a corner, as h is at E_1, he would not ignore the effect of his actions on his (potential) beneficiary.[5]

---

5. Since a selfish beneficiary maximizes $S_w = I_w + y$, she would maximize I_w alone when $y = 0$. An altruist maximizes

$$S_h = I_h + m_h I_w,$$

where $m_h I_w$ is the monetary value to him of w's income, and

$$m_h = \frac{\partial U}{\partial Z_w} \Big/ \frac{\partial U}{\partial Z_h}$$

Consequently, both an altruist and his selfish beneficiary maximize their combined income only as long as contributions are positive. Joint maximization would be more likely if the beneficiary were also altruistic and her utility function depended on the well-being of her benefactor. She would then contribute to him if her income were sufficiently large relative to his; that is, if the endowment were more favorable to her than the point of tangency of the family-income budget line and her indifference curve (point e_1 in Figure 8.4). He would contribute to her if the endowment were more favorable to him than the point of tangency of the budget line and his indifference curve (point e_0 in Figure 8.4). Neither wants to contribute when the endowment is between their points of tangency.

Both would maximize family income when either is contributing to the other: when the endowment is to the right or to the left of their points of tangency. If these points are identical—for example, if e_0 and e_1 in Figure 8.4 are the same—both always maximize family income regardless of the endowment or the effect on incomes of their actions. These points would be identical if they have the same utility function or, more generally, if the slopes of their indifference curves equal unity at the same values of Z_h and Z_w. However, these slopes would not equal unity at the same values if both are more selfish than altruistic in the sense that the marginal utility of own consumption exceeds that of the other's consumption when their consumptions are equal.[6]

---

is the slope of his indifference curve at the equilibrium position. If his contributions are positive ($y > 0$), $m_h = 1$ and he maximizes $I_h + I_w = S_h$, or family income. However, if his contributions are zero, $0 < m_h < 1$ and changes in her income are not ignored, although they are less important to him than equal changes in his own income.

6. The utility function of h can be said to be self-biased, neutral, or other-biased, as $\partial U/\partial Z_h \gtreqless \partial U/\partial Z_w$ when $Z_h = Z_w$, and similarly for w. If the utility functions of h and w are both other-biased, they want the impossible, because both want the other to consume more than they do. This conflict of "excessive" altruism is identical formally to the conflict of "excessive" selfishness when both utility functions are self-biased.

To see this, let point e_1 in Figure 8.4 now represent the equilibrium position preferred by h and point e_0 the position preferred by w. If the endowment is at E_0, both h and w want some contribution from h to w. However, w will refuse additional contributions as soon as she has received enough to place them at point e_0, unless h can induce w to accept more by offering her an all-or-nothing choice of either no contribution or a sufficiently large one to place them beyond e_0. Similarly, if the endowment is to the left of e_1, w wants to move them to e_0, but h will not want to accept contributions that place them to the right of e_1. When the endowment is between e_0 and e_1, both want to contribute, but neither will accept anything (see Mathematical Appendix, note C).

Multiperson Altruism and Envy

An altruist may have several beneficiaries, including children, spouses, parents, and siblings. The utility function and the budget equation of an altruist who contributes to several selfish children or other selfish beneficiaries are

$$U_h = U(Z_h, Z_1, \ldots, Z_p)$$

(8.9)

and

$$Z_h + \sum_{i=1}^{p} y_i = I_h,$$

where y_i is the contribution to and Z_i is the consumption and utility of the ith beneficiary, for $i = 1, \ldots, p$. Since

$$I_i + y_i = Z_i, \quad \text{for } i = 1, \ldots, p,$$ (8.10)

by substitution

$$Z_h + \sum_{i=1}^{p} Z_i = I_h + \sum_{i=1}^{p} I_i = S_h,$$ (8.11)

where S_h is the family income of the altruist. The first-order conditions are

$$\frac{\partial U}{\partial Z_i} = \frac{\partial U}{\partial Z_j}, \quad \text{for } i,j = h, 1, \ldots, p.$$ (8.12)

In equilibrium, an altruist receives the same utility from a small increase in own income or in the income of any beneficiary (assuming $y_i > 0$).

All the implications derived for a single beneficiary continue to hold when there are many. In particular, an altruist internalizes all external effects of his actions on different beneficiaries as he maximizes the sum of his own income or consumption and the incomes or consumptions of his beneficiaries. Moreover, each beneficiary, no matter how selfish, is induced by the reactions of the altruist to internalize the effects of his actions on the altruist's own income and consumption.

Would a selfish beneficiary neglect the effect of his actions on other beneficiaries when they would not retaliate? For example, would a selfish Tom raise his income by $1,000 if his action would also lower the income of his sister Jane by $1,500, assuming that neither Jane nor their altruistic father would know that Tom is the cause of Jane's misfortune? The Rotten Kid Theorem answers these questions in the negative.

Rotten Kid Theorem   Each beneficiary, no matter how selfish, maximizes the family income of his benefactor and thereby internalizes all effects of his actions on other beneficiaries.

To demonstrate this theorem, note that family income would fall by $500 if Tom takes the action that harms Jane. Since the consumption of both Tom and Jane would tend to be superior commodities to their altruistic father (see our earlier discussion), he would lower their consumption when his family income falls. He could lower Tom's consumption by reducing his contribution to Tom by more than $1,000 (assuming it exceeds $1,000 initially), and he could lower Jane's consumption by raising his contribution by less than $1,500. Since Tom is made worse off by this response of his father, he would not take the action. Indeed, Tom would even take actions that lower his own income if Jane's income were raised sufficiently, because his father would then increase his contribution to Tom by more than the reduction in Tom's income.

Although the Rotten Kid Theorem assumes that altruists know the utility functions and consumptions of their beneficiaries, they need not know the cause of changes in utility and consumption. In particular, their father can discourage Tom from actions that harm Jane and reduce family income without knowing that Tom is the cause of Jane's woes.

The Rotten Kid Theorem has a surprising extension to envious behavior.

Corollary   Each beneficiary, no matter how envious of other beneficiaries or of his benefactor, maximizes the family income of the benefactor, and hence helps those envied!

For example, Tom would not take actions that harm his envied sister and appear to help him if family income were thereby reduced, and would take actions that help her and appear to harm him if family income were thereby raised. Or the first wife of a polygynous husband would not take actions to harm an envied second wife if family income were thereby reduced, and would help her if family income were thereby raised.

To prove this corollary, write the utility function of envious Tom (or the envious wife) as

$$\psi = \psi(Z_t, Z_j), \tag{8.13}$$

where $\partial\psi/\partial Z_j = \psi_j < 0$ expresses his envy toward Jane. The utility function of their altruistic father depends positively on his own consumption, the utility of Tom, and the utility of a selfish Jane:

$$U_h = U[Z_h, \psi(Z_t, Z_j), Z_j]. \tag{8.14}$$

Although an increase in Jane's consumption directly raises the utility of their father because $\partial U/\partial Z_j = U_j > 0$, it also indirectly lowers the father's utility because $\partial U/\partial\psi > 0$ and $\psi_j < 0$. However, the positive direct effect must outweigh the negative indirect effect if their father initially contributes to Jane;[7] that is,

$$\frac{dU_h}{dZ_j} = \frac{\partial U}{\partial Z_j} + \frac{\partial U}{\partial\psi}\,\psi_j > 0 \quad \text{if } y_j > 0.$$

If the utilities of Tom and Jane (ψ and Z_j) are superior "commodities" to their father, Tom would be made worse off by actions harming Jane if family income is reduced and better off by actions helping Jane if family income is raised, because of induced changes in the contributions to Tom from his father. An envious Tom can be better off when Jane is better off if his own consumption increases sufficiently (see Mathematical Appendix, note B).

A shift of Tom's utility function toward greater envy would reduce his father's contribution to Jane; indeed, if Tom became sufficiently envious, the contribution to Jane might be reduced to zero. If it were, his father would attach less weight to a change in Jane's income than to an equal change in Tom's income. Then Tom might benefit from actions that harmed Jane sufficiently to reduce family income, because his father might not reduce his contribution to Tom by much. Of course, the father's utility function might only depend on Tom's consumption and not on Tom's utility function if the father *disapproved* of

---

7. In equilibrium, the father would receive the same utility from small increases in the consumption of Tom and Jane:

$$\frac{dU/dZ_j}{\partial U/\partial Z_t} = 1 = \frac{\partial U/\partial Z_j + (\partial U/\partial\psi)\psi_j}{(\partial U/\partial\psi)\psi_t} = \frac{\partial U/\partial Z_j}{\partial U/\partial Z_t} + \frac{\psi_j}{\psi_t} = 1.$$

The sum of the direct and indirect marginal rates of substitution between the consumption of Tom and Jane would equal unity. Since $\psi_j < 0$ and $\psi_t > 0$, the equilibrium direct marginal rates of substitution are larger than they would be without envy.

envy between his children (see the discussion of merit commodities in the next section).

Envy in a family is far more damaging, however, when not disciplined by the effective altruism of some members. For example, if a father is envious of his selfish children, they would try to *lower* rather than raise his utility. Whereas altruism induces selfish children and other beneficiaries to behave altruistically, envy induces children and other victims to behave enviously.

If a person, e, were envious of m selfish members of his family, their consumption can be considered negative inputs into the production of a commodity that reduces his envy:

$$E = f(Z_1, \ldots, Z_m), \quad \text{with } \partial E/\partial Z_k < 0 \text{ for } k = 1, \ldots, m.$$

The utility function of e would be

$$U_e = U(Z_e, E) = V(Z_e, Z_1, \ldots, Z_m), \text{ with } \partial U/\partial E > 0$$
$$\text{and } \partial V/\partial Z_k < 0. \quad (8.15)$$

An envier is willing to reduce his own consumption if the consumption of his victims is reduced sufficiently. If each dollar spent on a victim reduces the victim's consumption by one unit, the budget constraint of the envier and the consumption of his victims become:

$$Z_e + \sum_{k=1}^{m} y_k = I_e$$

$$(8.16)$$

and
$$I_k - y_k = Z_k,$$

where y_k is spent on the kth victim.

Substituting into Eq. (8.16), we have

$$Z_e - \sum Z_k = I_e - \sum I_k = R_e, \quad (8.11')$$

where R_e is the "envy income" of e, the difference between his income and that of his victims. He spends R_e partly on his own consumption (Z_e) and partly on the reduction of his envy (raising E). Since U_e is monotonically related to R_e (when the price of E is held constant), we have the following theorem:

Theorem I on Envy   An effective envier wants to maximize his envy income and takes all actions that raise the difference between his own income and the incomes of victims. In particular, he would be willing to lower his income if their incomes were lowered more and to raise his income if their incomes were raised less.

This striking theorem can be readily illustrated with Figure 8.5, where F_0 is the initial endowed position, R_e^0 is the envy income of the envier (e), the budget line joining F_0 and R_e^0 is assumed to have a slope of $+1$, and f_0 is the point that maximizes his utility. An increase in the difference between I_e and I_k increases his envy income and shifts his budget line to the right; for example, the new endowment might be F_1 if I_k were reduced by more than I_e, and the new budget line $F_1R_e^1$ would then be to the right of $F_0R_e^0$ because R_e^1 exceeds R_e^0. Clearly, e would take any action that raised R_e and shifted his budget line to the right.

The person envied, k, is worse off at f_1 than at f_0 because e increases his consumption of envy when he is better off. Hence k would take actions that lower R_e and harm e, because e would then reduce his expenditures on envy sufficiently to make k better off. More generally, all victims want to lower the envy income of the envier and harm him because he would then make them better off. Therefore, in contrast to the harmony between the altruist and beneficiaries produced by altruism, envy produces conflict between the envier and victims. However, envy produces harmony among victims just as altruism produces harmony among beneficiaries, since even selfish victims want to raise the

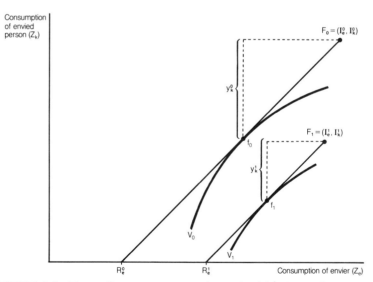

FIGURE 8.5 Expenditures on envy as determined by the preferences of the envier, his consumption, and the consumption of the person envied.

incomes of other victims (to hurt the envier). The behavior of victims can be formalized in the following theorem that corresponds to the Rotten Kid Theorem for altruism.

Theorem II on Envy   All envied victims want to minimize the envy income and utility of the envier. Hence they only take actions that lower the difference between the income of the envier and the incomes of victims. In particular, each would reduce his own income if the income of the envier were reduced more or if the incomes of other victims were raised more.

The Rotten Kid Theorem and the theorems on envy imply that for rotten kids to act rotten, they must have rotten parents—and that rotten wives must have rotten husbands. Even selfish and envious children or wives act as if they are altruistic toward their siblings and parents or husbands if these persons are altruistic toward them, and act as if they are envious toward their parents or husbands if these persons are envious toward them. The Rotten Kid Theorem does not imply, however, that families with altruistic members are perfectly harmonious. Selfish children want larger contributions from their parents, selfish wives want larger contributions from their husbands, and envious children or wives also want smaller contributions to their siblings or co-wives. Children cry, cajole, and use other techniques to delay weaning or reduce punishments, and generally increase the money, time, and effort spent on them. (See the discussion in Trivers, 1974.)

This conflict over the *distribution* of family income should not be confused with, and does not imply, any conflict over the *production* of income. Indeed, the Rotten Kid Theorem implies harmonious production of income in families with altruistic members: even selfish and envious children or spouses behave altruistically in all decisions that affect production[8] (except when the altruist is driven to a corner). Therefore, families with both altruistic and selfish members have neither perfect harmony nor pervasive conflict, but harmony in production and conflict over distribution. Of course, the conflict over distribution is

---

8. "I knew, for I had been told by each wife in turn, that they were jealous of the sheik's affections and felt rejected when he favored one woman's child over another, or brought gifts to one and not to the other two. Yet the three women depended on each other, and knew that their work would be much more difficult without the help of the others. The basic jealousies and petty dislikes were there, but they were submerged and mitigated by the necessities of daily living" (Fernea, 1965, p. 170).

smaller and the harmony in production is more robust when more members are altruistic.

An altruistic parent would be better off if his spouse were also altruistic and contributed resources to their children. Since the welfare of children would affect the welfare of both parents, contributions from each parent would depend on the contributions of the spouse. Indeed, each may try to free-ride on the other's contributions; see the discussion of public goods in Samuelson (1955) and Tideman and Tullock (1976).

The Rotten Kid Theorem can explain why a parent delays some contributions until later stages of his lifetime: he wants to provide his children with a long-run incentive to consider the interests of the whole family. Indeed, he might retain some contributions until after he dies so that he can have the last word.[9] He would not usually delay all contributions to the end, partly because he must establish good faith with his children.

This analysis can explain why altruistic parents leave bequests to their children even when the taxes on gifts *inter vivos* are lower than the taxes on bequests,[10] and even when gifts are more useful to children. It also implies that richer families can induce more altruistic behavior from older children than poorer families, because the rich contribute nonhuman as well as human capital, and nonhuman capital is more readily saved for bequests or gifts to older children.

The Rotten Kid Theorem can reconcile the implication of our earlier analysis that wealthy parents spend more nonhuman capital on less-endowed children with the evidence that bequests of parents to different children are often similar (see for example Menchik, 1980; Tomes, 1980a). Again, the distinction between bequests and gifts is crucial, because wealthy parents would compensate less-endowed children principally with gifts.[11] If gifts fully compensated these children, equal be-

---

9. If only King Lear had understood this:
Lear: Dost thou call me fool, boy?
Fool: All thy other titles thou hast given away, that thou wast born with.
—Shakespeare, *The Tragedy of King Lear*
I owe this reference, and the emphasis on the last word, to Hirshleifer (1977b).

10. The marginal tax rate on gifts has seemed lower than that on bequests, but a recent study (Adams, 1978) suggests that the true marginal rates on gifts and bequests may be similar.

11. The evidence on gifts is too limited to test this implication (see the discussion in Menchik, 1980).

quests would tend to elicit the same amount of altruism from all older children, whereas if bequests compensated, less altruism would be elicited from the better-endowed older children.

Even poorer parents might leave bequests if the annuity market were imperfect and they died prematurely (Tomes, 1979). Since poorer parents do not fully compensate less-endowed children (see Chapter 6), such "inadvertent" bequests to these children would be larger. In one sample of small estates, bequests tend to be larger to children with lower endowments (Tomes, 1980a).

The Rotten Kid Theorem also explains why contributions usually are not anonymous. Even an altruist wants beneficiaries to know their benefactor so that they can incorporate his interests into their behavior. Thus a giver's insistence on being identified does not imply that his gifts are really "purchases" of social prestige or explicit quid pro quos, but may only involve a recognition that even outright gifts can induce apparently altruistic behavior from selfish beneficiaries.

The threat of retaliation can induce members of completely selfish families to consider the effects of their actions on other members. However, the effectiveness of retaliatory threats declines as members age and fewer "moves" remain; and retaliation alone cannot induce fully altruistic behavior even at younger ages (see the discussion in Radner, 1979, 1980, and Telser, 1980). Moreover, accidents and acts of nature often are not easily distinguished from intentional harmful actions, for these can be disguised and innocence vigorously proclaimed. Although selfish families need not rely solely on the threat of retaliation, because they can negotiate contracts and other agreements to act altruistically, these arrangements too can be undermined by cheating, deceit, suspicion, and the cost of policing and enforcing agreements.

Altruistic families avoid these problems without negotiation (see also Kurz, 1977) because even selfish and envious members are induced to act altruistically. Policing and enforcement expenditures are unnecessary, and proclaiming innocence to disguise harmful actions is to no avail; altruists do not retaliate,[12] but respond automatically to changes in family income without regard to the causes. Indeed, even a little

---

12. This is recognized in the following dialogue from the comic strip *Dondi* (*Chicago Tribune*, December 17, 1979); I am indebted to Stephen Stigler for bringing it to my attention.

Adopted uncle of Dondi: Your grandma buy me these fancy skates 'cause she love me.

Dondi: That's not true, Charlie. She *bribed* you to quit bullying me!

Adopted uncle: Is same thing!

altruism can induce fully cooperative behavior when a finite but long sequence of moves is available to each participant. Altruistic families are partly immune to the "last move" problem as well, because selfish members are induced to act altruistically until the altruist dies or even later, by bequests and other delayed contributions.[13]

The effect of a little altruism on cooperative and efficient behavior can be illustrated by Good Samaritan situations (see the analysis in Landes and Posner, 1978). A selfish person who encountered someone drowning, being assaulted, or in other dire circumstances would refuse to help without the expectation of monetary or psychic compensation. An altruist, however, might help even if he were exposed to danger, and even if his altruism were sufficiently weak that he did not help in any way prior to the misfortune. Although the marginal utility from helping might have been small prior to the misfortune, the *total* increase in utility to the altruist from helping could exceed the disutility of the effort or risk involved because of the imminent large decline in the victim's welfare. This example shows not only how altruism can induce efficient behavior where selfishness fails, but also how altruism can significantly change behavior even when the altruism is weak.

Chapter 2 argues that the extensive specialization and division of labor in households, especially between women who bear and raise children and men who participate in the market sector, encourages shirking of responsibilities and other efforts to improve own well-being at the expense of other members. Since an altruist and his beneficiaries maximize family income and do not shirk their responsibilities or otherwise increase their well-being at the expense of others, altruism encourages the division of labor and an efficient allocation of resources.

Emile Durkheim (1933) asserted, contrary to Adam Smith and other economists, that the main advantage of an extensive division of labor is not increased production but a congruence of the interests and sentiments ("organic solidarity") of those participating in the division of labor.[14] I argue that a division of labor among selfish persons may encourage cheating and shirking, rather than organic solidarity. Contrary to Durkheim, I maintain that a congruence of sentiments is a

---

13. Selfish as well as altruistic families can use bequests to delay the last move.
14. "We are thus led to consider the division of labor in a new light. In this instance, the economic services that it can render are picayune compared to the moral effect that it produces, and its true function is to create in two or more persons a feeling of solidarity" (Durkheim, 1933, p. 56).

cause rather than a result of efficient division of labor. (See also the discussion of Durkheim in Hirshleifer, 1977a.) The only likely link from the division of labor to a congruence of sentiments is through the prosperity and survival of altruistic families and other organizations, a topic to be considered shortly.

Family Utility Functions

The analysis of altruism and envy is easily extended to many commodities if altruists or envious persons care about the *utility* of their beneficiaries or victims, as in

$$U_h = U[Z_{1h}, \ldots, Z_{mh}, \psi_1(Z_{11}, \ldots, Z_{m1}), \ldots, \psi_p(Z_{1p}, \ldots, Z_{mp})],$$
(8.17)

where Z_{ij} is the consumption of the ith commodity by the jth family member, for $j = h, 1, \ldots, p$, and ψ_k increases when the utility of the kth selfish beneficiary increases. The altruist h contributes "dollars" to his beneficiaries because his utility is maximized when they use these dollars to maximize their own utility. His budget equation would be

$$\sum_{i=1}^{m} \pi_i Z_{ih} + \sum_{k=1}^{p} y_k = I_h,$$
(8.18)

where π_i is the price of the ith commodity and y_k are the dollars contributed to the kth beneficiary. After substitution for y_k from the budget equation of k, the altruist's family income is:

$$\sum_{i=1}^{m} \pi_i Z_{ih} + \sum_{k=1}^{p} \sum_{i=1}^{m} \pi_i Z_{ik} = I_h + \sum_{k=1}^{p} I_k = S_h.$$
(8.11″)

The far left-hand side shows that family income is spent on the consumption of different commodities by the altruist and his beneficiaries.

All beneficiaries voluntarily maximize family income and the utility of the altruist, even when he does not have dictatorial power over their decisions, because their own utility increases and decreases along with his. Consequently, an altruistic family can be said to have a family utility function that is voluntarily maximized by all members regardless of the distribution of family income (as long as the altruist is not driven to a corner).

This derivation of a family utility function can be contrasted with the discussion in a well-known article on social indifference curves by Paul

Samuelson (1956). Without sufficient elaboration he refers to a consistent "family social welfare function," grafted onto the separate utility functions of different family members. In addition, he says that a family member's "preferences among his own goods have the special property of being independent of the other members' consumption. But since blood is thicker than water, the preferences of the different members are interrelated by what might be called a 'consensus' or 'social welfare function' which takes into account the deservingness or ethical worths of the consumption levels of each of the members" (p. 10). My difficulty with this statement is that the "deservingness" of the consumptions of different members should simply be incorporated into each member's preferences, as in my approach, rather than interrelated by a "consensus."

Samuelson also says (p. 21) that "if within the family there can be assumed to take place an optimal reallocation of income so as to keep each member's dollar expenditure of equal ethical worth, then there can be derived for the whole family a set of well-behaved indifference contours relating the totals of what it consumes: the family can be said to *act as if* it maximizes such a group preference function" (italics in original). In my approach the "optimal reallocation" results from altruism and voluntary contributions, and the "group preference function" is identical to that of the altruistic head, even when he does not have sovereign power.[15] Although his "indifference contours" do not simply depend on the family's total consumption of each commodity, family consumption is independent of the distribution of family income (aside from "corners"), is positively related to the level of family income, and is negatively related to the relative price of the commodity.

If h's utility function depends on the utility of another member (j), and at the same time j's utility function depends on h's utility, an infinite regress would be set in motion by giving. For example, a contribution from h to j directly raises the utility of j, which indirectly raises the utility of h because of his altruism, which in turn indirectly raises the utility of j because of his reciprocal altruism, and so on. Mathematically, this infinite regress can be expressed as

$$U_h = U(Z_{1h}, \ldots, Z_{mh}, \psi_h\{Z_{1j}, \ldots, Z_{mj}, \psi_j[Z_{1h}, \ldots, Z_{mh}, \psi_h(\ )]\}).$$
$$(8.19)$$

15. Samuelson (p. 9) appears to believe that the head must have sovereign power if the group preference function is the same as the head's function.

Nevertheless, a family utility function would still exist if suitable restrictions were placed on the degree of reciprocal altruism. The basic restriction implies that the marginal utility from own consumption tends to exceed the marginal utility from the other's consumption (see Mathematical Appendix, note C).

Even altruistic parents do not merely accept the utility functions of young children who are too inexperienced to know what is "good for them."[16] Parents may want children to study longer, not play with matches, or be more obedient than the children want to. Their consumption and other behavior is controlled until they accumulate more experience and education. Of course children (in modern times, especially adolescents) may believe that they do know enough and that their parents are out of touch with important changes, a clash of the generations that can be particularly bitter in dynamic societies. The conflict with older children is usually less severe, and altruistic parents are more willing simply to contribute dollars that the children can spend as they wish.

Parents sometimes want children to behave differently than children want to, not because parents are altruistic and consider themselves better informed, but because they are competitive with their children, gain prestige from their children's accomplishments, or for other "selfish" reasons. A parent's utility function could then be written as

$$U_h = U[Z_{1h}, \ldots, Z_{mh}, Q_1(Z_{11}, \ldots, Z_{m1}), \ldots, Q_p(Z_{1p}, \ldots, Z_{mp})],$$
(8.20)

where Q_k, the parent's benefit from his kth child's consumption, is *not* monotonically related to k's utility function. The parent would obtain little benefit from unrestricted contributions if Q_k were not closely related to k's utility function; indeed, he would be made worse off by unrestricted contributions if Q_k were negatively related to U_k. He might instead contribute particular goods, or restrict the ways his dollar contributions can be spent.[17]

The conflict between Q_k and U_k means that a common utility function for the family does not exist; different members maximize dif-

---

16. Perhaps better stated, the basic utility functions of young children would be accepted, but the children could not be trusted to maximize their utility because they would be poorly informed about household production functions.

17. One drunk says to another in a *Wizard of Id* cartoon, "Could you spare a buck for a bottle of wine?" The other answers, "How do I know you won't buy food with it?"

ferent utility functions. The conflict in such families therefore exceeds the conflict in altruistic families. Indeed, if Q_k and U_k were negatively related, the conflict would be similar to the conflict in envious families.

Altruism in the Family and Selfishness in the Marketplace

At the beginning of this chapter I suggested that selfishness is common in market transactions and altruism is common in families, but I did not explain why the same persons are altruistic in their families and selfish at their shops and firms. The reason is not that selfish parents and children or altruistic sellers and buyers are unknown—witness the neglected children and parents, and the utopian ventures into production and consumption. I believe that altruism is less common in market transactions and more common in families because altruism is less "efficient" in the marketplace and more "efficient" in families.

Despite the age and value of statements by Adam Smith and others about the prevalence of selfish behavior in market transactions, these assertions have not been derived from basic considerations. Recent discussions suggest that purposive (goal-oriented) behavior is more likely to survive market competition than random and other nonpurposive behavior (see the review in Hirshleifer, 1977a), but these discussions do not consider whether altruistic purposive behavior can survive as well as or better than selfish purposive behavior. Adam Smith (1853) tried to explain why people are more altruistic toward their families than toward strangers, but he did not consider what happens when altruistic and selfish behaviors compete in market transactions.

One naive argument is that altruism cannot compete against selfishness in market transactions because altruists earn lower money profits and other money income by charging below-market prices for their products and services. The argument is naive in that altruists receive psychic income in place of money income—they consume as they sell their products and services—and they can survive as well as money-income maximizers if they do not try to consume too much.[18]

---

18. Discriminators against blacks and other persons do not do as well as money-income maximizers because discriminators surrender money income to reduce psychic costs. Therefore, they cannot balance their lower money incomes with higher psychic incomes (see Becker, 1971).

Altruism is uncommon not because altruists receive psychic income in place of money income, but because altruism in market transactions is an *inefficient* way to produce psychic income. Consider, for example, a firm that for reasons of altruism prices its product below cost to some customers. The money value of the customers' gain from the altruism is approximately $\Delta p(x_0 + \frac{1}{2} \Delta x)$, where Δp is the price subsidy, x_0 would be the customers' consumption if they were not subsidized, Δx is the increased consumption induced by the subsidy, and $\frac{1}{2} \Delta p \, \Delta x$ is the consumer surplus from the subsidy. The firm's profits, on the other hand, are reduced by $\Delta p(x_0 + \Delta x)$, which exceeds the money value of the gain to these customers.

The firm and these consumer beneficiaries could obtain greater utility from the same reduction in profits, or the same utility from a smaller reduction in profits, if all customers were charged the same price and a cash gift were given to the favored customers. The cost to the firm would be the same if the gift equaled $\Delta p(x_0 + \Delta x)$, but the money value of the increase in utility to these customers, and hence also the value of the increase in utility to the altruistic firm, would be greater than $\Delta p(x_0 + \frac{1}{2} \Delta x)$, for the gift can be spent as desired and is not tied to the consumption of this product. The same argument implies that cash gifts are more efficient than higher wage rates to employee beneficiaries or than lower wage rates from employer beneficiaries.

The conclusion is that firms making cash transfers based on their altruism obtain greater utility than other firms *with the same preferences* and market opportunities who subsidize customers, workers, or suppliers. Consequently, firms making cash transfers are more efficient than firms using market transactions to convey their altruism. Although efficient participants in market transactions may be highly altruistic, they act as if they are selfish and maximize their money incomes. They express their altruism through cash transfers not tied to market transactions, as dramatically illustrated by the enormous charitable contributions of apparently selfish captains of industry in the United States at the end of the nineteenth and the beginning of the twentieth centuries.

This argument does not rule out family firms employing children or other relatives.The Rotten Kid Theorem indicates that beneficiaries are more likely to consider the firm's interests than other employees and to refrain from shirking, theft, and other behavior detrimental to the firm. (Moreover, firms might employ relatives even when they are not altruistic, since they know about the skills, character, and expenditures of relatives. They can use this knowledge to assign relatives to appropriate tasks and to detect whether their relatives are living "too well" as the result of stealing from the firm.) By specifying hours of work or by cash transfers in the form of bonuses, firms can pay employee-beneficiaries more than they are worth without inducing inefficient changes in their hours worked. We can understand why the small family firm has thrived in farming, services, and other sectors (see Chapter 2) even though altruism in market transactions is inefficient.

The average contribution to beneficiaries declines eventually as the number of beneficiaries increases. Since selfish beneficiaries take less account of the interests of their benefactor when contributions are small, an altruistic head of a large organization with many beneficiaries is readily pushed to a corner of zero contributions by detrimental actions of his beneficiaries: "The friend of all mankind is no friend of mine." Large firms are far more common than large households because economies of scale from specialized investments and the division of labor are more important to firms (see Chapter 2). Altruism is more common within households than within firms partly because altruism is more efficient in small organizations.

Altruism is common in families not only because families are small and have many interactions, but also because marriage markets tend to "assign" altruists to their beneficiaries. A selfish beneficiary compares her family income as the mate of her benefactor with the family income available from other participants in the marriage market. Her family income with her benefactor (Eq. 8.7) is

$$S_w = Z_w = I_w + y,$$

where Z_w is her consumption, y is his contribution to her, and I_w is her own income with an otherwise identical selfish participant. The family income of the altruist with his beneficiary (Eq. 8.4) is

$$S_h = Z_h + Z_w = I_h + I_w,$$

where I_h is the income of selfish persons who are otherwise identical to h. Since the wife's consumption counts twice (it enters both their utility functions), they are better off marrying each other than marrying similar persons who are neither benefactors nor beneficiaries.[19] Thus

---

19. A benefactor and his beneficiary are better off together than with selfish mates for the additional reason that marriages with altruism are more efficient and productive than selfish marriages.

we can readily explain why marriages with caring—or "love"—are likely to be part of the equilibrium sorting of mates (but see the discussion of extended families in Chapter 11).

Altruistic parents might not have more children than selfish parents, but they invest more in the human capital or quality of children because the utility of altruistic parents is raised by investment returns that accrue to their children (see also Ishikawa, 1975). Consequently, children from altruistic families tend to be more "successful" than children from selfish families, which raises the influence of altruistic families beyond their numbers. Moreover, their influence may grow over time by virtue of the fact that successful parents tend to have successful children, and altruism toward children is likely to be passed on from one generation to the next.

Our analysis also explains why parents usually are more giving to children than children are to parents.[20] Even if parents and children are equally altruistic, parents would give more because investments in children are more efficient. To show this, drop the assumption that giving merely transfers resources and revert to the more general and plausible assumption of earlier chapters that the productivity of contributions depends on a number of factors, including characteristics of recipients. Contributions to children tend to be more productive than contributions to parents because children have longer remaining lifetimes[21] and have not accumulated as much human capital as their parents, who are older. Parents would give more, then, even if children were equally altruistic.

Figure 8.6 assumes that parents and children have identical preferences and that the indifference curves U_0 and U_1 are symmetrical about the 45-degree line, with a slope of -1 along that line. If the endowed position (E) were on the 45-degree line, neither would give if each dollar given added one unit of consumption to the recipient. However, if the slope of their transformation curve AB exceeds unity at the 45-degree line because contributions to children are more productive than contributions to parents, the utilities of both would be maximized

---

20. This has been observed since biblical times. For example, the Apostle Paul wrote, "For the children ought not to lay up for the parents, but the parents for the children" (II Corinthians 12:14; I owe this reference to Nigel Tomes).

21. Biologists argue that contributions from nonhuman parents are also more productive than contributions from offspring because offspring have more reproductive potential remaining (Barash, 1977, p. 299).

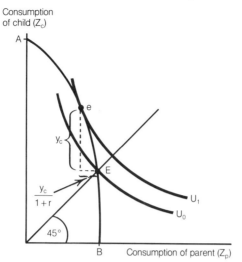

FIGURE 8.6   Contribution from parent to child when they have the same preferences and contributions are productive.

when parents give $y_c/(1 + r)$ and children receive y_c, where r is the rate of return on contributions to children.

Concluding Remarks

Even if altruism were confined to the family, it would still direct the allocation of a large fraction of all resources. Families in all societies, including modern market-oriented societies, have been responsible for a sizable part of economic activity—half or more—for they have produced much of the consumption, education, health, and other human capital of the members. If I am correct that altruism dominates family behavior perhaps to the same extent as selfishness dominates market transactions, then altruism is much more important in economic life than is commonly understood. The pervasiveness of selfish behavior has been greatly exaggerated by the identification of economic activity with market transactions.

Sophisticated models tracing the economic effects of selfishness have been developed during the last 200 years as economic science has refined the insights of Adam Smith. Much is now known about the way selfishness allocates resources in different markets. Unfortunately, an analysis of equal sophistication has not been developed for altruism. I

am hopeful that the analysis of altruism given in this chapter can become the foundation of a fuller development.[22]

Mathematical Appendix

A. Although this is a rather immediate implication of the maximization
of real family income, a proof may be instructive. If a particular action
directly changed the consumption of h and w by dZ_h^0 and dZ_w^0, the
change in the utility of the altruist would be

$$dU^0 = \frac{\partial U}{\partial Z_h} dZ_h^0 + \frac{\partial U}{\partial Z_w} dZ_w^0.$$

In equilibrium,

$$\partial U/\partial Z_j = \lambda_h, \quad \text{for } j = h \text{ or } w,$$

where λ_h is the marginal utility of income to h. Substitution gives

$$dU^0 = \lambda_h dZ_h^0 + \lambda_h dZ_w^0 = \lambda_h(dZ_h^0 + dZ_w^0) = \lambda_h dV^0,$$

where dV^0 is the value to h of the change in the consumption of h and
w. Both h and his selfish beneficiary w only take actions that raise h's
utility—that is, raise family income—because only these actions make
them better off. Since $\lambda_h > 0$,

$$dU^0 \gtreqless 0 \quad \text{as } dV^0 \gtreqless 0,$$

which was to be proved. The analysis is easily generalized to many
commodities consumed by h and w as long as h's utility function depends on the utility of w.

B. If $\psi_j < 0$ and Z_j increases, Tom would still be better off if
$d\psi = \psi_t dZ_t + \psi_j dZ_j > 0$, or

$$dZ_t + (\psi_j/\psi_t)dZ_j > 0.$$

---

22. Economic aspects of altruism are discussed also in Boulding (1973),
Phelps (1975), Hirshleifer (1977b), Kurz (1977), Collard (1978), and a few other
studies.

Actions of Tom that raise the income of Jane and the family would appear to make him worse off if

$$dI_t + (\psi_j/\psi_t)dI_j < 0, \qquad \text{when } dI_t + dI_j > 0.$$

However, increased contributions to Tom and possibly reduced contributions to Jane from their father would raise dZ_t relative to dZ_j to satisfy the first inequality and hence Tom as well as Jane and their father would be better off when the second set of inequalities holds. Similarly, actions that appear to make Tom better off because the second inequalities are reversed actually make him worse off. Reduced contributions to Tom and possibly increased contributions to Jane from their father lower dZ_t relative to dZ_j to reverse the first inequality.

C. Consider the Cobb-Douglas functions

$$U_h = [g_h(Z_{1h}, \ldots, Z_{mh})]^{a_h} U_j^{b_h}$$

and
$$U_j = [g_j(Z_{ij}, \ldots, Z_{mj})]^{a_j} U_h^{b_j},$$

where a_h, a_j, b_h, and b_j are greater than zero. By substitution,

$$U_h = g_h^{\frac{a_h}{1-b_hb_j}} g_j^{\frac{a_jb_h}{1-b_hb_j}} = g_h^{\alpha_h} g_j^{\beta_h}$$

and
$$U_j = g_h^{\frac{a_hb_j}{1-b_hb_j}} g_j^{\frac{a_j}{1-b_hb_j}} = g_h^{\beta_j} g_j^{\alpha_j},$$

where b_hb_j is independent of transformations on U_h and U_j that preserve the Cobb-Douglas form. The marginal utility from a change in the utility of the other person is bounded, and hence these utility functions would exist if, and only if,

$$b_hb_j = \left(\frac{\partial U_h}{\partial U_j}\bigg|_{g_h=g_h^0}\right) U_h^{-1}U_j \left(\frac{\partial U_j}{\partial U_h}\bigg|_{g_j=g_j^0}\right) U_j^{-1}U_h < 1,$$

or
$$\frac{\partial U_h}{\partial U_j}\bigg|_{g_h^0} \frac{\partial U_j}{\partial U_h}\bigg|_{g_j^0} < 1.$$

It is easy to show that this last inequality remains a necessary and sufficient condition when Cobb-Douglas functions are replaced by general utility functions.

Own consumption could be less important than the *utility* of the other person in the sense that a_h could be less than b_h and a_j could be less than b_j. However, since $\alpha_h\alpha_j > \beta_h\beta_j$ if $b_hb_j < 1$, own consumption must tend to be more important than the *consumption* of the other person:

A Treatise on the Family

$$\alpha_h \alpha_j = \left(\frac{\partial U_h}{\partial g_h} U_h^{-1} g_h\right)\left(\frac{\partial U_j}{\partial g_j} U_j^{-1} g_j\right) > \beta_h \beta_j,$$

where $\qquad \beta_h \beta_j = \left(\frac{\partial U_h}{\partial g_j} U_h^{-1} g_j\right)\left(\frac{\partial U_j}{\partial g_h} U_j^{-1} g_h\right),$

or $\qquad \dfrac{\partial U_h}{\partial g_h} \dfrac{\partial U_j}{\partial g_j} > \dfrac{\partial U_h}{\partial g_j} \dfrac{\partial U_j}{\partial g_h}.$

This condition too must hold for general utility functions: see also footnote 6.

CHAPTER 9

Families in
Nonhuman Species

Economic analysis is a powerful tool not only in understanding human behavior but also in understanding the behavior of other species. Clearly, all species must "decide" whether to mate in monogamous or polygamous systems, whether to produce many offspring and devote little care to each one or produce few and devote more care to each, whether to have a sharp division of labor by sex and in other ways, and whether to behave selfishly or altruistically toward offspring and others.

This chapter applies the analysis of human families developed in previous chapters to other species. In particular, Chapters 3 to 5 are used to understand the quantity and quality of offspring and the mating system chosen by different species, including birds, mammals, and amphibians.[1] We could apply the approach equally well to the division of labor, altruism (see Becker, 1976a), and other aspects of the family life of different species.

---

1. I have benefited greatly from the discussions in Fisher (1958), Lack (1968), Wilson (1971, 1975), Trivers (1972, 1974), Wiley (1973, 1974), Dawkins (1976), and Barash (1977).

Quantity and Quality of Offspring

Members of a species compete against one another for food, mates, and other limited resources. The strong, the clever, and the attractive are more successful in producing and rearing offspring because they can appropriate resources, including mates. Traits that are successful in producing offspring become more common in succeeding generations if they are inherited. This process of natural selection is the foundation of modern biology.

Inherited traits of individuals producing relatively many offspring and later descendants are selected, regardless of whether these traits are disadvantageous in other respects. Therefore, natural selection implies that the basic competition is in the production of kin, and traits are more likely to be selected when they are carried by individuals who devote all their time and energy to maximizing their surviving offspring and later descendants. Since inherited traits are carried by genes, natural selection implies that successful individuals maximize the replicas of their genes in subsequent generations (Dawkins, 1976)—biologists call this maximizing genetic "fitness."

We can think of fitness as determined by the production function

$$G = G(n,q), \tag{9.1}$$

where n is the number of replicas or offspring produced and q is the reproductive value of each offspring. Fitness is maximized subject to a limited supply of energy and time, and to production functions for n and q:

$$e = e_n + e_q,$$

$$n = n(e_n,\gamma), \quad \text{with } \frac{\partial n}{\partial e_n} > 0, \tag{9.2}$$

and

$$q = q(e_q,n,\delta), \quad \text{with } \frac{\partial q}{\partial e_q} > 0 \text{ and } \frac{\partial q}{\partial n} < 0,$$

where e_n and e_q are the resources spent on n and q respectively, e is the total supply of resources, and γ and δ represent other influences on n and q. Successful individuals produce more and higher-quality offspring because either they have more energy and other resources (more e) or they are more efficient (higher values of γ and δ).

If the production functions for n and q could be approximated by the simple functions

$$n = \frac{e_n}{p_n(\gamma)}$$

$$(9.3)$$

$$\text{and} \quad q = \frac{e_q}{p_q(\delta) + p(\delta)n},$$

the budget equation can be written as

$$p_n n + p_q q + pnq = e. \tag{9.4}$$

The term $p_n n$ is the cost of producing offspring that is independent of their "quality." These fixed costs are important for females in practically all species because they spend sizable resources on the production of eggs. Males usually can fertilize the eggs of females cheaply, but they may spend considerable resources competing for access to females. The term $p_q q$ is the fixed cost of adding to the quality of offspring that does not depend on their number. Females sometimes compete for favorable nesting sites where they can raise all their offspring with better chances for survival, or males may be able to defend many offspring as easily as a few. The term pnq is variable cost, which depends on both quantity and quality of offspring.

Fitness would be maximized subject to the budget constraint in Eq. (9.4) if resources were allocated between n and q to ensure that

$$\frac{\partial G}{\partial n} = G_n = \lambda(p_n + pq) = \lambda\pi_n$$

$$(9.5)$$

$$\text{and} \quad \frac{\partial G}{\partial q} = G_q = \lambda(p_q + pn) = \lambda\pi_q,$$

where π_n and π_q are the shadow prices of producing an additional unit of quantity and quality respectively. Even if p_n, p_q, and p are constant, π_n and π_q would not be constant because π_n depends positively on q and π_q depends positively on n. This interaction between quantity and quality has been systematically explored in Chapter 5 and is shown in Figure 9.1, where G_0 and G_1 are convex indifference curves of the fitness production function. The interaction between n and q implies that the boundary of the resource constraint in Eq. (9.4) is also convex, as shown by AB. If the boundary were less convex than the indifference curves—if the interaction between n and q were not "too" strong—the optimal combination of n and q would be at an internal po-

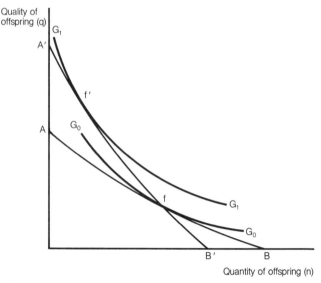

FIGURE 9.1   Interaction between quantity and quality of offspring.

sition, like point f in the figure. However, if the resource boundary were more convex than the indifference curves, the optimal combination would be at a "corner," with large n (or q) and negligible q (or n).

The interaction between n and q has the important implication that moderate changes in p_n, p_q, or p can have large effects on the optimal combination of n and q even if they are not close substitutes in the production of fitness. For example, an increase in p_n raises π_n relative to π_q, which induces a substitution toward q and away from n (the demand for n and q are negatively related to their relative prices). The substitution toward q and away from n further raises π_n relative to π_q because of the interaction between n and q, which induces an additional substitution toward q and away from n. The process is repeated until a new equilibrium is reached. In the figure a "compensated" increase in p_n changes the boundary from AB to A'B', and the optimal combination of n and q is changed substantially from point f to point f'.

The interaction between n and q can explain the fact that there are radical differences in reproductive "strategies" without assuming radical differences in underlying cost functions. For example, even if females typically have only moderately larger fixed costs of producing offspring than males, they desire far fewer offspring and would devote much more effort to raising them successfully than males would. As we shall see, the reproductive strategies of males and females do differ substantially in most of the biological world.[2]

Members of the same sex also follow different strategies. For example, males that can readily attract females seek many offspring and invest little in rearing them, whereas unattractive males try to rear their few offspring or other kin successfully.

Some species invest much in child care and "teaching" during long periods of child dependence, while others invest little. My analysis suggests that such differences among species are derived mainly from differences in the underlying costs of reproduction, especially in the fixed costs of quantity (p_n) and the variable costs of quality (p). Species with only moderately higher fixed costs or moderately lower variable costs[3] have far fewer offspring and invest much more in child care than do other species, again because of the interaction between quantity and quality.

Moderate and symmetrical differences among species in the underlying costs of producing and caring for children are transformed by the interaction between quantity and quality into large and positively skewed species differences in observed quantities and qualities of children. Moreover, species with relatively large quantities would tend to have relatively low-quality children. Biologists sometimes classify species into the two categories of r-strategists and K-strategists: the former have many offspring and invest little in each one, whereas K-strategists have few offspring and invest much in child care and learning (Wilson, 1975, pp. 99–100). I suggest that these two categories can usefully distinguish many species because the interaction between quantity and quality magnifies perhaps only moderate differences among species in underlying costs of reproduction and child care into major differences in quantity and quality that are negatively correlated across species.

Investments in the experience and skills of offspring are more productive, the more they will specialize in particular tasks (see Chapter 2)

---

2. Previous discussions have neglected the *interaction* between quality and quantity and have argued that the large differences in the reproductive strategies of males and females result from large differences in their costs of reproduction. See the pioneering discussion in Trivers (1972), essentially repeated by Wilson (1975, pp. 324–326) and Barash (1977, pp. 156–158).

3. A decrease in the variable cost p raises π_n relative to π_q if the total fixed cost of quantity ($p_n n$) exceeds the total fixed cost of quality ($p_q q$), which is likely to be the case for most species.

and the longer their life spans (see Chapter 1). K-strategists invest more in their offspring than r-strategists, partly because K-strategists live longer and in denser populations with greater specialization (see the summary table in Wilson, 1975, p. 101).[4] Their offspring are dependent for a longer period because greater investments in the young prolong the period of dependency.

Mating Systems

Previous chapters assumed that men and women choose mates and arrange their marriages in well-organized "markets." Some species, including fireflies, locusts, grouse, antelopes, and mountain sheep, literally form arenas (called leks) where males and females jockey for position, inspect the other sex, and choose mates for copulation and sometimes child rearing (Wilson, 1975; Wiley, 1973). Although most species do not form leks, the concept of a mating market appears to be applicable to nonhuman species, in that most species have developed sophisticated methods of finding and choosing mates.

Assume, therefore, that males and females of all species seek their mates in efficient mating markets. A market is efficient if all participants with the same characteristics expect to obtain the same fitness income, if higher-quality participants expect at least as much fitness as lower-quality participants, and if participants maximize their expected fitness, given the opportunities available.[5]

---

4. Investments in insect castes are also greater when insect colonies are larger and when insect life spans are longer. According to Wilson (1971, pp. 182 and 440), "the simplifying generalization [is] that, as mature colony size increases, the degree of caste differentiation increases" and "the most elaborate forms of social behavior occur in species with large, perennial colonies." More is invested in mother queens than in other castes, and the queens do live much longer (ibid., p. 428; see also the analysis in Oster and Wilson, 1978, p. 163).

5. The assumptions carefully presented in Altmann et al. (1977) are similar to those involved in the assumption of an efficient market, with the crucial exception that they assume that matings occur in sequence and that participants choosing mates at any moment neglect the effects of later arrivals. Therefore, expected fitness depends not only on personal characteristics but also on time of arrival. This is an unattractive assumption partly because the number of implications is severely limited unless the distribution of arrivals is specified, and mainly because selection favors those who can better anticipate the effects of subsequent arrivals. If these anticipations were correct on the average ("unbiased"), the Altmann model would be close to the model in this chapter.

Males differ because of the unequal incidence of inheritance, mutations, and other factors that affect strength, appearance, and various useful characteristics. More attractive males would be able to mate with several females, while less attractive males would be forced to remain bachelors. Females would prefer to mate with polygynous males, even when monogamous males are more attentive, if polygynous males offer them sufficiently greater protection and food or provide their offspring with sufficiently better genes. That is, females might prefer the partial attention of successful males to the full attention of "failures."

A polygynous male produces offspring with each mate and would allocate equal resources to each identical mate. If the production and care of the offspring of different mates were independent, and if all females were identical, Eqs. (9.1) to (9.5) imply that the fitness of the offspring produced by each mating of the ith male would be

$$G_{1k_i} = \alpha_i G(n_{1k_i}, q_{1k_i}) = \alpha_i G\left(\frac{e_m}{k_i}, e_f\right), \qquad (9.6)$$

where e_m and e_f are the total resources of a male and female respectively, k_i is the number of his mates, e_m/k_i and e_f are spent on the quantity and quality of the offspring of each mate, and α_i measures the efficiency of the ith male.

Since each female has a 50-percent genetic interest in the offspring she produces and no interest in the offspring produced by others (who are assumed to be unrelated), females prefer males "offering" the largest number of offspring—the largest G_{1k} in Eq. (9.6). If females know the offspring output available with all mates and are free to "choose,"[6] their competition for males offering the largest output would equalize the output with different males.

Therefore, the basic condition in well-informed efficient mating markets with identical females is that

$$\frac{1}{2} G_{1k_i} = \frac{1}{2} \alpha_i G\left(\frac{e_m}{k_i}, e_f\right) = C_f, \quad \text{for all } i, \qquad (9.7)$$

where C_f is the equilibrium fitness income of each female.[7] To simplify the analysis I assume that k varies continuously because it measures

---

6. This assumption rules out forcible matings or "rape"; on the use of force in matings, see Barash (1977, pp. 67–68).

7. Bride prices, dowries, and other capital transfers equalize the marginal products of identical participants in efficient marriage markets even when the distribution of married output between spouses is rigidly determined (see

the number of days or hours spent mating rather than just the number of mates.

An increase in k reduces the output per mate, regardless of any economies of scale in the production of fitness, because fewer male resources are available for each female (that is, e_m/k declines as k increases). The number of mates of more efficient males increases until this negative effect on the output with each mate just balances the positive effect of their greater efficiency. More efficient males with several mates have larger incomes because all females receive the same income. Indeed, the equilibrium income of the ith male is simply proportional to the number of his mates:

$$C_m = k_i^{\frac{1}{2}} G_{1k_i} = k_i C_f. \tag{9.8}$$

Less efficient males are forced to remain single when the number of females does not significantly exceed the number of males because efficient males attract several mates. Less efficient males remain single essentially because the price "asked" by females (C_f) exceeds the price these males are able to pay.[8]

Obviously, the distribution of mates is decisively influenced by the distribution of male efficiency; however, it also depends less obviously on the contributions of males and females to the production of fitness, and on the returns to scale in the fitness production function. This can be shown by differentiating Eq. (9.7) with respect to α and k, holding C_f, e_f, and e_m constant:

$$G + \alpha \frac{\partial G}{\partial(e_m/k)} \left(\frac{-e_m}{k^2}\right) \frac{dk}{d\alpha} = 0,$$

or $\quad\quad \epsilon(k,\alpha) = \dfrac{dk}{d\alpha}\dfrac{\alpha}{k} = \dfrac{1}{\epsilon(G,e_m)} = \dfrac{1}{\dfrac{\partial G}{\partial e_m}\dfrac{e_m}{G}}.$ $\tag{9.9}$

Chapter 4). Since nonhumans care only about the production of offspring, and since offspring rigidly inherit 50 percent of the genes of each parent, efficient mating markets cannot equalize marginal products, but instead equalize the fitness produced, as in Eq. (9.7). However, it may be readily shown that the equilibrium conditions in mating markets are equivalent to those in marriage markets when G is a Cobb-Douglas function.

8. Let the maximum output per mate, $\hat{G} = G(e_m/k, e_f)$ be attained when $k \leq k_0$. If k_0 is the equilibrium number of mates of males with efficiency α_0, all males with efficiency $\alpha_r < \alpha_0$ will remain single because they can only offer potential mates $\hat{C}_f = \frac{1}{2}\alpha_r\hat{G}$, which is less than the market price $C_f = \frac{1}{2}\alpha_0\hat{G}$.

Since the elasticity $\epsilon(G,e_m)$ measures the marginal contribution of males to the production of fitness, a change in efficiency has a larger effect on the equilibrium number of mates when the marginal contribution of males is smaller. If G is homogeneous of the tth degree in e_m and e_f, $t > 0$, the relation between $\epsilon(k,\alpha)$ and the contributions of males and females is simply

$$\epsilon(k,\alpha) = \frac{1}{\epsilon(G,e_m)} = \frac{1+r}{t} = b, \qquad (9.10)$$

where r is the ratio of the total contribution of females to the production and care of offspring to the total contribution of males, and G has decreasing, constant, or increasing returns to scale as $t \lessgtr 1$ (see Mathematical Appendix, note A).

This differential equation can be solved explicitly for k when b is a constant (that is, when G is a Cobb-Douglas function), for then

$$k = \bar{\alpha}^{-\frac{1+r}{t}} \alpha^{\frac{1+r}{t}} = \left(\frac{\alpha}{\bar{\alpha}}\right)^b, \qquad (9.11)$$

where $k = 1$ when $\alpha = \bar{\alpha}$.

The inequality in the distribution of mates can be measured by the standard deviation of the logarithm of k:

$$\sigma_{\log k} = \sigma_{\log c_m} = \frac{1+r}{t}\,\sigma_{\log \alpha}. \qquad (9.12)$$

The inequality in mates and in male income is proportional to the inequality in male efficiency; the factor of proportionality is positively related to the relative contribution of females to the production of fitness and is negatively related to returns to scale. If returns to scale were constant or decreasing ($t \leq 1$), the inequality in mates and male income would exceed the inequality in efficiency, and the difference would be large if females were important contributors to fitness. For example, if $t = 1$ and $r = 3$, mates and income would increase 16 times when efficiency doubled! Moreover, the distribution of mates and male income would be more skewed to the right than the distribution of efficiency: even a symmetrical distribution of efficiency implies a highly skewed distribution of mates and income if females contribute more to fitness.

The biological literature recognizes that the distribution of male efficiency and the relative contribution of females to the production and

care of offspring are important determinants of the incidence of polygyny (see for example Orians, 1969; Trivers, 1972; and Altmann et
al., 1977). However, these variables have not been combined to determine their interaction, nor have returns to scale been considered.
Consequently, this literature does not contain predictions about the
quantitative effect on the incidence of polygyny of a given change in
male efficiency or in the relative contribution of females.

Since females usually contribute much more than males to the
production and care of offspring, we can explain why species are polygynous without assuming large differences in male efficiency. Indeed, Eq. (9.12) implies that females would be very unequally distributed among males if males spent no time on child care. Male sage
grouse do not contribute to child care after mating in a lek, and 5 to 10
percent of the males in one study were responsible for over 75 percent
of the copulations (Wiley, 1973, pp. 107–109). Similarly, a few male
elephant seals were responsible for about 80 percent of the copulations
on an island in California (Le Boeuf, 1974, table 1).

Monogamy would be common when males contribute significantly to
child care if differences between males were not large and returns to
scale were not strongly decreasing. Practically all known species of
birds are monogamous (Lack, 1968, p. 150), and male birds usually
contribute greatly to child care during a long period of dependency as
eggs are hatched and offspring fed and protected. When bird species
are polygynous, as a rule only a small fraction have more than one
mate; for example, in a study of male indigo buntings, only 10 percent
did (Carey and Nolan, 1975). In general, monogamy or modest polygyny should be more common in K-strategist species, which emphasize quality of offspring, than in r-strategists, which emphasize quantity (Wilson, 1975, p. 243), inasmuch as the males tend to contribute
more to quality.

Some males are considered superior by females because they have
superior genes that are inherited by offspring, are more skilled at de-
fending and provisioning offspring, or have more energy and other
resources. If both production functions and effective stocks of resources differ among males, the income of identical females would be

$$\frac{1}{2} G_{1k_i} = \frac{1}{2} n(\alpha_i) G\left[\frac{m(\alpha_i)e_m}{k_i}, e_f\right] = C_f, \quad \text{for all } i,$$

$$\text{with } \frac{dm}{d\alpha} > 0 \text{ and } \frac{dn}{d\alpha} > 0,$$

(9.13)

where m measures differences in male effective resources and n measures differences in male efficiency. By differentiating with respect to α, we readily derive:

$$\epsilon(k,\alpha) = \epsilon(m,\alpha) + \frac{1}{\epsilon(G,e_m)}\,\epsilon(n,\alpha) > 1$$

$$\text{if } \epsilon(m,\alpha) + \epsilon(n,\alpha) \geq 1 \text{ and } t \leq 1,$$

(9.14)

where $\epsilon(m,\alpha) = (dm/d\alpha)(\alpha/m)$ and $\epsilon(n,\alpha) = (dn/d\alpha)(\alpha/n)$. The equilibrium number of mates is proportional to the level of resources because males of equal efficiency spend the same resources on each mate. Resources have been a major determinant of mates in polygynous human societies (see Chapter 3) and probably is important also in nonhuman societies.

The average fitness income of males relative to the fitness income of females is

$$\frac{\bar{C}_m}{\bar{C}_f} = \bar{k} = \frac{1}{s},$$

(9.15)

where s is the ratio of males to females in the mating market, and all unmated individuals are assumed to have zero income. The relative income of males is inversely related to the sex ratio of participants. If male and female offspring are equally costly to produce and rear, male offspring would be more valuable when adult males are scarcer than adult females, and less valuable when adult females are scarcer. Consequently, the sex ratio is kept near unity; selection favors parents with relatively many males when this ratio is below unity, and favors parents with relatively many females when it exceeds unity.[9]

Younger males are unable to compete for scarce females against stronger, "wealthier," and more experienced older males. We can readily understand, therefore, why males are older at their first mating in polygynous societies (see Wiley, 1973, pp. 137–139; Wilson, 1975, p. 329; and Barash, 1977, p. 141). The effect of polygyny on the age of females at their first mating is less clear-cut, because female income as given in Eq. (9.13) may not be closely related to the incidence of polygyny if the latter is mainly determined by male and female contributions to fitness. However, the difference in ages between male and female first mates should be greater when the incidence of polygyny is

---

9. This argument was first propounded by Fisher (1958, pp. 158–160). The formula given for humans in Chapter 3 is more complicated because humans do not simply maximize fitness.

greater (see the supporting evidence in Wiley, 1974, pp. 209–210; Wilson, 1975, p. 329).

Parents try to develop the strength and skills of male offspring, and males are willing to bear substantial costs and risks to acquire a competitive advantage in attracting females. Therefore, efficiency is determined by produced skills (h) as well as by luck or inheritance (u):

$$\alpha = u + h. \tag{9.16}$$

The production function for h is

$$h = \psi(e_m^*, u), \quad \text{with } \partial\psi/\partial e_m^* > 0 \quad \text{and } \partial\psi/\partial u > 0, \tag{9.17}$$

and, presumably, $\partial^2\psi/\partial e_m^{*2} < 0$ and $\partial^2\psi/\partial u \partial e_m^* > 0$, where e_m^* represents the resources spent on h.

Total resources

$$e_m + e_m^* = e_m^0 \tag{9.18}$$

are allocated between the indirect production of fitness (through the production of efficiency) and the direct production of fitness. The equilibrium condition[10] for an allocation that maximizes fitness income (C_m) is, if $m(\alpha) \equiv 1$:

$$\frac{\partial\psi}{\partial e_m^*} = \frac{\alpha}{e_m^0 - e_m^*} \frac{t}{1 + r}. \tag{9.19}$$

An increase in the relative contribution of females to the production of fitness (r) induces greater expenditure on efficiency until $\partial\psi/\partial e_m^*$ is lowered sufficiently. Since an increase in the contribution of females also encourages polygyny, the average male would invest more and would be more efficient when polygyny was more common.

This implication of the maximization of male fitness has been known since Darwin's discussion of competition for mates and the selection of secondary male characteristics.[11] Less well known is that an increase in the contribution of females raises the inequality in male efficiency by raising the inequality between abler and less able males.[12] Since po-

---

10. See the proof of a related formula in note D of the Mathematical Appendix to Chapter 3.

11. See Darwin (1872). Lack, studying birds, wrote, "It is also not surprising that the most elaborate male plumage and displays occur in promiscuous and polygynous species, because in these a successful male will acquire several mates, and hence there will be unusually strong selection for those characters which enable it to attract females" (1968, p. 159).

12. See the proof in footnote 26 of Chapter 3.

lygyny increases when the inequality in male efficiency increases, an increased contribution of females both directly and indirectly furthers polygyny; that is, an increase in r raises $\sigma_{\log k}$ in Eq. (9.12) by raising the coefficient of $\sigma_{\log \alpha}$, and also by raising $\sigma_{\log \alpha}$ itself.

The same analysis is applicable when females differ and males are identical. Then males might prefer to mate with a superior polyandrous female than with a "second-rate" monogamous female. An efficient mating market would distribute identical males among females to equalize the production of fitness with different females:

$$C_m = \frac{1}{2} \beta_i G \left(e_m, \frac{e_f}{\ell_i} \right), \tag{9.7'}$$

where C_m is the equilibrium income of males, and ℓ_i is the equilibrium number of mates "assigned" to females with efficiency β_i. The argument leading to Eq. (9.11) implies that if G is Cobb-Douglas,

$$\ell_i = \left(\frac{\beta_i}{\bar{\beta}} \right)^{1+(1/r)} t, \tag{9.11'}$$

where $\ell_i = 1$ when $\beta_i = \bar{\beta}$, and

$$\sigma_{\log \ell} = \frac{1 + (1/r)}{t} \sigma_{\log \beta}. \tag{9.12'}$$

Since females usually are the main contributors to the production and care of children, $1/r$ usually is small and much less than r. Therefore, a comparison of Eqs. (9.12) and (9.12') indicates that $\sigma_{\log \ell}$ would usually be much less than $\sigma_{\log k}$ even if the inequality among males and females ($\sigma_{\log \alpha}$ and $\sigma_{\log \beta}$ respectively) were the same. Moreover, our analysis implies that the inequality among males tends to exceed that among females because the former is larger when r is larger; a similar argument to that developed for Eq. (9.19) implies that the latter would be larger when $1/r$ is larger. Consequently, the incidence of polygyny, as measured by $\sigma_{\log k}$, should be much greater than the incidence of polyandry,[13] as measured by $\sigma_{\log \ell}$, both because r usually greatly exceeds $1/r$ and because $\sigma_{\log \alpha}$ exceeds $\sigma_{\log \beta}$.

Polygyny is, indeed, far more common than polyandry throughout

---

13. Clearly, my assumption that production with one mate is independent of production with other mates is not valid in a polyandrous family owing to uncertainty about who is the male parent. This uncertainty limits the incidence of polyandry by creating diminishing returns to "scale" (see Barash, 1977, p. 165, or Alexander et al., 1979, p. 413).

the biological world.[14] Moreover, the inequality among males does appear to exceed that among females; in particular, death rates among young males generally exceed those among young females. For example, Le Boeuf shows high death rates among young male elephant seals (1974, p. 169). The further implication of our analysis that more is invested in males than in females (because r is larger than $1/r$) is also supported empirically: males usually mature later, are taller (or have larger body size), and are stronger (see Wiley, 1974, pp. 209–211; Alexander et al., 1979).

Since $1/r$ is inversely related to r, polygyny and polyandry should not overlap much. Polyandry should be rare when polygyny is common (large r), and polygyny rare when polyandry is common (large $1/r$). The many polygynous species virtually never practice polyandry at the same time, nor do the few polyandrous species practice polygyny (see for instance Jenni, 1974). The inverse relation between r and $1/r$ also implies that investments in males relative to females would be greater when the incidence of polygyny is greater. Alexander and his associates (1979) show that the average male is larger relative to the average female when polygyny is more common (as measured by average harem size).

The ith male and the ith female would produce together (if they have no other mates) fitness equal to

$$n(\alpha_i, \beta_j) \; G[m(\alpha_i)e_m, f(\beta_j)e_f], \tag{9.20}$$

where $\partial n/\partial \alpha > 0$ and $\partial n/\partial \beta > 0$. It is plausible (see the discussion for humans in Chapter 4) that an increase in the efficiency of males usually raises the effect on fitness of mating with more efficient females, and vice versa; that is,

$$\partial^2 n/\partial \alpha \partial \beta > 0. \tag{9.21}$$

Chapter 4 shows that condition (9.21) implies positive assortative mating, that abler males and females would be assigned to each other by efficient mating markets. Positive sorting is common for most human traits and has been observed for other species as well (Fisher, 1958, chap. 6; Trivers, 1972, p. 170).

Males and females may prefer implicit polygamy with one superior

---

14. See Jenni (1974) or Barash (1977, p. 90). After showing that polyandry is rare among birds, Jenni says, "Whatever the adaptive value of simultaneous polyandry, *its evolution depends upon* the prior or concomitant evolution of *exclusive male incubation and parental behavior*" (pp. 140–141; italics added).

mate to explicit polygamy with several less superior mates. A female is likely to prefer implicit polyandry, even if her superior mate is explicitly polygynous, because females are the major contributors to the production of fitness. Her preference for implicit polyandry would be greater, the greater her contribution to fitness, the less polygynous her superior mate is, and the greater his superiority relative to her mates if she were explicitly polyandrous (see Mathematical Appendix, note B).

Therefore, *explicit* polyandry is rare also because *implicit* polyandry is preferred by superior females. If the several mates of superior males tend to be superior, females mated with polygynous males would have greater fitness, because both mates would tend to be superior. The evidence for red-winged blackbirds and yellow-headed blackbirds is consistent with this implication (Orians, 1972), but other evidence is not; for example, monogamous female marmots appear to have greater fitness than those mated with polygynous males (Downhower and Armitage, 1971). This suggests that the polygynous males of some species mate with inferior females.

Concluding Remarks

All individuals in different species maximize their utility while competing for mates and other resources. Nonhumans and even most humans do not consciously maximize, and may not maximize at all in the short run—but nonhumans can survive in the long run only if they maximize the production of replicas of their genes. Economic analysis provides powerful insights into the long-run behavior of nonhuman species because individual members maximize with stable preferences (the desire for offspring) in markets that reconcile the preferences of competing individuals, the principal defining characteristics of the economic approach (see Becker, 1976b, p. 5, and the Introduction to this book).

Lest I be misunderstood on a highly controversial subject, let me immediately indicate that the *analytical* continuity in the behavior of humans and other species does not imply that I believe human behavior is primarily biologically determined. Clearly, humans in modern societies do not simply maximize the production of children; they could readily have additional children who would live long and become well-educated and prosperous. The continuity between the behavior of humans and other species does not require a judgment about the relative importance of biological and cultural forces in explaining human behavior, although presumably cultural forces are of major importance and biological forces are not negligible. Human behavior can be determined by various combinations of cultural and biological forces, and utility still can be maximized with stable preferences in markets that reconcile the desires of different persons.

The continuity in behavior between humans and other species has led some biologists to conclude that human behavior must have a substantial biological component. Resisting the implications of this component, persons believing in the predominance of culture have often denied any behavioral continuity. The economic approach, however, implies that behavior is continuous because members of all species must allocate scarce resources among competing uses in market and nonmarket situations. Therefore, behavioral continuity has only modest implications for the importance of biological forces in the determination of human behavior.

To be sure, the theorems about human behavior would be sharper and more powerful if preferences were readily specified and were the same for all persons (Stigler and Becker, 1977). Since natural selection determines simple and identical preferences for other species, the economic approach may well be *more* powerful in understanding the long-run behavior of other species even though it was developed for human behavior. Indeed, modern biology is relying increasingly on explicit maximizing models similar to those used by economists.[15] Still, the economic approach does appear to provide a unified treatment of human and nonhuman behavior while recognizing that cultural forces are major determinants of human behavior and biological forces are decisive determinants of nonhuman behavior.

Mathematical Appendix

A. If G is homogeneous of the tth degree in e_m and e_f,

$$tG = \frac{\partial G}{\partial e_m} e_m + \frac{\partial G}{\partial e_f} e_f,$$

or

$$t = \epsilon(G, e_m) + \epsilon(G, e_f).$$

---

15. See for example the model of foraging by Charnov (1976), the treatment of insects by Oster and Wilson (1978), and the modeling of the experimental evidence on the behavior of pigeons, rats, and other animals in Rachlin et al. (1980).

If the relative contribution of males to fitness is defined by

$$r \equiv \frac{(\partial G/\partial e_f)e_f}{(\partial G/\partial e_m)e_m} = \frac{\epsilon(G,e_f)}{\epsilon(G,e_m)},$$

then

$$t = (1 + r)\,\epsilon(G,e_m).$$

B. The income of a female mated with a polygynous male is

$$C_{f_{k,j}} = \frac{1}{2}\,n(\alpha_i,\beta_j)G\left[\frac{m(\alpha_i)e_m}{k_i}, f(\beta_j)e_f\right],$$

where k_i is the number of his identical mates. If she were polyandrous with ℓ_j mates of efficiency $\alpha_j < \alpha_i$, her income would be

$$C_{f_{j,\ell}} = \frac{1}{2}\,n(\alpha_j,\beta_j)G\left[m(\alpha_j)e_m, \frac{f(\beta_j)e_f}{\ell_j}\right]\ell_j.$$

She is better off with the polygynous male if

$$C_{f_{k,j}} > C_{f_{j,\ell}},$$

or

$$\frac{n(\alpha_i,\beta_j)}{n(\alpha_j,\beta_j)} > \frac{G\left[m(\alpha_j)e_m, \dfrac{f(\beta_j)e_f}{\ell_j}\right]\ell_j}{G\left[\dfrac{m(\alpha_i)e_m}{k_i}, f(\beta_j)e_f\right]}.$$

If $n(\alpha,\beta) = \alpha\beta$, $G = e_m^{\frac{1}{1+r}} e_f^{1-\frac{1}{1+r}}$ and $m(\alpha) = f(\beta) \equiv 1$, this inequality becomes

$$\frac{\alpha_i}{\alpha_j} > (\ell_j k_i)^{\frac{1}{1+r}}.$$

She is more likely to prefer the polygynous male, the larger r and α_i/α_j and the smaller ℓ_j and k_i. For example, if $r = 3$, she would prefer to be the fifth mate of a polygynous male ($k_i = 5$) than the sole mate of three males ($\ell_j = 3$) who are half as efficient as he is ($\alpha_i/\alpha_j = 2$); whereas if $r = 1$, she would prefer the three inferior mates to being his second mate.

CHAPTER 10

Imperfect Information, Marriage, and Divorce

Previous chapters, in their consideration of marriage, division of labor, investments in children, and other family decisions, have neglected imperfect information and uncertainty. Imperfect information can often be disregarded without much loss in understanding, but it is the essence of divorce, search in the marriage market, contributions by children to elderly parents, a good reputation, and other behavior. For example, participants in marriage markets hardly know their own interests and capabilities, let alone the dependability, sexual compatibility, and other traits of potential spouses. Although they date and search in other ways to improve their information, they frequently marry with highly erroneous assessments, then revise these assessments as information improves after marriage.

The final two chapters of this book explore various consequences of imperfect information and uncertainty. This chapter concentrates on methods to improve information prior to marriage, and on the divorces that sometimes result when information becomes available after marriage. Information acquired during the first few years of marriage is frequently responsible for the quick termination of marriages in the United States and elsewhere.

Imperfect Information in Marriage Markets

Participants in marriage markets are assumed to have limited information about the utility they can expect with potential mates, mainly because of limited information about the traits of these mates. If they could search as "cheaply" for other mates when married as when single, and if marriages could be terminated without significant cost, they would marry the first reasonable mate encountered, knowing they would gain from even a less-than-optimal marriage. They would then continue to search while married. Since, however, marriage does limit access to single persons, and termination can be costly (chiefly because of children and other "investments" specific to a particular marriage), participants usually do not immediately marry the first reasonable prospect encountered, but try to learn about them and search for better prospects.

Increased search and better information raise the utility expected from marriage by improving the quality of marital choices. However, time, effort, and other costly resources must be spent on search, and the longer the search, the longer gains from marriage are delayed. A rational person would continue to search on both the "extensive margin" of additional prospects and the "intensive margin" of additional information about serious prospects until the marginal cost and marginal benefit on each margin are equal. In particular, rational persons marry even when certain of eventually finding better prospects with additional search, for the cost of additional search exceeds the expected benefits from better prospects.

Search in marriage markets takes diverse forms, including expenditures on grooming and personal appearance, parties, dating, church socials, coeducational schools, bars and apartment buildings for singles, residential segregation by income and other characteristics, and an exchange of curricula vitae that describe achievements and family back-

A Treatise on the Family

ground.[1] Occasionally, marriage brokers have been used, as among the Jews of Eastern Europe,[2] but informal methods of search have been far more common than commercial methods. Part of the explanation may be that participants are reluctant to seek commercial help when love and emotion are supposed to reign; but—more to the point—friends, relatives, schools, socials, and other informal channels of search are efficient whenever quality varies greatly and appropriate sorting is crucial. Informal channels are also important in labor markets, especially for skilled workers (Rees, 1966), and love seldom enters labor transactions (see Chapter 8).

Since the best way to learn about someone else is by being together, intensive search is more effective when unwed couples spend considerable time together, perhaps including trial marriages.[3] Yet when contraceptives are crude and unreliable, trial marriages and other premarital contact greatly raise the risk of pregnancy. The significant increase during this century in the frequency of trial marriages and other premarital contact[4] has been in part a rational response to major improvements in contraceptive techniques, and is not decisive evidence that young people now value sexual experiences more than they did in the past.

The information acquired from intensive search is used to estimate the traits of prospects. Difficult-to-assess traits are forecast partly by using the information on traits that are readily assessed—such as religion, education, family background, race, or appearance—because these and the less well-known traits often vary together in a systematic way. For example, the probability that a prospect is honest or amiable is related to the reputation of his family; his intelligence is related to his education.

Some readily assessed traits, proxies for unknown traits, thus have an influence that far exceeds their direct contribution to married output. Variables like appearance and family background have been valu-

---

1. Curricula vitae are still exchanged through friends and other intermediaries in Japan, even among Western-educated Japanese.

2. For an amusing fictional account of these brokers, see Aleichem (1969, bk. 5).

3. Similarly, trial employment is a more effective way for workers and firms to learn about one another than for workers to spend time in school or at other "screening" activities.

4. Various countries long ago developed bundling (or night-courting) and other forms of premarital contact that controlled the risk of pregnancy (see for example Shorter, 1975, pp. 44–50).

able guides to upbringing, genetic constitution, personality, and other traits of prospects that are difficult to assess directly.

Conversely, some difficult-to-assess traits traditionally have received little direct weight, even though they are significant contributors to marriage. In particular, the apparent disdain for love in traditional matchmaking does not imply that love is considered unimportant. Since lasting love is not easily distinguished from momentary infatuation, little confidence would be attached to any direct assessment of love prior to marriage. Indirect assessments of love would be used instead; for example, education and background would be important in part because love is more easily developed and sustained between persons with similar education and backgrounds.

Explicit attention to sexual compatability and other personal traits has increased substantially during the twentieth century; the growth of dating, coeducational schools, trial marriages, and other contacts between prospects has increased the reliability of direct assessments. Therefore, the greater attention paid to these personal traits instead of to proxies like background does not necessarily imply that personal traits have become more important to marital well-being than they were in the past (but also see Chapter 11).

The theory developed in Chapter 4 implies that most traits would be strongly positively sorted in the marriages generated by efficient markets with full information. Education, IQ, race, religion, income, family background, height, and many other traits are, in fact, strongly positively sorted. Usually only readily assessed traits are known to researchers, however; traits that are more difficult to assess by participants, such as love or capacity for growth, are also less readily assessed by researchers. Therefore, since traits more difficult to assess should be more weakly sorted than known traits, the degree of positive sorting found by researchers would exceed the degree of positive sorting for all traits.

Imperfect Information and Divorce

If participants in marriage markets have complete information about all prospects, divorce would be a fully anticipated response to a demand for variety in mates or to life-cycle changes in traits. Most divorces would then occur after many years of marriage, because traits change gradually. The facts, however, suggest the opposite: about 40 percent of all divorces (and annulments) occur prior to the fifth year of marriage, and separation usually precedes divorce by a year or more (U.S. Department of Health, Education, and Welfare, 1979).

If, however, participants had highly imperfect information, most divorces would occur early in marriage by virtue of the fact that information about traits increases rapidly after marriage. Several years of marriage is usually a far more effective source of information on love and many other traits than all the proxies available prior to marriage. I suggest that marriages fail early primarily because of imperfect information in marriage markets and the accumulation of better information during marriage. This suggestion is supported by the fact that unexpected changes in earnings and health do raise the probability of divorce (BLM,[5] 1977).

Women who divorced early in their marriage report that "difficult" spouses and value conflicts were major sources of their discontent, presumably because these traits are much better assessed after a few years of marriage. Personality conflict, sexual incompatibility, and similar traits should be less important sources of later than of earlier divorces; little additional information about these traits is acquired after a few years of marriage. On the other hand, some information, including information about other women and about earnings potential, is acquired more slowly and should be more important in later divorces. Indeed, another woman and/or financial conflict are frequently cited by women divorcing after ten years of marriage (Goode, 1956, pp. 128–129).

The major sources of discontent and divorce are not necessarily the major determinants of marital well-being. Education, age, physical appearance, and other easily assessed traits are not major sources of discontent because not much more is learned about them after marriage. Just as the emphasis on easily assessed traits in marriage markets does not imply that these traits contribute more to marital well-being than other traits, neither does the opposite emphasis on difficult-to-assess traits in "divorce markets" imply that those contribute more.[6]

---

5. The analysis and evidence in this section is partly taken from Becker et al. (1977), hereafter referred to as BLM.

6. Similarly, unsatisfactory working conditions, which do not lend themselves to advance assessment, constitute an important reason why people quit during the first few years on a job (Borjas, 1979); see also the distinction between "search" and "experience" goods in the discussion of consumer choices in Nelson (1970).

Marriage and Divorce [329

The more rapid accumulation of information during the first few years of marriage implies that divorce is more likely early in marriage than later. Divorce rates are highest during the first few years of marriage and decline steeply after four or five years, although the explanation is partly that those most prone to divorce tend to drop out early from the cohort of married persons (see Heckman, 1981, on the effects of heterogeneity).

Divorce is less likely later in the marriage for the additional reason that capital accumulates and becomes more valuable if a marriage stays intact ("marital-specific" capital). Children are the prime example, especially young children, although learning about the idiosyncrasies of one's spouse is also important (Heimer and Stinchcombe, 1979). Divorce is much less likely when there are children, especially young children—not only in the United States and other rich countries (Goode, 1963, pp. 85, 364; BLM, 1977), but also in primitive societies (Saunders and Thomson, 1979).

The accumulation of marital-specific capital is, in turn, discouraged by the prospect of divorce because, by definition, such capital is less valuable after a divorce. Presumably, trial or consensual marriages produce fewer children than legal marriages at least partly because the former are less durable (see the evidence in Kogut, 1972, on consensual and legal marriages in Brazil). Persons who marry outside their race or religion are far more likely to divorce than are others with similar measurable characteristics. Therefore, we can readily understand why marriages between persons of different races or religions have significantly fewer children even when intact marriages are compared (see the evidence for the United States in BLM, 1977), and why marriages between Indians of different castes have fewer children than marriages within a caste (Das, 1978).

Expectations about divorce are partly self-fulfilling because a higher expected probability of divorce reduces investments in specific capital and thereby raises the actual probability.[7] For example, consensual

---

7. Let

$$p = f(s,\alpha) \qquad \text{with } \partial p/\partial s = f_s < 0, \ \partial p/\partial \alpha = f_\alpha > 0,$$

and $\quad s = h(p,\beta) \qquad \text{with } \partial s/\partial p = h_p < 0, \ \partial s/\partial \beta = h_\beta > 0,$

where p is the probability of divorce, s is the investment in specific capital, and α and β are exogenous variables that raise p and s respectively. For example, α might be a dummy variable equal to 1 in consensual marriages and to 0 in legal marriages. Then

A Treatise on the Family

and trial marriages are less stable than legal marriages, and marriages between persons of different religions or races are less stable than those within a religion or race, partly because mixed marriages have fewer children. At the same time, as indicated, mixed marriages have fewer children partly because they are expected to be less stable.

Specific investment and imperfect information can explain why homosexual unions are much less stable than heterosexual marriages (Saghir and Robins, 1973, pp. 56–58, 226–227). Homosexual unions do not result in children, and generally they have a less extensive division of labor and less marital-specific capital than heterosexual marriages. Moreover, the opprobrium attached to homosexuality has raised the cost of search to homosexuals and thereby has reduced the information available to them. Furthermore, homosexual unions, like trial marriages, can dissolve without legal adversary proceedings, alimony, or child support payments.

Women have usually married earlier than men partly because the maturation and independence of men has been delayed by greater investments in their human capital. Since investments in men and women have become more equal over time as the demand for children has decreased (see Chapter 3), men and women now marry for the first time at rather similar ages. For example, the difference in the United States between the median age at first marriage of men and women declined from four years in 1900 to about two and a half years in 1970 (U.S. Bureau of the Census, 1971c).

Yet divorced women have *remarried* more slowly than divorced men[8] even when divorced at young ages. They almost always receive custody of children, a factor that discourages remarriage. For the same reason, women with illegitimate children marry for the first time more slowly than women without children (Berkov and Sklar, 1976).

Young children raise the cost of searching for another mate and significantly reduce the net resources of divorced women (Weitzman and Dixon, 1979). Possibly for these reasons they raise the probability that

---

$$\frac{dp}{d\alpha} = f_\alpha + f_s \frac{ds}{d\alpha} = f_\alpha + f_s h_p f_\alpha = f_\alpha(1 + f_s h_p) > f_\alpha.$$

The total effect on the probability of divorce of a rise in α (perhaps a shift from legal to consensual marriages) exceeds the effect of α alone, in that investments in specific capital (s) are reduced.

8. In one study 31 percent of the men and only 22 percent of the women remarried within two years of their divorce (BLM, 1977).

a remarriage will fail, even though children born during the remarriage lower this probability (BLM, 1977). It is noteworthy that illegitimate children and other pregnancies prior to first marriage also raise the probability of marital failure (Christensen and Meissner, 1953; Berkov and Sklar, 1976).

Divorced women might well remarry earlier than divorced men, just as single women without children marry earlier than single men, if divorced women did not receive custody of children. Indeed, perhaps 45 percent of divorced women would have remarried within the first two years of their divorce if they did not have custody, which is double their actual percentage (22) and considerably higher than the percentage for men (31). This estimate assumes that women without custody marry as rapidly as women without children. It is based on a regression equation that relates whether a woman remarries within a specified period of time to several variables, including number of children (BLM, 1977).

The Gain from Divorce

A husband and wife would both consent to a divorce if, and only if, they both expected to be better off divorced. Although divorce might seem more difficult when mutual consent is required than when either alone can divorce at will, the frequency and incidence of divorce should be similar with these and other rules if couples contemplating divorce can easily bargain with each other. This assertion is a special case of the Coase theorem (1960) and is a natural extension of the argument in Chapter 4 that persons marry each other if, and only if, they both expect to be better off compared to their best alternatives.

A risk-neutral couple would divorce with mutual consent if, and only if,

$$Z^m < Z^m_d, \qquad Z^f < Z^f_d, \tag{10.1}$$

where Z^m and Z^m_d are the husband's expected commodity wealth[9] from staying married and divorcing respectively, and Z^f and Z^f_d are defined

---

9. The relationship between utility and commodity income is discussed in Chapter 4.

similarly for the wife. If bargaining is cheap and easy, this necessary and sufficient condition can be stated more simply as

$$Z_{mf} \equiv Z^m + Z^f < Z^m_d + Z^f_d \equiv Z^{mf}_d. \tag{10.2}$$

Obviously, if the inequality in (10.2) does not hold, the inequalities in (10.1) could not hold. That (10.2) also implies (10.1) can be shown by assuming that, say, the husband's wealth would be reduced by divorce ($Z^m_d < Z^m$) even though their combined wealth would be raised ($Z^{mf}_d > Z_{mf}$). The wife could still "bribe" him to consent to a divorce by offering him a settlement that would offset his direct loss from divorce ($Z^m - Z^m_d$). She would also be better off as long as the settlement was less than their combined gain ($Z^{mf}_d - Z_{mf}$).

Less obvious perhaps is that (10.2), but not (10.1), is still a necessary and sufficient condition for divorce when either can divorce at will, or when only the husband can divorce at will, as in traditional Islamic societies. If he would gain from divorce ($Z^m_d > Z^m$) but their combined wealth would be reduced, she could bribe him not to seek a divorce by offering him a greater share of their married output.[10] Conversely, if he would lose from divorce but their combined wealth would increase, she could bribe him to seek a divorce by offering him a large settlement.

The history of divorce is filled with examples of settlements that induce recalcitrant spouses to consent. Only husbands could seek a divorce among Jews in the Arab world during the Middle Ages, yet "in many, if not most cases about which we have more detailed information, one gets the impression that the female partner was the initiator of the divorce proceedings, mostly, to be sure by *renouncing what was due her*" [her dowry and other marriage gifts] (Goitein, 1978, p. 265; italics added). And over 90 percent of the divorces in Japan between 1948 and 1959 were by mutual consent (Rheinstein, 1972, table 5), even though either spouse alone could initiate a divorce suit.

Still, one might reasonably argue that legal rules make a difference: the anger and other emotion generated by divorce proceedings make

---

10. Both want to remain married if

$$Z^{*m} = Z^m + \Delta > Z^m_d \quad \text{and} \quad Z^{*f} = Z^f - \Delta > Z^f_d,$$

where Δ is the bribe to him. Any bribe above $Z^m_d - Z^m$ and below $Z^f - Z^f_d$ would satisfy both inequalities.

bargaining costly and time-consuming, or a spouse might consent to a divorce only because his (or her) life is made difficult until he does (Friedman, 1969; Goitein, 1978, pp. 265–266; Saunders and Thomson, 1979). To obtain quantitative evidence on the effects of legal rules, consider the radical change in 1970 when California became the first state to grant divorce at the request of either spouse (no-fault divorce);[11] previously, divorce required either mutual consent or proof of "fault" in an adversary proceeding.

The average annual rates of growth of divorce rates in California and the rest of the country during the 1960s were 3.6 percent and 4.0 percent respectively. We can crudely estimate what the California rates would have been if the state had not gone to no-fault divorce by assuming that the rate of growth in divorce rates between any two years during 1969 to 1976 would have equaled the rate of growth for the rest of the country[12] multiplied by the ratio of their average growth rates during the 1960s (0.9 = 0.036/0.040). These "predicted" rates in Figure 10.1 are substantially below the actual rates for California in 1970 and 1971, slightly below in 1972, about equal to the actual rates in 1973 and 1974, and slightly above the actual rates in 1975 and 1976. The change to no-fault divorce does not appear to have had a lasting effect on the di-

---

11. No-fault divorce goes back at least to the Roman period. Lecky writes in his *History of European Morals* (1880):

> Another and a still more important consequence resulted from the changed form of marriage. Being looked upon merely as a civil contract, entered into for the happiness of the contracting parties, its continuance depended upon mutual consent. Either party might dissolve it at will, and the dissolution gave both parties a right to remarry. *There can be no question that under this system the obligations of marriage were treated with extreme levity* (p. 306; italics added).

However, after giving a few examples of Romans who divorced and remarried, he writes:

> These are, no doubt, extreme cases; but it is unquestionable that the stability of married life was very seriously impaired. *It would be easy, however, to exaggerate the influence of legal changes in affecting it.* In a purer state of public opinion a very wide latitude of divorce might probably have been allowed to both parties, without any serious consequence. The right of repudiation, which the husband had always possessed, was . . . in the Republic never or very rarely exercised (p. 307; italics added).

12. Only ten other states went to no-fault divorce between 1970 and 1974 (Foster and Freed, 1974).

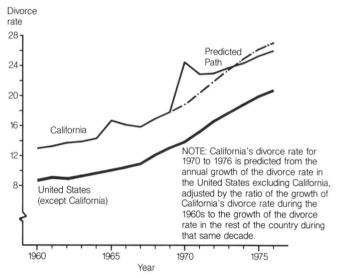

FIGURE 10.1   Rate of divorce per 1,000 married women for California and
for the United States except California, 1960 to 1976.

SOURCES: U.S. Bureau of the Census, 1963b, 1973e, 1977a and preceding issues,
1978; U.S. Department of Health, Education, and Welfare, 1979 and preceding issues;
information supplied by Alexander Plateris, Public Health Service, U.S. Department
of Health, Education, and Welfare.

vorce rates in California, although divorces may have been increased
for a couple of years.[13]

Even if the change from mutual consent and fault to no-fault divorce apparently had little lasting effect on divorce rates, the distribution of the gains from divorce, $Z_d^{mf} - Z_{mf}$ in (10.2), may have been
significantly altered. In particular, if men have been more willing than
women to divorce partly because they are not given custody of children and partly because they have many opportunities to meet other
women while still married, no-fault divorce reduces their incentive to

---

13. Since the 1970 law reduced both the minimum residency requirement
and the minimum waiting time between a petition for divorce and the final divorce decree, some divorces granted in 1970 and 1971 would have been granted
in 1972 and 1973 under the old law. Indeed, Schoen and his associates (1975)
claim that the jump in divorce rates in 1970 and 1971 can be almost entirely explained by these changes in timing and, to a much lesser extent, by the divorces
California residents would have obtained in Nevada. If, however, timing is the
main explanation, the predicted rates in 1972–1974 should have been much
above the actual rates; in fact this was not the case.

obtain their wives' consent with generous settlements. After 1970, alimony and child-support payments in California apparently did decline relative to father's income (Dixon and Weitzman, 1980, table 2).

The inequality in (10.2) is a simple and easily implemented criterion for analyzing the effects of different variables on the propensity to divorce. One has only to determine whether the joint wealth of a married couple would be increased by divorce, without worrying about how the increase is divided or about who has legal access to divorce. To illustrate, a negative income tax system or aid to mothers with dependent children raises separation and divorce rates among eligible families in that the incomes of divorced and separated persons are raised relative to the incomes of married persons. These programs, in effect, provide poor women with divorce settlements that encourage divorce.[14]

The expected wealth from remaining married would be raised if one spouse earns more than had been expected, or if any other trait of either spouse turns out to be better than expected. Nevertheless, and somewhat paradoxically, the marriage would be more likely to dissolve than if their expectations had been realized. The *combined* wealth of husband and wife from a divorce would be increased even more than their wealth from remaining together because they are no longer well-matched: the person with the better-than-expected traits should be matched with a "better" person than his spouse, and she should be matched with a "worse" person than he turns out to be. This implication of (10.2) is also supported empirically: marriages are more likely to dissolve when realized earnings, health, and fecundity exceed as well as fall short of expectations (BLM, 1977, section II.1).

If a husband were to find a good job elsewhere, but not his working wife—an increasingly likely issue since more wives have entered the labor force—their combined wealth might be maximized if he moved and she stayed. Their separation would, however, increase the likelihood of divorce because the advantages of remaining married are reduced by separation. Migration does seem to raise the propensity to divorce (see the analysis and evidence in Mincer, 1978).

Men with higher earnings or other income gain more from marriage than other men do because they can attract several wives or higher-

---

14. Divorce rates of participants in negative income tax experiments are analyzed in Hannan et al. (1977) and Keeley (1980); the effect of aid to mothers with dependent children on the number of female-headed households is considered in Honig (1974).

quality wives (see Chapters 3 and 4). This explains why they marry at younger ages and remarry faster when widowed or divorced (Keeley, 1974, 1977; BLM, 1977). Since an increase in the gain from marriage also increases the gain from staying married compared to the gain from a divorce, higher-income men should have lower propensities to divorce. This conclusion goes counter to popular opinion, but is supported by empirical evidence not only for the United States but for many other countries as well (Goode, 1963, p. 86).

Women with higher earnings gain less from marriage than other women do because higher earnings reduce the demand for children and the advantages of the sexual division of labor in marriage (Chapters 2, 4, and 5). Therefore, women with higher earnings should be more prone to divorce, a conclusion that is supported by several kinds of evidence (see BLM, 1977). Indeed, growth in the earnings of women during the last 30 years has been a major cause (also a result) of the growth in divorce rates during this period.

The instability of black families in recent decades has been the subject of considerable interest and comment—the controversial Moynihan report (U.S. Department of Labor, 1965), for instance. The greater instability of black families is not entirely explained by migration to the North or by the recent growth in welfare; black families have been much less stable than white families since the beginning of the century, and probably even earlier, in both the South and the North (Sanderson, 1980).

Black families should be less stable than white families, if only because blacks are much poorer and black women earn much more relative to black men than white women do relative to white men (Smith, 1977, 1979). Black-white differences in income, earnings, and unemployment can explain much of the difference in their marital instability during recent years (Ross and Sawhill, 1975, chap. 4). In view of the earning pattern of blacks over the past hundred years, we would expect black families to have been less stable than white families for a long time, whether or not they were similar in other respects.[15] Although slavery did not destroy the black family (Gutman, 1976), the lesser stability of black families in the United States is at least in part a legacy of slavery: black incomes were reduced relative to white incomes, and

15. Sanderson (1980) presents this argument, along with some evidence on the earnings of black men and women in the nineteenth century.

perhaps also the market productivity of black women was raised relative to black men (Goldin, 1977).

Why do some persons marry outside their religion, race, age, or educational class, when mixed marriages have much higher probabilities of divorce? These individuals do not appear to be ignorant of the risk. They have fewer children and in other ways act as if they anticipate a higher probability of divorce. Persons entering mixed marriages cannot simply be less religious or less "prejudiced" in favor of their own race or own educational level; for why then are their divorce rates so high? Nor do mixed marriages appear to provide advantages that compensate for the higher risk of divorce: earnings as well as fertility are lower. Consider the following equation giving earnings in 1967 (data from the Survey of Economic Opportunity):

$$E_m = 0.414 + 0.060S_m + 0.034e_m^2 - 0.0006e_m^2$$
$$(9.9) \qquad (14.5) \qquad (-15.1)$$
$$+ 0.067r + 0.028S_f + 0.0002S_mS_f, \qquad (10.3)$$
$$(0.9) \qquad (4.7) \qquad (0.5)$$

where E_m represents the log of earnings of married men in 1967, S_m their years of schooling, e_m their years of experience in the labor force, S_f the years of schooling of wives, r a dummy variable equal to one if the spouses are of the same race, and the t-statistics are shown in parentheses. The positive (but not statistically significant) coefficients of r and S_mS_f suggest that the earnings of men are not higher and may be lower in marriages that are mixed by race or education.[16]

The most plausible explanation is that persons enter mixed marriages even though they anticipate a higher probability of divorce because they do not expect to do better by further search and waiting. Perhaps they were unlucky in their search and became pregnant, or have aged and fear a diminishing market. Both women who become pregnant before marriage and persons not marrying until they are over thirty are more likely to marry outside their religion (Burchinal and Chancellor, 1962; Christensen and Barber, 1967).

Some persons enter mixed marriages not because they are unlucky but because they are inefficient at discovering suitable prospects or have other characteristics that lower their expected gains from mar-

---

16. Of course, this equation cannot determine whether mixed marriages lower earnings, whether men with lower earnings enter mixed marriages, or both.

riage. Such persons are likely to enter mixed marriages on second and later as well as on first marriages, whereas persons could expect average luck in the remarriage market if they were simply unlucky in their first marriage. The evidence in Table 10.1 indicates that bad luck is not the only major cause of mixed marriages. More than 40 percent of the Terman "geniuses" remarried outside their religion if their first marriage had been outside, whereas less than 20 percent remarried outside if they had previously married inside. Table 10.2 indicates that remarriage does not automatically raise the likelihood of mixed marriage: widowed Jews were less likely, while divorced Jews were much more likely, to marry a non-Jew than were Jews marrying for the first time.

Unlucky persons who enter mixed marriages have smaller expected gains from remaining married, since they anticipate average luck in the

TABLE 10.1   Proportion of Terman "geniuses" who married outside their religion, by order of marriage and previous behavior.

		Second marriage		Third marriage	
Current marriage	First marriage	Married within same religion on first marriage	Married outside own religion on first marriage	Married within same religion on second marriage	Married outside own religion on second marriage
Women:					
Married someone of *same* religion	0.88	0.81	0.44	0.40	0.50
Married someone of *different* religion	0.12	0.19	0.56	0.60	0.50
No. of observations	486	26	9	5	4
Men:					
Married someone of *same* religion	0.86	0.82	0.67	1.00	0.67
Married someone of *different* religion	0.14	0.18	0.33	0.0	0.33
No. of observations	689	38	18	4	3

SOURCE: BLM (1977, p. 1168). Data are from 1950 marital histories of high-IQ subjects in Terman's sample.

TABLE 10.2   Proportion of Jewish intermarriage in Indiana, 1960–1963.

| Type of marriage | Previous marital status of spouses | | |
	One or both widowed	Both single	One or both divorced
Inside religion	0.81	0.60	0.32
Outside religion	0.19	0.40	0.68
No. of observations	32	485	254

SOURCE: Rosenthal (1970, p. 436).

remarriage market, and therefore have higher propensities to divorce. Relatively small discrepancies after marriage between their realized and their expected information would make divorce an attractive alternative to remaining married. The same argument implies that the propensity to divorce is higher also for persons in mixed marriages because of characteristics that lower their expected gains from marriage. Inefficient searchers who enter mixed marriages may not have smaller expected gains from remaining married for the reason that they would be inefficient also in the remarriage market. However, they also should tend to have higher propensities to divorce as the result of entering marriage with less information about their mates (for a further discussion see BLM, 1977, and Wilde, 1980).

Divorce and Stigma

A couple divorces because unexpected information after marriage reduces their wealth from remaining married below their wealth from a divorce. They may not be as well matched as anticipated, or one (or both) may be less trustworthy or more quarrelsome than anticipated. Persons who are divorced because they are untrustworthy or quarrelsome are not attractive prospects in the remarriage market; unfortunately, there may be insufficient information to determine why their expected wealth from remaining married declined.

However, the average divorced person can be presumed to be more quarrelsome and in other ways less pleasant than the average person remaining married, because an unpleasant temperament is one cause of

A Treatise on the Family

TABLE 10.3 Probability of divorce by specific marital intervals, with regression coefficients on dummy variables indicating if previously married or previously widowed (white men and women in the United States, ages 15–65).

	Marriage interval (years)			
	Women		Men	
Explanatory variable[a]	0–5	5–10	0–5	5–10
Dummy = 1 if second	0.138	0.012	0.036	0.013
or third marriage[b]	(15.94)	(1.36)	(4.13)	(1.68)
Dummy = 1 if widowed	0.002	−0.018	−0.009	−0.009
in first marriage	(0.13)	(1.19)	(0.47)	(0.51)
R^2 (entire regression)	0.037	0.010	0.011	0.001
F (entire regression)	56.82	12.23	12.08	0.80
Sample size	11,960	9,627	8,688	6,948

SOURCE: BLM (1977, p. 1178).

[a] Figures in parentheses are t-statistics. Other variables included in the regressions are age, education, age at current marriage, for men their 1966 earnings, and for women the number of children from their current marriage measured at the beginning of each interval. As constructed, the first dummy variable's coefficient shows the effect on the probability of dissolution of being previously divorced compared to being in the first marriage, and the sum of the two dummy variables' coefficients shows the effect on the probability of dissolution of being previously widowed compared to being in the first marriage. The standardizations for age at current marriage, age, and especially duration of current marriage were decisive in these findings for men and women. The importance of these standardizations is explained largely by the fact that persons in first marriages were generally married longer and thus had more opportunity to divorce *sometime* during their marriage.
[b] Second or third marriage for men; second marriage for women.

divorce.[17] If the cause of divorce in particular cases is not easily determined, all divorced persons would be stigmatized as being less suitable marital prospects[18] (or employees, or borrowers, or neighbors) than the average person. Moreover, persons with two divorces would be more stigmatized than those with only one, and persons with three divorces more than those with two; the probability that a person divorced simply because he had had bad luck in his match would decline with the number of divorces.

17. This discussion was stimulated by Jovanovic (1978).
18. Stigma in the labor market is analyzed in Flinn and Heckman (1980).

If divorce carries a stigma, divorced persons can remarry only on less favorable terms than they had in previous marriages. Since a deterioration in the terms of marriage reduces the incentive to marry, the stigma attached to divorce implies that the probability of marriage declines with the number of prior divorces. Moreover, the evidence in Tables 10.1 and 10.2 also suggests that divorced persons expect to gain less from remarriage than they expected from prior marriages: divorced (but not widowed) persons are likely to remarry outside their religion even when they had previously married inside their religion.

The expected gain from remaining married was generally quite large in the nineteenth and early twentieth centuries. Fertility was high and few married women participated in the market sector (see Chapter 11 for a fuller discussion). Consequently, persons divorcing then must have been *very* badly matched or temperamentally *very* unsuited to marriage. The decline during this century in the gains from remaining married has encouraged persons with modest mismatches or moderately difficult temperaments to divorce. Therefore, the stigma attached to divorce would have declined over time along with the increase in divorces, even without increased "permissiveness" or greater tolerance of "deviant" behavior. The average divorced person is now considered temperamentally more normal than in the past.

Divorced persons usually gain less from remarriage than the average person gains from a first marriage because divorced persons tend to have more quarrelsome temperaments. Moreover, divorced persons gain less because they tend to have other characteristics that lower their expected gains from marriage, or they are inefficient searchers. Remarriages should then be more likely to dissolve than first marriages, especially remarriages of persons previously divorced more than once. Table 10.3 shows that the divorce rate on second marriages is much higher during the first five years of marriage, and a little higher during the second five years, than the rate on all first marriages, even when duration of the current marriage and several other variables are held constant. The divorce rate on third (or higher order) marriages of persons previously divorced twice (or more) appears to be extremely high (Monahan, 1958, table 5).

CHAPTER 11

The Evolution of the Family

Divorce rates, fertility, the labor force participation of married women, and other aspects of the organization and behavior of families have changed dramatically during recent decades. The magnitude and rapidity of these changes, and the attention they have received, should not be allowed to convey the impression that the family had stagnated previously. It was a radically different institution in primitive and peasant societies, one that has undergone a considerable transformation in the West during the last few centuries.

This last chapter uses the analysis developed in previous chapters to consider both the long-term evolution of the family and the ways the family has altered in the recent past. The discussion is speculative and sketched with broad strokes, for I am no expert on the historical and anthropological materials. I believe, however, that the sketch produced by the economic approach to the family portrays the main factors responsible both for the long-term evolution of the family and for contemporary developments.

Traditional Societies

All traditional societies have enormous problems coping with uncertainty and limited information. Witchcraft, sorcery, and superstition thrive on ignorance of the material world (Thomas, 1971). The majority of children die prior to age ten (see Chapter 5), and many persons become widowed before the tenth year of their marriage. Bad weather and pests can destroy a harvest, and predators or disease destroy herds and prey. Even ordinary transactions are fraught with uncertainty about the quality of merchandise and the honesty and reliability of buyers and sellers. A noted anthropologist has claimed that in all peasant market systems, "information is poor, scarce, maldistributed, inefficiently communicated, and intensely valued," and "the search for information one lacks and the protection of information one has is the name of the game" (Geertz, 1978, p. 29).

Traditional societies, as exemplified by primitive and peasant societies, generally do not experience cumulative change in the techniques used for farming, hunting, fishing, or other activities. Although families rise and fall because of the unequal incidence of luck and ability, and plagues and unusual weather may last for many years, the economy and social life tend to be static and stationary.

These societies cope with uncertainty and ignorance in various ways. Since they lack formal insurance programs, persons having a good harvest, catch, or kill are encouraged (even required) to share their good fortune with others.[1] Open fields with physically scattered plots of land are a crude and costly method of reducing fluctuations in income from crops, but they are common in peasant societies as the best available protection against the vagaries of weather and pests (McCloskey, 1976).

The family—or more accurately, the kinship group—is important in traditional societies in large measure because it protects members against uncertainty. The gifts that are so common in many primitive societies are mainly given to kin, and persons in distress can rely on their relatives for assistance (Herskovits, 1965; Posner, 1980). A kinship group is a reasonably effective "insurance company," in that even an extended group is sufficiently small to enable members to monitor other members—to prevent them from becoming lazy or careless, and in other ways taking advantage of the protection provided by their kin. Moreover, the characteristics of the members are known and their behavior easily observed, since they live together or close by.

---

1. Richard Posner (1980) examines this interpretation of the prevalence of gifts in primitive societies. Although my emphasis on the importance of uncertainty in traditional societies was independent in origin, its development has been greatly aided by discussions with Posner and by the analysis in his essay. Yoram Ben-Porath (1980) has an analysis that is similar in some respects.

In addition, altruism is more common in families than in other organizations, and even selfish members are induced by the *automatic* responses of altruistic members to incorporate the interests of altruistic members into their behavior. Otherwise, selfish members would be harmed by selfish behavior, because the time and other resources spent on them by altruistic members would be reduced. Chapter 8 demonstrates how the Rotten Kid Theorem induces even selfish members to act as if they were altruistic.

The importance of kin in protecting against uncertainty also reconciles the view that plots are scattered because of partible inheritances with the view that they are scattered to protect against fluctuations in income. Scattered plots of *family* members due to partible inheritances reduce fluctuations in family income, and thereby reduce fluctuations in the income of each member because of family insurance.

Older persons are held in esteem in traditional societies because they have accumulated knowledge that is especially valuable to younger persons in stationary environments (Brenner, 1979). Knowledge is passed to younger generations through the family mainly via the culture inherited by children, nephews, and other younger relatives. Specialized skills and knowledge of the elderly concerning their jobs, land, and so on are more readily conveyed to younger persons with similar family backgrounds (see Chapter 6 and Rosenzweig and Wolpin, 1979).

Since members monitor one another to protect against shirking and other "moral hazards" of insurance by kin, traditional societies encourage families to monitor members to detect crimes against other families, including nonpayment of debts. Encouragement often includes the punishment of whole families for antisocial acts by their members (Stone, 1977, p. 126; Posner, 1980).

Younger members tend to follow the same occupations and till the same land as their parents and other relatives because they acquire the specific knowledge of their elder relatives. Indeed, families can be considered small specialized schools that train graduates for particular occupations, land, or firms, and accept responsibility for certifying the qualifications of their graduates when qualifications are not readily ascertained. The importance of family "schools" in traditional societies explains why peasant farms remain in the same family for many generations, and why families specialize in producing soldiers (samurai), clergymen (Brahmins), merchants (bazari), farmers (peasants), servants, and other workers.

Often, families have the right only to produce graduates for specified occupations or other activities and are held accountable for badly prepared or dishonest graduates. The great Japanese ukiyoe artist, Andō Hiroshige, inherited the occupation of fire warden in Tokyo from his father and passed this right to his cousin, then to his son and grandson during the nineteenth century (Narazaki, 1968). One major implication is that caste and feudal systems did not simply redistribute wealth to upper-class families but these systems relied on families to train and certify their members for particular occupations, inasmuch as better methods for determining the distribution of persons among occupations were not available.

Families held accountable for the performance of their members would guide and, if necessary, force members into activities where they could contribute most to the reputation and opportunities of the whole family. Seventeenth-century England was an individualistic society by comparison with other countries (Macfarlane, 1979, chap. 7), but upper-class fathers there apparently still chose the occupations of their sons (Stone, 1977, esp. p. 179).

Marriages are among the most important events in traditional societies, so families want to avoid affiliation with dishonorable or badly managed families that will frequently ask for help or damage the family's own reputation. Therefore, families exercise considerable control over the mates chosen by their members. In a fourteenth-century French village, "many marriages were arranged by the family or friends of the people concerned without much attention being paid to their feelings," or "one married a domus [a family] rather than an individual marriage partner" (Le Roy Ladurie, 1978, pp. 188–189).

Two families sometimes cement an alliance by multiple marriages between members, as in the "connubium" of primitive societies (Fox, 1969). In describing a caste of Indian civil servants during the nineteenth century, Leonard said: "Multiple marriages were occurring among limited numbers of families. Sometimes as many as five marriages in one generation occurred between two families" (1978, p. 88). Marriage of cousins and other kin was common in some societies partly because risk of bad affiliation was reduced by marrying within the (extended) family.[2]

Under these circumstances marriage for love is not sanctioned unless it also contributes to the family's interests. In sixteenth-century

---

2. A Syrian proverb describes marriage between cousins: "Ill luck which you know is better than good luck with which you get acquainted" (Patai, 1971, p. 170).

A Treatise on the Family

England, "romantic love and lust were strongly condemned as ephemeral and irrational grounds for marriage" (Stone, 1977, p. 86). In the fourteenth-century French village studied by Le Roy Ladurie, "it was possible to love passionately," *but only* "within apparently rigid structures which predisposed towards and presided over the choice of a marriage partner" (1978, pp. 186–187). Concubines could be loved, and discreet affairs overlooked, but families had too great a stake in the marriages of members to allow love to thwart family objectives.

The families of an unhappily married couple in these societies would discourage them from divorcing if these families continued to benefit from the union. Instead, the husband, and sometimes the wife also, might be permitted to find solace with concubines and affairs. Since religious or social authorities might not be able to ascertain readily whether kin would agree to a divorce, they might prohibit or greatly discourage divorce, as in peasant societies and most of Western Europe prior to the middle of the nineteenth century.[3]

The importance of kin in traditional societies is indicated by the emphasis on kinship and descent, and by the many separate terms for different kinds of kin even in languages of primitive societies (Fox, 1969). In primitive and peasant societies a family line owns the farm; individuals and even nuclear families have only "usufruct" rights to work during their lifetimes the farm owned by their family lines (Herskovits, 1965, chap. 16; Nash, 1966, p. 34; Macfarlane, 1979, pp. 18 ff.).

In the United States a person can legally choose any family name, including the prefix *Von* or well-known names like Rockefeller or Carnegie, because a family name carries little advantage. Traditional societies, however, protect family names (when they have them) as vigorously as most countries protect business trademarks, because a family name in these societies can be a valuable asset or "trademark". Ancestors are usually respected and even worshipped in traditional societies for their accomplishments, and families do not tolerate criticisms of them.

Uncles, aunts, nieces, nephews, cousins, and other kin meet often to transfer gifts, plan family strategy, teach younger members, and inspect and monitor one another's performance and behavior. The pri-

---

3. For example, a divorce in England prior to the 1850s required an Act of Parliament, and fewer than two divorces were granted per year (Rowntree and Carrier, 1958). Many primitive societies, however, had high divorce rates; see Pryor (1977, pp. 335, 339) and the discussion in Posner (1980).

vacy of members is reduced by these frequent contacts and monitoring. Unmarried persons are chaperoned to prevent undesirable pregnancies and other entanglements, married women are secluded in Islamic societies to prevent affairs (see Maududi, 1975), and contacts with other families are controlled to prevent behavior that damages the family's reputation or increases its obligations. The privacy of members is invaded because the behavior of each member affects the well-being of other members. (For a more general discussion of the relation between privacy and "malfeasance," see Becker, 1980.)

Although members of poor and unsuccessful families have little physical privacy in most societies because they eat, live, and sleep in a small space, they usually have greater autonomy in their economic and social choices than do members of successful families. A poor person can choose his spouse and activities, for his family has little to lose from his behavior. Indeed, an ambitious poor person may move away from his family precisely to prevent his progress from being thwarted by their low status.

Modern Societies

In modern societies markets facilitate trade and production, and dynamic economic environments rapidly change technologies, incomes, and opportunities. The knowledge accumulated by older members is much less useful to younger members than in traditional societies because the young face a different economic milieu. Small family schools that prepare members for a traditional activity are not as efficient as large schools with students from many families that teach general knowledge adaptable to new environments. The "certification" provided by families in traditional societies is provided today by schools and examinations. Moreover, contracts and the possibility of repeat business reduce the need for prior certification; individuals who violate a contract can be punished by the legal system, and individuals who misrepresent themselves or are incompetent will not have repeat business.

Family insurance through gifts and loans to members in distress are less necessary in modern societies. Individuals can "self-insure" by borrowing in the capital market during bad times or by saving during good times. Moreover, market insurance based on the experience of thousands of families provides more effective protection against fire, death, old age, ill health, and other hazards than any single family can. Consequently, kinship is less important in modern than traditional societies because market insurance is used instead of kin insurance, market schools instead of family schools, and examinations and contracts instead of family certification. Not only are kin less concerned about monitoring and controlling members, they are also less able to do so because members scatter to find their best opportunities. Since kinship is less important in modern societies, elder members and ancestors receive less respect and attention; they are less likely to be defended against criticism by others and more likely to be criticized in public or in the privacy of a psychiatrist's office. Samuel Johnson had already made some observations on this subject in the latter part of the eighteenth century:

> In uncommercial countries many of the branches of a family must depend on the stock; so, in order to make the head of the family take care of them, they are represented as connected with his reputation, that, self-love being interested, he may exert himself to promote their interest. You have first large circles, or clans; as commerce increases, the connexion is confined to families. By degrees, that too goes off, as having become unnecessary and there being few opportunities of intercourse.[4]

The reduced importance of the family implies that members of middle-class and upper-class families gain the freedom and privacy of action available only to poor families in traditional societies. Children may begin by having the right to reject spouses chosen by their parents, then the right to choose subject to parental veto, and finally the right to choose with little concern about parental opposition. Dating, even by young teenagers, and search in marriage markets to find mates with desirable characteristics are more common in modern societies because personal, rather than family, compatibility is sought. In particular, individuals search actively (and often unsuccessfully) for mates they can love.

Unfortunately, love and other personal characteristics are less readily ascertainable prior to marriage than are family reputation and position, the important considerations in traditional societies. Many married persons discover that they are not still in love or are disappointed

---

4. Boswell (1959, p. 98). I owe this reference to Stone (1977, p. 259).

in other ways by their marital experiences. Some of these divorce to try again in the marriage market. Consequently, modern societies have what may appear to be a paradoxical combination of many love-marriages and high rates of divorce.

Parents have fewer children and more is invested in each child in modern than in traditional societies (see the discussion in Chapter 5). Moreover, in traditional societies much of the investment of time and other resources is made by grandparents, aunts, and other kin because of their interest in the children's well-being and behavior. As a result, modern parents are more shocked by the death of a child and generally more concerned about the welfare of each child because of their sizable commitment of time, money, and energy. In addition, the Rotten Kid Theorem implies that even selfish children gain by altruistic behavior toward parents who invest much in them, for the welfare of children whose parents invest much is closely dependent on the welfare of those parents.

Many historians have noted that nuclear families are more affectionate and closer in modern than in traditional societies, whereas cousins and more distant kin are closer in traditional societies (see for example Shorter, 1975, pp. 55 ff., 234 ff.; Stone, 1977, pp. 85 ff., 124). I argue here that modern spouses are closer, because love is more important in the selection of mates—and that present-day parents and children are closer, because quality rather than quantity of children is emphasized. Cousins and other kin are closer in traditional societies, because kin groups insure and train members and are more broadly responsible for them.

If modern society evolved from traditional society with the characteristics emphasized in this chapter, the individualism and nuclear familialism of modern society would have evolved from the extended families and kinship groups of traditional society. Many deplore individualism and lament the passing of the traditional family, but my analysis implies that individualism replaced familialism because many family functions in traditional societies are more effectively handled by markets and other organizations of modern societies. For example, family insurance and family provision and certification of training are less efficient than market insurance and market training in the dynamic environments of modern societies. Nostalgia for the supposed closeness of traditional families overlooks the restrictions on privacy and free choice, the very imperfect protection against disasters, and the limited opportunities to transcend family background.

A Treatise on the Family

The Last Half of the Twentieth Century

Figures 11.1 to 11.9 show the trends in the United States since 1950 of fertility, divorce, labor force participation of married women, school enrollment of young adults, elderly living alone, and a few other series indicative of family organization and structure. They leave no doubt that the family changed dramatically after the Second World War; for example, from 1950 to 1977 the legitimate birth rate declined by about one-third, the divorce rate more than doubled, the labor force participation rate of married women with young children more than tripled, and the percent of households headed by women with dependent children also almost tripled. Indeed, the family in the United States changed more rapidly than during any equivalent period since the founding of the colonies.

I believe that the major cause of these changes is the growth in the earning power of women as the American economy developed. The real weekly earnings of employed women over age fourteen grew by about 30 percent from 1950 to 1964 and by about 10 percent from 1964 to 1978 (see Figure 11.4). A growth in the earning power of women raises the labor force participation of married women by raising the foregone value of time spent at nonmarket activities. It also raises the

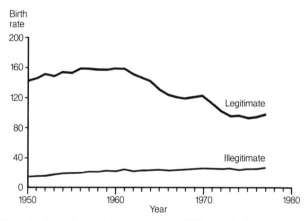

FIGURE 11.1   Legitimate birth rate per 1,000 married women ages 14–44 and illegitimate birth rate per 1,000 unmarried women ages 15–44 in the United States, 1950–1977.

SOURCES: U.S. Bureau of the Census, 1979c and preceding issues; U.S. Department of Health, Education, and Welfare, 1978.

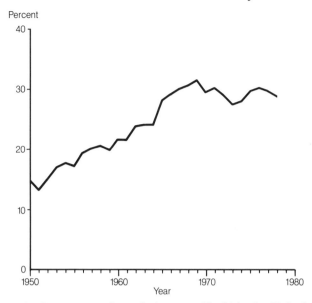

FIGURE 11.2   Percentage of population ages 18–24 in the United States enrolled in school, 1950–1978.

SOURCE: U.S. Bureau of the Census, 1979b and preceding issues.

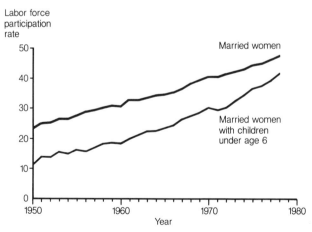

FIGURE 11.3   U.S. labor force participation of married women and of married women with children under 6 years, 1950–1978.

SOURCE: U.S. Bureau of the Census, 1975c, 1979c and preceding issues.

A Treatise on the Family

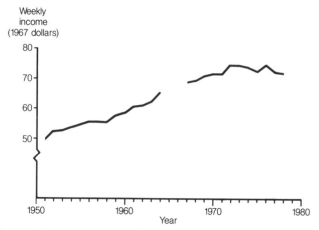

FIGURE 11.4   Real average weekly income of U.S. women in 1967 dollars, 1951–1978.

SOURCE: U.S. Bureau of the Census, 1967, 1980c and preceding issues.

relative cost of children and thereby reduces the demand for children because children require much time of their mothers (see the extended discussion in Chapter 5). Statistical studies (Butz and Ward, 1979b; Ward and Butz, 1980) suggest that the growth in the earnings and labor force participation of women have been important causes of the significant decline in fertility since 1957.

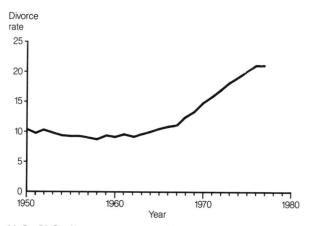

FIGURE 11.5   U.S. divorce rate per 1,000 married women, 1950–1977.

SOURCES: U.S. Bureau of the Census, 1979c and preceding issues; U.S. Department of Health, Education, and Welfare, 1979.

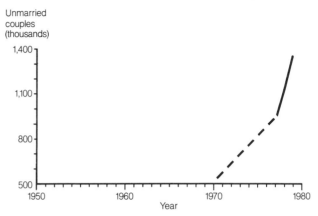

FIGURE 11.6   Number of unmarried couples living together in the United States, 1970–1979.

SOURCE: U.S. Bureau of the Census, 1979a, 1980a.

The gain from marriage is reduced by a rise in the earnings and labor force participation of women and by a fall in fertility because a sexual division of labor becomes less advantageous (see the discussion in Chapters 2 to 4). And divorce is more attractive when the gain from marriage is reduced. Michael's study (1978) of the interaction between fertility, divorce, and labor force participation since 1950 suggests that changes in the labor force participation rate of married women with

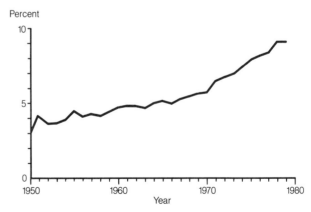

FIGURE 11.7   Percentage of families with female heads and own children under 18 years in the United States, 1950–1979.

SOURCE: U.S. Bureau of the Census, 1980b and preceding issues.

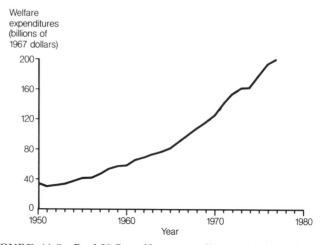

FIGURE 11.8   Real U.S. welfare expenditures, 1950–1977.

SOURCE: U.S. Bureau of the Census, 1975c, 1979c and preceding issues.

spouse present has been positively related to subsequent changes in the divorce rate. The decline in the gain from marriage and the increase in divorce have raised the number of unmarried couples living together and the percent of families headed by women (see Figures 11.6 and 11.7) and are partially responsible for the large growth in the illegitimate birth rate relative to the legitimate rate (see Figure 11.1).

Greater labor force participation of women (resulting from an in-

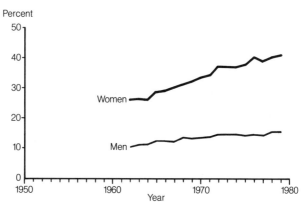

FIGURE 11.9   Percentage of men and of women ages 65 and over living alone in the United States, 1962–1979.

SOURCE: U.S. Bureau of the Census, 1980a and preceding issues.

crease in their wage rate, a decline in fertility, and/or an increase in the propensity to divorce) would itself raise the earning power of women and thereby reinforce the effects of economic development. Women invest more in market skills and experiences when they spend a larger fraction of their time at market activities, as we saw in Chapter 2 (see also Polachek, 1975).

Divorce rates, fertility levels, and labor force participation rates interact in other ways. For example, fertility is reduced when divorce becomes more likely, because children are more difficult to rear and may provide less pleasure after a marriage dissolves. Chapter 10 presents evidence that couples who anticipate higher probabilities of divorce have fewer children while married. The labor force participation of single and married women is also affected when divorce becomes more likely, for market experience is useful when a marriage dissolves and a woman must become the main financial support for her dependent children.

Economic development of the United States and the resulting growth in the earning power of women has not accelerated since 1950, yet both the divorce and the labor force participation rates of married women have risen more rapidly since then, especially during the last 20 years (Chiswick and O'Neill, 1977; Michael, 1978), and the decline in fertility between 1956 and 1976 exceeded the declines during any previous 20-year period (U.S. Department of Health, Education, and Welfare, 1979). Threshold effects of increases in female earning power on labor force participation of married women, fertility, and divorce are partly responsible for the accelerated changes in these series. When fertility is high and divorce and labor force participation of married women uncommon—as in the nineteenth and early twentieth centuries—a decline in fertility, say, due to an increase in female earning power, has relatively little effect on the participation of married women, who still spend most of their prime years having and rearing children. They would not invest much in market-oriented human capital, partly because they can spend only a short time in the labor force making use of such capital, and partly because their investment would depreciate significantly during the many years that they care for children (Mincer and Ofek, 1980). The effect on the divorce rate is also small in that the gain from marriage and an extensive sexual division of labor remains high.

Eventually, however, as female earning power continues to grow and fertility continues to fall, the time spent in child care is sufficiently reduced to permit married women to spend appreciable time in the labor force prior to their first child and after their last child has entered school. The expectation of greater participation at older ages encourages girls and young women to invest more in market-oriented human capital, which further increases earning power and participation, and further reduces fertility. Consequently, the increase in labor force participation and the decline in fertility eventually accelerate even when the growth in female earning power does not. Moreover, these two factors accelerate the increase in the divorce rate because the decline in the gain from marriage also accelerates. Furthermore, a growth in the divorce rate itself eventually encourages additional divorces; divorced persons become less stigmatized and can more readily find other divorcees to marry (see Chapter 10 and Becker et al., 1977).

The nature of the typical family may have changed especially rapidly during recent decades because of other events. Perhaps the contraceptive revolution ushered in by the introduction of ''the pill'' during the 1950s greatly reduced the number of unwanted children and thereby increased divorce and the labor force participation of married women. Although it has provided better control over the timing and number of children, I argue in Chapter 5 that the contraceptive revolution explains only a small part of the decline in fertility since the mid-1950s.

One aspect of the women's movement has encouraged women to reduce their childbearing, raise their labor force participation, and (when necessary) assert their independence by divorcing their husbands and becoming head of their own households. The movement undoubtedly provides emotional support and various arguments and evidence that help some women to take these steps. I believe, however, that the movement is primarily a response to other forces that have dramatically changed the role of women rather than a major independent force in changing their role.

The growth of the welfare state has been a powerful force that has changed the family in recent decades. Expenditures on social security, unemployment compensation, medicare and medicaid, aid to mothers with dependent children, food stamps, and other transfer programs grew in real terms by 123 percent from 1950 to 1963 and by 167 percent from 1963 to 1976 (see Figure 11.8). Aid to mothers with dependent children and other kinds of ''welfare'' grew rapidly during the earlier period, whereas medical care and social security flourished during the later period.

Payments to mothers with dependent children are reduced when the earnings of parents increase, and are raised when additional children are born or when fathers do not support their children. It is a program, then, that raises the fertility of eligible women, including single women, and also encourages divorce and discourages marriage (the financial well-being of recipients is increased by children and decreased by marriage). In effect, welfare is the poor woman's alimony, which substitutes for husband's earnings. The expansion of welfare, along with the general decline in the gain from marriage, explains the sizable growth in the ratio of illegitimate to legitimate birth rates despite the introduction of the pill and other effective contraceptives.

Before the days of unemployment compensation and medicare and medicaid, unemployed and sick persons commonly relied on parents, children, and other family members for assistance, in part through increased labor force participation of wives when husbands were unemployed (Mincer, 1966; Smith, 1979). Consequently, the growth of public programs, like the growth in the nineteenth century of private-market life insurance (Zelizer, 1978), weakened the ties of family members by further eroding the traditional role of the family in protecting members against hazards.

Several important public programs principally transfer resources between generations. For example, social security transfers from workers to retired persons, and "free" schools transfer from adults to children. Intergenerational transfers may not change the *combined* income of the average family with children (see the discussion in Chapter 7), but they still have important effects on family behavior and living arrangements.

Consider public support of education financed by taxes on the adult (mainly parent) population. Since parents reduce their own expenditures on the education and other human capital of children to recoup some of the resources for themselves that are taxed away to provide public education for children, public support may have a small net effect on the *total* investment in children (see Chapter 6). Public support and these parental responses, however, weaken the ties between parents and children and are partly responsible for the growing conflict between the generations in recent decades. If parents spend less on children because the state spends more, selfish children have less incentive to consider the effects of their behavior on the welfare of altruistic parents—a decline in parental welfare cannot harm the children as much. Selfish children then would have less incentive to obey parents who try to control their behavior by threatening to reduce or withdraw financial and other support.

Social security payments financed by taxes on the working popula-

tion reduce the amount spent by children to support retired parents because children recoup for themselves some of their resources taxed
away (Barro, 1978). Parents are less likely to heed or otherwise consider the interests of children who contribute less to their support. The
rapid increase during recent decades in the fraction of elderly men and
women living apart from their children, either in separate households
or in nursing homes (see Figure 11.9) is one manifestation of the weakened ties between children and older parents. Evidence presented by
Michael and colleagues (1980) suggests that the growth in social security payments has been an important cause of the decline in joint
households containing married children and widowed parents.

The earning power of women increased and the welfare state greatly
expanded in other Western countries also after World War II. If my interpretation of the change in the United States during this period is
valid, the family should have changed dramatically in these other countries as well. Figures 11.10 to 11.12 show that since 1964 fertility has
declined by about 30 percent in France, England and Wales, and
Sweden; the divorce rate has more than doubled in these countries;

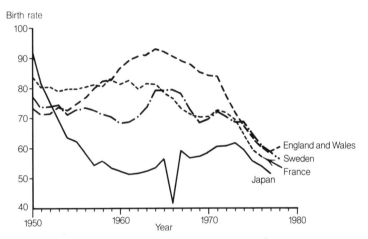

FIGURE 11.10   Birth rates per 1,000 women ages 15–44 in England
and Wales, France, Japan, and Sweden, 1950–1978. (Statistics for France
cover ages 15–49; for Japan, 10–49.)

SOURCES: France, Institut national de la statistique et des études économiques,
1978a and preceding issues; Great Britain Registrar General, 1975; Great Britain Central Statistical Office, 1980 and preceding issues; Japan Statistics Bureau, 1980 and
preceding issues; Sweden National Central Bureau of Statistics, 1980 and preceding
issues.

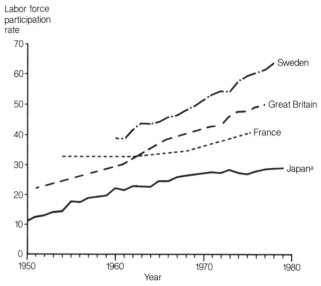

FIGURE 11.11   Labor force participation rates of married women in France, Great Britain, Japan, and Sweden, 1950–1979.

ª The percent of all women who are paid employees is shown for Japan.
SOURCES: France, Institut national de la statistique et des études économiques, 1956, 1964, 1971, 1978b; Great Britain Department of Employment, 1975, 1978; Japan Statistics Bureau, 1980 and preceding issues; Sweden National Central Bureau of Statistics, 1980 and preceding issues.

and the labor force participation rate of married women has increased by more than 20 percent in these countries. Japan is especially interesting: the women's movement has not been influential there and the pill has been banned, yet fertility has declined by more than 40 percent since 1950, the divorce rate has risen by almost 20 percent since 1960, and the percent of women who are paid employees has risen by more than 50 percent since 1955.

Although the major changes for the five countries depicted in these figures are similar, significant differences are also apparent. For example, the decline in fertility in England and Wales, Sweden, and France began several years after, and in Japan several years before, the decline began in the United States. And divorce rates increased by much less in Japan than in the other countries. These and other differences have not yet been satisfactorily explained. Still, the main message of these data, and those for other developed countries, is not diversity but uniformity: the family has changed in a similar revolu-

FIGURE 11.12 Divorce rates per 1,000 married women in England and
Wales, France, Japan, and Sweden, 1950–1978.

SOURCES: See Figure 11.10.

tionary manner in essentially all economically advanced countries
during the last several decades.

Both the welfare state and economic activity have grown much more
slowly in advanced countries since the early 1970s. The momentum
from the prior rapid changes explains why fertility continued to fall significantly, and divorce and labor force participation of married women
continued to rise sharply, throughout most of the 1970s. However, if
economic development continues to slow down and the expansion of
the welfare state continues to moderate,[5] the analysis in this chapter
predicts much less steep declines in fertility and less rapid increases in
divorce, labor force participation of married women, illegitimacy, and
female-headed households—and more gradual changes in many other
dimensions of family organization and behavior as well. Indeed, a sufficient slowing of the pace of development could eventually raise fertility
and also reverse the trends in other aspects of family behavior. I delib-

5. This is a shaky assumption because the causes of these slowdowns are
not well understood; see the relevant discussion by Edward Denison (1979) of
the attenuation of economic growth in the United States.

erately say "eventually" because not much is known about the timing of responses in fertility, labor force participation, and divorce.

These tentative forecasts of the future may be a fitting way to conclude a speculative chapter on long-run developments in the family. This chapter has tried to show that the economic approach provides a powerful framework for analyzing both the dramatic changes in the family during the last half-century, and the much slower, yet even larger changes extending over hundreds of years during the evolution from traditional to modern societies. Although the economic approach does not encompass all facets of human behavior, it does appear to focus attention on those aspects primarily responsible for changing the family over time.

The Family

and the State

Children are incapable of caring for themselves during many years of physical and mental maturation. Since their mental development is not sufficient for them to make reliable contractual arrangements with caretakers, laws and social norms regulate the production and rearing of children. Laws punish child abuse, the sale of children, and un-authorized abortions. They provide compulsory schooling, welfare payments to families with dependent children, stringent rules about divorce when young children are involved, and minimum ages of mar-riage.

Trades and contracts are efficient if no deviation from the terms would raise the welfare of all participants. An alternative criterion for efficiency is that the monetary gain to those benefiting from a deviation does not exceed the monetary loss to those harmed. Unfortunately, the immaturity of children sometimes precludes efficient arrangements between children and parents or others responsible for child care.

This supplement was written with Kevin M. Murphy and originally appeared in the *Journal of Law and Economics* 31 (1988): 1–18. Reprinted here, in slightly amended form, by permission.

This difficulty in establishing efficient relations within families provides the point of departure for our interpretation of the heavy state involvement in the family. We believe that a surprising number of state interventions mimic the agreements that would occur if children were capable of arranging for their own care. Stated differently, our belief is that many regulations of the family improve the efficiency of family activities. To be sure, these regulations raise the welfare of children, but they also raise the welfare of parents, or at least they raise the combined welfare of parents and children.

The efficiency perspective implies that the state is concerned with justice for children, if "justice" is identified with the well-being of children—for their well-being is the prime factor in our analysis. The efficiency perspective does not imply, however, that the effect on children alone determines whether the state intervenes. The effect on parents is considered too. The state tends to intervene when both gain, or when the gain to children exceeds the loss to their parents.

According to Richard Posner and others, the common law also improves efficiency when transaction costs are large. Posner (1986) says, "In settings where the cost of allocating resources by voluntary market transactions is prohibitively high—where, in other words, market transactions are infeasible—the common law prices behavior in such a way as to mimic the market" (p. 230).

We cannot *prove* that efficiency guides state involvement in the family. But we will show that state interventions in the market for schooling, the provision of old-age pensions, and access to divorce are consistent on the whole with the efficiency perspective.

The modern theory of regulation and public choice questions whether much government activity encourages efficiency and justice. Later in this supplement we sketch an analysis of interest-group behavior that can lead to government intervention to promote efficient family arrangements.

In order to interpret public policies, we develop an analysis of family behavior under different circumstances. The analysis greatly extends earlier work. My Woytinsky Lecture of more than 20 years ago shows that only parents who give their adult children gifts or bequests make optimal investments in children (Becker, 1967). Becker and Tomes (1986, and supplement to Chapter 7 of this volume) develop this approach further. Thompson and Ruhter (undated) reached the same conclusion, apparently unaware of this earlier literature.

Our discussion of the gains from government intervention in family

A Treatise on the Family

decisions generalizes the analysis of subsidies to schooling and other human capital found in my Woytinsky Lecture of 1967 and in this book. Thompson and Ruhter, in the paper cited, have a nice analysis with a similar interpretation of government intervention in families. Also relevant is the discussion of fertility by Nerlove et al. (1987).

Altruism toward Children

We assume that the large majority of parents are altruistic to their children in the sense that parental utility depends on the number of children and the utility of each child as well as on parents' own consumption. The altruism assumption is supported by the many sacrifices parents frequently make for children. Parents spend money, time, and effort on children through child care, expenditures on education and health, gifts, and bequests. More or less all parents spend on young children, but only some parents give sizable gifts to adult children or leave bequests.

Plato's *Republic* objects to the rearing of elite children by their parents. It advocates instead that "as soon as children are born, they will be taken in charge by officers appointed for this purpose . . . , while taking every precaution that no mother shall know her own child" (Cornford trans., 1951, p. 160). Plato's views attracted the attention of philosophers and stimulated experiments that invariably failed. Even the kibbutz movement has returned to giving parents responsibility for the care of children.

Parental altruism is the reason why essentially all societies have shown more common sense than Plato and give parents or other close relatives primary responsibility for child care. Altruistic parents are good caretakers, because they consider the effects of their actions on the welfare of children. They sometimes sacrifice their own consumption and comfort to increase that of their children.

Of course, some parents abuse their children, as examples of battered children depressingly illustrate. But even contemporary Western countries display great confidence in parents as caretakers, at least relative to feasible alternatives. Despite the anguish over parental abuse of defenseless children, governments seldom remove children from their parents. Fewer than two children per 10,000 below age eighteen are under state care in either the United States or England and

Wales (Dingewall and Eckelaar, 1984; American Humane Association, 1984).

Sometimes cited against the importance of parents' altruism is the fact that parents seldom insure the lives of their children. This evidence does not speak to the effect of a child's death on the utility of parents, however, because optimal insurance works to equalize the *marginal* utility of income in different states of the world. Even if a child's death enormously reduced parents' utility, the death would not be insurable if it hardly raised and perhaps reduced the marginal utility of money to parents. Support for the importance of altruism comes from the time and effort parents devote to lowering the probability of accidents, illness, or other harm to children. These "self-protection" activities respond not to the effect of a child's mishap on the marginal utility of parents' income, but rather to their effect on the *level* of parents' utility.

Our analysis recognizes that frequent contact among family members often raises the degree of altruism. That is to say, altruism may well have some of the properties of an addictive taste that is fostered by consumption of the good involved.[1] We believe that addictive aspects of altruism better explain the apparently larger bequests by parents to children who visit them more frequently than does the view that parents use bequests to "buy" visits.[2]

The Rotten Kid Theorem states that, under certain conditions, both altruistic parents and their perhaps selfish children work out efficient relations that maximize the combined resources of the family as a whole (see Chapter 8). If this theorem applies to most situations, state interventions in the family could not raise efficiency.

The Rotten Kid Theorem fails to hold, however, when parents do not give children gifts or bequests.[3] They may not give because their altruism is weak, but even parents with strong altruism may not give gifts and bequests when they expect their children to be much better off than they are. Children are better off than parents when economic growth is rapid and when their endowments of ability and other qualities are higher than those of their parents.

Bequests are large in rich families, fairly common among the middle

---

1. On addiction, see Becker and Murphy (1988b).
2. This view is developed in Bernheim et al. (1986).
3. Other qualifications are discussed in Bergstrom (1989).

class, and unimportant in poor families. One reason is that endowments of children tend to exceed those of their parents in poor families and to be less than those of their parents in rich families. Whatever the reason, the evidence on bequests implies that certain types of efficient transactions with children are less common in poorer than in richer families. Nevertheless bequests may cause other inefficiences, as we will show in the next section.

Investments in the Human Capital of Children

Since parents must reduce their own consumption (including leisure) to raise the time and resources they spend on child care and children's education, training, and health, even altruistic parents have to consider the trade-off between their consumption and the human capital of children. But altruistic parents who plan to leave bequests can avoid this trade-off by using bequests to help finance their investments in children. In effect, they can force even selfish children to repay them for expenditures on the children's human capital. These parents would want to invest efficiently in children because children's utility is raised thereby without costing the parents anything.

To make this clear, we assume a 4 percent rate of return on assets accumulated over the life cycle to provide either old-age consumption or gifts and bequests. If the marginal rate of return on investments in children exceeds 4 percent, parents who give gifts and bequests could invest more in children without lowering their own consumption by accumulating fewer assets. For example, if the marginal rate on human capital is 7 percent, an additional $1,000 invested in children raises their adult earnings by about $70 per year. If parents finance this investment through reduced savings of $1,000 and by reducing annual gifts by $40, their consumption at all ages would be unaffected by greater investment, while their children's income increases by $30 per year.

Clearly, then, altruistic parents who leave bequests will invest until the marginal rate of return on human capital equals the rate on assets. They are better off with efficient investments because they can trade between bequests and investments.

Some altruistic parents do not leave bequests because they get less marginal utility from consumption by their adult children than from their own consumption when elderly. They would like to raise their own consumption at the expense of their children's, but they cannot do this if they are unable to leave debts to children. Although children have been responsible for parents' debts in some societies, the practice is uncommon nowadays. Selfish and weakly altruistic parents would like to impose a large debt burden on their children. Social pressures can discourage this behavior in closely knit societies where elderly parents live with and depend on the care of children, but these pressures are not effective in mobile modern countries where the elderly do not live with children.

Parents who cannot leave debt can substitute their own consumption for that of their children by investing less in the children's human capital and instead saving more for old age. Therefore, in families without bequests, the equilibrium marginal rate of return on investments in children must exceed the rate on assets saved for old age; otherwise, parents would reallocate some resources from children to savings. These parents underinvest in the human capital of children.

When the rate of return on savings is less than the marginal rate on human capital, both children and parents could be better off with a "contract" that calls for parents to raise investments to the efficient level in return for a commitment by children to repay their elderly parents. Unfortunately, young children cannot be party to such contracts. Without government intervention, social norms, or "guilt" of parents and children, families without bequests would underinvest in children's human capital.

More generally, expenditures by an altruist are inefficient in the states of the world where that individual gives to a beneficiary if he does not give in other states. When he does give, an altruist would get the same utility from equally small changes in his own and in his beneficiary's consumption. Therefore, he would be willing to give more in these states in return for a commitment by the beneficiary to give him even a little in the other states. The selfish beneficiary also gains from such an agreement in that he receives much more in some states than he gives up in the others. Unfortunately, the beneficiary's promises to give may not be credible, just as children's promises to support elderly parents may not be credible.

State intervention in the provision of education and other human capital could raise investments in children to the efficient levels. Since poor parents are least likely to make efficient investments, such intervention would also reduce the inequality in the opportunities between children from richer and poorer families. The compulsory schooling laws in the United States that began in the 1880s and spread rapidly during the subsequent thirty years tended to have this effect. A state usually set minimum requirements at a level that was already exceeded by all but the poorest families in that state (Landes and Solmon, 1972). These laws raised the schooling of poor children but did not tend to affect the schooling of other children.

Subsidies to public elementary schools in the United States also began to grow in the latter half of the nineteenth century, and subsidies to public high schools expanded rapidly during the twentieth century. These subsidies appear to have raised the schooling of poorer families relative to richer ones, for the effect of parental wealth and education on the education of children declined over time as public expenditures on schooling grew (Featherman and Hauser, 1976).

Strong altruism of parents contributes to efficient investments in children by raising the likelihood that parents give gifts or bequests to adult children. Strong altruism may reduce efficiency in other ways, however, if children recognize that they will be rescued by parents when they get into trouble. For example, children who do not receive gifts now but expect gifts in the future from altruistic parents will save less and borrow more to increase their current consumption and reduce their future resources, since altruistic parents tend to increase their gifts when children are poorer.[4] Similarly, children may have fun in school and neglect their studies if they expect greater future support from their parents when their earnings are lower. Or children who receive gifts from altruistic parents may take big risks because they expect large gifts if they fail and yet can keep most of their gains if they succeed (gifts cannot be negative).

Parents will not give children such perverse incentives if they can precommit the amount of future gifts and bequests. With precommitment, children cannot rely on parents to bail them out of bad gambles or other difficulties. Precommitment is unnecessary if the altruism of parents declines enough when they believe that children have caused their own difficulties by gambling excessively, neglecting their studies, and so on.

Parents may choose not to precommit even when it is perfectly feasible. The Rotten Kid Theorem gives one advantage of retaining flexibility in future transfers. Flexibility can discourage children from

---

4. Bruce and Waldman (1986) and Lindbeck and Weibull (1987) develop similar arguments.

actions that help them but hurt their parents even more. With flexible gifts and bequests, parents would reduce their transfers sufficiently to make children worse off if they take these actions (see Chapter 8 and Bruce and Waldman, 1986). Parents may also choose not to precommit because they want to help children who get into difficulties through no fault of their own.

When precommitment is either not feasible or not desirable, parents may take other actions to give children better incentives in the future. They might *overinvest* in education and other training if children cannot run down human capital as readily as marketable wealth. They could also invest more in other illiquid assets of children, such as their housing.

Public policies can also discourage children from inefficient actions. Many countries require parental approval when children want to marry early, drop out of school, get an abortion, or purchase alcoholic beverages. Presumably, one reason is to prevent children who do not anticipate delayed consequences from taking actions that will make them worse off in the future. Another reason is that children may anticipate all too well the future help they will receive from parents if they get into trouble. The state then tries to reproduce the effects on children's behavior of an optimal degree of commitment by parents.

Social Security and Other Old-Age Support

Throughout history, children have been a major help to elderly parents. The elderly frequently have lived with children who care for them when ill and provide food and other support. In the United States a mere 40 years ago, only about 25 percent of persons over age sixty-five lived alone (Michael et al., 1980).

Richer families who leave bequests rely less on children because they are insulated from many risks of old age. For example, parents who live longer than expected can reduce bequests to finance consumption in the additional years. The opportunity to draw on bequests provides an annuity-like protection against an unusually long life and other risks of old age. If bequests are not a large part of children's assets, elderly parents get excellent protection against various hazards through the opportunity to reduce bequests, yet this does not have much influence on children's welfare. In effect, children help support their parents in old age, although their support is not fully voluntary.

Children in poorer and many middle-level families are willing to help support parents who agree to invest the efficient amount in the children's human capital. Few societies have contracts or other explicit agreements between parents and children, but many societies have social "norms" that pressure children to support elderly parents. Although little is known about how these norms emerge, it is plausible that they are weaker in modern societies with anonymous cities and mobile populations. Public expenditures on the elderly, together with public expenditures on children's education and other human capital, can fill the void left by the breakdown in norms.

Expenditures on the elderly in Western countries have grown rapidly in recent decades. United States governments at all levels spend more than $8,000 on each person aged sixty-five or over, largely in the form of medical and pension payments. Is the rapid growth in expenditures on the elderly mainly due to the political power of a growing elderly population? The media contain much discussion of generations fighting for a limited public purse (see for example Longman, 1985). Some economists support a balanced budget amendment to insulate present generations from heavy taxation of children and other future generations (see Buchanan and Wagner, 1977). In a widely cited and stimulating presidential address to the American Population Association, Samuel Preston suggested that growing public support for the elderly has been partly at the expense of public expenditures on children (Preston, 1984).

We would like to suggest the alternative interpretation that expenditures on the elderly are part of a "social compact" between generations. Taxes on adults help finance efficient investments in children. In return, adults receive public pensions and medical payments when old. This compact tries to achieve for poorer and middle-level families what richer families tend to achieve without government help; namely, efficient levels of investments in children and support to elderly parents.

Federal, state, and local expenditures on education, head-start programs, welfare, and the like are large: in recent years they have exceeded $2,500 per child under age twenty-two. Even though real expenditures per capita on the elderly in the United States grew at a rate exceeding 7 percent from 1950 to the 1980s, Table 11S.1 contradicts the impression that expenditures on the elderly grew at the expense of expenditures on children. Per capita public expenditures on the

TABLE 11S.1   Real per capita public expenditures in the United States on persons under age 22, and 65 and over (1980 dollars).

Year	Expenditures on children under 22, including higher education ($) (1)	Expenditures on persons 65 and over ($) (2)	(1)/(2) (3)
1920	122	a	—
1930	293	126	2.33
1940	393	1,022	0.38
1950	557	1,708	.33
1960	922	3,156	.29
1970	1,825	5,447	.34
1980	2,472	7,520	.33
1983	2,515	8,307	.30

SOURCES: U.S. Department of Health and Human Services, *Social Security Bulletin Annual Statistical Supplement* (various years). U.S. Department of Education, National Center for Education Statistics, *Digest of Education Statistics* (various years). U.S. Department of Commerce, Bureau of the Census, *Statistical Abstract of the United States* (various years).

a Cannot be estimated, but apparently a small amount.

young hardly changed between 1950 and 1983 relative to per capita expenditures on the old.

As Table 11S.1 shows, public expenditure on the elderly in the United States did not become important until 1940, long after public spending on education had become significant. If public spending on education and on the elderly are both part of a social compact, then the first generation of parents taxed to finance investments in children would be the first to receive public old age support. If education taxes start when a person is a young married adult, some thirty to forty years should elapse between the growth in spending on education and the introduction of social security. Perhaps the actual lag in the United States was longer because immigration was not really constrained until the early 1920s. A social security system introduced prior to that time might well have encouraged substantial immigration of older people.

The much greater per capita spending on the elderly ($8,300 versus $2,500) seems difficult to reconcile with a social compact between the young and the old. But these numbers are deceiving: the young, if anything, actually do better than the old. To show this, suppose young adults pay $2,500 to finance public investments in the human capital of each child. When adults reach age sixty-five they receive $8,300 annually for the remainder of their lives. These expenditures on children and the elderly continue until possibly a last future generation. Which generations would be better off with these expenditures?

Since the net reproduction rate in the United States is now close to unity, we assume that the representative parent at age twenty-five has a child, and has no more children after that. We also ignore offsetting reductions in parents' spending on children in response to public expenditures on children and offsetting reductions in children's support of parents in response to social security payments (our analysis applies directly if reduced parental spending equals reduced child support). In the United States, a twenty-five-year-old has a .79 probability of reaching age sixty-five, and a sixty-five-year-old can expect to live until age eighty-two. Therefore, each adult member of the initial generation would pay $2,500 annually from ages twenty-five to forty-six and expects to receive $6,557 (.79 × $8,300) from ages sixty-six to eighty-two. All subsequent generations receive a per capita government investment in their human capital of $2,500 until age twenty-two. The last generation does not invest in children, but it pays $6,557 from ages forty-one to fifty-seven to support the elderly of the prior generation. Each member of all in-between generations pays $2,500 from ages twenty-five to forty-six to support children of the succeeding generation, $6,557 from ages forty-one to fifty-seven to support the elderly of the prior generation, and expects to receive $6,557 from ages sixty-six to eighty-two.

Since estimated rates of return on schooling and other types of training exceed 5 percent (Psacharopoulos, 1973), and since most public expenditures on children are for schooling and other training, we assume conservatively that these have an average rate of return of 5 percent in the form of equal increases in earnings from ages twenty-three to sixty-five. Then $2,500 invested for twenty-two years would increase earnings each year by $5,939. The after-tax net earnings of each member of the last generation would increase by $5,939 from ages twenty-three to forty; they decrease by $618 ($6,557 − $5,939) from ages forty-one to fifty-seven while they are taxed to support the elderly of the previous generation; and they increase again by $5,939 from ages fifty-eight to sixty-five. The present value of this net earnings stream is positive for all nonnegative interest rates. Therefore, the last generation clearly gains from this exchange of child support for old-age support.

Unlike the last generation, generations between the first and the last must also support children of the succeeding generation but receive support when old. The reader can work out the arithmetic of their complicated net earnings stream, but the bottom line is that the present value of this stream is positive for nonnegative interest rates. Therefore, all generations between the first and the last also unambiguously benefit from the present combination of public spending on the young and the old.

The initial generation of adults does the least well. Each member pays $2,500 on child care from ages twenty-five to forty-six and gains $6,557 in old-age support from ages sixty-six to eighty-two. The internal rate of return on this series of gains and losses is a little less than 2 percent. This rate is slightly higher than the average interest rate (1.8 percent) on short-term U.S. government securities from 1948 to 1980 after adjustment for anticipated inflation (Barro, 1987), but it is considerably lower than the 4 percent average rate of return on tangible business capital in the United States during the post–World War II period (Prescott, 1986). Members of this generation do less well because their human capital is not augmented by public spending; however, they may still be better off even if this internal rate of return is less than the appropriate market rate of interest, because their utility is higher when the welfare of the next generation is higher (assuming altruism toward children).

Whatever the conclusion about the initial generation, our results sharply contradict the view that government payments to the elderly in the United States are large relative to government spending on the young. Indeed, any generation that benefits from the current level of public investments in children can easily use the higher earnings created by these investments to provide current levels of support for the elderly, and still have a considerable profit left over. Therefore, children would be happy to enter into a social compact with their parents whereby the children support their parents when old at current levels in return for a commitment to the current level of public support for children.

Our theoretical analysis implies that an efficient compact between the young and the old raises the human capital of children from poorer and middle-class families in return for contributions to the health and income of older members of these families. We indicated earlier that public spending on education favors the poor and middle class. Public spending on medical care also favors poorer families: the rapid growth in public spending on medical care during the past 20 years or so sharply reduced the effect of family income on medical care (Fuchs, 1975). In addition, poor and middle-level older persons are much more likely to live apart from their children than they were before social security became important (Michael et al., 1980).

Divorce

Virtually all societies forbid marriage prior to specified ages; many countries have banned marriages between men and women of different races, religions, and social classes; and Christian countries have not allowed polygamy. Regulation of divorce is equally common. The United States and other Western countries essentially did not allow divorce until the mid-nineteenth century. There were fewer than two (!) divorces per year in England from 1800 to 1850 (Rowntree and Carrier, 1958). Gradually, divorce laws in the West liberalized toward allowing divorce when one party committed adultery, abandoned his or her spouse, or otherwise was seriously "at fault." Divorce by mutual consent also began to be possible, especially when there were no young children. About 20 years ago, the United States and other countries started to allow either spouse to divorce without proving fault or getting consent.

Although some divorces badly sear the children involved, little is known about the usual effects of divorce on children. Among other things, the available evidence cannot distinguish the effect of a divorce from the effect of having parents who do not get along (see Emery, 1982). All altruistic parents consider the interests of children and are less likely to divorce when their children would be adversely affected. Even if we ignore the conflict between divorced parents in determining how much time and money each spends on their children,[5] altruistic parents might still divorce when their children are harmed. Parents who do not leave bequests might divorce even when the money value of the cost to children exceeds the money value of the gain to parents. The reason is that children do not have a credible way to "bribe" their

---

5. This issue is well analyzed in Weiss and Willis (1985).

parents to stay if they cannot commit to old-age support or other future transfers to parents contingent on the parents not getting a divorce.

The story is different in families with bequests. If divorce does not change the degree of altruism toward children and if divorce only affects future earnings and the value of other tradable resources, then children would also be made better off if their parents decide to divorce. The reason is that parents raise their gifts and bequests to compensate children for any losses from the divorce. This is an implication of the Rotten Kid Theorem discussed in Chapter 8.

Nevertheless, children may suffer from a divorce even by parents who give bequests if the divorce reduces the nontradable goods consumed by children. For example, children may be unhappy after a divorce because they seldom see their fathers. Parents cannot directly compensate children for the effect of a divorce on their happiness or other consumption. Indeed, if the effect on nontradables lowers the marginal utility to children of tradable resources, altruistic parents who divorce would *reduce* their gifts of tradables to children and thereby make children still worse off.

We claimed earlier that the degree of altruism is not fixed but often responds to the frequency and intensity of contacts with beneficiaries. In particular, over time a divorced father might become less altruistic toward his children as his contact with them declines. This would explain why many divorced fathers are delinquent in child-support payments,[6] and it strengthens our conclusion that a divorce may make children worse off even when their parents are quite altruistic prior to a divorce and even if they continue to give bequests after a divorce.

A divorce may greatly harm a wife who has many children and cannot earn much in the labor force, especially when her ex-husband fails to meet his financial and other obligations to the children. This consequence may occur even when divorce requires mutual consent, because in many societies husbands can intimidate wives into agreeing to a divorce under terms that are unfavorable to them.

It does not seem farfetched to suggest that the state has often regulated divorce to mimic the terms of contracts between husbands and wives and parents and children that are not feasible. Such contracts, for example, might greatly reduce the incidence of divorce when families have many children, since the aggregate loss to children (and mothers) from divorce would rise with the number of children. Many coun-

---

6. Weiss and Willis (1985) give other reasons.

tries did prohibit divorce when the typical family was large. Moreover, even when a divorce could not be easily obtained, marriages without children often could dissolve—could be "annulled." Divorce laws eased as birth rates began to decline in the nineteenth century. In recent decades, low birth rates and the much higher labor force participation of women stimulated a further easing toward no-fault divorce.

Some parents choose to separate from their children not through divorce but through the sale of their children. The universal ban on this practice strongly suggests that the sale of children lowers social utility. Young unmarried women and poor parents who need money are the two groups most likely to sell their children. Some children sold to prosperous families who want them may consider themselves better off than if they had remained with their parents. But even children who would suffer greatly might be sold because they have no way to compensate their parents for keeping them. Just as a ban on divorce may improve efficiency because certain contracts between parents and children are not feasible, so too may the ban on the sale of children improve efficiency. Nevertheless, Landes and Posner (1978) and Posner (1987) could be correct that a very limited right to sell babies is better than the present controlled adoption system. Note that subsidies to poor families with children through Aid to Families with Dependent Children and other programs encourage unmarried and other poor mothers to keep their children rather than give them up for adoption.

Optimal Population

With a heroic amount of additional imagination, we can consider not only the relation between parents and actual children but also contracts between parents and *potential* children. Such a thought experiment provides a new way of determining optimal family size and optimal population. The literature on optimal population has lacked an attractive guiding principle.[7]

Suppose that a potential child could commit to compensating his parents eventually if he is born. This "contract" would be Pareto improving (we assume that third parties are not hurt by births) if the child would still prefer to be born after compensation to parents that

---

7. See the criticisms of this literature in Meade (1967) and Friedman (1981).

makes them better off. Since such contracts are impossible, some children may not get born even when both parents and children could be better off. Fertility and population growth are too low when compensation from unborn children to their parents would be Pareto improving.

The first-order utility-maximizing condition with respect to number of children implies that parents are indifferent to a small increase in numbers. Unborn children want to compensate parents to change indifference into a positive preference for additional children. All parents might appear to welcome compensation, regardless of their altruism, because compensation lowers the net cost of additional children. This conclusion is correct for parents who do not provide gifts and bequests to children, for these parents would benefit from old-age support or other compensation from children.

The surprising result is that compensation *lowers* the utility of parents who do provide children with gifts and bequests. Compensation from potential children, in effect, reduces the net gift to these children. But parents do not need compensation to reduce gifts since they may reduce them in any case if they so choose. Therefore, families with gifts and bequests to children do have the Pareto-efficient number of children (neglecting effects outside the family): compensation from unborn children makes the parents worse off rather than better off.

This seemingly bizarre thought experiment with unborn children has a very concrete implication. We have shown that poorer families are less likely than richer ones to leave bequests. If commitments for compensation from unborn children are not feasible, fertility in poorer families is too low, and fertility in richer families (who give bequests) is optimal. Therefore, our approach implies—with any third-party effects ignored—that the aggregate private-fertility rate is below the Pareto-efficient rate.

A conclusion that poorer families may have too few children will shock some readers, because poorer families already have larger families than richer ones. But other factors raise fertility of poorer families, including welfare programs, subsidies to education, and limited birth control knowledge.

Thompson and Ruhter (undated) also conclude that parents who do not leave bequests tend to have too few children; but their argument, in contrast to ours, seems to depend on underinvestment in the human capital of each child by these families. Such an argument is incorrect, since underinvestment in children may induce families to have too many rather than too few children. The suboptimal expenditure per child "artificially" lowers the effective cost of an additional child through the interaction between the quantity and quality of children.[8]

Political Competition between Generations

Since public policy results from competition among interest groups, how does competition for political favors lead to efficiency-raising state interventions in the family? In this section we sketch out a possible answer when parental altruism is important.

Political competition between adults and children is hardly a contest; children cannot vote and do not have the means and maturity to organize an effective political coalition. If adults use their political power to issue bonds and other obligations, they can help support themselves when old by selling these obligations to the next generation of younger adults. Some economists support balanced government budgets and limits on debt issue to control such exploitation of the political weakness of children and later generations. Of course, this approach is not a problem if each generation can repudiate debt issues by previous generations. The issues involved in debt repudiation are beyond the scope of this article, so we will simply assume that debt is not repudiated.

Although present generations may be able to exploit future generations, altruism limits their desire to do so. Indeed, if all parents are altruistic and leave bequests, present generations have no desire to exploit future generations. After all, if they want to, they may take resources from future generations by leaving smaller bequests. Although families who do not leave bequests favor debt and other exploitation of the political weakness of future generations, their degree of altruism may greatly affect how they use their political power against future generations.

We have showed that families who do not leave bequests underinvest in the human capital of their children. They can increase the wealth of the children's generation by using their political power to raise education and other training through state schools and subsidies to other investments in children. Then the present generation may, if it wishes, issue obligations to future generations that extract this increase in children's wealth.

---

8. See the analysis in Becker and Murphy (1986) and Nerlove et al. (1986).

Although selfish parents try to extract as much as they can from children, altruistic parents may prefer to share some of the increased wealth with children. This means that future generations may also benefit from the political power of present generations. Therefore, even if the altruism of many parents is not strong enough to lead to positive bequests and efficient investments in human capital, it could be strong enough to ensure that future generations also gain when the present generation uses its political power to issue debt and other obligations to future generations.

This overly simplified analysis of political power and political incentives may help explain why public expenditures on children in the United States are not small compared to public expenditures on the elderly. The next generation gains enough from public expenditures on children by the current generation to pay for social security and other help to the elderly of the current generation, yet the next generation still has some profit left over from the public investment in their human capital.

We have tried to understand the widespread government intervention into family arrangements. We conclude that many public actions achieve more efficient arrangements between parents and children. Clearly, parents and children cannot always make efficient arrangements themselves because children are unable to commit to compensation of parents in the future.

Families who leave bequests can "force" children to repay parents for investments in human capital by reducing bequests. Therefore, these families do not underinvest in children's human capital. By contrast, families (often poorer families) who do not leave bequests do underinvest in children. The state may subsidize schools and other training facilities to raise investments in children by poorer families to efficient levels.

We consider not only subsidies to education and training but also social security and other old-age support, subsidies to births, laws that limit access to divorce and the sale of children, and laws that require parents' permission for early marriage and other choices of children. It is remarkable how many state interventions in family decisions appear to contribute to the efficiency of family arrangements.

BIBLIOGRAPHY

INDEX

Bibliography

Abel, Andrew. 1986. "Long-Run Effects of Fiscal Policy under Altruism and Endogenous Fertility." Unpublished memorandum, Harvard University.

Adams, James D. 1978. "Equalization of True Gift and Estate Tax Rates." *Journal of Public Economics* 9(1): 59–71.

Akerlof, George A. 1970. "The Market for 'Lemons': Quality Uncertainty and the Market Mechanism." *Quarterly Journal of Economics* 84(3): 488–500.

Aleichem, Sholom. 1969. *The Adventures of Menahem-Mendl,* trans. Tamara Kahana. New York: G. P. Putnam's Sons.

Alexander, Richard D., Hoogland, John L., Howard, Richard D., Noonan, Katherine M., and Sherman, Paul W. 1979. "Sexual Dimorphisms and Breeding Systems in Pinnipeds, Ungulates, Primates, and Humans." In *Evolutionary Biology and Human Social Behavior,* ed. Napoleon A. Chagnon and William Irons. North Scituate, Mass.: Duxbury Press.

Alström, Carl H. 1961. "A Study of Inheritance of Human Intelligence." *Acta Psychiatrica et Neurologica Scandinavica* 36(2): 175–202.

Altmann, Stuart A., Wagner, Stephen S., and Lenington, Sarah. 1977. "Two Models for the Evolution of Polygyny." *Behavioral Ecology and Sociobiology* 2(4): 397–410.

American Humane Association. 1984. *Highlights of Official Child Neglect and Abuse Reporting.* Denver.

Anderson, Norman. 1976. *Law Reform in the Muslim World.* London: Athlone Press.

Arrow, Kenneth, and Kurz, Mordecai. 1970. *Public Investment, the Rate of Return, and Optimal Fiscal Policy.* Baltimore: Johns Hopkins University Press.

Arthur, W. Brian. 1982. Review of *A Treatise on the Family. Population and Development Review* 8(2): 393–398.

383

Bibliography

Atkinson, A. B. 1975. *The Economics of Inequality.* Oxford: Clarendon Press.
———. 1981. "On Intergenerational Income Mobility in Britain." *Journal of Post-Keynesian Economics* 3(2): 194–217.
———. 1983. *Social Justice and Public Policy.* Cambridge, Mass.: MIT Press.
Azzi, Corry, and Ehrenberg, Ronald. 1975. "Household Allocation of Time and Church Attendance." *Journal of Political Economy* 83(1): 27–56.
Barash, David P. 1977. *Sociobiology and Behavior.* New York: Elsevier.
Barichello, Richard R. 1979. "The Schooling of Farm Youth in Canada." Ph.D. dissertation, University of Chicago.
Barro, Robert J. 1974. "Are Government Bonds Net Wealth?" *Journal of Political Economy* 82(6): 1095–1117.
———. 1976. "Reply to Feldstein and Buchanan." *Journal of Political Economy* 84(2): 343–349.
———. 1978. *The Impact of Social Security on Private Saving: Evidence from the U.S. Time Series.* Washington, D.C.: American Enterprise Institute for Public Policy Research.
———. 1987. *Macroeconomics,* 2nd ed. New York: Wiley.
Barro, Robert J., and Becker, Gary S. 1985. "Population Growth and Economic Growth." Paper presented at the Workshop in Applications of Economics, University of Chicago.
———. 1989. "Fertility Choice in a Model of Economic Growth." *Econometrica* 57(2): 481–501.
Bash, Wendell H. 1955. "Differential Fertility in Madison County, New York, 1865." *Milbank Memorial Fund Quarterly* 33(2): 161–186.
Becker, Gary S. 1956. "Fertility without Contraception." Unpublished memorandum, University of Chicago.
———. 1960. "An Economic Analysis of Fertility." In *Demographic and Economic Change in Developed Countries,* a conference of the Universities–National Bureau Committee for Economic Research. Princeton: Princeton University Press, for the National Bureau of Economic Research.
———. 1962. "Irrational Behavior and Economic Theory." *Journal of Political Economy* 70(1): 1–13.
———. 1964. *Human Capital,* 1st ed. New York: Columbia University Press, for the National Bureau of Economic Research. See also Becker, 1975.
———. 1965. "A Theory of the Allocation of Time." *Economic Journal* 75(299): 493–517.
———. 1967. "Human Capital and the Personal Distribution of Income: An Analytical Approach." Woytinsky Lecture no. 1, Institute of Public Administration, University of Michigan. Reprinted in Becker, 1975.
———. 1971. *The Economics of Discrimination,* 2nd ed. Chicago: University of Chicago Press.
———. 1973. "A Theory of Marriage: Part I." *Journal of Political Economy* 81(4): 813–846.
———. 1974a. "A Theory of Marriage: Part II." *Journal of Political Economy* 82(2, pt. 2): S11–S26.
———. 1974b. "A Theory of Social Interactions." *Journal of Political Economy* 82(6): 1063–93.
———. 1975. *Human Capital,* 2nd ed. New York: Columbia University Press, for the National Bureau of Economic Research.

———. 1976a. "Altruism, Egoism, and Genetic Fitness: Economics and Sociobiology." *Journal of Economic Literature* 14(3): 817–826.

———. 1976b. *The Economic Approach to Human Behavior.* Chicago: University of Chicago Press.

———. 1977. "A Theory of the Production and Allocation of Effort." National Bureau of Economic Research Working Paper no. 184. Cambridge, Mass.: National Bureau of Economic Research.

———. 1980. "Privacy and Malfeasance: A Comment." *Journal of Legal Studies* 9(4): 823–826.

———. 1981. *A Treatise on the Family,* 1st ed. Cambridge, Mass.: Harvard University Press.

———. 1985. "Human Capital, Effort, and the Sexual Division of Labor." *Journal of Labor Economics* 3(1, pt. 2): S33–S58.

———. 1989. "On the Economics of the Family: Reply to a Skeptic." *American Economic Review* 79(3): 514–518.

Becker, Gary S., and Barro, Robert J. 1985. "A Reformulation of the Economic Theory of Fertility." Discussion Paper no. 85-11. Chicago: Economics Research Center, National Opinion Research Center.

———. 1986. "A Reformulation of the Economic Theory of Fertility." Unpublished memorandum, University of Chicago.

———. 1988. "A Reformulation of the Economic Theory of Fertility." *Quarterly Journal of Economics* 103(1): 1–25.

Becker, Gary S., and Lewis, H. Gregg. 1973. "On the Interaction between the Quantity and Quality of Children." *Journal of Political Economy* 81(2, pt. 2): S279–S288.

Becker, Gary S., and Murphy, Kevin M. 1986. "Incomplete Markets and Investment in Children." Unpublished memorandum, University of Chicago.

———. 1988a. "The Family and the State." *Journal of Law and Economics* 31(1): 1–18.

———. 1988b. "A Theory of Rational Addiction." *Journal of Political Economy* 96(4): 675–700.

Becker, Gary S., and Posner, Richard A. 1981. "Sex Ratios, the Value of Men and Women, and the Incidence of Polygyny in Primitive Societies." Unpublished memorandum, University of Chicago.

Becker, Gary S., and Tomes, Nigel. 1976. "Child Endowments and the Quantity and Quality of Children." *Journal of Political Economy* 84(4, pt. 2): S143–S162.

———. 1979. "An Equilibrium Theory of the Distribution of Income and Intergenerational Mobility." *Journal of Political Economy* 87(6): 1153–89.

———. 1984. "Human Capital and the Rise and Fall of Families." Discussion Paper no. 84-10. Chicago: Economics Research Center, National Opinion Research Center.

———. 1986. "Human Capital and the Rise and Fall of Families." *Journal of Labor Economics* 4(3, pt. 2): S1–S39.

Becker, Gary S., Landes, Elisabeth M., and Michael, Robert T. 1977. "An Economic Analysis of Marital Instability." *Journal of Political Economy* 85(6): 1141–87.

Becker, Gary S., Murphy, Kevin M., and Tamura, Robert. 1990. "Human Capital, Economic Growth and Population Growth." *Journal of Political Economy* (in press).

Beesley, M. E. 1965. "The Value of Time Spent in Travelling: Some New Evidence." *Economica* 32(126): 174–185.

Behrman, Jere, and Taubman, Paul. 1976. "Intergenerational Transmission of Income and Wealth." *American Economic Review* 66(2): 436–440.

———. 1983. "Intergenerational Mobility in Earnings in the U.S." Unpublished memorandum, Center for Family and Household Economics, University of Pennsylvania.

———. 1985. "Intergenerational Earnings and Mobility in the United States: Some Estimates and a Test of Becker's Intergenerational Endowments Model." *Review of Economics and Statistics* 67(1): 144–151.

Behrman, Jere, Pollak, Robert, and Taubman, Paul. 1982. "Parental Preferences and Provision of Progeny." *Journal of Political Economy* 90(1): 52–73.

Ben-Porath, Yoram. 1973. "Economic Analysis of Fertility in Israel: Point and Counterpoint." *Journal of Political Economy* 81(2, pt. 2): S202–S233.

———. 1980. "The F-Connection: Families, Friends, and Firms and the Organization of Exchange." *Population and Development Review* 6(1): 1–30.

Ben-Porath, Yoram, and Welch, Finis. 1976. "Do Sex Preferences *Really* Matter?" *Quarterly Journal of Economics* 90(2): 285–307.

Bentham, Jeremy. 1963. *An Introduction to the Principles of Morals and Legislation.* New York: Hafner.

Bergstrom, Theodore. 1989. "A Fresh Look at the Rotten-Kid Theorem—And Other Household Mysteries." *Journal of Political Economy* 97(5): 1138–59.

Berkov, Beth, and Sklar, June. 1976. "Does Illegitimacy Make a Difference? A Study of the Life Chances of Illegitimate Children in California." *Population and Development Review* 2(2): 201–217.

Bernheim, B. Douglas, and Bagwell, Kyle. 1988. "Is Everything Neutral?" *Journal of Political Economy* 96(2): 308–338.

Bernheim, B. Douglas, Shleifer, Andrei, and Summers, Larry H. 1986. "The Strategic Bequest Motive." *Journal of Labor Economics* 4(3, pt. 2): S151–S182.

Bernstam, Mikhail S., and Swan, Peter L. 1986. "The Production of Children as a Claim on the State: A Comprehensive Labor Market Approach to Illegitimacy in the U.S., 1960–1980." Current Working Paper in Economics, Domestic Studies Program, Hoover Institution.

Bevan, D. L. 1979. "Inheritance and the Distribution of Wealth." *Economica* 46(184): 381–402.

Bevan, D. L., and Stiglitz, J. E. 1979. "Intergenerational Transfers and Inequality." *Greek Economic Review* 1(1): 6–26.

Bielby, William T., and Hauser, Robert M. 1977. "Response Error in Earnings Functions for Nonblack Males." *Sociological Methods and Research* 6(2): 241–280.

Bielby, William T., Hauser, Robert M., and Featherman, David L. 1977. "Response Errors of Black and Nonblack Males in Models of the Intergenerational Transmission of Socioeconomic Status." *American Journal of Sociology* 82(6): 1242–88.

Black, John D., and Black, Albert G. 1929. *Production Organization.* New York: Henry Holt.

Blake, Judith. 1968. "Are Babies Consumer Durables? A Critique of the

Economic Theory of Reproduction Motivation." *Population Studies* 22(1): 5–25.

———. 1981. "Family Size and the Quality of Children." *Demography* 18(4): 421–442.

Blau, Peter M., and Duncan, Otis D. 1967. *The American Occupational Structure*. New York: Wiley.

Blinder, Alan S. 1973. "A Model of Inherited Wealth." *Quarterly Journal of Economics* 87(4): 608–626.

———. 1974. *Toward an Economic Theory of Income Distribution*. Cambridge, Mass.: MIT Press.

———. 1976. "Inequality and Mobility in the Distribution of Wealth." *Kyklos* 29(4): 607–638.

Blinder, Alan S., and Weiss, Yoram. 1976. "Human Capital and Labor Supply: A Synthesis." *Journal of Political Economy* 84(3): 449–472.

Bloom, Benjamin S. 1976. *Human Characteristics and School Learning*. New York: McGraw-Hill.

Blurton Jones, Nicholas, and Sibly, R. M. 1978. "Testing Adaptiveness of Culturally Determined Behaviour: Do Bushman Women Maximize Their Reproductive Success by Spacing Births Widely and Foraging Seldom?" In *Human Behaviour and Adaptation*, ed. Nicholas Blurton Jones and Vernon Reynolds. Symposia of the Society for the Study of Human Biology, vol. 18. London: Taylor and Francis.

Bogue, Donald J., and Tsui, Amy O. 1979. "A Reply to Paul Demeny's 'On the End of the Population Explosion.' " *Population and Development Review* 5(3): 479–494.

Borjas, George J. 1979. "Job Satisfaction, Wages, and Unions." *Journal of Human Resources* 14(1): 21–40.

Boserup, Ester. 1970. *Woman's Role in Economic Development*. London: Allen & Unwin.

———. 1987. "Inequality Between the Sexes." In *The New Palgrave: A Dictionary of Economics*, ed. John Eatwell, Murray Milgate, and Peter Newman, pp. 824–827. New York: Macmillan.

Boswell, James. 1959. *Boswell for the Defence, 1769–1774*, ed. William K. Wimsatt, Jr., and Frederick A. Pottle. New York: McGraw-Hill.

Boudon, Raymond. 1974. *Education, Opportunity, and Social Inequality*. New York: Wiley.

Boulding, Kenneth E. 1973. *The Economy of Love and Fear*. Belmont, Calif.: Wadsworth.

Bowles, Samuel. 1972. "Schooling and Inequality from Generation to Generation." *Journal of Political Economy* 80(3, pt. 2): S219–S251.

Brenner, Reuven. 1979. "Human Capital and Changing Circumstances." Paper presented at the Workshop in Applications of Economics, University of Chicago.

Brittain, John A. 1977. *The Inheritance of Economic Status*. Washington, D.C.: Brookings Institution.

Bruce, Neil, and Waldman, Michael. 1986. "The Rotten-Kid Theorem Meets the Samaritan's Dilemma." Working Paper no. 402, University of California at Los Angeles.

Buchanan, James M., and Wagner, Richard E. 1977. *Democracy in Deficit: The Political Legacy of Lord Keynes*. New York: Academic Press.

Burchinal, Lee G., and Chancellor, Loren E. 1962. "Ages at Marriage, Occu-

Bibliography

pations of Grooms and Interreligious Marriage Rates." *Social Forces* 40(4): 348–354.

Butz, William P., and Ward, Michael P. 1979a. "The Emergence of Counter-cyclical U.S. Fertility." *American Economic Review* 69(3): 318–328.

———. 1979b. "Will U.S. Fertility Remain Low? A New Economic Interpretation." *Population and Development Review* 5(4): 663–688.

Cain, Glen G. 1966. *Married Women in the Labor Force: An Economic Analysis.* Chicago: University of Chicago Press.

Carey, Michael, and Nolan, Val, Jr. 1975. "Polygyny in Indigo Buntings: A Hypothesis Tested." *Science* 190 (4221): 1296–97.

Casteñeda, Tarsicio. 1979. "Fertility, Child Schooling, and the Labor Force Participation of Mothers in Colombia, 1977." Ph.D. dissertation, University of Chicago.

Cavalli-Sforza, Luigi L., and Feldman, Marcus W. 1973. "Models for Cultural Inheritance. I. Group Mean and Within Group Variation." *Theoretical Population Biology* 4(1): 42–55.

Champernowne, David G. 1953. "A Model of Income Distribution." *Economic Journal* 63(250): 318–351.

Chang, Fwu-Ranq. 1979. "A Theory of Joint Production." Unpublished memorandum, University of Chicago.

Charnov, Eric L. 1976. "Optimal Foraging: Attack Strategy of a Mantid." *American Naturalist* 110(971): 141–151.

Cheung, Steven N. S. 1972. "The Enforcement of Property Rights in Children, and the Marriage Contract." *Economic Journal* 82(326): 641–657.

Chiswick, Barry R. 1974. *Income Inequality.* New York: Columbia University Press, for the National Bureau of Economic Research.

Chiswick, Barry R., and O'Neill, June A., eds. 1977. *Human Resources and Income Distribution.* New York: W. W. Norton.

Christensen, Harold T., and Barber, Kenneth E. 1967. "Interfaith Versus Intrafaith Marriage in Indiana." *Journal of Marriage and the Family* 29(3): 461–469.

Christensen, Harold T., and Meissner, Hanna H. 1953. "Studies in Child Spacing: III—Premarital Pregnancy as a Factor in Divorce." *American Sociological Review* 18(6): 641–644.

Coale, Ansley J., Demeny, Paul, and Vaughan, Barbara. 1983. *Regional Model Life Tables and Stable Populations.* New York: Academic Press.

Coase, R. H. 1960. "The Problem of Social Cost." *Journal of Law and Economics* 3(1): 1–44.

———. 1976. "Adam Smith's View of Man." *Journal of Law and Economics* 19(3): 529–546.

Collard, David. 1978. *Altruism and Economy.* New York: Oxford University Press.

Conlisk, John. 1974. "Can Equalization of Opportunity Reduce Social Mobility?" *American Economic Review* 64(1): 80–90.

Cooper, J. P. 1976. "Patterns of Inheritance and Settlement by Great Landowners from the Fifteenth to the Eighteenth Centuries." In *Family and Inheritance,* ed. Jack Goody, Joan Thirsk, and E. P. Thompson. New York: Cambridge University Press.

Coulson, N. J. 1964. *A History of Islamic Law.* Islamic Surveys 2. Edinburgh: Edinburgh University Press.

Darwin, Charles. 1872. *The Descent of Man and Selection in Relation to Sex,* 2 vols. New York: D. Appleton.

———. 1958. *The Autobiography of Charles Darwin and Selected Letters,* ed. Francis Darwin. New York: Dover Publications.

Das, Man Singh. 1978. "A Cross-National Study of the Effect of Intercaste Marriage on Fertility in India and the United States." *International Journal of Sociology of the Family* 8(2): 145–157.

Davidovitch, David. 1968. *The Ketuba.* Tel Aviv: E. Lewin-Epstein.

Dawkins, Richard. 1976. *The Selfish Gene.* New York: Oxford University Press.

Dawson, Deborah A., Meny, Denise J., and Ridley, Jeanne C. 1980. "Fertility Control in the United States before the Contraceptive Revolution." *Family Planning Perspectives* 12(2): 76–86.

Demeny, Paul. 1979a. "On the End of the Population Explosion." *Population and Development Review* 5(1): 141–162.

———. 1979b. "On the End of the Population Explosion: A Rejoinder." *Population and Development Review* 5(3): 495–504.

Denison, Edward F. 1962. *Sources of Economic Growth in the United States.* Washington, D.C.: Committee for Economic Development.

———. 1979. *Accounting for Slower Economic Growth.* Washington, D.C.: Brookings Institution.

De Tray, Dennis N. 1973. "Child Quality and the Demand for Children." *Journal of Political Economy* 81(2, pt. 2): S70–S95.

———. 1978. "Child Schooling and Family Size: An Economic Analysis." R-2301-NICHD. Santa Monica, Calif.: RAND Corporation.

Dewey, John. 1889. "Galton's Statistical Methods." *Publications of the American Statistical Association* 1(7): 331–334.

Diamond, Arthur M., Jr. 1980. "Estimation of a Model of Intergenerational Mobility, with Special Attention to the Mobility of Blacks." Report no. 8031, Center for Mathematical Studies in Business and Economics, University of Chicago.

Dickemann, Mildred. 1979. "Female Infanticide, Reproductive Strategies, and Social Stratification: A Preliminary Model." In *Evolutionary Biology and Human Social Behavior,* ed. Napoleon A. Chagnon and William Irons. North Scituate, Mass.: Duxbury Press.

Dickens, Charles. 1867. *Bleak House.* Boston: Ticknor and Fields.

Dingewall, Robert, and Eckelaar, John. 1984. "Rethinking Child Protection." In *State Law and the Family,* ed. Michael D. A. Freeman. London: Tavistock Publications.

Dixon, Ruth B., and Weitzman, Lenore J. 1980. "Evaluating the Impact of No-Fault Divorce in California." *Family Relations* 29(3): 297–307.

Dorjahn, Vernon R. 1959. "The Factor of Polygyny in African Demography." In *Continuity and Change in African Cultures,* ed. William R. Bascom and Melville J. Herskovits. Chicago: University of Chicago Press.

Downhower, Jerry F., and Armitage, Kenneth B. 1971. "The Yellow-Bellied Marmot and the Evolution of Polygamy." *American Naturalist* 105(944): 355–370.

Drazen, Allan. 1978. "Government Debt, Human Capital and Bequests in a Life-Cycle Model." *Journal of Political Economy* 86(3): 505–516.

Durkheim, Emile. 1933. *On The Division of Labor in Society,* trans. George Simpson. New York: Macmillan.

Dyson, Tim, and Murphy, Mike. 1985. "The Onset of Fertility Transition." *Population and Development Review* 11(3): 1399–1440.

Easterlin, Richard A. 1968. *Population, Labor Force, and Long Swings in*

Economic Growth. New York: Columbia University Press, for the National Bureau of Economic Research.

———. 1973. "Relative Economic Status and the American Fertility Swing." In *Family Economic Behavior*, ed. Eleanor B. Sheldon. Philadelphia: J. B. Lippincott.

Eaton, Joseph W., and Mayer, Albert J. 1953. "The Social Biology of Very High Fertility among the Hutterites: The Demography of a Unique Population." *Human Biology* 25(3): 206–264.

Edwards, Linda N., and Grossman, Michael. 1978. "Children's Health and the Family." Working Paper no. 256. New York: National Bureau of Economic Research.

Ehrlich, Isaac, and Ben-Zion, Uri. 1976. "Asset Management, Allocation of Time, and Returns to Saving." *Economic Inquiry* 14(4): 558–586.

Emery, Robert E. 1982. "Interpersonal Conflict and the Children of Discord and Divorce." *Psychological Bulletin* 92(2): 310–330.

Epstein, Larry G., and Hynes, J. Allen. 1983. "The Rate of Time Preference and Dynastic Economic Analysis." *Journal of Political Economy* 91(4): 611–635.

Espenshade, Thomas J. 1977. "The Value and Cost of Children." *Population Bulletin* 32(1). Washington, D.C.: Population Reference Bureau.

———. 1984. *Investing in Children: New Estimates of Parental Expenditures*. Washington, D.C.: Urban Institute Press.

Featherman, David L., and Hauser, Robert M. 1976. "Changes in the Socioeconomic Stratification of the Races, 1962–1973." *American Journal of Sociology* 82(3): 621–651.

Feldstein, Martin S. 1974. "Social Security, Induced Retirement, and Aggregate Capital Accumulation." *Journal of Political Economy* 82(5): 905–926.

———. 1976. "Perceived Wealth in Bonds and Social Security: A Comment." *Journal of Political Economy* 84(2): 331–336.

Fernea, Elizabeth W. 1965. *Guests of the Sheik*. Garden City, N.Y.: Doubleday.

Finley, M. I. 1980. *Ancient Slavery and Modern Ideology*. New York: Viking.

Fisher, R. A. 1958. *The Genetical Theory of Natural Selection*, 2nd ed. New York: Dover Publications.

Flinn, Christopher, and Heckman, James J. 1980. "Models for the Analysis of Labor Force Dynamics." Paper presented at the Workshop in Applications of Economics, University of Chicago.

Flood, L. 1983. "Time Allocation to Market and Non-Market Activities in Swedish Households." Department of Statistics Research Report. Göteborg: University of Göteborg.

Foster, Henry H., and Freed, Doris J. 1974. "Divorce Reform: Brakes on Breakdown?" *Journal of Family Law* 13(3): 443–493.

Fox, Robin. 1969. *Kinship and Marriage*. Baltimore: Penguin.

France: Institut national de la statistique et des études économiques. 1956. *Recensement Général de la Population de Mai 1954: France Entière*. Paris: Imprimerie Nationale.

———. 1964. *Recensement Général de la Population de 1962: Population Active*. Paris: Direction des journaux officiels.

———. 1971. *Recensement Général de la Population de 1968: Population Active*. Paris: Imprimerie Nationale.

————. 1978a. *Annuaire Statistique de la France 1978,* vol. 83.
————. 1978b. *Recensement Général de la Population de 1975: Population Active.* Paris: Imprimerie Nationale.
Freeman, Richard B. 1981. "Black Economic Progress after 1964: Who Has Gained and Why?" In *Studies in Labor Markets,* ed. Sherwin Rosen. Chicago: University of Chicago Press, for the National Bureau of Economic Research.
Freiden, Alan. 1974. "The United States Marriage Market." *Journal of Political Economy* 82(2, pt. 2): S34–S53.
Freudenberger, Herman, and Cummins, Gaylord. 1976. "Health, Work, and Leisure before the Industrial Revolution." *Explorations in Economic History* 13(1): 1–12.
Friedman, David. 1981. "What Does 'Optimum Population' Mean?" *Research in Population Economics* 3: 273–287.
Friedman, Milton. 1955. "The Role of Government in Education." In *Economics and Public Interest,* ed. Robert Solo. New Brunswick, N.J.: Rutgers University Press.
Friedman, Mordechai A. 1969. "Termination of the Marriage upon the Wife's Request: A Palestinian Ketubba Stipulation." *Proceedings of the American Academy for Jewish Research* 37: 29–55.
Fuchs, Victor R. 1975. *Who Shall Live?: Health, Economics and Social Choice.* New York: Basic Books.
————. 1983. *How We Live.* Cambridge, Mass.: Harvard University Press.
Gale, David, and Shapley, Lloyd S. 1962. "College Admissions and the Stability of Marriage." *American Mathematical Monthly* 69(1): 9–15.
Galsworthy, John. 1949. *The Forsyte Saga.* New York: Scribner's.
Gardner, Bruce. 1973. "Economics of the Size of North Carolina Rural Families." *Journal of Political Economy* 81(2, pt. 2): S99–S122.
Geertz, Clifford. 1978. "The Bazaar Economy: Information and Search in Peasant Marketing." *American Economic Review* 68(2): 28–32.
Ghez, Gilbert R., and Becker, Gary S. 1975. *The Allocation of Time and Goods over the Life Cycle.* New York: Columbia University Press, for the National Bureau of Economic Research.
Ghiselin, Michael T. 1974. *The Economy of Nature and the Evolution of Sex.* Berkeley: University of California Press.
Girod, Roger. 1984. "Intra- and Intergenerational Income Mobility: A Geneva Survey (1950–1980)." Paper presented at the meeting of the International Sociological Association Research Committee on Stratification, Budapest, September 1984.
Goitein, S. D. 1978. *A Mediterranean Society.* Vol. 3, *The Family.* Berkeley: University of California Press.
Goldberger, Arthur S. 1978. "Models and Methods in the I.Q. Debate: Part I." Working paper, Social Systems Research Institute, University of Wisconsin-Madison.
————. 1979. "Family Data Analysis: Assortment, Selection, and Transmission." Proposal to the National Science Foundation.
————. 1985. "Modelling the Economic Family." Woytinsky Lecture, Institute of Public Administration, University of Michigan.
————. 1989. "Economic and Mechanical Models of Intergenerational Transmission." *American Economic Review* 79(3): 504–513.
Goldin, Claudia. 1977. "Female Labor Force Participation: The Origin of

Black and White Differences, 1870 and 1880." *Journal of Economic History* 37(1): 87–108.

Goldin, Claudia, and Parsons, Donald O. 1984. "Industrialization, Child Labor, and Family Economic Well-Being." Unpublished memorandum, University of Pennsylvania.

Goldschmidt, Walter. 1973. "The Brideprice of the Sebei." *Scientific American* 229(1): 74–85.

Gomez, Miguel. 1980. "An Analysis of Fertility in Mexico." Ph.D. dissertation, University of Chicago.

Goode, William J. 1956. *After Divorce*. Glencoe, Ill.: Free Press.

————. 1963. *World Revolution and Family Patterns*. New York: Free Press.

————. 1974. "Comment: The Economics of Nonmonetary Variables." *Journal of Political Economy* 82(2, pt. 2): S27–S33.

Goody, Jack. 1976. *Production and Reproduction*. London: Cambridge University Press.

Goody, Jack, Thirsk, Joan, and Thompson, E. P., eds. 1976. *Family and Inheritance*. New York: Cambridge University Press.

Goudy, Henry. 1911. "Roman Law." In *Encyclopaedia Britannica*, 11th ed., vol. 23, pp. 526–576. Cambridge: Cambridge University Press.

Great Britain: Central Statistical Office. 1980. *Annual Abstract of Statistics,* 1980 ed. London: Her Majesty's Stationery Office.

Great Britain: Department of Employment. 1975. "Labour Force Projections, 1976–1991: Great Britain and the Regions." *Department of Employment Gazette* 83(12): 1258–63.

————. 1978. "Labour Force Projections: Further Estimates." *Department of Employment Gazette* 86(4): 426–427.

Great Britain: Registrar General. 1957. *Statistical Review of England and Wales for the Year 1955*. Pt. 3, Commentary. London: Her Majesty's Stationery Office.

————. 1975. *Statistical Review of England and Wales for the Year 1973*. Pt. 2, Tables, Population. London: Her Majesty's Stationery Office.

Gregory, R. G., McMahon, P. J., and Whittingham, B. 1985. "Women in the Australian Labor Force: Trends, Causes and Consequences." *Journal of Labor Economics* 3(1, Supplement): S293–S309.

Griliches, Zvi. 1979. "Sibling Models and Data in Economics: Beginnings of a Survey." *Journal of Political Economy* 87(5, pt. 2): S37–S64.

Gronau, Reuben. 1970. "The Effect of Traveling Time on the Demand for Passenger Transportation." *Journal of Political Economy* 78(2): 377–394.

————. 1976. "The Allocation of Time of Israeli Women." *Journal of Political Economy* 84(4, pt. 2): S201–S220.

Gros, Daniel. 1983. "Increasing Returns and Human Capital in International Trade." Thesis seminar paper, Department of Economics, University of Chicago.

Grossbard, Amyra. 1976. "An Economic Analysis of Polygyny: The Case of Maiduguri." *Current Anthropology* 17(4): 701–707.

————. 1978. "The Economics of Polygamy." Ph.D. dissertation, University of Chicago.

Grossman, Michael. 1971. "The Economics of Joint Production in the Household." Report no. 7145, Center for Mathematical Studies in Business and Economics, University of Chicago.

———. 1972. *The Demand for Health: A Theoretical and Empirical Investigation.* Occasional paper no. 119. New York: Columbia University Press, for the National Bureau of Economic Research.

———. 1976. "The Correlation between Health and Schooling." In *Household Production and Consumption,* ed. N. E. Terleckyj. New York: Columbia University Press, for the National Bureau of Economic Research.

Gustafsson, Siv, and Jacobsson, Roger. 1985. "Trends in Female Labor Force Participation in Sweden." *Journal of Labor Economics* 3(1, Supplement): S256–S274.

Gutman, Herbert G. 1976. *The Black Family in Slavery and Freedom, 1750–1925.* New York: Pantheon Books.

Halpern, Joel M. 1972. "Town and Countryside in Serbia in the Nineteenth Century, Social and Household Structure as Reflected in the Census of 1863." In *Household and Family in Past Time,* ed. Peter Laslett. London: Cambridge University Press.

Hamilton, W. D. 1964. "The Genetical Evolution of Social Behavior: I, II." *Journal of Theoretical Biology* 7(1): 1–16, 17–52.

Hammel, E. A. 1972. "The Zadruga as Process." In *Household and Family in Past Time,* ed. Peter Laslett. London: Cambridge University Press.

Hannan, Michael T., Tuma, Nancy B., and Groeneveld, Lyle P. 1977. "Income and Marital Events: Evidence from an Income-Maintenance Experiment." *American Journal of Sociology* 82(6): 1186–1211.

Harbury, C. D., and Hitchens, D. M. W. N. 1979. *Inheritance and Wealth Inequality in Britain.* London: Allen & Unwin.

Hashimoto, Masanori. 1974. "Economics of Postwar Fertility in Japan: Differentials and Trends." *Journal of Political Economy* 82(2, pt. 2): S170–S194.

Hauser, Robert M. 1990. "Earnings Trajectories of Young Men." In *Social Stratification in Japan and the United States,* ed. D. J. Treiman and K. Tominaga. Forthcoming.

Hauser, Robert M., Sewell, William H., and Lutterman, Kenneth G. 1975. "Socioeconomic Background, Ability, and Achievement." In *Education, Occupation and Earnings,* ed. William H. Sewell and Robert M. Hauser. New York: Academic Press.

Hawthorne, Nathaniel. 1864. *The Scarlet Letter.* Boston: Ticknor and Fields.

Heckman, James J. 1976. "A Life-Cycle Model of Earnings, Learning and Consumption." *Journal of Political Economy* 84(4, pt. 2): S11–S44.

———. 1981. "Heterogeneity and State Dependence." In *Studies in Labor Markets,* ed. Sherwin Rosen. Chicago: University of Chicago Press, for the National Bureau of Economic Research.

Heckman, James J., and Hotz, V. Joseph. 1985. "The Labor Market Earnings of Panamanian Males." Unpublished memorandum, University of Chicago.

Heimer, Carol A., and Stinchcombe, Arthur L. 1979. "Love and Irrationality: It's Got to be Rational to Love You Because It Makes Me So Happy." Unpublished memorandum, University of Arizona.

Hemming, Richard. 1984. *Poverty and Incentives: The Economics of Social Security.* Oxford: Oxford University Press.

Henry, Louis. 1965. "The Population in France in the Eighteenth Century." In *Population in History,* ed. D. V. Glass and D. E. C. Eversley. Chicago: Aldine.

Bibliography

Herlihy, David. 1977. "Deaths, Marriages, Births, and the Tuscan Economy (ca. 1300–1550)." In *Population Patterns in the Past*, ed. Ronald D. Lee. New York: Academic Press.

Herning, William W., comp. 1809–1823. *The Statutes at Large: Being a Collection of All the Laws of Virginia*, 13 volumes. Vol. 9, pp. 226–227.

Herrnstein, Richard J. 1971. "I.Q." *Atlantic* 228(3): 43–58.

Herskovits, Melville J. 1965. *Economic Anthropology*. New York: W. W. Norton.

Hicks, J. R. 1957. *The Theory of Wages*. Gloucester, Mass.: Peter Smith.

Hill, M. S. 1981. "Patterns of Time Use." Unpublished memorandum, Survey Research Center, University of Michigan.

Himes, Norman E. 1963. *Medical History of Contraception*. New York: Gamut Press.

Hirshleifer, Jack. 1955. "The Exchange between Quantity and Quality." *Quarterly Journal of Economics* 69(4): 596–606.

———. 1977a. "Economics from a Biological Viewpoint." *Journal of Law and Economics* 20(1): 1–52.

———. 1977b. "Shakespeare *vs.* Becker on Altruism: The Importance of Having the Last Word." *Journal of Economic Literature* 15(2): 500–502.

Hodge, Robert W. 1966. "Occupational Mobility as a Probability Process." *Demography* 3(1): 19–34.

Honig, Marjorie. 1974. "AFDC Income, Recipient Rates, and Family Dissolution." *Journal of Human Resources* 9(3): 303–322.

Houthakker, H. S. 1952. "Compensated Changes in Quantities and Qualities Consumed." *Review of Economic Studies* 19(3): 155–164.

———. 1975. "The Size Distribution of Labor Incomes Derived from the Distribution of Aptitudes." In *Econometrics and Economic Theory*, ed. Willy Sellekaerts. New York: Macmillan.

Hume, David. 1854. "Of Polygamy and Divorces." In *The Philosophical Works of David Hume*, vol. 3. Boston: Little, Brown.

Inalcik, Halil. 1970. "The Rise of the Ottoman Empire." In *The Cambridge History of Islam*, vol. 1, ed. P. M. Holt, A. K. S. Lambton, and Bernard Lewis. Cambridge: Cambridge University Press.

India: Office of the Registrar General. 1976. *Census of India, 1971.* Ser. 1, India, Pt. II-c(ii), Social and Cultural Tables. New Delhi.

Iran: Statistical Centre. 1968. *National Census of Population and Housing, November 1966*. Tehran.

Ishikawa, Tsuneo. 1975. "Family Structures and Family Values in the Theory of Income Distribution." *Journal of Political Economy* 83(5): 987–1008.

Jacobson, Howard N. 1980. "A Randomized Controlled Trial of Prenatal Nutritional Supplementation." *Pediatrics* 65(4): 835–836.

Jaffe, A. J. 1940. "Differential Fertility in the White Population in Early America." *Journal of Heredity* 31(9): 407–411.

Japan: Bureau of Statistics. 1961. *Population of Japan, 1960 (Summary)*. Office of the Prime Minister. Tokyo.

———. 1962. *Japan Statistical Yearbook, 1962*. Tokyo.

———. 1977. *Japan Statistical Yearbook, 1977*. Tokyo.

———. 1989. *Japan Statistical Yearbook, 1989*. Tokyo.

Japan: Statistics Bureau. 1980. *Japan Statistical Yearbook, 1980*. Tokyo.

Jaynes, Gregory. 1980. "African Apocalypse." *New York Times Magazine*, November 16, pp. 74–86.

Jenni, Donald A. 1974. "Evolution of Polyandry in Birds." *American Zoologist* 14(1): 129–144.

Jensen, Arthur R. 1969. "How Much Can We Boost IQ and Scholastic Achievement?" *Harvard Educational Review* 39(1): 1–123.

Jovanovic, Boyan. 1978. "Adverse Selection under Symmetric Information." Paper presented at the Workshop in Applications of Economics, University of Chicago.

Juhn, Chinhui, Murphy, Kevin M., and Pierce, Brooks. 1989. "Wage Inequality and the Rise in Returns to Skill." Unpublished memorandum, University of Chicago.

Kaldor, Nicholas. 1956. "Alternative Theories of Distribution." *Review of Economic Studies* 23(2): 83–100.

Keeley, Michael C. 1974. "A Model of Marital Formation: The Determinants of the Optimal Age at First Marriage." Ph.D. dissertation, University of Chicago.

———. 1977. "The Economics of Family Formation." *Economic Inquiry* 15(2): 238–250.

———. 1980. "The Effects of Alternative Negative Income Tax Programs on Marital Dissolution." Paper presented at the Workshop in Applications of Economics, University of Chicago.

Kelley, Jonathan, Robinson, Robert U., and Klein, Herbert S. 1981. "A Theory of Social Mobility, with Data on Status Attainment in a Peasant Society." In *Research in Social Stratification and Mobility*, vol. 1, ed. Donald J. Treiman and Robert V. Robertson. Greenwich, Conn.: JAI Press.

Keniston, Kenneth, and the Carnegie Council on Children. 1977. *All Our Children*. New York: Harcourt Brace Jovanovich.

Kennedy, Finola. 1988. *Family, Economy and Government in Ireland*. Paper no. 143, Economic and Social Research Institute, Dublin.

Kenny, Lawrence W. 1977. "The Demands for Child Quality and for Educational Inputs, the Production of Child Quality, and Related Topics." Ph.D. dissertation, University of Chicago.

———. 1983. "The Accumulation of Human Capital during Marriage by Males." *Economic Inquiry* 21(2): 223–231.

Kimball, Miles S. 1987. "Making Sense of Two-Sided Altruism." *Journal of Monetary Economics* 20(2): 301–326.

Klapisch, Christiane. 1972. "Household Production and Family in Tuscany in 1427." In *Household and Family in Past Time*, ed. Peter Laslett. London: Cambridge University Press.

Kleiman, Ephraim, and Kop, Yaakov. 1978. "Who Trades with Whom—The Income Pattern of International Trade." Research Report no. 106, Department of Economics, Hebrew University of Jerusalem.

Knodel, John E. 1974. *The Decline of Fertility in Germany, 1871–1939*. Princeton: Princeton University Press.

Kogut, Edy L. 1972. "The Economic Analysis of Demographic Phenomena: A Case Study for Brazil." Ph.D. dissertation, University of Chicago.

Koopmans, Tjalling C., and Beckmann, Martin. 1957. "Assignment Problems and the Location of Economic Activities." *Econometrica* 25(1): 53–76.

Kotlikoff, Laurence J., Shoven, John, and Spivak, Avia. 1986. "The Effect of Annuity Insurance on Savings and Inequality." *Journal of Labor Economics* 4(3, pt. 2): S183–S207.

Kuratani, Masatoshi. 1973. "A Theory of Training, Earnings, and Employment: An Application to Japan." Ph.D. dissertation, Columbia University.

Kurz, Mordecai. 1977. "Altruistic Equilibrium." In *Economic Progress, Private Values, and Public Policy,* ed. Bela Balassa and Richard Nelson. New York: North-Holland.

Lack, David. 1968. *Ecological Adaptations for Breeding in Birds.* London: Methuen.

Laitner, J. P. 1979. "Household Bequests, Perfect Expectations, and the National Distribution of Wealth." *Econometrica* 47(5): 1175–93.

Landes, Elisabeth M., and Posner, Richard. 1978. "The Economics of the Baby Shortage." *Journal of Legal Studies* 7(2): 323–348.

Landes, William M., and Posner, Richard A. 1978. "Salvors, Finders, Good Samaritans, and Other Rescuers: An Economic Study of Law and Altruism." *Journal of Legal Studies* 7(1): 83–128.

Landes, William M., and Solmon, Lewis C. 1972. "Compulsory Schooling Legislation: An Economic Analysis of Law and Social Change in the Nineteenth Century." *Journal of Economic History* 32(1): 54–91.

Laslett, Peter, ed. 1972. *Household and Family in Past Time.* London: Cambridge University Press.

Lazear, Edward P. 1972. Econometric appendix for "On the Shadow Price of Children," by Robert T. Michael and Edward P. Lazear. Unpublished memorandum, University of Chicago.

———. 1977. "Schooling as a Wage Depressant." *Journal of Human Resources* 12(2): 164–176.

———. 1978. "Resource Allocation within an Organization Unit: Theory and Application to the Family." Unpublished memorandum, University of Chicago and National Bureau of Economic Research.

Le Boeuf, Burney J. 1974. "Male-Male Competition and Reproductive Success in Elephant Seals." *American Zoologist* 14(1): 163–176.

Lecky, William E. H. 1880. *History of European Morals,* vol. 2. New York: D. Appleton.

Leonard, Karen I. 1978. *Social History of an Indian Caste.* Berkeley: University of California Press.

Le Roy Ladurie, Emmanuel. 1978. *Montaillou,* trans. Barbara Bray. New York: George Braziller.

Levy, Frank. 1987. *Dollars and Dreams.* New York: Russell Sage.

Lewis, H. Gregg. 1986. *Union Relative Wage Effects: A Survey.* Chicago: University of Chicago Press.

Lillard, Lee A., and Willis, Robert J. 1978. "Dynamic Aspects of Earning Mobility." *Econometrica* 46(5): 985–1012.

Lindbeck, Asser, and Weibull, Jorgen W. 1987. "Strategic Interaction with Altruism: The Economics of *Fait Accompli.*" Unpublished paper, University of Stockholm.

———. 1988. "Altruism and Time Consistency: The Politics of *Fait Accompli.*" *Journal of Political Economy* 96(6): 1165–92.

Linder, Steffan B. 1961. *An Essay on Trade and Transformation.* New York: Wiley.

Lisco, T. E. 1967. "The Value of Commuters' Travel Time: A Study in Urban Transportation." Ph.D. dissertation, University of Chicago.

Livi-Bacci, Massimo. 1977. *A History of Italian Fertility.* Princeton: Princeton University Press.

Long, Clarence D. 1958. *The Labor Force under Changing Income and Employment.* Princeton: Princeton University Press, for the National Bureau of Economic Research.

Longman, Philip. 1985. "Justice between the Generations." *Atlantic Monthly* 255(6): 73–81.

Loury, Glenn C. 1976. "Essays in the Theory of Distribution of Income." Ph.D. dissertation, Massachusetts Institute of Technology.

———. 1981. "Intergenerational Transfers and the Distribution of Earnings." *Econometrica* 49(4): 843–867.

Lucas, Robert E., Jr. 1978. "On Size Distribution of Business Firms." *Bell Journal of Economics* 9(2): 508–523.

Lydall, Harold. 1968. *The Structure of Earnings.* Oxford: Clarendon Press.

McCarthy, Justin. 1979. "Age, Family, and Migration in Nineteenth-Century Black Sea Provinces of the Ottoman Empire." *International Journal of Middle East Studies* 10(3): 309–323.

McCloskey, Donald N. 1976. "English Open Fields as Behavior Towards Risk." In *Research in Economic History,* ed. Paul Uselding, vol. 1. Greenwich, Conn.: JAI Press.

McElroy, Marjorie B., and Horney, Mary Jean. 1981. "Nash-Bargained Household Decisions: Toward a Generalization of the Theory of Demand." *International Economic Review* 22(2): 333–349.

McFadden, Daniel. 1974. "The Measurement of Urban Travel Demand." *Journal of Public Economics* 3(4): 303–328.

Macfarlane, Alan. 1979. *The Origins of English Individualism.* New York: Cambridge University Press.

McInnis, R. M. 1977. "Childbearing and Land Availability: Some Evidence from Individual Household Data." In *Population Patterns in the Past,* ed. Ronald D. Lee. New York: Academic Press.

McNicoll, Geoffrey. 1988. Review of *The New Palgrave. Population and Development Review* 14(2): 347–350.

McPherson, Michael S. 1974. "The Effects of Public on Private College Enrollment." Ph.D. dissertation, University of Chicago.

Magnus, Sir Philip Montefiore. 1954. *Gladstone.* London: Murray.

Makhija, Indra. 1977. "The Economic Contribution of Children and Its Effects on Fertility and Schooling: Rural India." Ph.D. dissertation, University of Chicago.

———. 1978. "Adult and Child Labor within the Household and the Quantity and Quality of Children: Rural India." Unpublished memorandum, University of Chicago.

———. 1980. "High Yielding Varieties of Wheat and Rice, Schooling and Fertility: Rural India." Paper presented at the Agricultural Economics Workshop, University of Chicago.

Malaysia: Department of Statistics. 1977. *Social Statistics Bulletin, Peninsular Malaysia, 1975.* Kuala Lampur.

Malthus, T. R. 1933. *An Essay on Population,* vol. 1. London: J. M. Dent.

Mandelbaum, David G. 1970. *Society in India.* Berkeley: University of California Press.

Mandelbrot, Benoit. 1962. "Paretian Distributions and Income Maximization." *Quarterly Journal of Economics* 76(1): 57–85.

Martin, Teresa Castro, and Bumpass, Larry L. 1989. "Recent Trends in Marital Disruption." *Demography* 26(1): 37–51.

Bibliography

Maududi, S. Abul A'La. 1975. *Purdah and the Status of Women in Islam*, 2nd ed., trans. and ed. Al-Ash'ari. Lahore, Pakistan: Islamic Publications.
Mayer, Thomas. 1972. *Permanent Income, Wealth, and Consumption*. Berkeley: University of California Press.
Meade, James E. 1967. "Population Explosion: The Standard of Living and Social Conflict." *Economic Journal* 77(306): 233–256.
———. 1976. *The Just Economy*. Albany: State University of New York Press.
Menchik, Paul L. 1979. "Inter-generational Transmission of Inequality: An Empirical Study of Wealth Mobility." *Economica* 46(184): 349–362.
———. 1980. "Primogeniture, Equal Sharing, and the U.S. Distribution of Wealth." *Quarterly Journal of Economics* 94(2): 299–316.
Menken, Jane, and Bongaarts, John. 1978. "Reproductive Models in the Study of Nutrition-Fertility Interrelationships." In *Nutrition and Human Reproduction*, ed. W. Henry Mosley. New York: Plenum Press.
Mexico: Dirección General de Estadistica. 1976. *Mexican Fertility Survey*.
Michael, Robert T. 1966. "The Capital-Labor Ratio in Nonmarket Production." Unpublished memorandum, Columbia University.
———. 1973. "Education and the Derived Demand for Children." *Journal of Political Economy* 81(2, pt. 2): S128–S164.
———. 1978. "Causation among Socio-Economic Time Series." Working Paper no. 246, National Bureau of Economic Research.
Michael, Robert T., and Becker, Gary S. 1973. "On the New Theory of Consumer Behavior." *Swedish Journal of Economics* 75(4): 378–396.
Michael, Robert T., Fuchs, Victor R., and Scott, Sharon R. 1980. "Changes in the Propensity to Live Alone: 1950–1976." *Demography* 17(1): 39–56.
Mincer, Jacob. 1958. "Investment in Human Capital and Personal Income Distribution." *Journal of Political Economy* 66(4): 281–302.
———. 1962. "Labor Force Participation of Married Women." In *Aspects of Labor Economics*, a conference of the Universities–National Bureau Committee for Economic Research. Princeton: Princeton University Press, for the National Bureau of Economic Research.
———. 1963. "Market Prices, Opportunity Costs, and Income Effects." In *Measurement in Economics*, ed. Carl F. Christ et al. Stanford: Stanford University Press.
———. 1966. "Labor-Force Participation and Unemployment: A Review of Recent Evidence." In *Prosperity and Unemployment*, ed. Robert A. Gordon and Margaret S. Gordon. New York: Wiley.
———. 1974. *Schooling, Experience and Earnings*. New York: Columbia University Press, for the National Bureau of Economic Research.
———. 1978. "Family Migration Decisions." *Journal of Political Economy* 86(5): 749–773.
———. 1983. "Comment on June O'Neill's 'The Trend in Sex Differential in Wages.' " Presented at the conference on Trends in Women's Work, Education and Family Formation, Sussex, England, May 31–June 3, 1983.
Mincer, Jacob, and Ofek, Haim. 1980. "Interrupted Work Careers." Working Paper no. 479, National Bureau of Economic Research.
Mincer, Jacob, and Polachek, Solomon W. 1974. "Family Investments in Human Capital: Earnings of Women." *Journal of Political Economy* 82(2, pt. 2): S76–S108.
Mirrlees, J. A. 1976. "The Optimal Structure of Incentives and Authority within an Organization." *Bell Journal of Economics* 7(1): 105–131.

Mitchell, Wesley. 1937. "The Backward Art of Spending Money." In *The Backward Art of Spending Money and Other Essays*. New York: McGraw-Hill.

Modigliani, Franco. 1986. "Life Cycle, Individual Thrift and the Wealth of Nations." *American Economic Review* 76(3): 297–313.

Monahan, Thomas P. 1958. "The Changing Nature and Instability of Remarriages." *Eugenics Quarterly* 5(2): 73–85.

Montaigne, Michel de. 1958. *Essays*, trans. J. M. Cohen. Harmondsworth, Middlesex, England: Penguin.

Mosher, Steven W. 1983. *Broken Earth, the Rural Chinese*. New York: Free Press.

Narazaki, Muneshige. 1968. *Hiroshige Famous Views*. English adaptation by Richard L. Gage. Palo Alto: Kodansha International.

Nash, Manning. 1966. *Primitive and Peasant Economic Systems*. Scranton, Penn.: Chandler.

Nelson, Phillip. 1970. "Information and Consumer Behavior." *Journal of Political Economy* 78(2): 311–329.

Nerlove, Marc, and Schultz, T. Paul. 1970. "Love and Life between the Censuses: A Model of Family Decision Making in Puerto Rico, 1950–1960." RM-6322-AID. Santa Monica, Calif.: RAND Corporation.

Nerlove, Marc, Razin, Assaf, and Sadka, Efraim. 1986. "Some Welfare Theoretic Implications of Endogenous Fertility." *International Economic Review* 27(1): 3–31.

———. 1987. *Household and Economy: Welfare Economics of Endogenous Fertility*. Boston: Academic Press.

Oaxaca, R. L. 1973. "Male-Female Wage Differentials in Urban Labor Markets." *International Economic Review* 14(1): 693–709.

Ofer, Gur, and Vinokur, Aaron. 1981. "Earnings Differentials by Sex in the Soviet Union: A First Look." In *Economic Welfare and the Economics of Soviet Socialism*, ed. Steven Rosefielde. Cambridge: Cambridge University Press.

O'Hara, Donald J. 1972. "Change in Mortality Levels and Family Decisions Regarding Children." Santa Monica, Calif.: RAND Corporation.

Okun, Arthur M. 1975. *Equality and Efficiency: The Big Tradeoff*. Washington, D.C.: Brookings Institution.

O'Neill, June. 1983. "The Determinants and Wage Effects of Occupational Segregation." Working paper, Urban Institute, Washington, D.C.

———. 1985. "The Trend in the Male-Female Wage Gap in the United States." *Journal of Labor Economics* 3(1, Supplement): S91–S116.

Orians, Gordon H. 1969. "On the Evolution of Mating Systems in Birds and Mammals." *American Naturalist* 103(934): 589–603.

———. 1972. "The Adaptive Significance of Mating Systems in *Icteridae*." In *Proceedings of the XVth International Ornithological Congress*, ed. K. H. Voous, pp. 389–398. Leiden: E. J. Brill.

Oster, George F., and Wilson, Edward O. 1978. *Caste and Ecology in the Social Insects*. Princeton: Princeton University Press.

Papps, Ivy. 1980. "The Determinants of Brideprice in a Palestinian Village." Working Paper no. 31, Department of Economics, University of Durham, England.

Pareto, Vilfredo. 1971. *Manual of Political Economy*, trans. Ann S. Schwier. New York: Augustus M. Kelley.

Parfit, Derek. 1984. *Reasons and Persons*. Oxford: Clarendon Press.

Pasinetti, Luigi L. 1962. "Rate of Profit and Income Distribution in Relation to the Rate of Economic Growth." *Review of Economic Studies* 29(4): 267–279.

Patai, Raphael. 1971. *Society, Culture, and Change in the Middle East,* 3rd ed. Philadelphia: University of Pennsylvania Press.

Paukert, Felix. 1973. "Income Distribution at Different Levels of Development: A Survey of Evidence." *International Labour Review* 108(2–3): 97–125.

Peller, Sigismund. 1965. "Births and Deaths among Europe's Ruling Families since 1500." In *Population in History,* ed. D. V. Glass and D. E. C. Eversley. Chicago: Aldine.

Peltzman, Sam. 1973. "The Effect of Government Subsidies-in-Kind on Private Expenditures: The Case of Higher Education." *Journal of Political Economy* 81(1): 1–27.

Peter, H. R. H., Prince of Greece and Denmark. 1963. *A Study of Polyandry.* The Hague: Mouton.

Peters, H. Elizabeth. 1985. "Patterns of Intergenerational Mobility." Unpublished memorandum, University of Colorado, Boulder.

———. 1986. "Marriage and Divorce: Informational Constraints and Private Contracting." *American Economic Review* 76(3): 436–454.

Phelps, Edmund S., ed. 1975. *Altruism, Morality, and Economic Theory.* New York: Russell Sage.

Plato. 1951. *The Republic of Plato,* trans. Francis M. Cornford. New York: Oxford University Press.

———. 1953. *Laws,* bk. 6. In *The Dialogues of Plato,* vol. 4, trans. Benjamin Jowett. Oxford: Clarendon Press.

Polachek, Solomon W. 1975. "Differences in Expected Post-School Investment as a Determinant of Market Wage Differentials." *International Economic Review* 16(2): 451–470.

———. 1978. "Simultaneous Equations Models of Sex Discrimination." In *Income Inequality,* ed. John R. Moroney. Lexington, Mass.: Lexington Books.

Pollak, Robert A., and Wachter, Michael L. 1975. "The Relevance of the Household Production Function and Its Implications for the Allocation of Time." *Journal of Political Economy* 83(2): 255–277.

Popkin, Barry M., and Solon, Florentino S. 1976. "Income, Time, the Working Mother, and Child Nutriture." *Journal of Tropical Pediatrics and Environmental Child Health* 22(3): 156–166.

Posner, Richard A. 1979. "Privacy, Secrecy, and Reputation." *Buffalo Law Review* 28(1): 1–55.

———. 1980. "A Theory of Primitive Society, with Special Reference to Law." *Journal of Law and Economics* 23(1): 1–53.

———. 1986. *Economic Analysis of Law,* 3rd ed. Boston: Little, Brown.

———. 1987. "The Regulation of the Market in Adoptions." *Boston University Law Review* 67(1): 59–72.

Prescott, Edward C. 1986. "Response to a Skeptic." *Quarterly Review* (Fall), Federal Reserve Bank of Minneapolis.

Preston, Samuel H. 1975. "Estimating the Proportion of American Marriages That End in Divorce." *Sociological Methods and Research* 3(4): 435–460.

———. 1984. "Children and the Elderly: Divergent Paths for America's Dependents." *Demography* 21(4): 435–457.

Preston, Samuel H., and Richards, Alan T. 1975. "The Influence of Women's Work Opportunities on Marriage Rates." *Demography* 12(2): 209–222.

Pryor, Frederic L. 1973. "Simulation of the Impact of Social and Economic Institutions on the Size Distribution of Income and Wealth." *American Economic Review* 63(1): 50–72.

———. 1977. *The Origins of the Economy.* New York: Academic Press.

Psacharopoulos, George, with Keith Hinchcliffe. 1973. *Returns to Education: An International Comparison.* San Francisco: Jossey-Bass.

Rachlin, Howard, Kagel, John H., and Battalio, Raymond C. 1980. "Substitutability in Time Allocation." *Psychological Review* 87(4): 355–374.

Radner, Roy. 1979. "Monitoring Cooperative Agreements between Principals and Agents." Technical Report no. 3, Harvard University, for the Office of Naval Research.

———. 1980. "Collusive Behavior in Noncooperative Epsilon-Equilibria of Oligopolies with Long but Finite Lives." *Journal of Economic Theory* 22(2): 136–154.

Rawls, John. 1971. *A Theory of Justice.* Cambridge, Mass.: Belknap Press of Harvard University Press.

Razin, Assaf, and Ben-Zion, Uri. 1975. "An Intergenerational Model of Population Growth." *American Economic Review* 65(5): 923–933.

Rees, Albert. 1966. "Information Networks in Labor Markets." *American Economic Review* 56(2): 559–566.

Reischauer, Robert D. 1971. "The Impact of the Welfare System on Black Migration and Marital Stability." Ph.D. dissertation, Columbia University.

Rheinstein, Max. 1972. *Marriage Stability, Divorce, and the Law.* Chicago: University of Chicago Press.

Rivers, W. H. R. 1906. *The Todas.* London: Macmillan.

Robertson, Sir Dennis H. 1956. *Economic Commentaries.* London: Staples Press.

Rosen, Sherwin. 1978. "Substitution and Division of Labour." *Economica* 45(179): 235–250.

———. 1981. "The Economics of Superstars." *American Economic Review* 71(5): 845–858.

———. 1982. "The Division of Labor and the Extent of the Market." Unpublished memorandum, University of Chicago.

Rosenthal, Erich. 1970. "Divorce and Religious Intermarriage: The Effect of Previous Marital Status upon Subsequent Marital Behavior." *Journal of Marriage and the Family* 32(3): 435–440.

Rosenzweig, Mark R. 1977. "The Demand for Children in Farm Households." *Journal of Political Economy* 85(1): 123–146.

Rosenzweig, Mark R., and Schultz, T. Paul. 1980. "Market Opportunities, Genetic Endowment, and the Intrafamily Distribution of Resources: Child Survival in Rural India." Unpublished memorandum, Yale University.

Rosenzweig, Mark R., and Wolpin, Kenneth I. 1979. "An Economic Analysis of the Extended Family in a Less Developed Country: The Demand for the Elderly in an Uncertain Environment." Economic Growth Center Discussion Paper no. 317, Yale University.

———. 1980. "Testing the Quantity-Quality Fertility Model: The Use of Twins as a Natural Experiment." *Econometrica* 48(1): 227–240.

Ross, Heather L., and Sawhill, Isabel V. 1975. *Time of Transition*. Washington, D.C.: Urban Institute.

Rossi, Alice S. 1977. "A Biosocial Perspective on Parenting." *Daedalus* 106(2): 1–31.

Rowntree, Griselda, and Carrier, Norman H. 1958. "The Resort to Divorce in England and Wales, 1858–1957." *Population Studies* 11(3): 188–233.

Roy, A. D. 1950. "The Distribution of Earnings and of Individual Output." *Economic Journal* 60(239): 489–505.

Russell, Bertrand. 1967. *The Autobiography of Bertrand Russell, 1872–1914.* Boston: Little, Brown.

Saghir, Marcel T., and Robins, Eli. 1973. *Male and Female Homosexuality.* Baltimore: Williams and Wilkins.

Saksena, R. N. 1962. *Social Economy of a Polyandrous People*, 2nd ed. New York: Asia Publishing House.

Saller, Richard. Forthcoming. "The Structure of the Roman Family." Published in Italian in *Storia di Roma*, vol. 4, ed. Arnaldo Momigliano and Aldo Schiavone. Turin: Einaudi, 1989.

Salzano, F. M., Neel, J. V., and Maybury-Lewis, David. 1967. "Further Studies on the Xavante Indians. I. Demographic Data on Two Additional Villages: Genetic Structure of the Tribe." *American Journal of Human Genetics* 19(4): 463–489.

Samuelson, Paul A. 1955. "Diagrammatic Exposition of the Theory of Public Expenditure." *Review of Economics and Statistics* 37(4): 350–356.

———. 1956. "Social Indifference Curves." *Quarterly Journal of Economics* 70(1): 1–22.

———. 1958. "An Exact Consumption-Loan Model of Interest with or without the Social Contrivance of Money." *Journal of Political Economy* 66(6): 467–482.

Sanderson, Warren C. 1980. "The Economics of Marital Dissolution, the Black Family, and the Legacy of Slavery." Paper presented at the Workshop in Applications of Economics, University of Chicago.

Santos, Fredricka P. 1975. "The Economics of Marital Status." In *Sex, Discrimination, and the Division of Labor,* ed. Cynthia B. Lloyd. New York: Columbia University Press.

Sargent, Thomas J., and Wallace, Neil. 1975. " 'Rational' Expectations, the Optimal Monetary Instrument, and the Optimal Money Supply Rule." *Journal of Political Economy* 83(2): 241–254.

Sattinger, Michael. 1975. "Comparative Advantage and the Distributions of Earnings and Abilities." *Econometrica* 43(3): 455–468.

Saunders, Margaret O., and Thomson, James T. 1979. "A Theory of Hausa Marriage (or Gary Becker in Hausaland)." Paper presented at the annual meeting of the American Anthropological Association.

Sayles, G. O. 1952. *The Medieval Foundations of England*, 2nd ed. London: Methuen.

Schmelz, U. Oskar. 1971. *Infant and Early Childhood Mortality among Jews of the Diaspora.* Jerusalem: Institute of Contemporary Jewry, Hebrew University.

Schneider, H. K. 1969. "A Statistical Study of Brideprice in Africa." Paper presented at the annual meeting of the American Anthropological Association.

Schoen, Robert, Greenblatt, Harry N., and Mielke, Robert B. 1975. "California's Experience with Non-Adversary Divorce.'' *Demography* 12(2): 223–243.

Schultz, T. Paul. 1973. ''Explanation of Birth Rate Changes over Space and Time: A Study of Taiwan.'' *Journal of Political Economy* 81(2, pt. 2): S238–S274.

Schultz, T. Paul, and DaVanzo, Julie. 1970. ''Analysis of Demographic Change in East Pakistan: A Study of Retrospective Survey Data.'' R-564-AID. Santa Monica: RAND Corporation.

Schultz, Theodore W. 1963. *The Economic Value of Education*. New York: Columbia University Press.

———. 1975. ''The Value of the Ability to Deal with Disequilibria.'' *Journal of Economic Literature* 13(3): 827–846.

———. 1980. ''Nobel Lecture: The Economics of Being Poor.'' *Journal of Political Economy* 88(4): 639–651.

Schumpeter, Joseph A. 1951. *Imperialism and Social Classes*, trans. Heinz Norden. New York: Augustus M. Kelley.

Scrimshaw, Susan C. M. 1978. ''Infant Mortality and Behavior in the Regulation of Family Size.'' *Population and Development Review* 4(3): 383–403.

Shavell, Steven. 1979. ''Risk Sharing and Incentives in the Principal and Agent Relationship.'' *Bell Journal of Economics* 10(1): 55–73.

Shaw, George Bernard. 1930. *Man and Superman*. In *The Collected Works of Bernard Shaw*, vol. 10. New York: William H. Wise.

Shell, Karl, Fisher, Franklin, Foley, Duncan K., and Friedlaender, Ann F.; in association with James J. Behr, Jr., Stanley Fischer, and Ran D. Mosenson. 1968. ''The Educational Opportunity Bank: An Economic Analysis of a Contingent Repayment Loan Program for Higher Education.'' *National Tax Journal* 21(1): 2–45.

Sheps, Mindel C., and Menken, Jane A. 1973. *Mathematical Models of Conception and Birth*. Chicago: University of Chicago Press.

Sheshinski, Eytan, and Weiss, Yoram. 1982. ''Inequality within and between Families.'' *Journal of Political Economy* 90(1): 105–127.

Shorrocks, Anthony F. 1979. ''On the Structure of Inter-Generational Transfers between Families.'' *Economica* 46(184): 415–425.

Shorter, Edward. 1975. *The Making of the Modern Family*. New York: Basic Books.

Simon, Herbert A. 1979. ''Rational Decision Making in Business Organizations.'' *American Economic Review* 69(4): 493–513.

———. 1986. ''Rationality in Psychology and Economics.'' *Journal of Business* 59(4, pt. 2): S209–S224.

Simon, Julian L. 1974. *The Effects of Income on Fertility*, Monograph no. 19. Chapel Hill: Carolina Population Center, University of North Carolina.

Singer, Burton, and Spilerman, Seymour. 1974. ''Social Mobility Models for Heterogeneous Populations.'' In *Sociological Methodology, 1973–1974*, ed. Herbert L. Costner. San Francisco: Jossey-Bass.

Singh, Ram D. 1988. *Economics of the Family and Farming Systems in Sub-Saharan Africa*. Boulder: Westview Press.

Singh, Ram D., Schuh, G. Edward, and Kehrberg, Earl W. 1978. ''Economic Analysis of Fertility Behavior and the Demand for Schooling among Poor Households in Rural Brazil.'' Agricultural Experiment Station Bulletin no. 214, Purdue University.

Smith, Adam. 1853. *The Theory of Moral Sentiments.* London: Henry G. Bohn.

———. 1937. *An Inquiry into the Nature and Causes of the Wealth of Nations.* New York: Modern Library.

Smith, James E., and Kunz, Phillip R. 1976. "Polygyny and Fertility in Nineteenth-Century America." *Population Studies* 30(3): 465–480.

Smith, James P. 1977. "Family Labor Supply over the Life Cycle." *Explorations in Economic Research* 4(2): 205–276.

———. 1979. "The Distribution of Family Earnings." *Journal of Political Economy* 87(5, pt. 2): S163–S192.

———. 1984. "Race and Human Capital." *American Economic Review* 74(4): 685–698.

Smith, James P., and Ward, Michael P. 1985. "Time-Series Growth in the Female Labor Force." *Journal of Labor Economics* 3(1, supplement): S59–S90.

Soltow, Lee. 1965. *Toward Income Equality in Norway.* Madison: University of Wisconsin Press.

Stafford, Frank P. 1980. "Women's Use of Time Converging with Men's." *Monthly Labor Review* 103(12): 57–59.

Stigler, George J., and Becker, Gary S. 1977. "Degustibus Non Est Disputandum." *American Economic Review* 67(2): 76–90.

Stiglitz, J. E. 1969. "Distribution of Income and Wealth among Individuals." *Econometrica* 37(3): 382–397.

Stoffaës, Christian. 1974. "Analyse Multicriteres, Optimalité des Choix Collectifs et Marché des Mariages." In *Théorie de la Décision et Applications.* Paris: Centre National d'Information pour la Productivité des Entreprises.

Stone, Lawrence. 1977. *The Family, Sex and Marriage in England, 1500–1800.* New York: Harper and Row.

Summers, Larry H. 1981. "Capital Taxation and Accumulation in a Life Cycle Growth Model." *American Economic Review* 71(4): 533–544.

Sun, Te-Hsiung, Lin, Hui-Sheng, and Freedman, Ronald. 1978. "Trends in Fertility, Family Size Preferences, and Family Planning Practice: Taiwan, 1961–76." *Studies in Family Planning* 9(4): 54–70.

Sweden: National Central Bureau of Statistics. 1980. *Statistical Abstract of Sweden 1980,* vol. 67. Stockholm.

———. 1986. *Statistical Abstract of Sweden 1986,* vol. 72. Stockholm.

Sweet, James A. 1974. "Differentials in the Rate of Fertility Decline: 1960–1970." *Family Planning Perspectives* 6(2): 103–107.

Taiwan: Directorate-General of Budget, Accounting and Statistics, 1976. *Report on the Survey of Personal Income Distribution in Taiwan Area, Republic of China, 1975.*

Taiwan: Ministry of the Interior. 1974. *1973 Taiwan Demographic Fact Book, Republic of China.*

———. 1976. *1975 Taiwan-Fukien Demographic Fact Book, Republic of China.*

Tamura, Robert. 1985. "A Note on the Dynastic Family." Paper presented at the Workshop in Applications of Economics, University of Chicago.

Telser, Lester G. 1980. "A Theory of Self-Enforcing Agreements." *Journal of Business* 53(1): 27–44.

Theil, Henri. 1952. "Qualities, Prices, and Budget Enquiries." *Review of Economic Studies* 19(3): 129–147.

Thomas, Keith. 1971. *Religion and the Decline of Magic*. London: Weidenfeld and Nicolson.

Thompson, Earl A., and Ruhter, Wayne E. Undated. "Parental Malincentives and Social Legislation." Unpublished memorandum, University of California at Los Angeles.

Tideman, T. Nicolaus, and Tullock, Gordon. 1976. "A New and Superior Process for Making Social Choices." *Journal of Political Economy* 84(6): 1145–59.

Tinbergen, Jan. 1970. "A Positive and a Normative Theory of Income Distribution." *Review of Income and Wealth* 16(3): 221–234.

Tomes, Nigel. 1978. "A Model of Child Endowments, and the Quality and Quantity of Children." Ph.D. dissertation, University of Chicago.

———. 1979. "Inheritance and the Intergenerational Transmission of Inequality: Theory and Empirical Results." Paper presented at the Workshop in Applications of Economics, University of Chicago.

———. 1980a. "Inheritance and Inequality within the Family: Equal Division among Unequals, or Do the Poor Get More?" Paper presented at the Workshop in Applications of Economics, University of Chicago.

———. 1980b. "Notes on Child Endowments and the Quality and Quantity of Children." Unpublished memorandum, University of Western Ontario.

———. 1981. "The Family, Inheritance, and the Intergenerational Transmission of Inequality." *Journal of Political Economy* 89(5): 928–958.

———. 1984. "Inequality within the Family and Regression to the Mean." Unpublished memorandum, University of Western Ontario.

Tomes, Nigel, and Becker, Gary S. 1981. "Assortative Mating, the Demand for Children, and the Distribution of Income and Intergenerational Mobility." Unpublished memorandum, University of Chicago.

Trivers, Robert L. 1972. "Parental Investment and Sexual Selection." In *Sexual Selection and the Descent of Man, 1871–1971*, ed. Bernard Campbell. Chicago: Aldine.

———. 1974. "Parent-Offspring Conflict." *American Zoologist* 14(1): 249–264.

Tsai, Shu-Ling. 1983. "Sex Differences in the Process of Stratification." Ph.D. dissertation, University of Wisconsin.

United Nations. 1953. "The Determinants and Consequences of Population Trends." *Population Studies*, no. 17. New York: United Nations.

———. 1972. *Demographic Yearbook, 1971*. New York: United Nations.

———. 1974. *Demographic Yearbook, 1973*. New York: United Nations.

United Nations Food and Agriculture Organization. 1962. *Nutrition and Working Efficiency*. FFHC Basic Study no. 5. Rome: UNFAO.

U.S. Bureau of the Census. 1963a. Census of Population: 1960. *Educational Attainment—Subject Reports*. Final Report PC(2)-5B. Washington, D.C.: Government Printing Office.

———. 1963b. Census of Population: 1960. Vol. 1, *Characteristics of the Population*, pt. 6, California. Washington, D.C.: Government Printing Office.

———. 1965. *Statistical Abstract of the United States, 1965*. Washington, D.C.: Government Printing Office.

———. 1967. *Trends in the Income of Families and Persons in the United States, 1947–1964*. Technical Paper no. 17. Washington, D.C.: Government Printing Office.

———. 1971a. Census of Business, 1967. Vol. 1, Retail Trade—Subject Reports. Washington, D.C.: Government Printing Office.

———. 1971b. Census of Business, 1967. Vol. 3, Wholesale Trade—Subject Reports. Washington, D.C.: Government Printing Office.

———. 1971c. Current Population Reports. Series P-20, no. 212. "Marital Status and Family Status: March 1970." Washington, D.C.: Government Printing Office.

———. 1972. Current Population Reports. Series P-20, no. 243. "Educational Attainment: March 1972." Washington, D.C.: Government Printing Office.

———. 1973a. Census of Agriculture, 1969. Vol. 2, General Report, chap. 4, "Equipment, Labor, Expenditures, Chemicals." Washington, D.C.: Government Printing Office.

———. 1973b. Census of Population: 1970. Age at First Marriage—Subject Reports. Final Report PC(2)-4D. Washington, D.C.: Government Printing Office.

———. 1973c. Census of Population: 1970. Educational Attainment—Subject Reports. Final Report PC(2)-5B. Washington, D.C.: Government Printing Office.

———. 1973d. Census of Population: 1970. Vol. 1, Characteristics of the Population, pt. 1, United States Summary—sec. 1. Washington, D.C.: Government Printing Office.

———. 1973e. Census of Population: 1970. Vol. 1, Characteristics of the Population, pt. 6, California, sec. 2. Washington, D.C.: Government Printing Office.

———. 1975a. Census of Mineral Industries, 1972. Subject Series: General Summary, MIC72(1)-1. Washington, D.C.: Government Printing Office.

———. 1975b. Current Population Reports. Series P-20, no. 287. "Marital Status and Living Arrangements: March 1975." Washington, D.C.: Government Printing Office.

———. 1975c. Historical Statistics of the United States, Colonial Times to 1970. Bicentennial ed., pt. 1. Washington, D.C.: Government Printing Office.

———. 1976a. Census of Manufactures, 1972. Vol. 1, Subject and Special Statistics. Washington, D.C.: Government Printing Office.

———. 1976b. Census of Selected Service Industries, 1972. Vol. 1, Summary and Subject Statistics. Washington, D.C.: Government Printing Office.

———. 1977a. Current Population Reports. Series P-20, no. 306. "Marital Status and Living Arrangements: March 1976." Washington, D.C.: Government Printing Office.

———. 1977b. Statistical Abstract of the United States, 1977. Washington, D.C.: Government Printing Office.

———. 1978. Statistical Abstract of the United States, 1978. Washington, D.C.: Government Printing Office.

———. 1979a. Current Population Reports. Series P-20, no. 338. "Marital Status and Living Arrangements: March 1978." Washington, D.C.: Government Printing Office.

———. 1979b. Current Population Reports. Series P-20, no. 346. "School Enrollment—Social and Economic Characteristics of Students: October 1978." Washington, D.C.: Government Printing Office.

———. 1979c. Statistical Abstract of the United States, 1979. Washington, D.C.: Government Printing Office.

———. 1980a. *Current Population Reports*. Series P-20, no. 349. "Marital Status and Living Arrangements: March 1979." Washington, D.C.: Government Printing Office.

———. 1980b. *Current Population Reports*. Series P-20, no. 352. "Household and Family Characteristics: March 1979." Washington, D.C.: Government Printing Office.

———. 1980c. *Current Population Reports*. Series P-60, no. 123. "Money Income of Families and Persons in the United States in 1978." Washington, D.C.: Government Printing Office.

———. 1989. *Statistical Abstract of the United States, 1989*. Washington, D.C.: Government Printing Office.

U.S. Bureau of Labor Statistics. 1978. "Employment and Unemployment Trends during 1977." *Special Labor Force Report* no. 212. Washington, D.C.: Government Printing Office.

———. 1979. "Work Experience of the Population in 1977." *Special Labor Force Report* no. 224. Washington, D.C.: Government Printing Office.

———. 1984. *Statistical Abstract of the United States, 1984*. Washington, D.C.: Government Printing Office.

U.S. Department of Agriculture. 1976. "Changes in Farm Production and Efficiency." Statistical Bulletin no. 561, Economic Research Service. Washington, D.C.: Government Printing Office.

———. 1979. *Agricultural Statistics, 1979*. Washington, D.C.: Government Printing Office.

U.S. Department of Commerce. 1932. *Statistical Abstract of the United States, 1932*. Washington, D.C.: Government Printing Office.

U.S. Department of Health, Education and Welfare, Public Health Service. 1978. *Vital Statistics of the United States, 1975*. Vol. 1, *Natality*. Washington, D.C.: Government Printing Office.

———. 1979. *Vital Statistics of the United States, 1975*. Vol. 3, *Marriage and Divorce*. Washington, D.C.: Government Printing Office.

U.S. Department of Labor, Office of Policy Planning and Research. 1965. *The Negro Family: The Case for National Action*. Washington, D.C.: Government Printing Office.

Uzawa, Hirofumi. 1968. *Time Preference, the Consumption Function, and Optimum Asset Holding*, ed. J. N. Wolfe. Chicago: Aldine.

Vandenberg, Steven G. 1972. "Assortative Mating, or Who Marries Whom?" *Behavior Genetics* 2(2–3): 127–157.

Vining, Daniel R., Jr. 1983. "Illegitimacy and Public Policy." *Population and Development Review*. 9(1): 105–110.

Wahl, Jenny Bourne. 1985. "Fertility in America: Historical Patterns and Wealth Effects on the Quantity and Quality of Children." Ph.D. dissertation, University of Chicago.

Wallace, Alfred R. 1905. *My Life*, vol. 1. New York: Dodd, Mead.

Walsh, Brendan M. 1972. "Trends in Age at Marriage in Postwar Ireland." *Demography* 9(2): 187–202.

Ward, Michael P., and Butz, William P. 1980. "Completed Fertility and Its Timing." *Journal of Political Economy* 88(5): 917–940.

Weiss, Yoram, and Willis, Robert J. 1985. "Children as Collective Goods and Divorce Settlements." *Journal of Labor Economics* 3(3): 268–292.

———. 1989. "An Economic Analysis of Divorce Settlements." Working Paper no. 89-5. Chicago: Economic Research Center/National Opinion Research Center.

Bibliography

Weitzman, Lenore J. 1974. "Legal Regulation of Marriage: Tradition and Change." *California Law Review* 62(4): 1169–1288.

Weitzman, Lenore J., and Dixon, Ruth B. 1979. "Child Custody Awards: Legal Standards and Empirical Patterns for Child Custody, Support and Visitation after Divorce." *University of California, Davis, Law Review* 12(2): 471–521.

Wessels, Walter J. 1976. "The Theory of Search in Heterogeneous Markets: The Case of Marital Search." Ph.D. dissertation, University of Chicago.

West, E. G. 1970. *Education and the State,* 2nd ed. London: Institute of Economic Affairs.

Westoff, Charles F. 1974. "Coital Frequency and Contraception." *Family Planning Perspectives* 6(3): 136–141.

Westoff, Charles F., and Ryder, Norman B. 1977. *The Contraceptive Revolution.* Princeton: Princeton University Press.

Whiting, Beatrice B. 1977. "Changing Life Styles in Kenya." *Daedalus* 106(2): 211–225.

Wildasin, David E. 1985. "Nonneutrality of Debt with Endogenous Fertility." Unpublished memorandum, Indiana University.

Wilde, Louis L. 1980. "Information Costs, Duration of Search, and Turnover: Theory and Applications." Social Science Working Paper no. 306. Pasadena: California Institute of Technology.

Wiley, R. Haven. 1973. "Territoriality and Non-Random Mating in Sage Grouse, *Centrocercus urophasianus.*" *Animal Behaviour Monographs* 6(2): 85–169.

———. 1974. "Evolution of Social Organization and Life History Patterns among Grouse." *Quarterly Review of Biology* 49(3): 201–227.

Wilkinson, L. P. 1978. "Classical Approaches: I. Population and Family Planning." *Encounter* 50(4): 22–32.

Williams, Anne D. 1979. "Fertility Determinants in the United States: A Test of the Relative Income Hypothesis." Unpublished memorandum, University of Pennsylvania.

Willis, Robert J. 1973. "A New Approach to the Economic Theory of Fertility Behavior." *Journal of Political Economy* 81(2, pt. 2): S14–S64.

———. 1985. "A Theory of the Equilibrium Interest Rate in an Overlapping Generations Model: Life Cycles, Institutions, and Population Growth." Discussion Paper no. 85-8. Chicago: Economics Research Center/National Opinion Research Center.

———. 1986. "Externalities and Population." In *Economic Consequences of Population Growth in Economic Development.* Washington, D.C.: National Academy Press.

Wilson, Edward O. 1971. *The Insect Societies.* Cambridge, Mass.: Belknap Press of Harvard University Press.

———. 1975. *Sociobiology.* Cambridge, Mass.: Belknap Press of Harvard University Press.

Wilson, William Julius. 1987. *The Truly Disadvantaged: The Inner City, the Underclass and Public Policy.* Chicago: University of Chicago Press.

Winch, Robert F. 1958. *Mate-Selection.* New York: Harper.

Wolf, Margery. 1968. *The House of Lim.* New York: Appleton-Century-Crofts.

Wolff, P. de, and van Slijpe, A. R. D. 1973. "The Relation between Income,

Intelligence, Education and Social Background." *European Economic Review* 4(3): 235–264.

Yitzhaki, Shlomo. 1984. "On the Relation between Return and Income." Unpublished memorandum, Hebrew University.

Young, Kimball. 1954. *Isn't One Wife Enough?* New York: Henry Holt.

Zabalza, Anton, and Tzannatos, Zafaris. 1985. "The Effects of Britain's Antidiscriminatory Legislation on Relative Pay and Employment." *Economic Journal* 95(379): 679–699. Previously published under the same title as Discussion Paper no. 155. London: London School of Economics, 1983.

Zelder, Martin. 1989. "Children as Public Goods and the Effect of Divorce Law upon the Divorce Rate." Ph.D. dissertation, University of Chicago.

Zelizer, Viviana A. 1978. "Human Values and the Market: The Case of Life Insurance and Death in 19th-Century America." *American Journal of Sociology* 84(3): 591–610.

Index

Abel, Andrew, 159n
Abortions, 140, 143, 144, 362, 369
Abuse within family, 14–15, 364
Adams, James D., 293n
Addictive behavior, 365, 365n. *See also*
Altruism, increased by contact
Adoption, 45, 141, 194
Adultery, 48, 49, 124, 129, 328, 346, 374
Adverse selection, 140–141
Age
and bride price, 129n
and household productivity vs. wage
rates, 42
and human capital investment, 26–27,
31, 40, 73, 244, 302, 311–312
and living alone, 50, 350, 354, 358, 369,
374
respect for, 344, 346, 348
See also Assortative mating, of traits;
Marriage, age at
Agriculture. *See* Farming
Aid to mothers with dependent children,
135, 139, 335, 356, 357, 376
Akerlof, George A., 141
Aleichem, Sholom, 326n
Alexander, Richard D., 319n, 320
Alimony, 44, 330, 335, 357. *See also* Divorce, settlement
Alström, Carl H., 117
Altmann, Stuart A., 312n, 316
Altruism, 5–13, 16, 31, 53, 124, 190, 191,
307, 349, 357, 364–365
allocation of resources with one selfish
beneficiary, 278–285
allocation of resources with several ben-
eficiaries, 287–289

automatic response of, 11, 284, 288, 294,
344
behavior of children, 288–295, 298,
368
compensation for harm, 284–285
conflict and harmony, 14, 284, 286n,
291–293
efficiency, 295, 299–301, 365, 368–
369
families with, 9, 296, 302
family utility functions, 296–299
function, 159–160
increased by contact, 12, 365, 375. *See
also* Conflict
influence of number of children, 7,
157–162, 168
influence on number of children, 162,
164, 167, 173, 177–178
influence on total consumption of beneficiary, 162, 164, 167, 175–176, 178,
280, 285
maximization of family income, 282–
283, 285–286, 287–288, 296
per child, 7–8, 158, 160, 261
and presumption of parental care of children, 364–365
reciprocal, 286, 297–298
role in economic activity, 303
substitution between siblings, 188–190,
262
utility of parents dependent on utility of
children, 155–158, 180, 236, 240, 257,
364
utility-possibility boundary, 280
See also Bequests; Dynastic utility
function; Gifts; Merit goods

411

Index

Index